Hawaii Early Learning Profile (HELP)

ACTIVITY GUIDE

By
Setsu Furuno, Katherine A. O'Reilly,
Carol M. Hosaka, Takayo T. Inatsuka,
Toney L. Allman, Barbara Zeisloft

VORT Corporation, Palo Alto, California 94306

Funded by P.L. 91-230 Bureau of Education
for the Handicapped, U.S. Office of
Education, Grant No. OEG-0-72-4859

Library of Congress Catalog Card No. 79-66849
ISBN 0-89718-090-9

Published by:
VORT Corporation
P.O. Box 11132
Palo Alto, California 94306

To the families
of the
Enrichment Project for Handicapped Infants

ACKNOWLEDGEMENTS

HELP has many meanings for us. Besides serving as the acronym for our publication, it expresses the considerable help we received from many sources. Foremost are our parents and children for the rich experiences and insights they provided us about child development and human resources. We are grateful to Mary Alger, Bernard Garon, Betty Nakaji who assisted us with the first draft, and to Joe Rosenthal and Gloria Boylan who worked so sensitively with our parents. To Drs. Sharon Bintliff and Pauline Stitt, our gratitude for their medical consultation and support.

Carolyn Fletcher assisted us with the final editing to provide overall consistency. We appreciate her assistance and thank also Tom Holt, our publisher, for his patience and understanding throughout the preparation of this publication. To Marjorie Slaght, we owe much thanks for her painstakingly continuing efforts in typing the manuscript.

Special thanks go to all the participants in the field testing; they provided us considerable encouragement by their positive responses and their efforts to disseminate the use of the chart and guide.

Finally we express our gratitude to the Bureau of Education for the Handicapped and the School of Public Health of the University of Hawaii for allowing us the opportunity to conduct the demonstration project.

CONTENTS

INTRODUCTION

From 1971 to 1975, the staff of the Enrichment Project for Handicapped Infants worked with over one hundred handicapped infants, birth to three years of age, and their families. These children were referred by physicians, public health nurses, parents themselves, and health agencies. This demonstration project was conducted under the auspices of the School of Public Health of the University of Hawaii. Funds were provided by the Bureau of Education of the Handicapped of the Department of Health, Education and Welfare.

In planning an individual program for children with a wide range of handicaps and diagnoses, we saw the necessity of using a single instrument which could provide the developmental sequences in small incremental steps. Additionally, we saw the need for a comprehensive visual picture of the child's functioning levels. Such a visual picture would facilitate planning and allow us to focus on the whole child, i.e., building his strengths as well as helping us work on his specific handicap.

The Hawaii Early Learning Profile (HELP) was developed to meet this need. To facilitate assessment, we developed the HELP Charts in a format similar to the horizontal continuum of other screening tests. To assist in planning and task analysis, we developed the HELP Activity Guide.

Numerous growth and developmental scales and standardized tests* were utilized during the development of the HELP Charts and Guide. Both the Charts and Guide were field-tested by all the programs for infants with handicaps in Hawaii since the programs were established following the demonstration project. Additionally, the materials have been used and reviewed by programs in 35 states and 7 different countries, each of which provided us with constructive feedback on how to improve the products. Based upon the field-testing and review information, we have updated both the Charts and Guide to provide a month-to-month sequence of normal developmental skills in six different areas. These small incremental steps are helpful in demonstrating to the parent the gains the child can make in the program. *Although the HELP Charts and Guide were developed while working with handicapped children, parents and teachers working with normal children will find the materials useful because they are based on sequential development of skills.*

The age references provided for the skills on the Charts and in the Activity Guide are based on a synthesis of research and project data. These age references represent "approximations" since each child is unique and differs in his or her ability to demonstrate specific skills. Your child may successfully display skills before or after the indicated age range. Since each child is unique, you should not be concerned if your child does not display skills exactly within the specified age range. The skills detailed in the Charts are not necessarily all critical to the child's development. Many are included because of their teachability and amenability to intervention. It is assumed that a child will not necessarily accomplish all skills listed. A normal child may very well omit some skills and these omissions will not necessarily affect the course of his development. A child may very well complete a skill out of sequence.

---

*See Bibliography.

The Charts are arranged by listing skills according to the age range in which they *normally* begin. The skills are arranged within blocks, but this does not mean they end at a specific age level. Some are lifetime skills and others change to more complex skills. Arrows used at the thirty-six month level indicate that these skills may begin at a time beyond thirty-six months. All items on the Charts are numbered to coincide with the numbers in the Activity Guide. These numbers are for cross-references only and *do not* reflect developmental sequence.

We have footnoted some items because of the need for brevity in the Charts. Footnote 1 indicates additional information and definition of skills may be obtained by referring to the Guide. As an example, skills related to reflexes are written to indicate when they are inhibited, i.e., responses one would not want to teach a child. It is the inhibition of these skills which is significant in development, and activities in the Guide are focused in that direction. We strongly suggest the Charts and Guide be used together.

Footnote 2 refers to skills that should not be taught although they do relate to behaviors typical for the child's age, i.e., they occur as a natural part of the child's development. Suggestions are provided in the Activity Guide for handling these behaviors.

The Language Development section relates only to language expression. It was difficult to separate language from cognitive skills, particularly in relation to receptive language. As a result, we decided to include receptive language items as part of the Cognitive Development section and placed these items at the bottom of that section.

In the Gross Motor Development section the word "position" has been left out in some cases to avoid repetition and is implied, e.g., "In side-lying (position)," "In prone (position)."

The Activity Guide was developed to provide staff with activities that would help teach skills recorded on the HELP Charts. These activities are the result of many helpful suggestions from books and guides* and from programs on enrichment for normal as well as handicapped infants and children and most importantly, from the ideas of staff and parents as they planned and worked together to assist the child in his development. The Activity Guide is divided into the same six sections as the HELP Charts. The word "mother" is used in the Guide synonymously with "primary caretaker" which can mean the father, a grandparent, or a foster parent.

The Guide also lists activities specifically "for the older delayed child." Since activities in the Guide are written for skills as they occur sequentially, those designated "for older delayed children" relate to special efforts on our part to present appropriate activities for the older child who is functioning at a younger level. *The activities in the Guide are all* suggestive *and should therefore be utilized flexibly and according to individual interest and need. Use caution and your own best judgment in using all suggested Guide activities and seek professional assistance on all questions.* We should emphasize that these materials do not replace the professional person in the assessment and the treatment of handicapped infants and children. Consultation with therapists is necessary, particularly for contraindications and precautions related to certain disabilities. The written style of each section may vary according to the nature of the subject. It is vital for the success of each activity to ensure a warm, relaxed atmosphere at all times for the child.

---

*See Bibliography.

There was not always agreement in growth and development literature as to when a skill begins. We used our best judgment in determining the placement of the skills on the Charts. We should also add that we have *randomly used both genders and personal names* in the text.

As a final comment, may I say that while I served as the Director of the project and was responsible for reviewing all of the materials and preparing them for publication, my colleagues with their respective expertise were responsible for preparing the different sections: <u>Cognitive</u>: Carol Hosaka, teacher; <u>Language</u>: Barbara Zeisloft, speech therapist; <u>Gross Motor</u>: Katherine O'Reilly, physical therapist; <u>Fine Motor and Self Help</u>: Takayo Inatsuka, occupational therapist; and <u>Social-Emotional</u>: Toney Allman, psychologist.

Setsu Furuno

INSTRUCTIONS

To facilitate use of the HELP Charts and Activity Guide, we would like to outline the procedures we found most useful for our staff and for the programs we worked with in Hawaii:

I. Assessment

1. Conduct a formal and/or informal assessment. This usually involves one staff member working with the child and the parent, while other staff members observe and suggest tasks for the child to do. The parent is asked to assist by presenting some of the tasks and this may serve to ease the situation for the child. This procedure reduces: 1) the handling of the child by many strangers, 2) the amount of time for assessment, and 3) the duplication of tasks requested of the child.

2. Interview the parents for additional data about family background, child's handicapping conditions, etc. This could be done by a social worker or a parent counselor who would also assess parents informally so a program for them could be developed.

3. Have parents sign release papers granting permission to obtain additional data from the physician and the referral source.

II. Recordkeeping using the HELP Charts

4. Record personal identifying information about the child in the blanks provided on the Chart. Each child should have a set of Charts.

5. Review the child's assessment information from steps 1-3 above.

6. Select a color to be representative of the assessment information obtained as of the respective assessment date. Identify this color with the assessment date in the space provided on the Charts.

7. Color in each of the skill items on the Charts displayed by the child as of the assessment date. By use of multi-colors according to different assessment dates, a comprehensive picture of the child's present and previous attained skills is provided. For an older child, it is not necessary to record assessment data from birth. Thus, some of the blocks at the child's earlier age levels may not be colored. It should be expected that the development of a handicapped child will be less uniform than that of a normal child.

8. Periodically additional assessments should be conducted for the child, and the Charts updated using a different colored pen according to each new assessment date.

III. Writing behavioral objectives

9. Review the requirements of a well written behavioral/instructional objective. An objective must be: measurable/observable; have a time reference; and contain a criterion reference,

i.e., specific conditions representing fulfillment of the objective as, for example, the number of trials, etc.

10. Review the child's HELP Charts. Review each of the six developmental areas and determine which area is a current goal or priority area. Review each specific skill item that is not yet colored (deficit). Select at least one skill item per developmental area as a basis for writing objectives. Write one objective for each different skill item. Use the Guide for assistance in preparing your instructional objective. For example, if you have selected in the Cognitive area skill item no. 86, "Places square piece in formboard," you could develop an objective from this as follows: *Child will place round and square pieces in circle and square formboard in four out of five trials by June 10, 1979.*

11. Do not develop objectives for skill items on the Charts referenced by a Footnote 2. (See the Introduction.)

IV. Programming through use of the Guide

12. Review the skill item in the Guide using the reference number. Use the Skill Reference Listing on page 191 for a complete overview of all the skills in each developmental area.

13. Study the activities in the Guide for that skill item. Decide on appropriate tasks for the individual child which would help direct him towards achieving the objective. These activities should be planned so they can also be carried out at home. We tried to suggest fun activities for the child and for the family members. When planning the activities on a weekly basis for the families, we recommend that these activities be carried out in general play activities of the family throughout the day and not in a single work period during each day.

V. Continuation of recordkeeping

14. Update the Charts when the child has mastered the objective by using a color to fill in the block containing the item.

15. Color only the beginning of the block, if the child can perform the skill only partially, e.g., by using an assistive device or by moving very slowly or awkwardly.

16. Outline the block with the appropriate color, if the child has accomplished a skill to the best of his ability but not in a normal way, e.g., by using an assistive device.

17. Repeat steps 5 to 17.

NOTE: Each child is unique and may master skills at a rate and age different from other children. The age references in this Guide are approximations. You should not be concerned if your child does not display skills exactly within the specified age ranges. See the Introduction for additional clarification.

1.01 QUIETS WHEN PICKED UP (0-1 mo.)

The child stops crying, momentarily, when picked up.

1. Try to anticipate the child's needs, in this way you are prepared to meet the immediate needs. For example:
   a. Prepare a bottle or make sure the backrest you need for breast feeding is ready. Your child will be hungry after a three hour nap.
   b. Prepare clean diapers and whatever else you need to change the child's diapers quickly.
2. Call the child's name when approaching her to let her know you are coming. Pick the child up gently and slowly, not quickly with a jerk. Keep your voice calm.
3. Hold the child firmly so he feels secure being picked up and in your arms. Place the child snugly against your body. Do not hold the child too tightly, restrict her movements or hold her partially suspended.
4. Mold your body to the child's so she fits securely against your body. Lean slightly back to compensate for the child's weight and the angle at which she is held.
5. Pick up the child and gently rub or pat her back as you soothingly talk to her.
6. Rock gently and sing softly as you pat the child's back.

1.02 SHOWS PLEASURE WHEN TOUCHED AND HANDLED (0-6 mo.)

1. Talk to the child as if he understands everything you are saying to him. As you share and talk, activities are made more pleasant for you and for the child.
2. Gently stroke the child's head, hold his hand or rub his arm while you cuddle and feed the child from the bottle or breast.
3. Tap and rub the child's back very gently, and at times, playfully, when burping him.
4. Carry and rock the child to the beat of rhythmic music.
5. Pat and rub the child's legs and arms when checking to see if he is cold or hot.
6. Talk to the child, sing simple songs or nursery rhymes while bathing him.
7. Use terry cloth towels or smooth materials to rub different parts of child's body, naming parts as you go along.
8. Blow on the child's stomach, hair, face, toes, or fingers.
9. Play a game like "This Little Piggy Went to Market" with the child's toes.
10. Sing nursery rhymes, such as "Hickory Dickory Dock." Use your two hands as the "mouse," and run up the child's body from toes to chin.
11. Sit in back of the child supporting him in sitting and do motions to songs, such as hands up, to the side, waving, rolling, tapping stomach or legs.

1.03 RESPONDS TO SOUNDS (0-1 mo.)

The child may show she has heard the sound in a number of different ways. She quiets after having been active, she changes her breathing pattern, she becomes more active after having been quiet by kicking her feet, moving her arms, widening her eyes or making a verbal sound.

1. Shake a bell eight to ten inches from the child's chest first to the left and then to the right of her head while the child is in supine.
   a. Use bright colored rattles with *low* tones, such as a wooden rattle.
   b. Use bright colored rattles (yellow) with *high* tones.
   c. Use rattles with faces on them.
   d. Use a squeak toy.
   e. Clap your hands suddenly (be careful not to scare her).
2. Shake the bell or rattle loudly and softly.
3. Repeat activity #1 with the child in different positions:
   a. In prone.
   b. In a carrying seat or held in sitting against an adult.
   c. In an upright position over the shoulder of an adult.
4. Place the rattle in the child's hands so she can feel its texture and shape. Assist the child in shaking the rattle to produce a sound.
5. Rock or move to a song on the radio. Stand very still when the music stops.
6. For the older delayed child:
   a. Place him in different positions when ringing a bell or rattle. Touch the cheek or arms of the child so she feels the vibration of the sound. Use a triangle or tuning fork.
   b. Hold the child very still and listen for a sound another person makes or for environmental sounds, such as a ringing telephone or flying airplanes. Turn the child toward the source of the sound.
   c. Make different sounds by knocking on wood or cans, or by using toys, such as xylophones, jack-in-the-boxes. Immediately acknowledge the sound by smiling and showing pleasure. Show excitement by asking, "Did you hear that?" or "That was a clown!"

1.04 RESPONDS TO VOICE (0-2½ mo.)

Initially, the child shows his awareness of a sound by a response, such as an eyeblink or a startle response depending on the intensity of the sound. He quickly adjusts to the sound and his response diminishes. The child adjusts to almost any kind of environmental noise and sleeps in quiet or noise, whichever is typical of his environment. A change either way to more noise or more quiet is apt to result in a response of increased activity or alertness demonstrating his awareness of the change.

1. Comfort the child by soothing him and by talking to him during the first few weeks. Speak to him in a soft, friendly voice. This will help quiet him when he is upset, provided he is not hungry or in pain.

2. Encourage the child to respond to your voice by talking to him in a soothing manner as you care for him. He will begin to associate your voice to the handling and care which accompanies it.
3. Use many verbal cues. Stimulate the child by encouraging eye contact and eye movement toward sounds. Activities which require listening are necessary for development. Activities for cognitive and language development from this very early age are limited to stimulation. Language is total communication. Tone of voice, facial expression, touching and gestures are as much a part of communication as words.
4. Refer to 5.02 (Regards face).

1.05 INSPECTS SURROUNDINGS (1-2 mo.)

The child visually begins to explore the environment.

1. Give the child opportunities to look at his surroundings.
2. Carry the child securely and comfortably, but in different positions when you go places:
   a. In front facing you.
   b. In front facing outward.
   c. Over your left shoulder.
   d. Over your right shoulder.
3. Place the child in different positions as he plays with a toy:
   a. In supine.
   b. In prone.
   c. In side-lying.
   d. In sitting in the adult's lap leaning against the adult.
4. Place the child in different areas of the living room with a toy.
5. Let the child lie on different textures, such as blankets, rugs. Let the child touch the different textured clothing of people carrying him.
6. Hang appropriate mobiles over the crib with mobile figures facing the child's face about eight to ten inches from the child.
7. Present the child with different rattles and toys to see, touch, smell, hear, taste.
8. Decorate the child's room with large, bright colored, simple pictures of animals, objects, and people. Colorful animal place mats are effective and easy to clean.
9. For the older delayed child: Change the location of his crib so the windows and door are at different angles to him.

1.06 SHOWS ACTIVE INTEREST IN PERSON OR OBJECT FOR AT LEAST 1 MINUTE (1-6 mo.)

The child interacts with a person or object for one minute.

1. Face the child so she can see your face easily whenever you feed, bathe or pick her up. Talk to her throughout these everyday activities naming body parts, clothing, foods, actions.

2. Encourage the child to reach and touch your face when you diaper or play with her. Nod your head or turn it; children are attracted to movement. Use touching, rubbing, or caressing to reinforce the child for looking at you, "talking" to you or interacting with you in any way.
3. Rock and bounce the child to music as she faces you. Sing with the music too. Rock the child facing you on your knees, in prone, etc.
4. Play blanket swing to songs, especially those you can sing. Place the child on her back on a sturdy blanket or large towel. Pick up four ends and gently swing side to side. Make sure the child can see you. When two people do this the child has a clear view of the persons. The child need be only a few inches off the floor and rocked very gently. Another day try rocking forward and back. Change the child's position so she has experience with different positions.
5. Hang a musical mobile within reach of the child's hands while the child is in different positions, in side-lying, in supine or in supported sitting. Show the child how she can bat at and move the mobile to produce sounds. The mobiles should be sturdy and securely fastened to the crib or to a rope strung across the crib or playpen. *Use caution* to determine the length of the rope to prevent entanglement by the child.
   a. Use a mobile that makes sounds the child likes. Test the child's responsiveness to the high and low tones of the mobile before buying or making your own.
   b. Hang or place it in different locations of the crib, such as on the side at first, then to the other side, in the middle (midline), slightly closer, then farther, etc.
   c. Use mobiles that can move in different ways, such as swaying sideways, bouncing up and down because they are attached to elastic.
   d. Check to see that objects or pictures on mobiles are facing the child. If she is looking up, animals should be parallel to her eyes, not to the person standing over her.
6. Play with the child using a rattle. Vary the sounds, textures, design and color. Refer to 1.13 (Begins play with rattle).
7. Attach an interesting toy to the baby's high chair or stroller to play with while eating or going for a walk. *Use caution* in determining the length of the string so the child cannot get entangled.
8. Place the child in front of a mirror with a toy so she can watch herself do different things with the toy.
9. Use toys that rock and make music, such as roly poly clowns, Japanese rocking dolls and other toys that return to an upright position after they are moved or hit sideways. These toys can be used with the child in prone, in supine, in side-lying, over a wedge or roll, or in supported sitting.
10. Give the child a soft squeeze toy. If the child shows no interest, show her how to squeak it by poking, hitting, holding and squeezing it for her. Let her reach, touch and grasp the toy.

11. For the older delayed child: Sit or kneel at a busy box attached on the wall at the correct level for the child. Explore the different things. Talk to her, describe what she is doing, the effect, the movement, the color, the sounds.

1.07 LISTENS TO VOICE FOR 30 SECONDS
   (1-3 mo.)

The child soberly regards the face of the adult speaking to him and seems to listen intently as the adult continues to talk.

1. Talk to the child as you feed, dress and change him. Use a friendly tone of voice. Tell him how wonderful and beautiful he is. Tell him what you are doing.
2. Talk to the child at close range when playing. Make funny sounds. Entertain him. Encourage your older children to talk to him with your supervision. They will enjoy the child's attention and your approval.
3. Keep the child in the room with you when you talk to other people, when you read or tell stories to your older children. The child should be able to see you.
4. Sing to the child. A good voice or ability to carry a tune is unnecessary.
5. Whistle or hum to the child.
6. Refer to 5.02. (Regards face) and to 5.07 (Responds with smile when socially approached).

1.08 SHOWS ANTICIPATORY EXCITEMENT
   (1½-4 mo.)

The child shows that he can anticipate something that is about to happen to him: a change in the surrounding environment, such as mom smiling and talking to him; a change in his situation, such as getting picked up; or a change in his condition, such as being fed.

A child shows his anticipation in a variety of ways: kicking, smiling, vocalizing, tensing his body, quieting or becoming more active from a quiet state.

1. Call the child's name and tell him you are coming whenever you approach the child. Tell him what you will do, such as "Time to sunbathe," "We're going to take a bath now," or "Mommy's bringing your milk." Start talking before he can see you or before you enter the room and continue until you reach him. As you approach, his visual picture of you and your voice level will increase.
2. Walk naturally, not necessarily quietly, so the sound of your footsteps will let him know you are approaching, and your sudden appearance or approach will not startle him.
3. For the older delayed child:
   a. Use commercially available milk bottles with faces or animal shapes. This sometimes helps the child to focus on the bottle. There are also different colored bottles. Find one the child responds to and use it consistently.
   b. Make a covering for the bottle with a sock or with bright colored cloth that attracts the child's attention. Use different textures to encourage exploration and the patting and touching of the bottle.
   c. Play the "I'm going to tickle you" game. The adult or sibling leans over the child so she can see his expressions and wiggling fingers. The adult says gleefully, "I'm going to tickle you" (intonation and inflection are very important), and then tickles the child by wiggling his fingers along the child's trunk saying, "tickle, tickle," and laughing.
   d. If the child is eating solid foods, before feeding him, show the child the spoon and bowl or jar that the food is in. Let him smell the food and see it so he knows what is coming.
   e. Refer to 1.21 (Continues a familiar activity by initiating movements involved, Activity #4). Show the child the blanket while telling him what you will be doing. Help the child anticipate the activity.
   f. Place the child in prone. Tell him the game you will be playing or what you will be doing. Lift him a few inches off the floor and say, "Ready, set, go," and gently swing the child from side to side, back and forth or up and down. The way you say, "Ready, set, go" indicates to the child something different and fun will be happening. Play the game only if the lifting is enjoyable for the child. Start with very gentle movements which take the child only a few inches off the ground. You can later increase the height and the amount of movement.
4. For the breast fed child, talk to the child to let him know it is time for eating. Perhaps show him something he may associate with feeding time, like a burp towel. This lets the child know what is going to happen. Many times just the positioning of the child, or the mother starting to undo her clothing lets the child know it is time for milk. During this time it is important for the child's hands to be free to explore and touch mommy's clothes and breast while drinking.
5. From approximately three-and-a-half months, the baby who is bottle fed will recognize the bottle visually and react to its appearance. As with activity #1, tell the child you are approaching and you are bringing his bottle. When you reach the child, pick him up and show him his bottle for a moment, say, "Bottle, Tony's bottle," then feed him. It is important the child's hands and arms are not pinned behind mother or held away from the bottle. Touching is important to learning.
6. Extend your hands to the child and say, "Come up" or "Come, let's go see Daddy" before you pick him up. Give the child a few seconds to see your arms and look at your smiling face as you talk. Let him know he will be picked up. Being picked up should be a pleasant experience; avoid jerking the child with a sudden lift.
7. Play a game involving anticipation of a sound or movement. Tell the child "Daddy is going to wind the toy radio." At this young age, the child does not understand what is said, but he associates the intonation of the words and the winding noise. The child has a visual picture of daddy winding the toy, hearing the forthcoming

music, daddy singing or humming, picking him up to "dance," or rocking gently with him. Musical mobiles are great fun too.

1.09 REACTS TO DISAPPEARANCE OF SLOWLY MOVING OBJECT (2-3 mo.)

The child watches a slowly moving object disappear and continues to search for it for a few seconds at the place at which it disappeared.

1. Play face to face with a child, and slowly move behind a nearby barrier, such as a big box. Draw the child's attention to your face by your expressions, smiles and conversation and slowly make your face disappear until only the top of your head and your eyes are visible. Reappear slowly the way you disappeared.
2. Talk and play with the child for awhile without toys; play tickle games or rock to music. Slowly move while the child is watching until you disappear behind a couch, chair, box or any barrier. As soon as you disappear, quickly reappear at the place you disappeared behind the barrier. See if the child is still watching the place where your face disappeared. If the child seems to lose you, do the activity again but do not stop talking when you disappear. Keep up the conversation until you reappear.
3. For the older delayed child:
   a. Attach a balloon to the stroller, high chair or wrist of the child. Let her play with it and watch it bounce and move. When the balloon settles partially or completely behind things, call attention to where it disappeared. Let the balloon come into view again where it disappeared. See if the child will linger with a glance at the point of disappearance. Do not use a dangerously long string (over twelve inches) for this activity.
   b. Use a piece of cloth and a toy on a strong. Pull the toy so it disappears under the cloth. The toy's shape will be evident. Pull the toy out again from where it disappeared. If the child follows the toy and continues to "look" at it even when it was covered, try the next activity.
   c. Use a toy attached to a string and slowly pull it behind a low barrier so part of the top can be seen. Pull the toy out again. Increase the barrier's height by adding a block and repeat the activity. See if the child lingers with a glance at the place at which the toy disappeared.
   d. Play with toys on a string, facing the child. Take one of the toys the child likes, and pull the string behind you as the child watches. See if the child continues to look at the place at which the toy disappeared. If the child immediately loses it, pull it back out. Try this several times. If the child still loses it, use a toy that moves with a sound so the child can follow the sound.
   e. Play with a texture ball. Roll it slowly behind a couch or low box while the child is looking at it. If the child

does not linger with a glance, move the barrier to show part of the ball and roll it again. If the child can move, encourage her to find the ball. If she does not move well, roll the ball so only a part of it disappears.
   f. Take the child out for a walk in a stroller or carry him out. Point out, talk about and touch, flowers, leaves, tree trunks, parked cars, grass, cement. Point out something big and bright in the environment whenever you come to a tree or large natural barrier. Let the child focus on it, then slowly move past the barrier until the object disappears. Ask the child where it is, go back to it, then slowly move again to see if the child will linger with a glance at the point where the object disappeared.

1.10 SEARCHES WITH EYES FOR SOUND (2-3½ mo.)

In these activities the adult must make sure the child is in a position to search for a sound by using his eyes (not by turning his head). The child searches for the sound but need not find it and look toward it.

1. Ring a bell eight to ten inches from the child's face to one side of his eyes. If the child does not respond, slowly move it toward the front of his eyes until he does.
2. Use a rattle. If the child does not respond, touch or tap his cheek on the side he is to look for the sound.
3. Try activities numbers one and two while the child is in different positions and make different sounds with:
   a. Bright colored (yellow) rattles with low tones.
   b. Bright colored rattles with high tones.
   c. Rattles with faces on them.
   d. Squeak or musical toys.
   e. Hands clapping or banging objects.
   f. Loud and soft sounds.
4. Sing or hum a tune with your head or lips against the child's head so she "feels" the song and turns to you. Encourage the child to look at and touch your mouth.
5. Sing your favorite song to the child. Encourage him to touch your mouth. Occasionally place his hand over your mouth so the singing stops. Let him watch your mouth as you sing again. Sing the song to the child while he is not looking and see whether he searches for you.
6. Wear bright colored lipstick to encourage the child to focus on your mouth. Talk or sing to the child, turning his head, if necessary, to focus on your mouth and face. When the child is paying attention, move your face slowly to the left or right and help the child follow, if necessary. Move upwards and downwards also.
7. Place the child's hand on a rattle, bell, or tuning fork so he turns toward the sound and vibration. If the child does not, gently turn his head so he sees the object producing the sound or moves the object into his field of vision.
8. Help the child hold and shake the toy so he feels his own movements with the sound. If the child searches, guide the rattle in front of him until he finds it.

9. When a sound is heard, bring the child close to touch and see it, if possible.
   a. When the telephone rings let the child touch it while it is vibrating.
   b. When an airplane or loud truck passes, go to or turn the child toward the window and point saying, "Look at the truck," "The truck goes *(make sound)*."
10. Call the child as you approach him either when you enter the room or when you move closer to him. Reinforce him verbally, with touching or by lifting him when his eyes search for you in response to your voice. If the child does not look for you, touch his face while you call his name and talk to him. Reward the response.
11. Hang a sound mobile, like the chime mobile, at a distance to the left or right of the child so the child's random movements can activate the mobile. This is a passive activity and is recommended for those times when mother cannot directly interact with the child.

1.11 INSPECTS OWN HANDS (2-3 mo.)

The child looks at and really inspects her hands, moving them, watching what they do without a toy.

1. Bring the child's hands to a position where he can inspect them if he does not do so spontaneously. Place the child in supine, in prone, in side-lying or in supported sitting.
2. Place the child in prone on different textures, such as grass, grass mat, blanket and encourage her to explore its texture.
3. Place your finger in the child's hand. After he grasps your finger, bring it to where he can see you wiggle your finger and his.
4. Place a colorful wrist band with a bell on each wrist or hand.
5. Provide a variety of textured and auditorily stimulating toys and objects for the child to play with and explore.
6. Focus the light from a flashlight on the child's hands to attract his attention to them.
7. For the older delayed child:
   a. Use a texture box or textures which are available in the home, such as clothing, objects, household things. Pat and rub the different textures on the child's hands, fingers, feet, and toes in play. Describe the textures and tell the child what body part you are rubbing. Other uses for good times:
      (1) Bathtime. Use your hand or soft terry-cloth while washing. (Or, sew a glove by connecting two small hand towels together or one large towel cut in half to wash or rinse the child.)
      (2) Diapering. Gently rub the clean diaper on her hands or let the child play with an extra cloth diaper, touching, sucking, mouthing it as the child is lying on her back.
      (3) After diapering, say, "Give me your hands." Tap the child's hands and pull the child to sitting. Clap her hands together and say

"Good girl!"
   b. While carrying the child at home, at school, out shopping, anywhere—
      (1) Allow and encourage the child to touch her environment, especially the adult's clothes.
      (2) Draw attention to her hands once in a while by kissing or blowing on them, providing tactile and verbal stimulation.
      (3) Allow the child to use her hands to explore your face. Should she get them in your mouth, playfully pretend to munch on them using your tongue and lips to give sensory stimulation to the child.
8. For the child with an asymmetrical tonic neck reflex:
   a. Place the child in supine with head in midline. Bring her hands to midline, providing support at the shoulders or arms. Position her hands so she can inspect them.
   b. Place the child in side-lying with elbows flexed and hands where she can see them.

1.12 WATCHES SPEAKER'S EYES AND MOUTH (2-3 mo.)

1. Hold the child in such a way he has a direct view of your face.
2. Take the child's hand and place it on your mouth, nose and eyes.
3. Cradle the child in your arms in such a way that the child can see your face when you are feeding him. When the child looks at you, smile and verbalize.
4. Make faces and smile to draw attention to your eyes and mouth.
5. Refer to 1.07 (Listen to voice for 30 seconds).
6. Use bright colored lipstick to draw the child's attention to your face.
7. Use funny facial expressions to entertain the child.

1.13 BEGINS PLAY WITH RATTLE (2½-4 mo.)

The child plays with a rattle placed in her hand by regarding, shaking, mouthing or waving it for very short periods of time. Choose rattles that do not break easily, expose sharp edges or have small particles which fall out.

1. Refer to 4.13 (Grasps toy actively).
2. Help the child by gently tapping or moving her arms at the elbow.
3. Move the child's arm so the rattle is in midline about eight to ten inches away from the child's chest; help the child shake the rattle.
4. Encourage the child to explore the rattle with his mouth.
5. Talk to the child and describe what he is doing.
6. Change the child's position.
7. Use a variety of rattles such as:
   a. Rattles with easy to grasp handles.
   b. Rattles with different tones so you can see which one the child likes best.

c. Rattles with faces on them to attract the child's attention.

d. Rattles with intense colors.

e. Rattles with different textures.

f. Rattles which are opaque. These are especially useful for a child with visual problems. Place the child near a source of light that can filter through the rattle.

8. Give the child the experience of holding the rattle in his left as well as in the right hand.

1.14 ENJOYS REPEATING NEWLY LEARNED ACTIVITY (3-4 mo.)

The child purposefully hits or moves a toy at least three to four times to keep it active, in movement or in sound or both.

1. Attach bells to elastic or cloth and put them around a child's wrist or ankle so when she moves, the bells will ring. Place them on the child's hands and another time on her ankles. Later try both wrists and ankles but use different tones so the sounds are different.

2. Refer to 1.06 (Shows active interest in person or object for at least one minute, Activity #5).

3. Use or make mobiles of different textures with sounds (bells) attached or contained within the objects.

4. Use toys that rock and make music such as roly poly clowns, Japanese rocking dolls and other toys that go back to an upright position after they are hit or pushed. These toys can be used with the child in supine, in side lying, over a wedge or roller and in supported sitting.

5. For the child who is unable to use his hands for a while, such as a child being fed intravenously through his arms, hang a mobile near his feet so he can kick at it. "Thumper" is a good toy to attach to a crib or playpen when he must remain there alone. Refer to 3.11 (Kicks reciprocally)

6. For the older delayed child: Use toys with a suction on one end so they can be attached firmly to wheelchairs or other structures. This type of toy can be attached in different places easily and at different heights and angles to the child.

1.15 USES HANDS AND MOUTH FOR SENSORY EXPLORATION OF OBJECTS (3-6 mo.)

The child explores objects by mouthing, patting, touching, rubbing, hitting them with his hands or banging them against another object.

1. Refer to 6.09 (Brings hand to mouth with toy or object).

2. Place two rattles near the child so she can look at them and choose the toy she would like to play with.

3. Use textured teethers and a variety of objects to provide different experiences for the child. The feel of bumps, lines, and holes in teethers or rattles is fun and important for exploration. Grooved rubber balls are good play things because the child can grip them and easily bite

and mouth them. Textured balls for patting, rubbing, and mouthing provide good stimulation. If a child does not respond to different textures, use one texture at a time. Encourage touching and mouthing of soft things, then, smooth things, bumpy things, scratchy things, rough things.

4. Toys and objects which make noises help motivate the child to move the toys. This gives different viewpoints and changing areas of exploration, also, a sustaining interest in toys. Colors, faces and designs on toys can be attractive and of more interest to explore.

5. Give the child toys which are of different temperatures. Some toys can be refrigerated for a brief period (even a metal can cover with no sharp edges) or some toys contain water that can be frozen. This is especially fun to explore and mouth when a child is teething. Warm water is also good to explore. Rubbery things (that may remind the child of bottle nipples) placed in hot water until warm are fun to chew and explore.

6. If other ways of encouraging the child to explore are unsuccessful after repeated efforts, place a *small* amount of honey on a rattle or teether. This may *start* some exploration with the child's mouth. Infant cereal may also be used. The honey should be used only to encourage exploration and eliminated as soon as possible.

1.16 TURNS EYES AND HEAD TO SOUND OF HIDDEN VOICE (3-7 mo.)

The child turns to mother's voice when she is near and later localizes it even when she is hidden from view.

A. Localizes mother's voice.
   1. Talk to the child so he responds to your voice and his name during everyday activities:
      a. When feeding the child and he is facing you.
      b. When picking him up after he awakens from sleep.
      c. While bathing him.
      d. When entering the room and you greet him and call his name, talking as you go to him so he can see where the voice is coming from.
      e. While carrying and rocking the child so he associates your voice with the pleasure of the movement.
      f. While playing with the child as he explores his hands, feet, fingers; touch them and name them when the child focuses on you.
   2. Do the above activities and call with a loud, soft, high-pitched or low-pitched voice. Try to determine if the child responds preferentially to a particular tone. Check her favorite musical toys or rattles to see if they are high or low in pitch.
   3. Talk to the child and encourage her to touch and explore your face while the child is in a variety of positions. Tell her what she is touching, "Nose, mommy's nose."
   4. Slowly move to the left or right during an activity when you are talking to the child and she is paying

6

attention to you. Encourage the child to follow your face and voice. If she does not, gently guide her in the proper direction. Give the child a chance to follow your voice. If the child stops following, stop talking. Talk again to gain her attention (even if you must go directly in front of her), move to the sides, then up and down.

B.   Localizes hidden voice.
1.   Move so you are partially behind a barrier, such as the crib bars, chair back, a book or small towel when the child is following your voice. If the child does not follow, try a transparent barrier and later an opaque one.
2.   Quietly approach the crib and remain hidden. Call the child's name. If the child does not respond by turning correctly to where you are, call again and continue talking until he does. If the child is unable to locate the direction of your voice, move to where he is looking, call his name and then pop up and reinforce the child.
3.   Play hide-and-seek with the child and a sibling or a friend. Let the sibling call the child and mother from another room or outside from behind trees, bushes or the side of the house to find the sibling. Mother can make it an exciting, suspenseful game by her movements, voice and the rest of her behavior.
4.   For the older delayed child who can move independently, play hide-and-seek indoors. Let the person hiding stay behind a couch or a reasonably close barrier. Let her call out so the child can find her. If the child needs encouragement the person hiding can extend a leg or an arm to help the child.

1.17 PLAYS WITH OWN HANDS, FEET, FINGERS, TOES (3-5 mo.)

At this time, the child touches, clasps his hands, and reaches for his feet and toes. The child need not look at what he is doing. In general, the activities described for play with hands can be done with other body parts with little or no modification.

1.   Refer to 1.11 (Inspects own hands).
2.   Play simple movement games with the child on his back, or sitting in your lap at home, riding in a car or bus.
  a.   "Ten Little Indians" with fingers and toes.
  b.   "Twinkle Twinkle Little Star."
  c.   "This Little Piggy Went to Market."
  d.   "The Foolish Man Built His House Upon the Sand."
  e.   "Wheels on the Bus."
  f.   Make up your own games and songs.
3.   Use colorful mittens on a cold day for the child to wear. Draw the child's attention to his hands by securely attaching anything light that makes a sound, like little bells to the mittens. Do this with booties also.
4.   For the older delayed child:
  a.   Use bracelets or make colorful toys out of different textures which produce sounds that encourage movement, touching and playing.

b.   Dip the child's fingers in cream and help him spread it over his hands and body.
c.   Let the child put some food on her fingers. Let her put it into her mouth to suck and explore its taste. Use honey, poi, plain yogurt, or later some creamy peanut butter.
d.   Stick a colorful sticker, rolled masking tape or scotch tape to the child's hands. If the child does not respond by touching, by mouthing, or by removing it, help him. A bandaid may also be fun to try.
e.   Sing and do bicycling exercises for fun or as a relaxing activity for the child. Rub the child's legs and play with his toes as well.
f.   Attach something on the child's crib or playpen for her to kick. This will result in a tactile and auditory response.
g.   Use a non-toxic, large felt pen and make designs or faces in the child's palm, on the back of his hand, or on his fingers to attract his attention to his hands. You can paint his finger nails but do not use nail polish.
h.   Focus light (flashlight) on the child's fingers to help him maintain interest in his fingers.
i.   Sit the child in a hole with sand to support him and encourage the exploration of wet and dry sand in his hands at the beach. Drop wet sand and dry sand on his hands. If the child is willing, bury his hands in the sand to be "found" when he moves or pulls them out.

1.18 AWAKENS OR QUIETS TO MOTHER'S VOICE (3-6 mo.)

The primary reason for using the soothing voice in conjunction with awakening or quieting is to begin the development of a good feeling, a sense of security with a melodic human voice.

1.   Wake a sleeping child by gently calling her name. Continue talking softly as the child awakens. In this way, awakening becomes a good experience.
2.   Use the same soothing voice to quiet a crying child and help the child feel secure and sleepy. Often, just speaking softly and quietly to the child will be sufficient. Soft humming or singing will also help the child feel secure.
3.   Sing or talk to the child as you put him to sleep.

1.19 LOCALIZES SOUND WITH EYES (3½-5 mo.)

The child finds a sound that is close by, to the left, right, above and below his eyes. The child must be in a position in which he is physically capable of finding the sound by using his eyes.

1.   Refer to 1.10 (Searches with eyes for sound).
2.   Ring a bell seven to ten inches from the child's face to the left or right of his eyes. If the child does not locate the bell, slowly move it toward the child's face (ringing it) until he does.

3. Shake a bell seven to ten inches from the child's eyes to the left of his face if he is looking to the right and vice versa when he is sitting on your lap. If the child does not locate it with his eyes gently move his head, with the side of your head, until he does.
4. Touch the area of the child's face closest to the direction of the sound.

1.20 FINDS A PARTIALLY HIDDEN OBJECT
(4-6 mo.)

The child successfully uncovers a partially covered, non-symmetrical toy or object (e.g., doll or car).

1. Start with uniform objects or large toys and gradually change to non-symmetrical smaller ones.
2. Gather familiar favorite toys. Place the child in front of a mirror in sitting, in prone, or in side-lying position. Let the child look at himself in the mirror. Pick up a musical toy and hold it behind the child so the child can see it clearly in the mirror. Show the toy to him, ringing it and moving it to attract his attention. If the child does not turn to find it, help him by turning his face. Do the same with other toys, some without sounds so the child can find the toys by its reflection only.
3. Find a favorite non-uniform toy and show it to the child. When the child wants it and begins to reach for it, quickly cover it with a transparent screen. Plastic covers from containers or coffee cans work well. Soft plastics such as plastic bags or wrap should *not* be used. If the child does not continue to look for the toy, lift the cover and show him the toy. Let the child play with the toy, then try again.
4. Use a familiar, non-uniform toy and cover half the toy as the child reaches for it. Use a cloth, a towel, a part of the sheet the child may be lying on or a newspaper as the cover.
5. Cover half the toy with fallen leaves or if dad is mowing the lawn, the fresh cut grass. Encourage the child to find the toy and shake the leaves or grass off.
6. Pile a few toys together so the toys are partially covered by each other. Encourage the child to pull out his favorite toys. The same can be done with the child's toys in a toy box or a cardboard box designated as the child's toy box. Let the child "rummage" through the box to pull out toys to play with.
7. Play with the child by burying half of a toy with sand. Ask the child to help you find it again or to help you pull out the whole toy. This can be done at the beach or in a sandbox or with dirt or mud. Cover part of the child's foot or hand with sand and pull it out.
8. Hide a toy behind something like a couch or pillow with one end showing. Attract the child's attention to it and encourage him to pull it out.
9. Place a toy or a common household article, such as a large spoon in your apron pocket. Allow part of the spoon to show and encourage the child to pull it out. Place pens in daddy's pockets.

10. For the older delayed child: Give him toys from behind, from above, from his side, from angles he is not used to seeing them. Use toys that are uniform, such as pop beads. Later use toys that are non-symmetrical, such as stuffed animals and rattles which have different bottoms.

1.21 CONTINUES A FAMILIAR ACTIVITY BY INITIATING MOVEMENTS INVOLVED
(4-5 mo.)

The child must indicate she wants to continue a pleasant familiar activity by appropriately moving the specific body part involved.

1. Find an action or sound toy which is likely to interest the child, such as a musical jumping jack, a top, a wind-up toy animal, or another similar toy. Be sure the child can devote his full attention to the toy. Make sure he is not involved in another play activity and that there are no environmental distractions. Play appropriately with the action toy so the child can see how it moves or produces sound. Stop the activity abruptly. See if some gesture stands out in the child's reactions. He might hit his hand on a surface, kick his legs, vocalize, or make some other general movement.
2. Do activity #1. Look for a *specific gesture* that may stand out in reaction to an abrupt cessation of a pleasant action. Repeat the activity several times to see if the child reacts with the same procedure or specific gesture.
3. Place the child in prone on someone's stomach. Bounce the child and then stop abruptly. See if the child will push up with his arms to bounce with his body or if the child will push downward.
4. Swinging in a blanket or a big towel is a fun activity. Place the child in the center, then each person takes an end (two people) or if there is only one person she takes all four ends. Gently swing the child side to side or forward and back just a little above the floor while smiling and humming a tune. Stop the activity abruptly. The child can still be suspended or be placed down on the floor. See if the child will rock by himself or pull purposefully on the blanket sides to restart the activity.
5. Bounce the child on your knee, sitting the child sideways or have her straddle your knees. As you bounce, sing a short song or nursery rhyme, hum, or repeat a syllable like "ma" or "da" to a melody. Abruptly stop the verbalizing and the bouncing. Observe if the child tries to restart the activity by moving a specific body part appropriately, bouncing by himself using his own legs to go up and down, pushing purposefully on your knee or perhaps wiggling his bottom to restart the bouncing.
6. Rock the child in sitting, in puppy position or extended puppy position and stop abruptly. Again see if she will continue on her own or push against your hands if you are holding her. If you rock the child in your arms before this activity, it is harder to recognize whether the child

is moving a specific body part to restart the rocking or is just excited and therefore moving her whole body.

1.22 LOCALIZES TACTILE STIMULATION BY TOUCHING THE SAME SPOT OR SEARCHING FOR OBJECT THAT TOUCHED BODY (4-6 mo.)

The child searches for the object he felt or localizes the body part touched. Use normal firm pressure when touching and rubbing.

1. Use your finger tips to tickle, rub, and stimulate a place on the child's body, such as his stomach or toes. When the child looks for the place or touches your hand, reward him with praise.
2. Touch the child's hand or leg with a toy that is attractive to him, that vibrates and makes a sound or that feels soft or smooth. Help the child, if necessary, to reach for and pick up the toy, and to explore and play with it.
3. Play with just one body part, such as the child's hands. When he is not looking, touch his hands with a variety of toys which provide different kinds of clues.
    a. Toys which vibrate and make different sounds such as bells, rattle, squeaks .
    b. Toys which have different textures, such as texture balls, bumpy, soft, and smooth toys.
    c. Toys or objects with different temperatures, such as a bottle with warm milk or cold water, a cold or warm teething ring, cold fruit, a utensil like a spoon or a wet washcloth.
    d. Objects with different smells.
4. Touch different body parts which are easy to see first. Later, touch the area around the child's mouth and her cheek.
5. Touch different parts of the child's body with one texture or try a variety of textures. Encourage him to find what touched him and where. Allow him time to find the object or the place he was touched. Continue to touch and rub till he does. Keep the different textures in the box (texture box).
6. Dangle a toy so it rubs against or touches the back of the child's head while he is sitting or on his stomach. If he does not look for it, move it to the side. See if he will turn and reach for it or for the place on his head it had touched. Move the toy to the front, if needed, and help him touch and look at it. Repeat this in front of a mirror.
7. Quickly attach an elastic bracelet of beads, bells, to the child's leg or hand while she is looking away. If the child does not feel the slight snap or added weight, as well as the tactile sensation, aid her by showing it to her and moving it around against her skin.
8. Use something sticky, such as colored masking tape or plastic tape which is rolled up. The size, color and movement, in addition to the stick, attracts the child's attention. If it does not, show it to him and remove it or stick it on while he is watching. Use colorful dot stickers, too.

9. Slowly roll a ball or an attractive, light vehicle, like a toy car when the child is watching. If he does not react to the bump, teach him to touch the place where it bumped him. When the child is *not* watching, roll a ball to him so it bumps into him. Encourage him to find the ball or to touch the place where it bumped him.
10. For the older delayed child: Attach some colorful clothespins to the child's shirt. The weight and clicking sounds of the pins may stimulate the child's localizing or searching behavior.

1.23 PLAYS WITH PAPER (4½-7 mo.)

The child enjoys crumpling, tearing and pulling paper.

1. Give the child the opportunity to play with paper. Encourage him to feel its texture by crumpling, stretching and tearing it. Let him explore paper using all his senses. At this age everything goes to the mouth; this is okay so long as other exploration takes place as well. (A small amount of paper eating is often unavoidable.) *Never* use plastic wrap or plastic bags.
2. Types of paper that can be used:
    a. Sturdy butcher paper
    b. Brown paper bags cut open
    c. Magazine pages
    d. Newspaper
    e. Wax paper
    f. Colorful construction paper
    g. Napkins
    h. Kleenex tissue
    i. Colorful tissue paper
    j. Large masking tape or scotch tape
3. Add mild scents to the paper after the child has explored it in its natural form. Be sure what you add is non-toxic and pleasant. Perfumes taste horrible and should be avoided.
4. Make a paper texture box placing different types of paper and a few paper products, such as plates, cups, and napkins in the box. Explore the different textures with the child and describe them as she touches, mouths and tears them.

1.24 TOUCHES TOY OR ADULT'S HAND TO RESTART AN ACTIVITY (5-9 mo.)

The child begins to learn that objects can have independent actions. He watches the performance of an action toy. When it stops, he tries to start it again by touching the toy or the hand of the person who started the action.

Later the child learns to explore for direct causes of the action he observes and eventually tries to start it the way he sees it started.

1. Play a simple game that will interest the child, such as banging blocks or spinning a toy. Stop the activity abruptly. Leave both your hand and the toy within

reach of the child. See if the child tries to start the game by *touching the toy or your hand.*

2. Play other games.
    a. Play hand games where you drum, scratch or make your fingers crawl on a surface.
    b. Shake or bang a rattle.
    c. Play "Pat-a-Cake."
    d. Play peek-a-boo with your hands or a cloth.
    e. Play with a busy box or busy bath toy.
    f. Splash or stir the bath water to make a floating toy bob. Quickly catch the toy and keep it in your hand when you stop splashing or stirring.

1.25 REACHES FOR SECOND OBJECT PURPOSEFULLY (5-6½ mo.)

The child holds an object in one hand and reaches for a second object purposefully. He reaches for the object with either hand, whether or not he has a toy in it. The child need not be successful in obtaining the second object.

1. Offer the child a second and more attractive object while he plays with a toy or object small enough to be held in one hand. See if the child will reach for it. Usually bright musical toys are attractive.
    a. If the child does *not* respond by reaching:
        (1) Bring the object to the child's free hand and encourage him to track it with his eyes. Place the object in his hand. Reward him through play and verbalization for having an object in each hand.
        (2) Bring the object to the child's free hand and encourage him to track it.
        (3) Tap the hand on the palm to encourage palmar grasp of the toy. Reinforce through play the feel and pleasure of having two objects to shake and bang.
    b. If the child moves toward the object:
        (1) Immediately help complete the attempt by moving the child's hand to the object. Reward the effort with play and praise.
        (2) Move the object closer and tap the child's arm beneath the elbow to get extension toward the object.
    c. If the child lets the first object go, catch it as the fingers extend. Encourage the child to retain it while reaching.
2. Use your watch, bracelet or an object that dangles which the child has seen you wear for the second object. Objects which the child has seen you "play" with are attractive to him.
3. Position the child so he can see clearly, is relaxed, and feels secure. Attempt different positions, such as in sitting, in prone, in supine, in side-lying or in puppy. Use easy to grasp toys. The attractiveness of the toys, visually, tactually, auditorily, is determined by the child's response to it. The spatial position of the offered toy is

important. The toy should not be so far away that even a good try is unsuccessful. The child's approach is sometimes a sweeping circular motion and not a direct approach, so allow for this as well.

1.26 WORKS FOR DESIRED, OUT OF REACH OBJECT (5-9 mo.)

The child reaches repeatedly for a toy or object without necessarily obtaining it. Give the toy to the child after a few attempts if the child does not succeed. The child's persistence is achieved only if he experiences repeated success in obtaining the object. Be careful not to tease the child.

1. Refer to 5.21 (Lifts arms to mother).
2. Place a favorite toy out of the child's reach so he must stretch or move to obtain it. Do this when the child is in sitting, in prone, in supine or on hands and knees. Place and offer objects to the child from different angles, different distances or a combination of both.
3. Place the child's toys in different places depending on his locomotion skills.
    a. Place toys on a sofa to encourage the child to pull to standing.
    b. Place toys on a low shelf or table to encourage the child to reach while in hands and knees.
    c. Place a toy where the child must pivot on his stomach to obtain it.
    d. Place toys at a distance to be "rolled to."

1.27 DISTINGUISHES BETWEEN FRIENDLY AND ANGRY VOICES (5-6½ mo.)

The child responds in a different manner to pleasant and angry voices even when she cannot see the facial expression.

1. Give the child the opportunity to hear voices showing a variety of emotions, but avoid very strong negative inflections since they may frighten the child.
2. Let the child hear you when you scold the dog for barking or the cat for coming in the house in a mildly angry voice when it is appropriate.
3. Comfort the child if he suddenly begins crying (or shows fear in other ways) when you scold or become angry at someone else. Some children react by becoming very quiet. Notice the child's reaction and reassure him when necessary.
4. Occasionally, children become frightened by loud, angry voices on TV or the radio. Help the child avoid these experiences if they upset him.

1.28 HAND REGARD NO LONGER PRESENT (5-6 mo.)

If the child has been progressing sequentially, the child has many things to do and has much to see and play with by this developmental age. He should not be looking at his hands con-

stantly or for any period of time. If hand regard occupies much of the child's day, seek professional help.

1.29 BRINGS FEET TO MOUTH (5-6 mo.)

After the child plays with her feet, she begins to explore bringing them to her mouth.

1. Play games like "How Does the Animal Walk?" while the child is in supine. Make up different movements for different animals with the child's feet.
   a. Elephant—feet up and down slowly with big strides.
   b. Horse—galloping movements.
   c. Mouse—short, quick movements.
2. Splash water with the child's feet, look at them through the water, rub them together. Do this while bathing the child, while at the beach, or outdoors during yard play with a tub of warm water.
3. Play a game like "This Little Piggy Went to Market" with the child's toes.
4. For the older delayed child who is beginning to bear weight on her feet, give her experiences on different textured surfaces.
   a. Sofa—soft, bouncy, hard, fuzzy or smooth.
   b. Cement—hard, bumpy, warm or cool.
   c. Ground—grass, dirt, wet or dry.
   d. Floors—smooth, rugged, hard or soft.

1.30 SHOWS INTEREST IN SOUNDS OF OBJECTS (5½-8 mo.)

The child shows interest in the sounds objects make by actively hitting, banging, and shaking different toys. The child uses a single toy to make different sounds by doing different things with it, hitting it on or against different surfaces.

1. Tie some yarn with a bell securely attached to it around the child's wrist or ankle so the child's movements will produce a sound.
2. Give the child a plastic squeak toy. If the child shows no interest, show her how to squeak it by poking, holding or hitting it on the floor, etc.
3. Clap your hands, clap the child's hands. Play "pat-a-cake" together.
4. Place the child in prone, tap, then scratch the rug or floor with your fingers.
5. Let the child listen to sounds.
   a. Quiet sounds, such as the ticking of a clock or a watch.
   b. Seeing and hearing running pipe or bath water.
   c. Helping turn on and off lights and hearing the click.
   d. Watching and listening to the wind and rain.
6. Let the child actively search and listen to new sounds, especially during holidays, such as the tooting and rattles at Halloween, the rustling and tearing of wrapping paper at Christmas.
7. Let the child bang the top, sides and insides of coffee cans with big spoons, small spoons, metal, wooden and plastic spoons. Let him bang xylophones, pianos, drums.
8. Let the child find and touch objects with sound vibrations, such as telephones, bells, tuning forks, cymbals or use two pot covers, musical triangles, a jack-in-a-box, an organ, piano, or let him hit a pot cover with a spoon.
9. Go about the house with the child knocking on wood, rugs, walls, the refrigerator, cushions listening to the sounds they make.
10. Do activities #2, 4, 6-9, and make the sounds loud and soft.
11. For the older delayed child:
    a. Hide behind a sofa or chair and make a sound using paper or a toy to attract the child's attention. Make the sound until she finds you. Use toys which make different sounds for this game.
    b. Use lots of blow things, such as horns to toot and whistles to blow.

1.31 ANTICIPATES VISUALLY THE TRAJECTORY OF A SLOWLY MOVING OBJECT (5½-7½ mo.)

The child appropriately switches his glance from the point of disappearance of an object to the expected point of reappearance.

1. Creep backwards behind a carrier, such as a box or chair, as the child watches you. Before you disappear completely, your back should reappear on the other side of the barrier. If the child does not see your back, wiggle and draw attention to it, so the child switches his glance to the other side of the barrier or screen. Do this activity again but creep behind the barrier head first. Repeat the activity, using a screen big enough to hid behind completely before you reappear.
2. Refer to 1.09 (Reacts to disappearance of slowly moving object, Activity #3,c.). Do activity #3, c., except the toy should be pulled until it goes behind the screen and out the other side.
   a. Use a toy with a sound the child can track as it moves behind the barrier and reappears.
   b. Vary the size of the toy.
   c. Vary the color or pattern of the toy.
   d. Vary the width of the barrier.
3. Refer to 1.09 (Reacts to disappearance of slowly moving object, Activity #3,b.). Do activity 3,b., but continue to pull the toy until it reappears on the other side of the cloth.
4. Refer to 1.09 (Reacts to disappearance of slowly moving object, Activity #3,d., 3,e., 3,f.). Make appropriate modifications as in activity #3 above.
5. Build barriers and tunnels out of sand and use sand toys that travel slowly and reappear out of the tunnels or around the dunes.
6. Use a light, sturdy balloon and attract the child's attention. Let it float down behind a table or chair. See if the

child looks for the reappearance of the balloon in the appropriate place. The transparency and the size of the barriers can be varied according to how much help the child needs in predicting where the object will reappear.

1.32 FINDS HIDDEN OBJECT USING 1 SCREEN, 2 SCREENS, THEN 3 SCREENS (6-9 mo.)

The child finds an object she sees hidden under a screen. DO NOT move the screens around and make this a guessing game.

A. Hidden Object Using One Screen.
1. Show the child one of his favorite toys and as the child reaches for it, cover it with a transparent screen such as a plastic cover or wax paper, plastic coffee lid or cup. If the child has difficulty controlling his arm and finger movements, use a tall transparent plastic cup so a simple movement can uncover the toy. Later use a handkerchief, plain piece of cloth, towel, diaper, part of a blanket or mat, zabuton, pillow. Use cardboard boxes, tin cans, or plastic containers.
2. Give the child a toy to play with when changing his diaper. After you have changed him, use another diaper or hand cloth and cover the toy (with the child still holding it). Ask the child where the toy is. Let the child shake the screen off to find the toy.
3. Let the child's brother or sister hide under a sheet and call the child. Encourage the sibling to talk and wiggle from under the sheet until the child pulls it off. Let the child hide with a sibling while someone else finds them and pulls the sheet off.
4. Use the palm of your hand or use both hands together to hide small toys. Play games in which the child tries to open your hands or fingers to get the toy balloon out or to find a miniature car.
5. Hide a cracker under a napkin on the child's plate and encourage him to find it.
6. Cover body parts or toys with sand and find them again at the beach. Cover pails, shovels, plastic dolls, toys, even lava rocks found in the water.
7. Hide a toy in a box with an easy to open cover and encourage the child to take the top off. Hide a spoon or a cup in a pot with a cover.
8. Hide a toy in a box of shredded paper or a box of packing material (foam pieces) and encourage the child to search for the toy. *Supervise* so the child does not put any paper or foam pieces in his mouth.
9. Play "cover the toy" by placing a diaper over a toy the child is looking at when dressing the child in sitting. Encourage the child to uncover the toy. She need not let go of the diaper to be successful.
10. Cover a floating toy with a small washcloth when giving the child a bath. If necessary, help the child shake the water or pull the cloth off to find the toy.
11. Hide a toy behind your back while he is watching and see if he can find it. If he does not, begin to move sideways so part of the object appears, then the child should be able to find it.
12. Cover a familiar object in the environment, like a busy box that is attached to the wall. See if the child notices it.
13. Place a toy in a cup and lay it on its side facing away from the child while the child is watching. Encourage her to find the toy. If the child has difficulty, use a transparent cup first and then an opaque one. Use a transparent jar for variation.
14. Place one of the child's favorite toys or familiar objects in a wax paper bag while the child is watching. Let him get the object. Do not twist or crumple the end of the bag. Use a brown paper bag on another occasion. When the child can find the toy and enjoy the game, crumple or twist the end of the bag slightly.
15. Place some toys in a large brown bag or shopping bag while the child watches. Let the bag remain open and standing upward. Encourage the child to find the toys and empty them out from the bag.
16. For the older child who is blind, use an object like an apple and a bag or paper sack. Place the apple in the child's hands. Guide her hands with the apple into the bag and leave the apple in the bag. Describe everything as you do it. Ask the child to give you the apple.

B. Hidden Object Using Two Screens, Then Three Screens.
1. Place two identical and uninteresting screens (diapers, cups, large leaves, sand mounds) in front of the child and show him a toy or object. When he indicates that he wants it, hide it under one screen while he watches. Encourage the child to get the toy.
    a. Place the screens far enough apart so the child does not go for both at the same time.
    b. The toy should not be so large that its bulge will indicate to the child where it is.
    c. Choose the screens according to what is available and the motor ability of the child to uncover the desired object. For example if the child has arm muscle involvement and his control is poor, place the screens far apart and use tall cups so a sweeping movement can uncover the toy.
    d. Use whatever toy, object or foods (cereal, cracker, piece of cheese) that is desirable to the child.
    e. To prevent the child randomly looking for the toy—allow the child to remove only one screen. If it is incorrect, you uncover the correct screen and show the object to the child. Try the activity again. The child learns he has only one change to get the toy.
    f. Always place the object under the same screen,

for example—always under the left screen and let the child see you hide it each time. The screens should be identical.

   g. When the child is successful three times consecutively go on to #2.

2. Use two screens. Hide an object alternately under either of two screens. Do activity #2 only this time vary the screen you place the toy under. When the child can find the toy three times consecutively go on to #03.

3. Use three screens. The child must find the toy or object he saw you hide under one of three identical screens in front of him. Vary the placement of the toy. When the child correctly finds the toy go on to #4.

4. Use three screens. Place three screens in a row in front of the child. Show the child a small toy and as he watches, pass the toy under all the screens starting on the child's left and continuing to the third screen. Let the toy show between screens. Leave the toy under the last screen and encourage the child to find it.

1.33 PLAYS PEEK−A−BOO (6-10 mo.)

The child responds with delight when his eyes, face or his parent's face is uncovered suddenly.

1. Respond with delight and surprise as the child's head reappears from under the shirt while dressing or undressing the child.

2. Play peek-a-boo with the wash cloth when it momentarily hides the child's face whenever you clean the child's face.

3. Use your hands to play peek-a-boo even while riding the bus or the car and the child is in his car seat. Cover your eyes with your hands while the child watches and then quickly remove them. Verbalize what you are doing and pause before you "reappear."

4. Hide your face behind something, such as a sofa, table, pillow, and say "Where's Daddy?" when the child is looking at you. Quickly reappear and say "Here's Daddy." This can be done when playing with a child or when entering the room.

5. Use a handiwipe, paper, or a light cloth to play this game. While smiling and playing with the child, bring the cloth between your face and the child's so your face is gradually covered from the child's view. When your face is completely hidden from the child's view, pause, and remove the cloth. Appropriate verbalizations such as "I'm going to hide Mommy," and "Here's Mommy," should be used.

6. Use a tissue and drape it over the child's face. Play peek-a-boo by peeking under it and around the sides or by flowing it off. Talk to the child with phrases like "Where's Paisley?", "I see you," or "Marcelle, where are you?"

7. Drape a small wash cloth, a soft extra diaper or an extra shirt over the child's face and head. Talk to the child so he still knows you are there but pretend you do not

know where he is. Encourage the child to remove the cloth, but should the child appear frightened, quickly remove it and greet him with a smile and a calm "Here I am" or "There's Jesse." Try again with the cloth on your face instead. At the beginning you may need to help the child remove the cloth by helping him hold the cloth in his hands, pulling the cloth off for him, or helping him shake his head to get the cloth off. All attempts should be praised and encouraged. Maintain physical contact with the child when he is "hiding."

8. Play or sing a short song rocking with the child facing you in your lap. If the child will allow you, clap her hands to the music and at appropriate pauses in the song cover the child's eyes with her hands briefly. Uncover them with a "There you are" and the continue the game.

9. Play peek-a-boo with your hands and encourage the child to imitate you with her hands.

1.34 SMELLS DIFFERENT THINGS (6-12 mo.)

The child uses her sense of smell to explore her environment. The following are specific activities to encourage the child to use this sense in learning about her environment and in discriminating differences.

1. Encourage the child to smell the perfume or aftershave lotion you are wearing.

2. Bring flowers into the room and house and have the child smell the flowers.

3. Allow the child to play near or in a high chair where she can smell the aromas cooking in the kitchen. Be careful!

4. Encourage the awareness of the smell of fruits and vegetables, and fish and crab, etc., when marketing.

5. Let the child smell the soap you use to wash him with and the toothpaste you use to brush his teeth.

6. Rub hand cream or baby oil on the child's hands and encourage him to smell them.

7. Point out the different things as well as the different smells when outdoors. Pause to smell trees, flowers, etc.

1.35 PLAYS 2-3 MINUTES WITH SINGLE TOY (6-9 mo.)

The child is actively involved with a single toy for two to three minutes.

1. Use toys that can teach a variety of skills and demand the use of a variety of senses. Use toys that make sounds, have different textures to feel and taste, can be squeezed, banged, are colorful, have a face that can be related to the child's, have movement possibilities, etc.

2. Help the child notice the different aspects of a toy by putting it in his hand and helping him to shake it, mouth it, and hit different things like the rug, table, floor, or another toy.

3. Use squeeze toys for the child to hit, bang, touch, look

at, taste different parts, etc.
4. Play with the toy with the child watching if she resists playing with it. Talk about what you are doing. "Oh, I see the eyes on the doll," or "The baby is wearing a red dress." Touch, pat, pick up, pretend to rock, stand up, dress or undress a doll, brush its hair, give it something to drink, kiss and hug it, make its arms and legs move, smell it, turn the doll upside down. Lie on the floor and toss the doll up in the air. Play games like "peek-a-boo" with the doll. If the child shows interest, touch, hug or pat the child with the doll.
5. Change the child's position to create a different perspective of a toy. This will encourage a longer play period, especially if the child seems to lose interest in a toy quickly.
6. Play with a roly poly toy. Refer to #1.14 (Enjoys repeating newly learned activity, Activity #4).
7. Place the child in sitting in front of a busy box attached to the wall. Talk to him describing what he is doing, the effects, the movement, the color, the sounds.
8. Place the child in front of a mirror with a toy so she can watch herself play.
9. For the older delayed child: Use a bath toy or give him cups and containers he can pour water in and out of while he is bathing. Use floating toys he can watch and play with.
10. For the child who has difficulty with fine motor co-ordination:
    a. Toys can be attached to something stable in the environment, such as the stroller or the wall. (A ball can be suspended so it will return to the same position.)
    b. Place the child so if a toy should roll or get pushed away, it cannot go far because of natural barriers (e.g., couch).

1.36 SLIDES TOY OR OBJECT ON SURFACE (6-11 mo.)

The child slides the toys or objects as a way of exploring the object and the environment.

1. Encourage the child to touch different things, such as rubbing her hands on rugs, couches, mom or dad's clothes, trees, grass, sand.
2. Let the child play with toys or household objects which roll or involve a general sliding movement.
3. Encourage the child to imitate you as you slide a toy on a surface. Toys that make sounds as well as move are more attractive than those that only move. If the child does not imitate, help the child by doing it with him.
   a. Find different surfaces which produce different sounds in the toy, bumpy cement or dirt, grass, grass mats, linoleum, rugs, panelled walls.
   b. Find toys which make interesting sounds when they come in contact with surfaces, squeeze toys, popping toys.
   c. Use toys which have different textures like bumps or

protrusions which also add to the movement and effect.
   d. Use easy to grasp toys.
   e. Use objects and toys such as rattles, small cars, paper, blocks, keys on chain, bottle on table, sponge, cloth to do this activity.
4. Let the child watch whenever you clean the car, wipe the dishes, wipe the table or mop the floors. Explain all your activities to him.

1.37 FOLLOWS TRAJECTORY OF FAST MOVING OBJECT (6-8 mo.)

The child follows and finds a rapidly moving or falling object with his eyes after it passes behind obstacles.

1. Hold the child when riding the bus, so she can look outside and see the trees, cars, quickly passing. Name objects or people, describe, and point to them. If there is a window sill or railing, these can act as narrow barriers behind which objects disappear and reappear.
2. Do activity #1 while riding the car with the child safely in his car seat.
3. Use a large object that can make a noise as it hits the floor as well as move across the floor such as a large year ball with bells attached. Hold it above the child's head. When the child focuses on it, drop it to the right or left side of him. If the child follows the movement of the object successfully, drop the object so it follows a path (trajectory) that is partially hidden behind a desk or tray. See if the child continues to follow the object with his eyes.
4. Drop an object so the last portion of the path is hidden behind a barrier. Encourage the child to search for the object in the direction in which it fell.
5. Repeat activity #3 and 4. Use small light-weight objects that drop quietly such as a cotton ball, plastic car, flower, paper, etc. If the child is unsuccessful in any part of the activity, teach him by pointing, telling, and showing him where to look. Reward him with the toy or with praise when he is successful, even if he is successful with assistance.
6. Use a tether ball attached to the ceiling.
   a. Play with it showing the child how it moves, letting him touch and explore it.
   b. Place a large roll or barrier upright in front of the child so that when the ball is swung it will swing behind the roll and reappear on the other side. Place the child so he will see this happening, and make sure he is looking at the ball before you let it go.
   c. Start with someone else on the other side to catch the ball. Swing it again in the opposite direction so the child follows it in a different direction.
   d. Let the ball swing freely so the child must follow it quickly in both directions.
7. Use a toy truck, car, or any vehicle that moves, or a ball. Play with the toy appropriately and occasionally send it quickly to another person or to the child. Set up a

screen so the trajectory of the moving toy will be invisible for a short period or for the length of the distance. See if the child can follow and find the toy.

8. For the older delayed child: Make bridges or tunnels out of blocks or large cylinders and have miniature cars go through them.

1.38 LOOKS FOR FAMILY MEMBERS OR PETS WHEN NAMED (6-8 mo.)

1. The child should hear the names of her brothers and sisters and other family members and see their faces whenever appropriate. Make a habit to face the child toward whomever you are talking to, instead of carrying the child over the shoulder with her back to whoever is in front.

2. In the mornings, greet the family members with "Hi Dad" or "Good morning, Bryan." Whenever leaving say, "Good-bye, Jesse."

3. When you call family members to dinner or pick them up at school, encourage the child to look for them and greet them when appropriate. Remember to use everyone's name. When a sibling, for instance, approaches, say, "There's Bruce, Hi Bruce." Encourage family members to greet the child whenever they see him.

4. Encourage siblings to play with the child and to use their own names a often. So instead of "Throw the ball to *me*," they use their names instead of the natural pronouns.

5. Play a game of "Let's find Daddy" or a sibling. Call Dad's name and wait for a reply. Then together, go and find Daddy. When you find him say "Here's Daddy" and if possible, Daddy takes the child and swings him or plays with him.

6. Play peek-a-boo games with family members using their names as they cover their faces with cloth.

7. Ask the child "Where is Grandpa?" Encourage the child to look for the person or point to him. If the child does not, help him by turning his body and help him point to the person. Take the child to the person and let him touch or be touched, smiled at and played with by the person.

8. For the older delayed child: Use a book made of photographs of family members. Look at and name the person in the photo, point out and compare the photograph with the person by holding it next to his face.

1.39 RESPONDS TO FACIAL EXPRESSIONS (6-7 mo.)

The child's facial or bodily movements change appropriately in response to adult emotions.

1. Use animated facial expressions.
2. Play peek-a-boo and look surprised when you see the child.
3. Show pleasure when the child laughs, smiles, vocalizes or coos.

1.40 RETAINS TWO OF THREE OBJECTS OFFERED (6½-7½ mo.)

The child reaches for an object and retains it while reaching for a second object. When a third object is offered, the child retains both objects or drops one as he reaches for the third object. The child retains the third object.

1. Place the child in sitting at a low table or in his high chair and allow him to play with a number of small toys such as cubes, pegs, toy bus, people, rattles, etc. Encourage him to pick up two toys and bang them on the table.

2. Encourage the child to transfer the first object he has grasped to the free hand, to pick up another object, and then reach for a third object. Refer to 4.38 (Transfers object).

3. Offer the child a toy small enough to be held in one hand. Let the child explore and play with it. Then offer the child a second object and encourage her to reach for it with the free hand. If the child does not respond by reaching and retaining the second object, bring her arm toward the object and encourage grasp. Refer to 1.25 (Reaches for second object purposefully).

4. Let the child play with toys or objects which are small, with adult supervision.
   a. Try sand or leaves.
   b. Try corn meal, or a box of foam pieces.
   c. Do some paper play with magazine pages, newspaper, wax paper which the child likes to crumple, tear and pull apart. Refer to 1.23 (Plays with paper).

5. For the older delayed child: Play with toys that come apart, such as:
   a. Pop beads.
   b. Colored stacking cones.
   c. A long dowel with wooden or plastic shapes that slide on and off.
   d. A string of wooden beads the child can take off the string.

6. For the hemiplegic child or a child involved on one side more than the other, encourage him to use the involved side as an assister by holding one object with the involved arm against his body or by placing the object into the assisting hand.

1.41 TURNS HEAD AND SHOULDERS TO FIND HIDDEN SOUND (7-10 mo.)

The child turns her head and shoulders to locate hidden sounds at a distance.

1. The toys your child likes to play with or is most responsive to are important. Make a note whether the child likes loud or soft sounds, high or low sounds or a sound peculiar to a certain material, such as a "wrinkling paper sound."

2. Use the sound the child likes and make the sound behind him while he is playing with a quiet toy. When he

turns, show him how you made the sound and, if possible, let him do it too. Repeat the activity, only this time make the sound behind you. Vary the place the sound is hidden as well as the distances he may need to travel to find the sound. Do this while the child is in different positions.

3. Help the child notice sounds from outdoors, at stores or at home. Respond to sounds made by things the child can look for, perhaps touch or even smell, such as pots and pans rattling during cooking or dish washing, airplanes and helicopters in the sky, popcorn being popped, music from a speaker, the telephone if it is in another room.

4. Place the child in a swing at the play ground. The child and swing can be easily turned to find the sounds in the environment, such as passing cars, buses, birds, other children. Later when the child can hear sounds that are hidden, you can both go and look for them.

5. Hide an object that can make a sound and encourage the child to take off the screen or box covering it.

6. Play hide-and-seek indoors with a person hiding behind a couch or a reasonably close barrier and makes sounds with a toy so the child can find him. If the child needs encouragement briefly show the sound maker, who again hides and continues to make sounds.

7. Turn the radio or phonograph on in another room and encourage the child to locate the sounds. Reward the child by "dancing" with her to the music.

1.42 IMITATES FAMILIAR, THEN NEW GESTURE (7-11 mo.)

The child imitates gestures she can do spontaneously and then imitates gestures which are new to her.

A. Imitates Familiar Gestures
 1. Observe the motor behaviors the child shows spontaneously toward objects or toys. At this time, they are behaviors such as banging an object on the table, waving an object, etc. When the child is not engrossed in any activity, perform this familiar action in front of him and then see if he makes any movement in response to you or imitates the behavior performed.
 2. Take the child's hand and help him imitate you if he does not respond. If the child succeeds with two or three behaviors, go on to the imitation of new patterns.

B. Imitates New Gesture
 1. Play with the child and imitate one of the child's gestures; then encourage the child to imitate your gesture (one that is familiar to the child). After imitating familiar gestures once or twice, do a simple new gesture when it is your turn.
 2. Pick new gestures similar to the ones the child knows, such as "patting the floor" if he knows "patting your stomach."
 3. Try new gestures which are less similar, such as

"patting the floor" to "rubbing the floor" to "rubbing the toy," as the child shows he understands the game.

1.43 RESPONDS TO SIMPLE REQUESTS WITH GESTURES (7-9 mo.)

The child responds with an appropriate gesture to a simple verbal request. The verbal request is accompanied by a gesture.

A. Reaches arms to be lifted.
 1. Hold the child and say "Up Bruce," or "Come Travis," when it is time to pick him up. The child should move both arms and hands upward toward you and lift his head.
 2. Tap the arms of the child upward so he learns what you are asking him to do if he does not respond by raising his arms. When the child first starts to raise his hands, pick him up quickly and reward him. Adjust your distance accordingly. If you are too close the child will not need to reach to get to you (your hands), and if you are too far he may become discouraged. Good times during the day to do this are:
  a. After changing his diaper.
  b. When you are going outside.
  c. Picking him up after feeding to burp him.
  d. Picking him up after a nap or in the mornings.

B. Crawls, rolls to person in response to "Come Jesse" with the person gesturing using fingers, hand and arms.
 1. Praise the child's attending or vocalizing to your call. This is a first step.
 2. Start by getting in front of the child while he is moving and say "Come Carl." Do *not* move further back as the child gets closer. When the child gets to you, reward him with praise, patting, rubbing; or whatever the child likes.
 3. Start about one foot away from the child with her favorite toy or bottle (if it is time for it) next to you. Call the child and gesture; show her the toy or bottle to help motivate her. If the child does not come, reach over and help the child move toward you. As you do this, repeat the word "come" so she associates it with the movement toward you. When the child reaches you, pick up the child and the toy, praise her, then sit and play together with the toy.
 4. Increase the distance a foot at a time that the child must travel in response to "come" with your gestures.
 5. Encourage the child to come by patting the place in front of you, patting your lap or pointing to yourself in addition to the "come" gesture.

C. Lifts arm, or moves wrist or fingers to "Wave bye-bye" while you also demonstrate.
 1. Wave and say "bye-bye" whenever you are leaving someone. Encourage the child to wave too.
 2. Help the child wave bye-bye by moving her arms

whenever appropriate. You can even wave at inanimate objects which the child likes so she learns waving "bye-bye" is an indication of leaving someone or something—"Bye-bye house."

3. Assist the child by tapping his arms upward saying "Wave bye-bye, John."

4. The child need not do a perfect imitation of the arm, wrist or finger movement. Any arm, wrist or finger movements which indicate he knows what you are saying should be praised. Some children start by making finger movements to themselves, making the movement the way *they see others wave to them*. This is all right.

D. Responds to "Dance Paisely" with movement of body or arms.
    1. Listen to music and "dance" with the child while carrying him. Bounce the child on your lap, rock in sitting or snap and clap your hands to the beat of the music.
    2. Tap the child's arms to encourage waving and shaking in dance movement. Hold him in standing so he can bounce, etc.

1.44 LOOKS AT PICTURES ONE MINUTE WHEN NAMED (8-9 mo.)

The child enjoys looking at pictures for one minute with an adult who names and points to the pictures.

1. Choose books the parent and the child can enjoy together. Sitting in Daddy's lap or lying side by side on the floor with Mom while looking at pictures can be part of the fun of books for the child. The pleasure and excitement of books is conveyed by the voice and interest of the adult.

2. Make texture books. Cut out textured squares and glue them onto railroad board or cardboard, bind them together with large metal rings. Together with the child, turn pages and feel the different textures. Tell the child what he is touching, such as cloth, sandpaper, sponge, scouring pads, etc. and describe the textures to the child. Make a texture book using rug scraps or rug samples bound together.

3. Make books using railroad boards, cardboard or another firm material. Glue or attach actual objects in the books such as combs, toothbrushes, paper plates, wooden spoons, forks, so the child can touch the objects as you describe and talk about them.

4. Use animal squeak books. The child can make the pages squeak by patting or pushing the pages down.

5. Use animal books with realistic animal pictures. Tell the child the names of the animals and make the sounds of the animals. Children love to hear the different sounds and see Mom or Dad make them.

6. Make a book with photographs of familiar objects, such as the child's bottle, the car, spoon, cereal.

1.45 RETAINS TWO AND REACHES FOR THIRD OBJECT (8-10 mo.)

The child retains an object in each hand and reaches to secure a third object without dropping one. The child may try to obtain the third object by using his mouth or by purposefully putting one toy down to reach for the third object.

1. Give the child a cube for each hand. Quickly offer a third toy or object. Hold the third object within easy reach in midline in front of the child. Observe how he secures the third object. If the child repeatedly drops one of the objects, teach him to transfer the object to the other hand to reach for the third object or place one object down to reach for the third object.

2. Use two similar small toys, such as two plastic or wooden peg dolls or animals, and offer a third object more desirable to the child than either of the first two, such as a cracker, your wrist watch, his bottle, favorite rattle.

3. For the older delayed child:
    a. Play a game of picking up lots of things or scooping up lots of toys and placing them in a container. Model and help the child move his arms and hands, showing him how to pick up lots of little toys by bringing his palms together. Drop the toys into a container that will make a sound as the toys hit the bottom. Use peg people, pop beads, macaroni, foam pieces, scraps of paper, flowers, leaves, fresh cut grass to play this game. The child learns to hold many objects at the same time.
    b. Play the game in activity #3,a. using one hand to see how many toys can be picked up at once. If the child has a difficult time, place several toys in the child's palm, so she has the feel of holding several toys.

1.46 OVERCOMES OBSTACLE TO OBTAIN OBJECT (8-11 mo.)

The child obtains a toy or object by reaching over or around an obstacle or by removing the barrier.

1. Use a toy the child wants and place it just within reach of her hands. When she reaches for it, place a transparent screen in front of the toy. Use a smooth piece of clear glass or plastic. The child should reach over or around it. If the child does not, show her how to obtain the object; try again but place the barrier so only half the toy is blocked and the child can pull it from the side. When she can do this, repeat the original activity.

2. Show the child a toy that she wants. As she watches slowly move it behind a partial see-through barrier such as a clothes basket turned upside down. The child can see the toy through the basket but must remove or go around it to obtain the toy.

3. Face each other sitting on the floor. Shake a small toy until the child looks at it. Move it along the floor slowly until it is behind your back. See if the child crawls or creeps behind you to find the toy. If the child does not,

move to the side so he can see part of it. Use other barriers that are hard to move so the child goes around or over them.

4. Use a musical toy or another interesting object the child shows he wants. Place it just within reach of his hands. As he reaches for it, place a barrier between the child and the toy. Use toy blocks, milk carton blocks, a cardboard box upside down, pillows or a big toy truck as a barrier. If the child stops, draw his attention by tapping the barrier or shaking the toy.

1.47 RETRIEVES OBJECT USING OTHER MATERIAL (8-10 mo.)

The child pulls the material on which a toy or object rests to obtain the toy.

1. Model and tell the child what you are doing in everyday situations.
   a. Gently pull the blanket the child is lying on and pick him up. As you do this say, "Pull the blanket, here's Julian."
   b. Say, "Pull the bag to Mommy, and here's your bottle" when you are holding the child and need something in the diaper bag.
   c. Obtain a toy and say, "Pull your toy box, here's your doll."
2. Place a soft toy or rattle on the edge of a firm pillow next to the child so he can see the toy when he is lying on his back or side. Encourage the child to reach for the toy. Place the pillow in such a way that gross movements by the child will result in the toy tumbling down to the child.
   a. Place the toy on the pillow so additional tugging is necessary to obtain the toy.
   b. Change the toy unless the child remains interested in the same one. Be sure the toys are ones which will not hurt the child when they tumble down near or on the child.
3. Place a light toy just out of reach on a diaper when the diaper's edge is near or under the child's hands. Give the child a chance to pull or move the diaper nearer to obtain the toy. Any repeated effort should bring the toy within reach.
   a. Help the child by placing your hand over the child's hands. Help pull the diaper closer to obtain the toy.
   b. Model for the child by pulling on the diaper and encouraging the child to imitate you.
   c. Place the toy three or four inches away from the child's hands so she must work a little harder to obtain the toy.
4. Give the child a cracker on a napkin for a snack. Place the cracker and napkin on the table in such a way that the child must move the napkin closer to obtain the cracker.

1.48 LISTENS SELECTIVELY TO FAMILIAR WORDS (8-12 mo.)

The child shows signs of understanding familiar words. If you ask a child to "Get the ball," the child shows signs of looking, scanning or appearing to know the word "ball," which are appropriate responses. He does not actually "get" the ball, but it is important that he show to you he understands the word "ball" or any other familiar word.

1. Repeat words and names of things which are important to the child. Use his name, "mama," "daddy," "bottle," "come," "uhoh," "diaper."
2. Name familiar objects as the child looks at, touches, plays with, smells and mouths them.
3. Talk to the child about things he sees everyday. Use the same words to describe common things.
4. Name the child's clothing and body parts as you dress her. For example, say, "Shirt. Put your shirt on. Shirt. Over your head. One arm, other arm. Now your shirt is on."
5. Tell the child what you are doing. Describe what is happening, what will happen or what did happen. "We're going to visit Grandma. We will ride in the car. First you must get dressed. Let's put on your shirt."
6. Use words that child appears to understand at this point in the development of her receptive language. Use lead phrases such as:
   a. Here's the juice.
   b. Look at the bus.
   c. I can't find the cracker.
   d. Let's find the ball.
   e. Where's the book?

1.49 FINDS HIDDEN OBJECT UNDER THREE SUPERIMPOSED SCREENS (9-10 mo.)

The child finds an object she sees hidden under three layers of screens placed one at a time on the object.

1. Refer to 1.32 (Finds hidden object using one screen, two screens, then three screens).
2. Start with just two screens, if necessary. Place the toy or object the child wants in front of him and cover it with one screen, then cover that with a second screen, and then a third. Arrange the screens so the child cannot remove them all at once with one swipe of the hand. Encourage the child to find the object. The screens need not be identical. A bowl, diaper, and a cardboard piece or cover may be used.
3. Place a toy or object in a box with an easy to remove cover or wrap it in one of the screens (newspaper, diaper, towel) while the child watches. Cover the toy or object with the two remaining screens (one at a time) and encourage the child to find it.
4. Hide a small toy in a towel. Place it in a box of shredded paper and cover the box.

1.50 GUIDES ACTION ON TOY MANUALLY (9-12 mo.)

The child attempts to make an action toy, which has stopped, perform by manually putting it through its action.

1. Use a wide variety of toys and games, such as:
    a. A friction toy car, truck, bus.
    b. A wind-up toy car.
    c. A mechanical toy duck that wobbles, dog that wiggles its tail, clown or monkey that claps its hands, bear or soldier that hits a drum.
    d. A tether ball attached to the ceiling or any toy that will swing when pushed.
    e. A spring toy that shakes and wiggles when pulled or shook.

1.51 THROWS OBJECTS (9-12 mo.)

The child throws an object and observes where it goes and its effects.

Throwing objects may develop accidentally as the child, in learning voluntary release, shakes his hands to remove objects and finds they get flung a distance and they bounce and roll. These kinds of observations and experiences are important to learning. Throwing objects should not be the primary or only interaction between child and object. It is a behavior that develops naturally and is part of children's play, in addition to other play behaviors. Provide lots of appropriate toys and experiences for throwing. Do not become overly concerned about the throwing of objects. All this will help the child move on to developing other schemas. Throwing things just to get attention, even if the attention is negative, is different from the play activity.

1. Throw balls of different textures and sizes.
2. Throw bean bags of different weights, shapes, textures.
3. Crinkle paper and throw it in the trash can or a box.
4. Throw leaves in boxes, throw clothes in hampers or clothes baskets.
5. Throw cloth blocks into a container.
6. Provide a time outside on the grass where the harder toys can be flung without people being hit or things broken.
7. Prevent the child from throwing objects at people. If it is not possible, he may need to be told "no throwing" but do not say, "Bruce is a bad boy." Let the child know that the *act* is what is being reprimanded, not the child himself. Do not degrade or otherwise belittle the child.
8. Refer to 4.50 (Releases object voluntarily).

1.52 DROPS OBJECTS SYSTEMATICALLY (9-12 mo.)

The child drops objects repeatedly and intentionally. This behavior appears as the child learns to let go of things, observing the path of moving objects and listening to the sounds objects make when they hit the floor.

1. Give the child a box full of unbreakable objects as she sits in her high chair or at the table. Observe the child's play to see if she drops the toys repeatedly, systematically, or looks down to see where they fall. If the child does not do these things, when she accidentally loses some object, draw her attention to the missing toy or the drop of the toy, and look for it with the child. Find it and give it back to the child. You might also draw the child's attention to a toy and "accidentally" drop or tip it over the side of the tray, then help the child look for it if she does not do so immediately.
2. Play a game of drop the bean bags into a box on the floor. Use a large box and occasionally change its position. Encourage the child to aim and drop the bags. The child and you should watch to see if the bean bags dropped into the box.
3. Refer to 4.50 (Releases object voluntarily).
4. Teach the child that food and utensils are not for dropping. *Do not reinforce* this behavior when it occurs. The child will drop spoons, cups and his toast, etc. as part of learning. When you pick these up say "Toast is for eating" or "eat toast." Do not smile and make a game of "baby drops and Mommy picks up." Give the child time to play with toys he can drop for fun. Children are confused when sometimes a spoon is for dropping and Mommy smiles and plays, and sometimes the same action makes mommy angry. Try to be consistent about play things and non-play things. If the child continues dropping food for you to retrieve, she is probably not hungry. Remove the food and play with toys on the floor instead.
5. For the older delayed child: Play throw the ball into a container. The container can be placed further out and in different areas around the child.

1.53 USES LOCOMOTION TO REGAIN OBJECT AND RESUMES PLAY (9-12 mo.)

The child plays with a toy that has at least two essential parts. When one part is moved, the child uses a form of locomotion to regain the part then resumes play. A child may push, drag or carry one part of the toy to resume play.

1. If a child uses a toy to bang a can or the floor, when exploring sounds, see if you can obtain the toy by distracting him. Move the toy. Then see if the child will go and pick it up and resume banging.
2. Use a banging toy with two parts, such as a xylophone, drum, spool can and spool, bench and hammer, etc. Let the child play with the toy then pull one part away or move the hammer a few feet away but still in view. Allow the child to regain the part and resume play.
3. Use a container, such as a coffee can with objects such as spools that the child has learned to put into the can. While the child reaches for a spool to put into the con-

tainer, move the container a few feet from him. Encourage the child if he does not do so independently, to retrieve the can or to take his spools to the can to resume play.

4. Allow the child to splash and to play in the tub of water with toys. While the child is playing move some of the toys. See if the child will retrieve the toys and resume playing. Turn on the hose and place it in the tub as the child watches. Pull the hose out of the tub and wait for the child to pick it up and put it back in.

5. Play with paper. Crumple newspaper to put in a container. Move the paper so the child must retrieve it, crumple it, and return to put it in a container.

6. If the child is able to stack rings, place one or two of the rings out of reach. See if the child will get them and resume stacking his rings. Do the same with pop beads that the child can pull apart and put in a large container.

7. For the older delayed child:
   a. Have the child find partially hidden Easter eggs and put them in a basket placed at a distance. Have the child put toys in decorated Easter baskets.
   b. Ask the child to help you put clothes in the laundry basket or leaves in the trash can. Place the clothes or leaves near the container. Place a few pieces of clothing or leaves where the child must move to get them.

1.54 LISTENS TO SPEECH WITHOUT BEING DISTRACTED BY OTHER SOURCES (9-11 mo.)

Children may become so engrossed in their immediate activities and play they are unaware of or appear undistracted by the external environment.

It is very important the child attends only to the "important" sounds. Everyone should be able to screen out unimportant sounds, such as traffic noises and some conversations.

1. Do the following activities to help the child develop selective listening.
   a. Expose the child to normal environmental sounds.
   b. Help the child identify or recognize sounds by showing him how they are made or what they mean. A child will attend to an unusual sound or one he does not understand more than ones with which he is familiar and unconcerned.
   c. Help the child attend to you and your speech through eye contact as well as physical contact.
   d. Play background music quietly when the child is playing.

2. Do the following activities if your child seems distracted by sounds to the point where he loses interest or cannot block out appropriately the extraneous sounds or cannot "attend" to what he is involved in.
   a. Place the child in a quieter room.
   b. Study the time of day or the type of noises which cause the most confusion to your child.
   c. Check with a specialist if you feel your child has a difficult time and is overly distracted and/or confused by external sounds and noises.

1.55 KNOWS WHAT "NO—NO" MEANS AND REACTS (9-12 mo.)

The child stops what he is doing for a brief moment when an adult says "No."

1. Never punish the child for failing to respond to "no." He does not yet have the control or the understanding to be consistent.

2. Use "no" only for dangers or hazards which cannot be removed from the environment. The more often you say "no" at this period, the more likely the child will use it later. A good way to avoid the extreme use of "no" by the child at the negativity stage is to avoid any excessive use yourself.

3. Teach the child the meaning of "no" by responding to his attempts at telling you "no." The beginning of an understanding of the concept "no" is seen when the child turns away to indicate he does not want something, often food. You can take advantage of this by verbalizing and shaking your head saying, "You're telling me *no*! You do not want it." Over exaggerate by shaking your own head and repeat "no." Accept the child's refusal.

4. Remove the child physically from danger as you say "No—No." Do not expect the child to control herself.

5. Substitute the appropriate word for "No—No." Use for example, "hot!" or "sharp" or say, "No—sharp!" or "No—hot!" to help the child understand why you are saying "No—No." Otherwise "No—No" remains nebulous and meaningless.

1.56 RESPONDS TO SIMPLE VERBAL REQUESTS (9-14 mo.)

The child learns to respond to verbal requests, such as "Come here," "Up," "Don't touch," without the gestures which usually accompany such requests. The child responds with gestures.

1. Refer to 1.43 (Responds to simple request with gestures). Do not use gestures to accompany the verbal request.

2. "Child proof" your house, so there are few restrictions the child needs to learn at this time. When the child is older, he can learn to avoid touching many more things. At this age, the restrictions should relate to absolutely dangerous or potentially dangerous things, such as electrical outlets and lamp cords which cannot possibly be taped down. When the child approaches these hazards, say, "Don't touch the stove." Quickly pick up the child to remove him from the situation and play with him with a toy. Help the child to learn that he can touch most things but not everything.

1.57 REMOVES ROUND PIECE FROM FORMBOARD (10-11 mo.)

A formboard is a shape puzzle; the round shapes are easiest to remove.

1. Place the formboard in front of the child. Let the child explore it. If the child does not take the round piece out of the formboard, show her how to do it and verbally describe what to do. Let the child try to remove the round piece on her own. If the child still has difficulty help her by placing your hand over the child's hand and pick up the round piece with her. Start with a board with one or two pieces.
2. For the child who has physical involvement in the hands and has difficulty with grasp, add a small drawer knob or a small spool to the top of the round piece to facilitate grasp.
3. Make two matching holes on a show box top. Pass a large spool through the hole from underneath and encourage the child to pull it out. (Spools may be kept in the box.)
4. Make your own formboards out of wood, heavy cardboard, inverted ice cream cups, styrofoam, inverted spray can covers, or flat sponge pieces.

1.58 TAKES RING STACK APART (10-11 mo.)

The child removes all the rings on the ring stack toy with some adult encouragement.

1. Allow the child to use any method of removing the rings from the ring stack. The child can tip the stack on its side to take them off, rub them off at one time with the ring stack vertical. Five rings are enough to be successful so if a large ring stack is used, simply remove the excess rings and put them away (not lying around).
2. Stack the rings so the smallest ring is on the bottom and the largest ring is on the top.
3. Start with two to three rings on the ring stack. Let the child play with the ring stack and see if he will spontaneously pull the rings off. If the child pulls some off, reward with praise and patting or rubbing; if the child pulls a ring off partially help him continue until he gets it off completely and reward him. If the child does not attempt to remove the ring demonstrate how to do it. If necessary, help him by putting both his hands on the ring and lift them up. The child may do better if you sit behind him and you put your arms around him and help him direct his arms to get the rings off.
4. Tilting the ring stack, hold it steady or hold it horizontal to the child if she needs assistance. As she is successful and enjoys the game gradually reduce the assistance.

1.59 DEMONSTRATES DRINKING FROM A CUP (10-15 mo.)

Give the child a child size cup or a play cup similar to one the child uses. The child should "drink" although there is nothing in it.

1. Give the child appropriate experiences with a cup drinking juice, milk, water from a cup. During these ex-periences allow the child to look at, examine, and handle the cup and try to drink as independently as possible.
2. Let the child drink from a cup in different places, such as drive-ins, restaurants, the relatives' or sitters' home and from different cups such as one and two handle cups, paper cups, large and small cups.
3. Show the child how you or a sibling drinks from a cup. Point the cup out to the child, say "Cup, Joanne drinks with a cup." Show the child pictures of people and es-pecially babies drinking from a cup.
4. Use a play cup and a mirror. Let the child play with the cup in front of a mirror. If he does not demonstrate drinking, do so yourself with another similar cup or the child's cup.
5. Use a cup with something in it and help the child drink while watching himself in a mirror. Use a transparent cup so the child can see the milk or juice in the cup.

1.60 ENJOYS LOOKING AT PICTURES IN BOOKS (10-14 mo.)

The child enjoys looking at pictures in books with some adult participation.

1. Refer to 1.44 (Looks at pictures one minute when named).
2. Sew a cloth book for the child. Felt and other scrap materials cut in familiar shapes or added to pen drawings on cloth are captivating and fun to touch.
3. Press pictures between wax paper and make a book that can be easily wiped. Trim the tops and bottoms with pinking shears to decorate. (Use ring reinforcers.)
4. Use a variety of materials to make books, such as cardboard box sides with large rings, brown paper bags with staples or an old clean shower curtain cut in squares with rings for binders.
5. Make a book with photographs of the members of the immediate family, grandparents, baby sitters, and nurses and doctors if the child is hospitalized, other familiar and important people. Large, clear and recent pictures should be used. Place the child's picture on the first page and then a picture of another person on each page. There should be only one picture to a page and one person to a picture. A photo album is good because the clear plastic covers protect the pictures from drool and handling. The pictures should be talked about by Mom, Dad, and others and patted and touched by the child. The printed name of the person may be added below the picture. Capitalize only the first letter of the name and put the rest in smaller case letters. Look at the pictures with the child, tell him who each person is and something about the person, such as "Kristine played with you today."
6. Make a book with magazine pictures of objects familiar to the child. Construction paper can be used and bound together by strong staples, with yarn strung through punched holes or use binders (plastic binders for term papers). Lamination or clear contact paper will help

keep the pictures in good shape.

7. Use a scrapbook. Set aside a special time during the week when you and the child look through old magazines and pick out a picture. Quickly cut and paste it in the book while the child watches. This book will keep changing as you add pictures to it.

8. Use schematic (outline) pictures to see if the child prefers them. Some children may be attracted to schematic drawings instead of photographs at this age. The attention to pictures and the parent-child's enjoyment of the activity are important. Use a combination of schematic drawings and photographs.

9. Compare books which have several objects on a page to books which have one large picture on a page to see which is preferred by the child.

1.61 UNWRAPS A TOY (10½–12 mo.)

The child obtains an object loosely wrapped with paper.

1. Place a favorite toy or food in a pice of waxed paper and gently crumple the top while the child watches you. Allow the child to unwrap the paper and obtain the toy or food. Help the child only if necessary after she had time to shake, tear, or unwrap the toy. Start with large toys which make a noise, which are generally smooth and easy for paper to slide off so the child can use big arm movements.
    a. Use toys which are small and have shapes which are harder to unwrap, such as bells, rattles, keys, as the child becomes more skillful.
    b. Give the paper a twist at the top as the child learns to manipulate the paper.
    c. Use transparent paper such as cellophane.

2. Do activity #1, using colored tissue paper. It is easy to tear, but the child cannot see through it. Try newspaper and napkins as well when appropriate.

3. Place toys in a paper sack while the child is watching and crumple the top closed. Shake the bag and give it to the child encouraging her to get the toy.

4. Encourage the child to open his own gifts at Christmas or on his birthday. Help by starting a hole in the paper and leave flaps of wrapping paper for the child to pull and tear. Spread it out so the child opens one or two days before Christmas, one or two Christmas eve, a few on Christmas day, and a few after Christmas. Birthday presents can also be spread out to encourage unwrapping.

5. Do activity #1 using cloth such as a towel or see through material. Wrap the toy in the cloth and put it in a box with a loose cover. See if the child will search for and then unwrap the toy.

6. Use foil to wrap a musical toy and loosely crush it around the object. If the child needs help, make a hole in the foil and leave the ends open for the child to pull.

1.62 HIDDEN DISPLACEMENT ONE SCREEN (11-13 mo.)

The child finds an object hidden by displacement. The child watches as an object is placed into a container. The container is hidden under a screen and the child cannot see the object being removed from the container and left under the screen. The child searches for the object by looking into the container and then by looking under the screen.

1. Work on an area with sound absorbing material such as a rug. Place a screen such as a diaper, a hand towel, clothes in front of the child. Use a small object of interest to the child such as a small car or doll. Place it in a container such as a cardboard box or towel roll deep enough so the toy is hidden from the child. As the child watches, place the container under the screen and let the object fall out of the container. Show the empty container to the child and encourage him to find the object.

2. Use your fist in place of the container in the activity described above. Place the toy in your hand and hide it with your fingers. Hide your hand under a box, a blanket, in the sand, in a pocket, in a bag or purse. Leave the toy behind the cover. Show your fist to the child who then searches for the toy in your hand and where it was left.

1.63 PLACES CYLINDERS IN MATCHING HOLE IN CONTAINER (11-12 mo.)

The cylinder can be a spool, juice can or peg.

1. Place the container in an upright position in front of the child. Show the child how to put the cylinders through the hole if he does not do so spontaneously. If the child needs assistance place your hand on his and take him through the movements.

2. Flex the child's wrist, tap or stroke the back of his hand if he has difficulty releasing the cylinder.

3. Outline the hole on the lid or cover using colored tape, ink or paint to make the hole stand out.

4. Position the container with the hole facing the child to obtain more wrist extension. Raise the container to a higher level to encourage reaching or arm flexion. Position the container at arm's length to encourage elbow extension.

5. Make containers out of coffee cans, large plastic jars or boxes. Cut round holes in the lid or cover to match the size of the thread spools, balls, large round beads, or sponge circle cut-outs.

6. Make faces or other animated structures on thick cardboard or wood with holes and cylinders to match. For example, make a face with holes for the eyes, nose, and mouth; a clown with holes down the front of his clothes for "buttons"; or a leopard with holes for spots.

7. Use only the round holes and cylinders of commercially made materials. Cover the inappropriate holes on materials with multiple shapes.

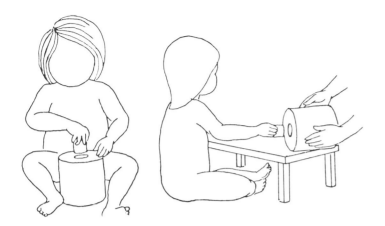

3. Bounce the child to music while carrying her or on your knee or in your lap.
4. Move to the rhythm of things you see in the environment, e.g., look together at swaying trees and sway in imitation while you tell the child the wind makes the trees bend and rock. When it rains and the windshield wiper is on, sing songs such as "Rain, Rain, Go Away" or "It's Raining, It's Pouring," and gently rock to the beat of the windshield wiper.
5. Play movement games like "Row, Row, Row, Your Boat."
6. Swing the child rhythmically in your arms, in a blanket, on the swings.
7. Play musical instruments to the beat of familiar fun songs.

1.64 STACKS RINGS (11-12 mo.)

The child stacks rings in any order using a ring stack with a center that is uniform in size.

1. Start with two rings. Place one ring on and encourage the child to imitate you by placing the other ring on. Give the child assistance as needed. Check the manner in which the child holds the rings and, if necessary, tilt the ring stack center.
2. Use the following suggestions if the child has a lot of difficulty.
   a. Place the ring on the pole. Let the child complete the task by putting the ring down or by letting the ring drop the base.
   b. Place the ring in position above the pole and let the child complete the task.
   c. Sit in back of the child and guide the child's arms until the ring is above the pole. Let the child complete the task.
3. Play a game in which the child chooses the rings for you to stack. You then pass the rings back to the child for her to stack. Name the colors of the rings as you do this.
4. If the child has difficulty placing the rings on the pole, find or paint the rings the same color and make the pole a contrasting color. The pole should be at an appropriate height for the child.
5. Refer to 1.58 (Takes ring stack apart, Activity # 5).

1.65 MOVES TO RHYTHMS (11-12 mo.)

The child spontaneously moves his whole body rhythmically in response to music, but not necessarily in time with the music.

1. Give the child experience in movement to rhythmic music. Let the child initiate the movement. If he does not, give visual cues such as you moving, verbal cues, or start the child moving and let him continue it.
2. Rock the child to music with a definite beat using records, tape recorders, the radio. Sing to the child in the car, at home, while waiting for buses or doctors' appointments.

1.66 IMITATES SEVERAL NEW GESTURES (11-14 mo.)

The child imitates several new gestures and combines two simple gestures in imitation.

A. Several New Gestures
   Refer to 1.42 (Imitates familiar, then new gestures).
B. Imitates Complex Gestures
   1. Take a simple familiar behavior that the child spontaneously performs and incorporate it into a more complex action pattern. When the child is not involved in any activity, perform this activity for him. If the child does not respond, help him do it, then gradually decrease the amount of aid given. For example:
      a. If the child shakes objects, show the child how to put blocks inside a container and shake it.
      b. If the child bangs on surfaces with objects, show the child how to take a block in each hand and hit them together.
   2. Play singing games with lots of repetitive simple movements or movements in a series. Encourage the child to imitate the motions. Use songs or activities such as:
      a. "Pat-A-Cake"
      b. "Row Row Row Your Boat"
      c. "Twinkle Twinkle Little Star"
      d. "The Wheels on the Bus"
      e. "If You're Happy and You Know It"
      f. "Hands"
      g. Peek-a-boo
      h. "This is The Way We Wash Our Hands"
      i. Dance to music
      j. "Rub a Dub Dub"
      k. "Rain, Rain, Go Away"

1.67 HANDS TOY BACK TO ADULT (12-15 mo.)

The child understands that you caused the action of a toy. He tries to continue the action of the toy when it stops by giving the toy back to you and waits for you to activate it again.

1. Use a toy that moves when you activate it. Activate the toy, then stop it or wait for it to stop if it is a wind up toy. Leave your hand and the toy within the child's reach. If the child does not pick up the toy and give it to you, try again. If the child does not respond to the activity, take his hand and together make the toy perform the action. If he still does not react refer to 1.24 (Touches toy or adult's hand to restart an activity) and 1.50 (Guides action on toy manually) and play more of these games.

2. Uses the following toys and materials:
   a. Wind-up toy, musical ferris wheel, radio, music box.
   b. Push or pull toys like the popcorn popper or spinning top.
   c. Mechanical toy animals which jump, run, bark or wiggle.
   d. Animal or people pop up toys.
   e. Balloons and soap bubbles to blow.

1.68 ENJOYS MESSY ACTIVITIES SUCH AS FINGERPAINTING (12-18 mo.)

A. General Suggestions.
   1. Show the child how much fun it is to touch the paint and move it all over the paper. Encourage the child to join you.
   2. Show pleasure in fingerpainting if the child is afraid or refuses to touch the paints. Draw many different things in the paint and tell the child what you are doing and how it feels. Use voice and facial expressions to show your enjoyment.
   3. Have a bucket of water ready to wash the child's fingers if he looks at his hands and becomes fearful. Show him how quickly the paint washes off.
   4. Add different textures (refer to B.02.c.) to the paint after the child enjoys many successful experiences. Use different colors and mix colors on the paper.

B. Materials.
   1. Paper
      a. Use fingerpaint paper. Place the dull side of the paper on the table. The fingerpaints can be easily spread on the shiny smooth side of the paper.
      b. Use other strong papers such as butcher paper. Wet the paper with water before adding the paint.
      c. Use cardboard, table tops, oil cloth or the inside of an inflatable swimming pool for a surface.
   2. Paint
      a. Buy or make your own non-toxic fingerpaints.
      b. Use the child's favorite color or a bright color like yellow. Use only one color and let the child explore this new activity. Do not start

with the color red. Some children associate this color with blood and it frightens them.
      c. Change the texture of the paint by adding sand, coffee grounds, rice.
   3. Smocks and Clean-up.
      a. Being messy is part of the fun of fingerpainting. Cleaning should generally be done at the end of the activity. Exceptions are times when paint is splashed near the child's eyes (it would not be harmful, only uncomfortable) or when the child becomes fearful of the color on his hands or body. Avoid the constant cleaning which can signal to the child that being messy in this activity is not okay and that painting is dirty.
      b. Let the child wear only diapers or nothing at all on a sunny day.
      c. Use smocks to protect the child's clothes. However, protecting clothes should be less important than exploring and having fun.
      d. Dress the child in old clothes.

C. Recipes for Fingerpainting.
   There are many recipes for fingerpainting, but are for older children who no longer mouth things, e.g., soapflakes. Always check your ingredients if very young exploring children will be fingerpainting.
   1. Wheat paste fingerpaint.
      Mix wheat paste with water until desired thickness is achieved. Spoon mixture on wet paper and sprinkle tempra paint on it (wet or power form).
   2. Starch fingerpaint.
      Spoon liquid starch such as Vano onto wet paper. Add tempra paint to it (wet or powder form).
   3. Salt and flour fingerpaint.
      Mix 1 cup flour and 1½ cups of salt with 3/4 cups water. Add food coloring.

D. Do other messy play activities using sand and dirt.

1.69 REACTS TO VARIOUS SENSATIONS SUCH AS EXTREMES IN TEMPERATURE AND TASTE (12-18 mo.)

The child reacts with facial expressions or body movements.

1. Give the child experiences with cold things. Verbalize the concept, "cold ice," "cold apple." Let the child touch these objects using hands and other body parts.
2. Provide experiences with hot (warm) foods and drinks. Point out the need to be careful. Point to the steam and discuss it. Let the child touch toys warmed by the sun and clothes just out of the dryer.
3. Provide experiences with sweet and sour foods. Let the child taste naturally sweet and sour foods, such as grapefruits, lemons, limes, tart oranges, guavas, pineapples, starfruits.

1.70 SHOWS UNDERSTANDING OF COLOR AND SIZE (12-18 mo.)

The child shows a preference for a certain color(s). Awareness of size is seen in the exploratory use of formboards and nesting cans.

1. Describe the *properties* of familiar objects. For example, instead of stressing "ball" say "Big ball," "Little ball," "Red ball," "Round ball." *Introduce one concept at a time.*
2. Take neighborhood walks and pause to look at and point to things in the child's environment. Describe, do not just name, the things you see. Say, "Big house," "White house," "Small flower," "Red flower," "Green grass." Remember, size is relative. Label as "big" those things which are bigger than the child. Use "small" or "little" for objects smaller than the child.
3. Make specific "kits" or boxes of colors. Find an old purse (e.g., green purse) and place green objects in it. As the child puts the objects in and takes them out, talk to her about the green paper, green ball, green crayon, etc.
4. Look at picture books which contain color and size descriptions.
5. Make a book that emphasizes one concept.
   a. A book of common familiar objects of one color.
   b. A book with a pair of pictures on each page. The objects should be the same except for size.
   c. A book of round things—oranges, balls, balloons, rocks, cookies.

1.71 PLACES ROUND PIECE IN FORMBOARD (12-15 mo.)

A formboard is a shape puzzle; the round pieces are easiest to insert.

1. Let the child place small juice cans in matching holes cut in a milk carton.
2. Let the child place pegs in a pegboard.
3. Teach the child to help you put round lids on containers such as thermos bottles, dusting powder containers. (He cannot twist them yet.)
4. Make round indentations in the sand or dirt while at the beach or at home and let the child place rocks of the same size and shape into these indentations. Other materials which can be used for this game are bottle covers, poker chips, and circles made from foam, wood, plastic or sponge.
5. Formboards—General Suggestions:
   a. Start with one circle piece and one hole in the formboard.
   b. Start with deep holes cut into the formboard and with pieces which fit in completely. Let the child see the difference in putting it completely in, having it on the board or having it partially in.
   c. Start with a piece with a large knobbed handle. Handles can be made by gluing on small, empty spools of

thread, large beads, wooden knobs, etc. Later, use smaller handles made with small pieces of wood, plastic, sponge, large screws or nails to replace the larger handles.
   d. Let the child feel the round puzzle piece and the inside edges of the formboard where the round piece fits. You may want to line parts of the puzzle with textures to aid the child.
   e. Give the child time to learn by trial and error before you begin to direct some of his efforts.
   f. Ask the child to put the circle back in the board after he has removed it. Point to the hole if the child does not respond or appear to understand. If more help is needed, show the child how to put the round piece into the hole and describe to the child what you are doing. Encourage the child to repeat your action.
   g. If the child cannot get into the hole and appears to be tiring or becoming frustrated, help her. Place your hand near the hole. The child can use your hand as a backstop and you can help slide the piece in the hole.
   h. Help the child by guiding the piece in the hole by holding the piece with the child. The child need not let go of the piece as long as he can consistently put it in the hole.
6. Use a board or make one with one large and one small circle. Let the child try to put the pieces in correctly. Should the child place the small one in the large hole, do *not* say "No, that's the wrong hole" or "No, put it here." Let the child make his own corrections. If he does not correct himself, point out the error in a friendly, helpful way. Encourage him to try again.

1.72 NESTS TWO THEN THREE CANS (12-19 mo.)

The child fits together two round containers by placing the smaller one into the larger container. The child then fits together three containers. The child may place the middle container into the largest container and then add the smallest one, or she may place the smallest one into the middle container and place both inside the largest one.

A. Basic Directions.
   1. Use two cans. Place the two cans in front of the child. Allow the child to play with them. Show the child how to put the cans together if the child does not spontaneously try to nest them. Describe what you are doing, "Look, I put the small can into the big can." Allow the child to try on his own. If the child tries to put the big can into the small can and does not correct himself, spread the two cans out and tap the correct can to be nested.
   2. Use three cans. Teach the child how to nest three cans after he learns to nest two cans.
B. Possible Suggestions for the Use of Visual and Tactile Cues to Aid the Child.
   1. Two Cans.

a. Start with two cans of the same color. The child learns to place the smaller can into the larger can through trial and error. If the child has a difficult time nesting because he seems unaware of size differences, draw a small flower or a happy face on the smaller can.

b. Use two different colored cans, the larger having the brighter more intense color.

c. Add a strip of soft material, sandpaper, or contact paper around the smaller can for tactile cues.

2. Three Cans.

a. Make the two larger cans identical and the smallest can different. Use visual and tactile cues.

b. Make the largest and smallest cans identical and the second can different.

C. List of Possible Nesting Materials.

1. Emply cans of varied sizes with all sharp edges eliminated by hammer and/or tape.

2. Aerosal spray can covers of varied sizes.

3. Cups of varied sizes.

4. Plastic bowls of varied sizes.

5. Measuring cups.

6. Jar covers of varied sizes.

7. Commercially made:

a. Nesting drums.

b. Nesting eggs.

c. Nesting cups.

d. Nesting barrels.

1.73 UNDERSTANDS POINTING (12-14 mo.)

The child visually follows your pointing or points with her index finger at people and things.

A. The child learns to look as you point to an object.

1. Find a time in the day when a familiar person, an adult or child, leaves or comes home. Each day the person (for example, Dad) should call the child's name and say, "I'm home," drawing the child's attention. Dad should do this from the same place. When the child turns and looks, Dad should immediately reinforce this by saying things as "Hi John" and picking him up, patting him, etc.

2. Repeat activity #1 above and modify it so Mom points to Dad and says, "Look, there's Dad!" before he greets the child. When the child responds Dad greets and praises the child.

3. Vary the place Dad stands to greet the child. Greet the child at other times, in other places, at different distances.

4. Point to a familiar, large, stationary object such as the parked family car. Draw the child's attention with appropriate verbal directions—"Look, Mommy's car!" Tap the car if necessary so the child turns toward it. Continue to point and touch the car saying, "Yes, Daddy's car" or "Baby's car." Do this whenever you approach or look for the car after shopping, picking up brother, visiting friends, etc. If a bus is more familiar or more exciting to the child do the same activity with appropriate modifications. Gradually increase the distance from which you point to the car or bus.

B. The child uses his index finger to point.

1. Let the child use his index finger to make holes in the sand at the beach. Point to the holes and let him imitate you.

2. Place small objects in containers with narrow necks. Encourage the child to poke the objects.

3. Let the child poke squeak toys.

4. Let the child explore bumps and indentations with his fingers.

5. Let the child poke holes in play dough.

6. Let the child play with finger puppets.

7. Encourage the child to use his finger to make designs in fingerpaint.

8. Let the child gently touch fragile things with one finger. Say, "Gently with one finger."

9. Accept whatever gesture the child, who is physically unable to point, uses.

10. Refer to 4.51 (Pokes with index finger) and 4.63 (Points with index finger).

1.74 PULLS STRING HORIZONTALLY TO OBTAIN TOY (12-13 mo.)

The child obtains a toy, which is out of reach, by pulling on a string attached to it. The stringed toy is placed on a table so the child pulls horizontally.

1. Use toys which have long sections the child can grasp to pull the toy to himself, such as a stuffed animal with a long neck or tail.

2. Use toys which make sounds as they are pushed or pulled along the floor. Encourage the child to pull the toys independently. If he does not, take the child for a ride on the wagon with him holding the toy string. As you pull the wagon, tell the child he is pulling the toy. Use ducks which waddle, trains, xylophones.

3. Attach a small yellow balloon to a string and tie it onto the child's wrist if he does not mind. Encourage him to pull the balloon toward himself or move his arms so the balloon will follow. If the child does not want it tied to him, tie the string in a loop and attach the balloon with a safety pin to his sleeve or shirt.

4. Attach a musical toy or bell with a string to a stroller or crib bar. Show the child that by pulling and waving the string, he can make the bell ring.

5. Tie a piece of cloth around a toy in place of a string or use a belt with the buckle as the reward.

6. Let the child play with an object that has a string attached to it, such as a colorful ring with a piece of yarn tied to it. Show or allow the child to dangle the object using the string or vice-versa.

7. Take a favorite toy and as the child watches, tie a string around it. Place the toy horizontally out of the child's reach and the string near the child's hand. See if she will pull the string to obtain the toy. If the child wants the toy but does not pull the string, demonstrate several times by pulling the string until the toy is close. See if she will imitate. To discourage climbing toward the toy, seat the child at a table or in a high chair that makes seeing the toy possible, but climbing too difficult. If the child does not pull the string after demonstration, help her pull it to obtain the toy. A hand-over-hand pull is not necessary for this item. Any method, however awkward, is acceptable as long as the child's interest settle on the toy and not the string.

8. For a child with poor grasp, attach a large ring or bead at the end of the string to make grasping easier.

1.75 MAKES DETOURS TO RETRIEVE OBJECTS (12-18 mo.)

The child goes around obstacles to obtain something he desires if he cannot crawl or creep directly to it.

1. Roll a ball under the sofa and out the other side. Get the ball if the child does not go around the sofa himself. Show it to the child and encourage him to come and pick up the ball.
2. Play hide and seek with the child where he can see and hear you call, but must go around a barrier to actually get to you.

1.76 LOOKS AT PLACE WHERE BALL ROLLS OUT OF SIGHT (12-13 mo.)

The child observes a ball roll out of sight and continues to look for it at the point it disappeared.

1. Play with a large texture ball. Roll it slowly behind a couch or low barrier while the child is watching. If the child does not search for it, move the barrier to show part or all of the ball. Roll the ball again and encourage the child to find it. The child need not obtain the ball.
2. Use balls of different sizes and colors. Use balls which have noise makers either inside or attached to it as an individual aid if it is needed.

1.77 RECOGNIZES SEVERAL PEOPLE IN ADDITION TO IMMEDIATE FAMILY (12-18 mo.)

The child may indicate his recognition by looking at or pointing to the person named. Recognition may also be indicated by a lack of stranger anxiety and by a willingness to interact freely.

1. Refer to 1.38 (Looks for family members or pets when named).

2. Smile, wave, and greet the child from a distance on first meeting or when reacquainting oneself with a child. Usually a casual greeting instead of a loud, sudden one is more appropriate. Approach the child slowly, but if the child shows signs of anxiety, stop, and try again at a later time.

1.78 HIDDEN DISPLACEMENT TWO SCREENS (13-14 mo.)

The child finds an object hidden by displacement when two screens are used. Refer to 1.62 (Hidden displacement one screen). Modify the activities to include two screens. Be sure to leave the object under the same screen.

1.79 PULLS STRING VERTICALLY TO OBTAIN TOY (13-15 mo.)

The child observes a desired object which is attached to a string as it is lowered beneath a barrier. The child pulls the string upward to obtain the object.

1. Tie a big balloon to a string and let the child play with it. Tie the balloon to the child's stroller, high chiar or to her hand if she will allow it. The balloon will settle to the floor and be partially out of view. You can encourage the child to pull it up into view again.
2. Place the child where the balloon, when it settles to the floor, will be out of sight. See if the child will pull the string to obtain the balloon or to get it into view again.
3. Tie a string or yarn around a favorite toy while the child watches. Lower the toy behind a table or desk. Keep the end of the string near the child's hand. If the child does not pull the string to obtain the toy, pull the toy to the level of the desk so the child will see it and will want to pull the string himself. Encourage the child by gestures, wiggling the string and verbal directions to pull the string and get the toy. If the child has a hard time grasping the string, use a thicker cord, a rope, or add a large bead or plastic ring to the end of the string.
4. Repeat activity #3, using a small table so the child can move back and see the toy hanging under the table or on the side of it. Let the child pull the string and watch the toy go up and over the edge of the table. Use toys which make a noise as they dangle on the string.
5. Repeat activity #3, using a floor table so the child can see the toy when the string is stretched out. Let the child pull the string. The toy will briefly disappear from view as it nears the table. Use a toy which is light and easy to pull.

1.80 HIDDEN DISPLACEMENT THREE SCREENS (14-15 mo.)

The child finds an object hidden by displacement when three screens are used. Refer to 1.62 (Hidden displacement one screen). Modify the activities to include three screens. The object should be under the same *screen.*

1.81 HIDDEN DISPLACEMENT TWO SCREENS ALTERNATELY (14-15 mo.)

The child finds an object hidden by displacement when it is randomly hidden under one of two screens. The child finds the object by removing the correct screen. The child should not randomly search under all the screens, but should look only under one screen.

1. Refer to 1.62 (Hidden displacement one screen). Modify the activities to include two screens. Randomly hide the object under either of the two screens.
2. Remove the correct screen to show the hidden object if the child's first choice is incorrect.

1.82 PATS PICTURE (14-15 mo.)

1. Refer to 1.44 (Looks at pictures one minute when named).
2. Refer to 1.60 (Enjoys looking at pictures in books).
3. Cut pictures of babies from magazines, photographs, and newspaper advertisements. Paste and make a book with these pictures. Place a shiny piece of foil on one of the pages so the child can see his reflection as one of the "pictures." Let the child point and pat the pictures as you talk about what the babies are doing, wearing or playing with. Give the child the opportunities to look at the pictures by himself and see if he spontaneously pats them.

1.83 HELPS TURN PAGES (14-15 mo.)

The child assists the adult in turning the pages of a book.

1. Turn pages of books correctly and purposefully as you enjoy the pictures together. Let the child experiment with the way pages turn and make noise. Treat the book with respect and the child will learn to also.
2. If the child tears the pages purposefully and not accidentally, he is interested in what he can do with paper. Remove the book and provide him with newspaper or waxpaper and let his rustle, crumple, and tear it.
3. Let the child turn the pages after you separate and lift them half way over. If the child does not attempt to flip the page over, take his hand and help him turn it. The child should need only a simple downward movement in the correct direction. Increase what the child does by himself as he learns to assist in turning the pages.

1.84 IMITATES "INVISIBLE" GESTURE (14-17 mo.)

An "invisible" gesture is one the child cannot see himself perform.

1. Observe the child's play with several different toys and objects to determine a familiar gesture. Choose one gesture, such as blinking her eyes, shaking her head and hair, nodding her head. Get the child's attention and perform the familiar invisible gesture when the child is not engrossed in another activity. If the child does not respond, try again and assist the child. See if she will imitate independently.
2. Do activity #1 in front of a mirror so she can see herself perform. Remove the mirror when she learns and enjoys the game.
3. Play simple singing games involving movement and familiar invisible gestures.
   a. "If You're Happy and You Know It."
   b. "This is the Way We Wash Our Clothes."
   c. Dance and wiggle to music.
4. See if the child will imitate an unfamiliar invisible gesture. Ask the child's mother if the gestures you choose are unfamiliar to the child.

1.85 MATCHES OBJECTS (15-19 mo.)

The child identifies objects which are exactly the same with at least one object which is not the same.

A. General Suggestions.
   1. Use simple, familiar objects.
   2. Use objects which are identical in size, shape, color, texture, as the matching pair.
   3. Choose distinctly different pairs of objects, such as a pair of small white blocks and a pair of large blue shoes.
   4. Choose pairs of objects which are equally attractive to the child.
   5. Reduce the number of clues as the child improves.
B. Activities.
   1. Help the child attend to and become familiar with the common names of objects and body parts. Compare similar ones.
      a. Discuss, show, touch and have the child touch a body part such as her hand, then her other hand.
      b. Discuss, show, touch and have the child touch a body part such as her foot, then the foot of the adult or sibling.
      c. Discuss, show, touch and have the child touch a body part such as her head and the head of a doll.
   2. Discuss similar objects choosing common, familiar objects and toys around the house.
      a. Point out the identical spoons at mealtime.
      b. Let the child notice his shoes when dressing him.
      c. Pick leaves from the yard which are the same size, color, shape, weight, texture.

3. Use two sets of identical objects such as two spoons, two lids of baby food jars. Let the child hold the spoons. Discuss the similarity. Do the same with the lids. Then, place one spoon and one lid in front of the child. Hand the other spoon to her. Ask her to pick up the matching object. Do the same with the lids.
4. Do activity #3. Change the objects. Slowly increase the number of choices as the child learns the game.
5. Use pairs of objects which are similar in category, such as cups and spoons, toothbrush and toothpaste tube, combs and brushes.
6. Use similar objects which differ in size, color, shape weight, texture, and smell, such as two wooden cooking spoons and two dessert spoons.
7. Use objects similar in one dimension but different in another, such as two yellow plastic spoons and two silver dessert spoons.
8. Use foods, such as two pieces of banana and two cheese squares which the child can eat after successfully matching them.
9. The fine discriminations—matching by size, color, texture, smells, weights, sounds, objects to pictures, and picture to picture—are more difficult and develop later.

1.86 PLACES SQUARE PIECE IN FORMBOARD (15-21 mo.)

A formboard is a shape puzzle.

1. Refer to 1.71 (Places round piece in formboard, Activity #5). These suggestions apply to a formboard for square pieces.
2. Make square holes in the sand at the beach using square boxes, pieces of wood, blocks. Let the child put the square object into the matching hole.
3. Use a formboard with circles and squares.
4. Suggestions for making formboards out of scrap materials.
   a. Use heavy cardboard to make a formboard. Cut out squares with a razor knife. Glue the squares together to make the puzzle piece. Glue the rest of the cardboard together to make the puzzle board. The thickness of the puzzle piece may be greater than the puzzle board.
   b. Use heavy cardboard for the formboard but a different material for the shaped pieces. Inverted plastic ice cream cups and spray can covers can.be used for circles. Half pint milk cartons or wood or plastic toy blocks make good squares.
   c. Use styrofoam and sponge. Packing styrofoam and sponge are easily cut for appropriate shapes.
   d. Use an old telephone directory for the formboard. The depth of the holes can be quickly changed by flipping the pages.

1.87 INDICATES TWO OBJECTS FROM GROUP OF FAMILIAR OBJECTS (15-18 mo.)

The child points to, touches, or picks up two different objects at the same time out of a group of three to five objects upon request.

1. Play a "Give me" game. Use very different objects and ask the child to give you one of the objects. Let the child select the requested object out of a group of two objects. Gradually increase the group of objects. Ask the child to give you two objects at one time. Ask for related objects to make it easier.
2. Ask the child to give you his shoe and socks when dressing him.
3. Ask the child to give you his cup and spoon after a meal.
4. Let the child pick out his shovel and bucket from his toys when you go to the beach.
5. Ask the child to bring her doll and blanket from her room when you go on an outing.
6. Ask the child to point to the dog and cat in a picture book.

1.88 BRINGS OBJECTS FROM ANOTHER ROOM ON REQUEST (15-18 mo.)

The child must bring something from the same room before she can bring an object from another room.

1. Ask the child to bring an object which is in the same room.
2. Ask the child to bring an object from another room after she can successfully bring an object from the same room.
3. Suggestions for choosing objects.
   a. Ask for a familiar object.
   b. Ask for objects which can be immediately used by you or the child.
   c. Ask for objects she can immediately see as she enters the room.
   d. Ask for objects which she can easily reach and are kept in a specific place.
   e. Ask for objects the child can carry easily.
   f. Ask for objects located in the next room.
4. Give the child assistance if he needs it.
   a. Go with the child and show him the object. Bring it back together.
   b. Go with the child to the appropriate room and let him look for the object.
   c. Point to the appropriate room. Follow the child to the room and let him find the object.
5. Do not scold or appear disappointed if the child forgets the task or brings the wrong object. Thank her for the object she brings to you. Gently repeat your original request.
6. Make this activity a game, not a chore. If the child does not want to play, cheerfully say, "Okay, Mommy will get it."
7. Play along if the child brings you the wrong object as a joke.

8. Let the child use aids for locomotion, such as crawligators or walkers if necessary.

1.89 TURNS TWO OR THREE PAGES AT A TIME (15-18 mo.)

The child turns pages by pushing many pages over at a time. The child learns to turn one page at a time at a later age.

1. Encourage the child when he shows an interest in turning pages independently. The child may push up from the lower right hand area, he may turn the pages with the palm instead of the fingers or he may turn the pages from the upper right area of the page and push down.
2. Use familiar books with worn pages. New pages are too slippery and are hard to turn.
3. Use large books with simple pictures which have small, loose bindings. The pages will be easier to turn and will stay down after they have been turned.
4. Let the child turn pages without insisting he stop to look at the pictures. The child may be very interested in simply turning pages.
5. Let the child go backwards through a book if he does so at this stage. He need not start at the beginning. Do not encourage this but at this time do not bother or correct the child.

1.90 IDENTIFIES SELF IN MIRROR (15-16 mo.)

The child identifies himself in a mirror. He may point to his image or indicate in other ways he recognizes himself. A child may find it easier at first to recognize members of his family in the mirror.

1. Let the child sit and play in front of the mirror. Use a large mirror which is attached to the wall, close to the floor. Talk to the child, show, touch and point to what he is wearing and doing. Use the child's name often, "I see Tommy's face and nose," or "Sally is wearing a red dress today." Use your name and point to your reflection.
2. Play peek-a-boo by draping a cloth in front of the mirror.
3. Encourage the child to pat or kiss himself in the mirror.
4. Let the child wipe off carefully selected glass polish. As he "swipes" at the mirror with a cloth, his image appears.
5. Do finger plays and songs with gestures in front of the mirror. Assist and encourage the child to join you.
6. Encourage the child to look at herself in the mirror when she is wearing something new or special like a baseball cap.
7. Use a mirror tile, a shiny cookie sheet or a coffee can with a shiny bottom in place of a large mirror.

1.91 IDENTIFIES ONE BODY PART (15-19 mo.)

The child identifies one body part by pointing, touching or moving the part named.

A. The child learns his body parts.
1. General Suggestions.
   a. Start with body parts the child can see.
   b. Start with body parts used most often.
   c. Start with body parts that are distinct.
2. Name the body parts the child uses or touches, such as emphasize her "hands" when the child washes or claps her hands.
3. Name the body parts the child explores on your face, such as "That's Mommy's mouth," "bushy beard," "Where's Daddy's nose?".
4. Name and gently touch the child's mouth as you feed her. Make appropriate comments such as, "In your mouth, the spoon is in your mouth."
5. Name body parts as you wash the child. Name body parts on yourself as you bathe.
6. Name body parts when giving a haircut or clipping nails.
7. Tickle the child's stomach as you change her diaper. Tell her you are tickling her stomach. Tickle and label other parts of her body.
8. Discuss, rub, and touch the child's body parts while dressing and undressing him.
9. Use a mirror for the child to explore and to look at herself. Rub different body parts with textures such as terrycloth, a silk glove, or a small velvet cushion.
10. Use a cloth puppet to rub and point to the child's body parts.
11. Play games and sing to the child about his body parts.
12. Do finger plays with the child such as:
    a. "Ten Little Fingers."
    b. "Ten Little Fingers and Ten Little Toes."
    c. "Two Little Eyes and One Little Nose."
    d. "Two Little Cheeks and One Little Chin, And Here's a Little Mouth Where the Food Goes In!"
    e. "One Little Body.
       Two little hands to clap, clap, clap!
       Two little feet go tap, tap, tap!
       Two little hands go thump, thump, thump!
       Two little feet go jump, jump, jump!
       One little body turns around,
       One little body sits quietly down."
13. Sprinkle sand on the child's hands or feet at the beach or, bury parts of his body and have them pop out again.

B. Some children learn body parts on dolls before they learn them on themselves.
1. General Suggestions.
   a. Buy sturdy dolls which do not come apart (many children are frightened when dolls come apart; they identify with the dolls).
   b. Buy anatomically correct dolls, if possible.

  c. Use dolls with distinct features.
  d. Do not worry if your child—boy or girl—likes to take off the doll's clothes, many children simply prefer their dolls this way.
  2. Make a doll that resembles the child e.g., use identical dress materials. Teach the child to:
    a. Hold the doll's hands and play "Row, Row Your Boat."
    b. Tickle the doll's feet.
    c. Pat the doll's back or head.
    d. Place "This Little Piggy" with the doll's toes.
    e. Kiss the doll's eyes.
    f. Brush the doll's hair.
    g. Clap the doll's hands.
    h. Feed the doll, put the food into his mouth.
    i. Play peek-a-boo by covering the doll's face.
    j. Whisper in the doll's ears.
    k. Put a bracelet on the doll's arm.
    l. Place a hat on the doll's head.
    m. Put a band-aid on the knee, let, arm of the doll.
    n. Powder the stomach of the doll.

1.92 RECOGNIZES AND POINTS TO FOUR ANIMAL PICTURES (16-21 mo.)

The child points to or touches the appropriate picture out of a choice of four pictures when asked.

1. Provide the child with many first hand experiences with animals. Let the child see, touch, smell and ride animals. Take the child to pet stores, the Humane Society, county, state or farm fairs.
2. Point out and name pictures of animals and objects in the everyday environment.
    a. Use pictures on cereal boxes or pictures hung on the kitchen wall.
    b. Look at pictures on tablecloths, clothes, napkins.
    c. Point to posters in windows, on cars, on walls.
    d. Look at murals in banks, museums, libraries.
3. Use animal pictures the child sees repeatedly and has heard you talk about. Ask the child to point to the animal picture you name.
4. Take your zoo book or your farm animal book when you visit the zoo or the farm. Compare the animal with the picture of the animal. Books with photograph pictures instead of drawings are best.
5. Take your camera to the zoo or farm and make your own animal book.
6. Sing "Old MacDonald Had a Farm" to the child. Use pictures of animals as you sing and make the noises the animals make.
7. Find an animal sticker book. These are inexpensive books with pictures of animals on gummed paper which are removed and pasted in the correct animal outlines. This fun activity lets the child name the animals and provides for good pasting practice.

1.93 UNDERSTANDS MOST NOUN OBJECTS (16-19 mo.)

The child knows the names of most common objects in her environment and looks at or points to them on request.

1. Label objects for the child. Discuss things around him.
2. Discuss body parts and clothing when you bathe and dress the child.
3. Discuss the food, the utensils, the kitchen furniture and things when you feed the child.
4. Give the child simple directions to see if he knows the names of things.
5. Discuss what you routinely see when you ride the car, such as traffic lights, stop signs, trucks, buses, fire stations.

1.94 SERIES OF HIDDEN DISPLACEMENTS: OBJECT UNDER LAST SCREEN (17-18 mo.)

The child finds an object, when hidden by a series of displacements, under the last screen.

1. Refer to 1.62 (Hidden displacement one screen) for a description of "displacement."
2. Place three screens in a row in front of the child. Place a small desired object in your hand as the child watches. Pass your hand with the object completely hidden under the screen on the child's left and continue under the second and third screens. The child should see your hand as it passes between screens. Leave the object under the last screen. Show your empty hand to the child and encourage her to find the toy. Repeat the activity until the child knows where to look for the toy. Reverse the direction, going from right to left. Check whether the child can follow and find the object.
3. Put a large toy in a package while the child watches. Pretend to hide the toy by pausing behind three large chairs or obstacles as the child watches. Take the toy out of the package behind the third chair and leave it there. Give the package to the child to look in then encourage her to find the toy. The child should search directly in the last place.

1.95 SOLVES SIMPLE PROBLEMS USING TOOLS (17-24 mo.)

The child purposefully uses an unrelated object to obtain a desired result.

1. Provide the child with play experiences which involve using an object in a variety of ways or using extensions of an object to obtain the object.
    a. Refer to 1.74 (Pulls string horizontally to obtain toy).
    b. Refer to 1.79 (Pulls string vertically to obtain toy).
    c. Show the child he can pull toys around in his wagon or on a blanket.
    d. Let the child carry toys in her pocket, purse or paper bag.

2. Ask the child to help clean up some of her toys. Suggest fun ways to clean up.
   a. Show the child how several toys can be carried in the shirt or dress by holding the edges and making a cradle.
   b. Let the child use a large dump truck or wagon to transport the toys.
   c. Let the child use a paper bag or box to carry the toys to the appropriate shelf.
   d. Show the child how several toys can be carried in a small blanket or towel by holding the four corners and making a sack.
   e. Provide the child with a special place for her own belongings, such as a large box, a basket, a special corner or a shelf.
3. Provide games in which tools are used.
   a. Let the child hit a suspended ball using a paddle.
   b. Let the child use a paddle to keep a balloon afloat in the air.
   c. Let the child bowl using plastic bowling pins or empty milk cartons.
   d. Let the child blow bubbles.
   e. Let the child throw bean bags at a ball placed within a circle. The child can try to hit the ball out.
   f. Let the child throw bean bags at a target that jingles when hit.
4. Ask the child to bring an object which is out of her reach, after you placed a stool near the object. If the child does not use the stool, suggest it to her conversationally.
5. Ask the child to bring the ball you placed under a low sofa. Place a yard stick nearby. See if the child will use it to hit the ball from under the sofa.

1.96 IMITATES SEVERAL "INVISIBLE" GESTURES (17-20 mo.)

Refer to 1.84 (Imitates "invisible" gesture). Increase the number of invisible gestures the child imitates.

1.97 POINTS TO DISTANT OBJECTS OUTDOORS (17½-18½ mo.)

1. Point to objects and encourage the child to do the same.
2. Point to objects or people within reasonable range. Gradually increase the distance.
3. Point to another person at a distance. Point and wave as the person approaches the child.
4. Point to and identify objects at a distance. Move closer to touch the objects, if possible.
5. Point to passing fire engines, dogs, cars, people. Watch as they move farther away.
6. Point out objects in the air, such as airplanes, helicopters, birds.
7. A child who is not physically able to point with his index finger may use a gross arm movement, fisted hand, or eye movement toward the object.
8. Refer to 4.63 (Points with index finger).

1.98 ATTEMPTS AND THEN SUCCEEDS IN ACTIVATING MECHANICAL TOY (18-22 mo.)

The child searches for a way to reactivate a toy that ceased its movement. The child searches although she did not see the toy activated.

1. Demonstrate the procedure of winding, pressing a switch, if the child explores for ways to activate the toy. Activate the toy for the child. Stop it or let it stop if it is a wind-up toy. Let the child activate the toy. Encourage and help him as needed. Introduce an unfamiliar toy when the child can independently activate a toy. He should immediately look for or find a way to activate the new toy without demonstration. Be sure the wind-up toys can be easily wound.
2. Use mechanical dogs, monkeys, drummer boys, which activate with a switch.
3. Use jack-in-the-boxes, pop-up animals and other toys which activate with several push buttons or with dials which turn easily.
4. Use music boxes with handles to crank and spinning tops which activate by pushing down quickly and repeatedly.

1.99 USES PLAYDOUGH AND PAINTS (18-24 mo.)

The child explores and manipulates playdough. He enjoys a variety of painting activities.

A. Playdough.
   1. Make playdough with the child. Use theraplast for a child who needs special exercises for hand and fingers. The thickness and texture of playdough can be varied by increasing or decreasing the amount of flour. Use three cups flour, one cup salt, three-fourths to one cup water. A small amount of oil will keep the dough moist for weeks. Add food coloring if desired.
   2. Invite the child to play. Play with the playdough yourself exploring and describing its properties if the child does not want to touch the playdough. Make some of your favorite things and invite the child to join you. Try again another day if the child still does not wish to play.
   3. Explore the dough without tools.
      a. Poke holes, squeeze, pat and pound.
      b. Stretch, twist, break apart.
      c. Roll long pieces. Roll balls.
   4. Give the child a few tools.
      a. A tongue blade or popsicle stick to poke, cut, scoop, scrape.
      b. A rolling pin for bilateral grasp.
      c. Cookie cutters.

5. For a hemiplegic child:
   a. Encourage the use of both hands as much as possible.
   b. Let the child press the dough or cookie cutter on the table with the affected hand. Working for weight bearing with wrist and finger extension.
   c. Let the child stand while weight bearing on her hands for elbow extension.
   d. Encourage the child to poke the playdough with each finger and thumb for individual finger extension.
   e. Add textures, such as sand, coffee grounds, beans for fun and learning. Caution: Do not add beans if the child puts things into his mouth.

B. Painting Activities.
   1. Sponge Printing.
      Cut a sponge into various sizes and shapes. Use a thick paint. Tape a large piece of paper to the table or to the wall. Show the child how to place the sponge in the paint and to pat the paper with it. Describe the action and the results for the child.
   2. Block Printing.
      Follow the directions for sponge printing. Let the child use wood pieces, spools, erasers, or raw potato slices with shapes and designs in place of the sponge.
   3. Crayon Resist.
      Let the child scribble with crayons on butcher paper. After he is finished help him cover the paper with diluted tempera paint using a sponge. The crayon will stand out and the sponge wash will add a nice background.
   4. Tapa Printing.
      a. Let the child crumple sturdy butcher paper several times. Dip the paper into diluted brown tempura paint and let it dry. Let the child block print geometric designs on it.
      b. Let the child crayon color a piece of paper. Let him crumple the paper several times. Dip it into diluted brown tempera paint and hang it up to dry.
   5. Yarn Painting.
      Attach short pieces of thick yarn to clothespins. Let the child dip the yarn into thick paint and pull it around the paper. Let him make designs using the clothespin handle.
   6. Hand and Foot Printing.
      a. Let the child dip her hands into thick tempera paint and place them on paper.
      b. Tape a large piece of paper to the floor while the child sits on a chair next to the paper. Paint the bottoms of her feet. Place her feet on the paper or let her walk with help across the paper. Wash the paint off by having the child sit on a chair with her feet in a bucket of water.

7. Drip and Fold.
   Cut the paper into different shapes. Fold the paper in half. Open the paper and let the child squeeze or drip thick tempera paint from plastic catsup containers or eye droppers. Fold the paper again and let the child spread the paint by rubbing the paper. Let the child open the paper for a nice surprise.
8. Marble Painting.
   Cut a piece of paper to line the bottom and sides of a box. Allow about two-inches of paper around the sides of the box. Put a marble on a spoon and dip it into thick tempera paint until covered. Let the child roll the painted marble around, tipping the box to make various designs.
9. Cornstarch Play.
   a. Add just enough water to wet the cornstarch to make a putty-like mixture. Encourage the child to explore the mixture. See Activity A.3. Explore the dough without tools.
   b. Thicken tempera paint with cornstarch. Let the child paint with a large brush. After the paint dries, encourage the child to close his eyes and use his fingers to feel the picture.
10. Tissue Collage.
    Let the child help you cut or tear tissue paper into shapes. Let the child use a large brush to cover her paper with diluted liquid starch or glue. The child then pats the shapes one at a time onto the wet, sticky surface.
11. Fold and Dip.
    Fold a paper towel or roll it into a spiral. Let the child dip the ends and the middle into colored water made with food coloring. Help the child unfold the paper. Cut out snowflakes and other designs with the colored paper.

1.100 PASTES ON ONE SIDE (18-24 mo.)

The child applies paste on one side of a shape and turns it over to stick on paper.

1. Let the child watch you paste stamps on letters, trading stamps in books, recipes on cards. Explain what you are doing and describe the steps you take.
2. Use things which are sticky on one side, such as band-aids, masking tape or scotch tape. Let the child feel the tape and help you use it. For example, let the child hand you the tape you cut to hang his paintings and drawings.
3. Use soft, easy-to-apply school paste or glue and construction paper. Help the child scoop some paste on her fingers and spread it around the paper she is pasting.
4. Use gummed paper and water. Let the child wet his fingers on a sponge and apply the water to the sticky or shiny side of the paper. Help the child turn the paper over and stick it onto another paper. This activity can be used to make holiday cards. Colored

gummed paper can be purchased or use leftover
Christmas and Easter seals, magazine order stickers,
holiday stickers.

5. Outline a rabbit on a large sheet of paper. Give the
child two ears and a tail to paste onto the rabbit outline. As the child improves in this skill add more
features.

1.101 PAINTS WITHIN LIMITS OF PAPER (18-24 mo.)

*The child paints or colors inside the limits of her large
paper (approximately eighteen by twenty-two inches).*

1. Let the child trace the outline of the paper with his
hand. Tell the child the paint goes on the paper. Place
the paper on a wooden board, a styrofoam board, or a
thick cardboard the same size as the paper. Should the
brush, sponge, hand, or crayon go off the paper, the
child will have a kinesthetic as well as a visual cue he is
not on the paper. Help the child, if necessary. Emphasize the importance of painting "on the paper."
2. Match one corner of a paper with a table corner. Place
the child at the corner of the table. The cues which will
define the edge of the paper will be more distinct on
the corner two sides of a paper. Observe the child.
Reinforce her with praise if she tries to avoid going off
the paper and the table.
3. Use an easel or small chalkboard to color or paint on.
4. Contrast the child's paper with the background. Place a
yellow paper on a red paper, on a white table or on some
newspaper.
5. Use masking tape to border the child's paper. Be sure
to discuss and to trace with the child the edge of her
paper.

1.102 POINTS TO SEVERAL CLOTHING ITEMS ON REQUEST (18-20 mo.)

1. Discuss and name the child's clothes when dressing or
undressing him.
2. Ask the child to pass you her clothes as you dress her
after a bath.
3. Ask the child to select the shirt he would like to wear out
of a choice of two shirts. Do this with pants and other
familiar clothing items.
4. Ask the child to help you gather her extra clothes to take
to the park or to the beach. Spread the clothes out and
ask the child to point to specific clothing items.
5. Ask the child to identify clothes on herself or on a doll.

1.103 EXPLORES CABINETS AND DRAWERS (18-24 mo.)

1. Provide times when the child is free to explore the rooms
in the house. Give as much or as little supervision as
necessary. Fill bottom bureau drawers and low cabinets
with old, but interesting objects. Let the child empty and
fill "his" drawers as often as he wishes.
2. Caution: This does not suggest the child is allowed to
play with anything in all drawers. The adult should
"child proof" drawers and cabinets and eliminate fragile
things or dangerous things, such as poisons or cleaning
fluids. The adult should lock those places the child
should not open at all.

1.104 MATCHES SOUNDS TO ANIMALS (18-22 mo.)

*The child shows his understanding of the sounds animals
make. The child spontaneously vocalizes the sound of animals
when she sees them. The child points to the correct animal
when another person vocalizes the animal sound. The child
responds correctly when asked, "What does the (animal) say?"*

1. Ask the child to identify an animal by the sound it makes.
Say, "I see something that says, 'ruff-ruff.' Whenever you
see a dog nearby. Praise the child if he can point to the
dog. If he does not point, say, "The dog says 'ruff-ruff.'"
2. Refer to 1.92 (Recognizes and points to four animal
pictures, Activity #1).
3. Sing animal songs, such as "Old MacDonald Had A Farm."
Let the child use stuffed toy animals. Let the child
stand and make the animal sound at the appropriate
place in the song.
4. Do the above activity using animal puppets for songs,
games and stories.
5. Tape record sounds of animals. Listen to the sounds and
match them to the correct stuffed animals or animal pictures.

1.105 RIGHTS FAMILIAR PICTURE (18-24 mo.)

*The child spontaneously corrects a familiar picture pre-
sented to her upside down, or moves herself to the other side
of the picture.*

1. Swing the child upside down in frolic play. Describe what
is happening to her.
2. Show the child a familiar toy or object. Turn it over or
upside down. See if the child will right it.
   a. Use a cup. Give the child his juice when he rights the
   cup.
   b. Use a plate. Put a few raisins on the plate when he
   rights it.
   c. Use a puzzle. Turn the board upside down or turn a
   few of the pieces over.
3. Let the child lie on a large piece of paper and draw an

outline of her with a crayon or felt pen. Add the body parts and perhaps paint in a dress. Hang it on the wall upside down. If the child does not respond or notice how you have hung it, have her stand next to it. Together decide it must be upside down and correct it.

4. Present pictures of objects and favorite books upside down.

1.106 ENJOYS NURSERY RHYMES, NONSENSE RHYMES, FINGERPLAYS, POETRY (18-30 mo.)

1. Use large attractive pictures depicting the rhyme.
   a. Point to the appropriate people, animals, or actions as you say the rhyme.
   b. Add textures to the pictures.
   c. Use a series of two or three pictures for the rhyme story.
2. Use objects which the child can touch, see, hear, smell, or taste to illustrate the rhyme.
3. Use real animals whenever possible. Recite an appropriate rhyme, such as "Hey Diddle, Diddle" if a cat should appear.
4. Use lots of body, hand, facial expressions and gestures to accompany the poem or rhyme.
5. Pick books which contain the rhymes you would like to do with the child.
6. Sing or listen to recordings of the rhyme.
7. Add appropriate sound effects, such as "Old Mother Hubbard went to the cupboard to get her poor dog— 'ruff-ruff'—a bone."
8. Be selective about rhymes and poems. Take your child's interests and present fears (bodily damage or scary things like spiders) into consideration. "Little Miss Muffet" can be avoided because it frightens a child, but it can teach a child not to be frightened of a spider by making light of it.
9. Do parts of a rhyme. Do not feel you must do all of the rhyme or poem or use it exactly as it is written. Have fun.
10. Repeat rhymes outdoors, in the car, with other children, at stores. The more familiar the rhyme, the more the child enjoys it. Repetition is very important.

1.107 MATCHES OBJECTS TO PICTURE (19-27 mo.)

The child puts the object on or points to the matching picture out of a choice of three to four pictures.

1. Start with photographs of the objects. If they are not available find pictures which closely resemble the objects.
2. Show the child a familiar object. Name it or if the child can verbalize, let her name it. Show the child a picture of the same object. Name it or have the child name it. Show the child both the object and the picture and com-

pare them. Talk about their sameness, point out the obvious similarities.
3. Show the child a familiar object. Then show him two pictures (one of the object, the other of a very dissimilar object). Ask her to point out the picture which matches the object.
4. Show the child a familiar picture of a familiar object. Then show him two objects (one identical to the picture, the other, very dissimilar). Ask him to give you the object which matches the picture.
5. Show the child a picture of a familiar object in the house or classroom. Have the child find the actual object in the house or classroom. Be sure it is near the child and within his reach.

1.108 SORTS OBJECTS (19-24 mo.)

The child separates objects into three groups. Each group has three to five identical objects.

1. Discuss similar objects which are found in and around the house and are placed in the same containers. Point out crayons in the crayon box, clothespins in the bag, leaves in the trash bag, potatoes in the basket, records in record holders, books on a bookshelf, sister's curlers in a bag.
2. Point to and discuss tires stacked in garages, buses at the bus terminal, airplanes at the airport when taking a drive or riding the bus.
3. Point to and discuss the racks of identical clothes and objects, such as balls, dolls, apples, carrots, while at the market or a department store.
4. Let the child help you whenever you are sorting.
5. General Suggestions.
   a. Start with two kinds of objects to sort. Later, sort three to four types of objects into containers.
   b. Choose very different kinds of objects to sort. Later, objects can be used which are similar in size, shape, color, texture, weight, smell.
   c. Start with objects that are familiar to the child. Later, include unfamiliar objects.
   d. Start with two of each kind of object. Increase the numbers to about four or five.
6. Place an object into a container and a dissimilar object into a second container while the child watches. Give the child one object. Ask him to drop it into the appropriate container. Continue until all the objects have been sorted.
7. Repeat activity #6 above but give the child two or three objects to drop into the appropriate container. Continue to give the child objects to sort in small groups. Later, give the child all the objects he will sort at one time. The child may sort by picking up an object at random to drop into the appropriate container or he may sort by dropping all the objects of one kind into the appropriate container before doing this with the second type of object.
8. Encourage the child to sort his shirts from his pants

after they are washed.
9. Let the child sort blocks and beads during clean-up time.
10. Let the child sort rocks and seaweed while at the beach.
11. Let the child sort poker chips and spools into containers which have matching holes.
12. Let the child sort spools and pegs, putting the pegs into the pegboard and the spools into a container.
13. Let the child sort spoons and forks at a picnic. Let the child help briefly in the kitchen, sorting the silverware, cups, plates, bowls.
14. Let the child sort hairpins and curlers whenever Mom sets her hair.
15. Let the child pick out grass, leaves, rocks whenever Dad cleans the yard.

1.109 ASSEMBLES FOUR NESTING BLOCKS (19-24 mo.)

Nesting blocks are square containers of different sizes which fit together.

1. Refer to 1.72 (Nests two then three cans). Use the basic directions and suggestions for visual and tactile cues; follow the same procedure.
2. Give the child only as much help as he needs to be successful.
3. Use the following materials:
   a. Wooden boxes.
   b. Cardboard boxes.
   c. Three cardboard boxes and one block.
   d. Shoe boxes of different sizes.

1.110 RECOGNIZES SELF IN PHOTOGRAPH (19-24 mo.)

The child points to or picks up his photograph from a choice of two photographs. Each photograph should have only one person in it. A child may find it easier to recognize members of his family before recognizing himself in photographs.

1. Point out the child's reflection in a restroom mirror, a showcase glass, garden or pond water, shiny metals.
2. Let the child play in front of a mirror. Point out body parts, make faces, etc. Discuss who is in the mirror. Place a photograph on the mirror so the child can see his face and his photograph at the same time.
3. Look at family photo albums. Discuss and find familiar people in different pictures. Pay special attention to pictures of the child. Use his name often. Occasionally point to, pat, or tap the child to indicate a photograph of him. Place two pictures in front of the child. Ask the child to "show you," "touch" or "point to" himself.
4. Place two photographs in front of the child and ask him to pick up his picture. If the child reaches for the wrong photograph, direct his hand to his photograph. Praise him and try again. If the child picks up the incorrect photograph, pick up the correct one and say, "Here is

Ricky's picture." Point to the photograph the child has and say "That is a picture of Joshua." Say this with a positive attitude and tone of voice. Do not punish the child for responding incorrectly. He needs many positive information-receiving experiences. The two photographs should be very different at first. If the child is a girl with long hair, make the other picture a boy with very short hair.

1.111 IDENTIFIES THREE BODY PARTS (19-22 mo.)

Refer to 1.91 (Identifies one body part).

1.112 UNDERSTANDS PERSONAL PRONOUNS, SOME ACTION VERBS AND ADJECTIVES (20-24 mo.)

The child shows understanding of a pronoun by carrying out a simple direction which is given without gestures. The child performs a simple familiar action on request.

1. Use personal pronouns accompanied by gestures and then without gestures in reference to people.
   a. "Give it to him (her, me)." Point appropriately.
   b. "Don't forget Daddy! Give him a kiss!" Daddy points to his cheek.
   c. "That's Susan's. Take it to her." Points to Susan.
2. Discuss the child's activities. Discuss what he and other people do.
3. Read books together. Imitate the depicted familiar actions, such as eating or walking. Ask the child to imitate.
4. Use adjectives when you talk to the child. The first ones children learn are hot, cold, heavy, big, funny, pretty, nice. Use these in a variety of situations in the activities of daily living.

1.113 SERIES OF HIDDEN DISPLACEMENTS: OBJECT UNDER FIRST SCREEN (21-22 mo.)

The child finds an object, when hidden by a series of displacements, under the first screen.

1. Refer to 1.62 (Hidden displacement one screen) for description of "displacement."
2. Refer to 1.94 (Series of hidden displacements: object under last screen, Activity #2, 3). Modify the activities by leaving the object under the first screen. Continue to move to the last screen. Observe the child's search for the hidden object. See if she looks under the last screen first, the middle screen, and then the first screen. This search pattern is appropriate.

1.114 PLACES TRIANGULAR PIECE IN FORM-BOARD (21-24 mo.)

A formboard is a shape puzzle.

1. Refer to 1.71 (Places round piece in formboard). Be sure to point out the triangle's angles and points.
2. Cut triangles out of wood, foam, sponge, plastic or find triangular boxes and containers. Take them to the beach and make triangular holes in the sand. Let the child put the triangular objects into the matching holes.
3. Use a formboard with a combination of triangles, circles and/or squares.
4. Refer to 1.86 (Places square piece in formboard, Activity #4) for suggestions on making your own form-board.
5. Use a formboard with three triangles of different sizes. Let the child remove the triangles from the formboard. Arrange the triangles so the correct triangle is next to the hole in which it belongs. Place the triangles at random after the child can successfully match them to the correct hole.

1.115 REMEMBERS WHERE OBJECTS BELONG (21-24 mo.)

The child can with adult assistance put some of his toys and familiar objects away.

A. Puts Toys Away.
   1. Encourage the child to help put away his toys. You may be doing almost all the work in the beginning.
   2. Do not ask the child if he wants to put his toys away since at this age children are indecisive and negative, say, "Time to put your toys away. We are going to the store." Should you inadvertently ask the child to clean up and you receive a "no" response, you will have to respect the child's decision and matter-of-factly do it yourself. Should the child join in, accept the help with pleasure. *Remember the child is only two years old. It will be a few years before he can do these things completely and consistently.*
   3. Give the child a five to ten minute warning before she must put her things away. Say, "We are going to the store. You'll need to put your toys away soon." Say it casually. If the child says "no," do not get into an argument. Respond with something pleasant, such as "It's not time yet; you may still play."
   4. Give the child a good reason to put her toys away, such as, picking Daddy up, seeing Grandma and Grandpa, going for a walk. She may put her toys away as you put your things away.
   5. Start with short, easy tasks, such as putting blocks into their own container, collecting the three books to put on the shelf or, "parking" the toy car on the shelf.
   6. Make up games, such as "You put the yellow car away, I'll put the red one away," or "Let's take turns."
   7. Give reminders, if needed. The child will occasionally get sidetracked. This is natural at this age.
   8. Be sensitive to the child's moods and health. Putting toys away will be an added frustration if the child is over tired, slightly sick, or having a bad day.
   9. Let the child show you where toys belong. Let the child put the first block into the can or bring the can to you. Reinforce his behavior and describe to her what she is doing, such as "That's right, the blocks go into the block can." Should the child make a mistake, do not say "No, not in here," or "That's the wrong place." Put a similar toy into the correct place and say, "This is where the blocks belong."

B. Puts Other Things Away.
   The child can put away things other than her own toys.
   1. Give the child the opportunity to explore the rooms of the house with your supervision, the kitchen one day while you are cooking, the bathroom before bathing the child. Discuss the name of the objects in the room.
   2. Take time, whenever appropriate, to show the child where things belong. If he wants a drink say, "A cup of milk for John. I will get your cup from the top shelf."
   3. Discuss where things are found before you use them. Say, "Time to brush your teeth. We need your toothbrush. Where is it? In the bathroom, your toothbrush is in the bathroom. Let's go to the bathroom to brush your teeth."
   4. Ask the child to show you where his spoon is kept just before it is time to eat.
   5. Look at books and pictures which show where things belong. The books need not be specifically written for this purpose, but you and the child can spend a few minutes naming all the objects in the picture where "the little bear is eating."
   6. Let the child help you put your purchases away after grocery shopping. Ask him where the toilet paper goes. Let him put away the butter.
   7. Let the child put his clothes away in the appropriate drawer. Provide a special place to hang his towel, a shelf for his shoes, his own hamper or clothes basket for his soiled laundry.

1.116 TURNS PAGES ONE AT A TIME (21–24 mo.)

1. Use books with worn pages and with binders which allow the binding and pages to lie flat.
2. Let the child practice opening and turning the magazine section of the Sunday paper. Start with one page. Add pages as she can turn one page over at a time.
3. Make a book using folder dividers as pages or add divider tabs to an old familiar book. Show the child how to lift

the tab to turn the page.

4. Make a book using tracing paper. Paste only one picture on each page. Place large and small pictures on alternate pages to provide for contrast. Show and explain to the child how to check if more than one page has been turned.

5. Make a book using two different textures and weights of paper. Alternate the lighter and heavier pages.

6. Make a book using two distinctly different colored pages, such as green and red. Alternate the page colors to help the child distinguish the different pages.

7. For the older delayed child: Let him wet the tips of his fingers on a sponse before he turns a page. If the child still finds it extremely difficult to turn pages, secretary wax or rubber finger tips may help.

1.117 POINTS TO FIVE–SEVEN PICTURES OF FAMILIAR OBJECTS AND PEOPLE (21-30 mo.)

The child points to or touches the appropriate picture out of a choice of four pictures when asked.

1. Collect familiar common objects with the child which are relatively small and flat, such as sticks, leaves, balloons, paper forks and spoons. Place these objects between two sheets of wax paper. Place the wax paper between the two sheets of paper. Press the edges with a warm iron to seal the objects in the wax paper. Hang these objects as pictures around the house or loosely bind the sealed objects to make a book. Let the child point out the "pictures" as she progresses.

2. Take familiar objects which can be flattened, such as plastic balls, balloons, and paper cups. Show the objects to the child in their usual form. Flatten them while the child watches. Explain how the air comes out of a ball or balloon, how to press a cup flat, etc.

3. Compare familiar objects with pictures of the objects. Start with things which appear two dimensional like pants, shirts, combs, plates. Name the object, outline the shape with your hand then show the picture of the object. Place the object next to the picture and compare them. Outline the shape of the object which is in the picture.

4. Point to and name pictures of animals and objects in the everyday environment. Use pictures the child sees repeatedly and has heard you talk about. Ask the child to point to the objects as you name them.

5. Use a camera which develops pictures instantly. Photograph pictures of favorite toys and objects. Compare the object in the picture to the actual object. Make a book with the photographs.

6. Find a sticker book. These are inexpensive books with pictures of animals and objects which are removed and pasted in the appropriate outlines. This fun activity lets the child name objects and provides for good pasting practice.

7. Let the child look through magazines, newspapers and catalogues for pictures she can select for you to cut out. Together paste them into a scrapbook. The child can use this book to point to named objects and to name the pictures of familiar objects.

8. Bind together and make a booklet of postcards or old Christmas cards with people, candles, bells.

1.118 MATCHES SOUNDS TO PICTURES OF ANIMALS (22-24 mo.)

The child demonstrates her understanding of the sounds animals make using pictures of the animals.

1. Refer to 1.104 (Matches sounds to animals).

2. Refer to 1.92 (Recognizes and points to four animal pictures).

3. Use books with large, simple photographs of animals. Look at the pictures of the animals with the child. Make the sounds the animals make. Say, "The dog says 'ruff-ruff.' Can you say 'ruff-ruff'?" or "What does the dog say?"

4. Look at animal books which have textures or sound-makers in the pages.

5. Show the child two pictures, one of an animal and the other of an object. Make the animal sound and point to the correct picture. Make the animal sound and ask the child to point to the correct picture.

6. Make individual animal books with photographs, magazine pictures, drawings.

1.119 IDENTIFIES SIX BODY PARTS (22-24 mo.)

Refer to 1.91 (Identifies one body part).

1.120 PLAYS WITH WATER AND SAND (24-36 mo.)

The child uses water and sand imaginatively and purposefully.

A. Bathtub Play: Never leave the child alone or unsupervised in the bathtub.
1. Have the child fill a pan with water using a small cup.
2. Hide toys under bubble bath suds and let the child find them.
3. Put floating toys, sponges and containers in the bath tub. Encourage splashing and the filling of containers with water by using the sponges.
4. Let the child take a bubble bath. Encourage the child to poke at the bubbles or pop them using his fingers and thumb. Have him pop the bubbles with his toes or elbow.

B. Outdoor–Indoor Water Play.

1. Let the child pour colored water out of cups. Use a different cup from the one she uses for meals.
2. Use a plastic swimming pool, a tub or a tire cut in half and fill it with water for outdoor play.
3. Use toys which float and sink.
4. Use a large brush and paint with water on the sidewalk, etc.
5. Give the child eye droppers to "paint" the sidewalk with water.
6. Give a doll a bath using a cloth or sponge.
C. Sand Play.
    1. Sand painting. Help the child make a design with glue by spreading it on paper. Let her sprinkle sand on the design before the glue dries. This makes a sand picture.
    2. Play with wet sand and compare it to dry sand.
    3. Use plaster of paris for sand casts. Let the child make foot or hand impressions in sand. Fill the impressions with plaster.
    4. Dig holes with hands and shovels. Fill containers with sand, using cups, spoons, shovels.
    5. Make sculptures out of sand using different containers as molds.
    6. Make sandcastles by dripping wet sand on a mound.
    7. Make impressions in wet sand, dry sand, damp sand.

1.121 PASTES ON APPROPRIATE SIDE
(24-30 mo.)

The child independently applies paste to the appropriate side of a shape and turns it over to stick it onto a paper.

1. Refer to 1.100 (Pastes on one side). Make the right side of the shape distinctly different and more attractive than the wrong side.
2. Use distinctive "right side" cues, such as glitter, pieces of cloth or other texture, designs, corrugated cardboard, plastic with bumps on one side.

1.122 DEMONSTRATES AWARENESS OF CLASS ROUTINES (24-27 mo.)

The child anticipates the next classroom activity when given environmental or verbal cues. A routine helps the children feel more comfortable in the classroom. They know there is a certain order to the class day and are able to anticipate activities (e.g., putting in their name card after their arrival at school, snacking at a certain time of day). A routine allows them to be more independent and helps in teaching time concepts.

1. General Suggestions.
    a. Prepare the child for school in the morning by talking to the child about school and what he will do there (name general activities in chronological order).
    b. Let the child relate to only one person rather than all the staff members or volunteers when he first comes to school.
    c. Allow enough time for each child to settle in and feel comfortable with the school atmosphere.
    d. Label the child's things, i.e., apron, name ard, cup, bowl and utensils, seating area or chair, cubby hole. This helps to establish and maintain the routines.
    e. Use cues to signal the end of an activity or to alert the child to the next activity. For example, use a bell to signal snacktime or sing the same song to end music time.
    f. Verbalize to the child the sequence of events as they occur. For example, say while the child washes his hands, "Yes, we wash our hands and then we sit down at the table for our snack."
    g. Routines at home are also helpful for the child.

1.123 UNDERSTANDS CONCEPT OF ONE
(24-30 mo.)

The child points to a set of one out of a choice of two sets, such as a set of one apple and a set of two bananas. Also the child answers verbally or with gesture the question, "How many do you have?"

1. Use the word "one" with concrete objects such as one dog, one block, and not just "one." Should a child point and say one bus when there are two or more say, "two buses," or "many buses." Whenever the child is actively involved with one object, label it, such as "One ball, let's play with the one ball," "One shoe, we only have one shoe."
2. Play games with body parts as contrasting pairs, such as two legs, two hands, two ears, with one nose, one mouth.
3. Point out and label the set of one in books or everyday situations, such as "One dog, three cats," "The boy has one yellow balloon."
4. Play games or do things involving the use of one of something at a time.
    a. String leis and beads and have the child "help" you by passing "only one" at a time. Give short, clear directions, such as "Give me just one flower, thank you, now give me another one, one flower."
    b. Build with blocks or do puzzles. Stack blocks with the child passing one block at a time to you. Take turns stacking by passing the blocks to the child to stack.
    c. Ask the child to get one diaper so you can change his diaper or one clothes pin as you hang clothes. Ask the child to bring one of something from another room.
5. Go on a walk with one brown package. Collect objects, such as one red flower, one leaf, one twig. At home, spread out your treasures on paper and name them again. Glue, tape or paste them to make a collage.
6. Sing songs and do fingerplays with gestures and pictures involving the concept of one. Do some favorites with modification, such as "Twinkle, Twinkle, Little Star" with one hand, then use two hands.
7. Watch *Sesame Street* on television.

1.124 IDENTIFIES ROOMS IN OWN HOUSE (24-28 mo.)

The child, on request, goes to or points to different rooms in the house, such as the kitchen or bathroom.

1. Identify the different rooms for the child when he is doing something in a room, for example, "Bryan is playing in the kitchen."
2. Look for things normally used in the different rooms and make it a game.
3. Ask the child to bring you a familiar object from a certain room. Vary the rooms from which you "need" things. Ask the child to take something to a particular room, for example, "Take the book to Allison's room."
4. Ask the child where a room is located, "Where's the bathroom, can you take me there?" or "Show Amber the playroom."
5. Play hide and seek in different rooms. Pick a room you will hide in and tell the child where you will be. The child waits until you give a signal then finds you. On another occasion tell the child what room to hid in, then go and look for him.
6. Play hiding games with objects or toys. Hiding eggs at Easter time is especially fun.

1.125 DEMONTRATES USE OF OBJECTS (24-28 mo.)

The child responds correctly to questions involving the functions of objects, such as comb, telephone or shoe, e.g., "What do you do with a shoe?" A gesture is acceptable.

1. Demonstrate the use of three to five common objects. Describe to the child what you are doing when you use the common objects with him. For example, when you are combing the child's hair say, "Here's the comb, let's comb your hair." Allow the child to do these things himself and give him as much assistance as necessary. Use other common objects such as cups, comb, telephone, hairbrush, spoon, toothbrush, wash cloth, towel, napkin, soap, broom, sponge.
2. Give the child the object and ask the child to show you how to use the object. Reinforce the child when he is correct. Use pictures which demonstrate the use of the object to help the child respond correctly. Say, "What do you do with the comb?"
   a. The child may demonstrate on himself or you.
   b. The child may demonstrate on a doll.
3. Familiarize the child with the car.
   a. Let the child sit in Mommy's or Daddy's lap in the driver's seat (while car is parked). If the child does not want to verbalize car noises, provide the auditory stimulation, vroom, beep-beep, etc. for her. Do not leave the child in the car unattended.
   b. Use a toy with a steering wheel. Let the child play with the steering wheel, horn. Pretend with him he is driving a car, "Oh, turn the wheel," "Beep-beep."
   c. Play with the toy cars with the child— give him a toy car and take one for yourself. Make the sounds of a car while you push it. Combine playing cars with other activities, such as building bridges with blocks or sand, parking in garages, playing a stop and go game to music as the music stops and goes.
4. Plays games involving trains or buses.
   a. Have children hold on to each other at the hips or shoulders or just line up single file and play "train"— shuffling feet and making noises, raising arms to blow whistle.
   b. Play with an electric or wind up train set. Set up a small circular track with the child. Show her how the train starts. Let the child play with it and see if she can start the train.
   c. Line up two or three blocks or cubes and push them. Let the child build his own train, lining his cubes up. Refer to 4.79 (Imitates three block train using cubes).

1.126 IDENTIFIES CLOTHING ITEMS FOR DIFFERENT OCCASIONS (24-28 mo.)

The child indicates appropriate clothing for several specific activities or occasions.

1. Talk about the choice of clothing when dressing the child for a specific activity or occasion.
   a. Tell the child he is wearing his boots and raincoat because it is raining. Show him how they prevent him from getting wet.
   b. Ask the child to pick out the pajama he would like to wear to bed. Emphasize he is wearing pajamas because he will be going to sleep soon.
   c. Talk about the clothes the child wears for birthday parties, pool or beach activities.
2. Ask the child to bring or choose the clothes she will need for a specific activity. For example, tell the child she is going to the beach and ask her to pick out her swim suit.
3. Play games which involve dressing the child's doll for different occasions.
4. Point out in books and magazines the appropriate clothing children or adults are wearing for an activity.

1.127 ENJOYS TACTILE BOOKS (24-29 mo.)

Tactile books are books which have pop-up pictures, textured pieces glued on the pages, things for the child to do such as pull a tab, open a flap, scratch, smell, turn a wheel between two pages, manipulate moving or pressing parts on a page. These books generally need to be handled more gently than ordinary books and are usually more costly if bought or require more time if made.

1. Buy inexpensive books and adapt them using your creativity.
   a. Glue material or other pieces of texture on appropriate objects, such as clothes, animals.

b. Buy two identical books; cut pictures out of one and superimpose them on the pictures in the other book.

c. Put small flat objects on or beside pictures of the objects. Place the pictures with the objects between wax paper. Place the wax paper between two pieces of cloth and lightly press with a warm iron. Make a book using these pages.

d. Sew a cloth book. Sew felt pieces on the pages.

e. Add diluted food extracts to appropriate parts of the book or page for olfactory awareness and stimulation.

2. Introduce the tactile book as you would other books. If the child does not spontaneously manipulate parts of the book tell her what to do and then show her while describing what you are doing. You may also want to do it together with the child.

3. If the child is unable to handle a costly book without damaging it, avoid anger and frustration for both parent and child, and do not allow unsupervised use. Even a child who can manipulate the book may get excited or pull a little too hard once in a while. Keep in mind that a loved book is a worn, smudged and tattered book, not one that remains crisp and white and new looking.

1.128 FINDS DETAILS IN FAVORITE PICTURE BOOK (24-27 mo.)

The child looks at and points at several fine details in favorite pictures in books both spontaneously or when named.

1. General Suggestions.
   a. Begin with simple pictures that have a limited number of details.
   b. Use books with large pictures.
   c. Point out details which are generally seen alone, not always part of another object, such as trees in the background as opposed to leaves on an apple stem.

2. Point out interesting details in addition to the main object or person when reading or look at pictures in books. This should not be done on every page, nor should every detail be scrutinized. Pointing out a few on two or three pages is a good start.

3. Use familiar and well liked books which have a main character or a character, such as a small animal, insect or person which is repeatedly used. Ask the child to find the character in the pages which contain it. *Inch by Inch* by Leo Lionni has a small inch worm in the pictures that can be sought by the child. Many of Richard Scarry's books use small animals repeatedly.

4. Use nursery rhyme posters or other familiar pictures. Ask the child to locate then point to a familiar "detail" in the picture. Start with objects or people that are separate from the main character and later ask for things that are part of the main character, such as his hat, shoe, button. Should the child have difficulty locating the object, describe where it is and use your hand to guide the child's eyes to the right part of the page.

1.129 RECOGNIZES FAMILIAR ADULT IN PHOTOGRAPH (24-28 mo.)

1. Show the child a large recent photograph of Mom. Put the photo next to Mom so the child can compare the photo with Mom herself. Talk about the picture of Mom.

2. Show the child two pictures, one of Mom, another of a complete stranger. Ask the child to point to Mom. (Make sure the photographs are of equal attractiveness so the child is not attending to the color size.)

3. Make a picture book with photographs of the child's mother, father, grandparents, aunts. Put one picture on each page. Have a picture of all the family members. Encourage the child to name each person.

4. Look through the family album with the child. Point out family members. After several pictures ask the child if he can find the picture of Mom, Dad.

5. Show the child family pictures and have her find different members. Have her point to the picture and then to the person.

6. Use a name chart at school. Give each child and the teacher a name card with his picture on the left side followed by his name. Let the child look at the picture of the teacher and compare it to the teacher. Later, show the child the picture of the teacher and one of someone else. Ask the child to point to the picture of the teacher.

1.130 ENGAGES IN SIMPLE MAKE–BELIEVE ACTIVITIES (24-30 mo.)

The child begins to initiate make believe activities at this age. He begins to separate reality and fantasy, but the two are still often mixed. The activities the child engages in are short, discrete pieces of drama and are active imitations of actions previously seen or experienced. Should an adult participate, the child is usually unable to reverse the role of the adult, that is, the child cannot respond as if the adult is the child, even if he is pretending to be Daddy or Mommy.

1. Give the child the opportunity to act out frightening experiences in order to learn how to cope with his feelings. For a child who has been hospitalized, "doctor things" should be provided.

2. Be cautious about pretending to be monsters or wild animals. Reality and fantasy are not clearly differentiated.

3. Suggestions for play materials:
   a. Pots and pans.
   b. Old shoes and pocketbooks.
   c. Stethoscopes.
   d. Hats.
   e. Strong, well constructed dolls with moveable arms, legs, eyes.
   f. Cameras.
   g. Shaving toys.

1.131 KNOWS MORE BODY PARTS (24-28 mo.)

The child increases the number of body parts he can identify to include smaller parts of the body, such as the wrist, elbow, knees.

1. Refer to 1.91 (Identifies one body part).
2. Name and touch body parts while the child rides a swing. Stand in front of the swing and as the child swings close by touch and name her knees.
3. Name body parts in the bathroom. Around this time, children are being toilet trained and it is a natural time for them to play with their genitals. Name these parts as you would any other body part. Do not make a big fuss over these parts either by silence or with scolding. Do not teach the child that part of him is mysterious or "dirty."

1.132 SELECTS PICTURES INVOLVING ACTION WORDS (24-30 mo.)

The child points to several pictures depicting familiar actions on request.

1. Teach by naming the actions as he does them or observes them being done by someone else (i.e., "Oh, You're eating now," or "Look at Daddy sleeping.").
2. Play pretend games with the child, "house" or other simple games. Refer to 1.130 (Engages in simple make believe activities). Talk to the child about what you did together.
3. Play a game where the child describes the action you are demonstrating, sleeping, walking, sitting, running.
4. Teach the child action words by showing him pictures of familiar actions—eating, running, cooking, sewing, hammering.
5. Ask the child to point or pick out the appropriate picture out of a choice of two pictures, "Point to the boy sleeping."
6. Have the child point to several different actions in one picture. Say to him, "Show me the boy *running;* where is the girl *eating?"*
7. Look for pictures of one action at a time. Look for pictures of someone sleeping, sitting, eating, brushing teeth, drinking, etc. in magazines with the child.
8. Make a book with pictures showing familiar actions from magazines.

1.133 OBEYS TWO PART COMMANDS (24-29 mo.)

The child obeys a simple command related to two objects but requiring only one action, such as "Give me the shoe and the ball."

1. Play the games in which the child is asked to do something with a toy with two parts, e.g., "Bring the doll and the doll dress."
2. Play games in which the child is asked to do something with a toy that cannot function without the other part, e.g., "Please bring the ring stack and the rings."
3. Play games in which you ask the child to obey a simple command related to two familiar nonrelated objects such as "Bring me the bear and the book." Make sure both are in sight and very near to you and the child. If the child does not comprehend the directions, help him with carrying out the task together. Give reinforcement while doing so.
4. Have the child repeat the direction to himself. A question such as "What are you going to bring Mommy?" is helpful.
5. After the child is able to obey two object commands teach him to carry out two action commands. This occurs around 33-35 mo.
6. Start with two familiar action commands and combine them. Give directions slowly. Make sure commands are related to each other, such as "Pick up the ball and put it away."
7. Use clues, such as "First you," "then," "after."
8. Some suggestions for two-part action commands:
   a. "Run to the door and touch the door."
   b. "Open the door and go outside."
   c. "Take off his shoes or slippers and go into the house."
   d. "Close the book and put it away."
   e. "Pick up the ball and put it in the box."
   f. "Put the ball on the floor and kick the ball."
   g. "Drink your juice and put your cup on the table."

1.134 UNDERSTANDS COMPLEX AND COMPOUND SENTENCES (24-27 mo.)

The child remembers and understands more complex language structures as her language experiences and her skills increase.

1. Use complex and compound sentences. See if the child can remember and understand the sentences.
   a. When we get home you may have a cookie.
   b. We will buy a toy when we go to the store.
   c. We will have dinner after Daddy gets home.
   d. Susan can take her doll and you can take your teddy bear.
   e. Give the ball to Daddy and give the book to me.
2. Avoid the short, simple phrases used in conversing with the child when she was younger. Daily conversation should include more complex statements such as, "It's time to get dressed to go to Grannie's house."
3. Refer to 1.133 (Obeys two-part commands).
4. Refer to 1.125 (Demonstrates use of objects), 1.127 (Enjoys tactile books), 3.113 (Imitates simple bilateral movements of limb, head, and trunk) for activities in which complex and compound sentences can be used.

1.135 GIVES ONE OUT OF MANY (25-30 mo.)

The child gives or takes one of something from a larger grouping. Be careful that unintentional cues are not given.

1. Refer to 1.123 (Understands concept of one, Activities #1-3, 5, 6).
2. Ask the child to give you "one cup" when she is playing with a small number of toys that are different, such as a doll, cup, spoon. Since the child has only one cup she will be successful.
3. Ask the child for an object, which is one of two identical objects, when the child is playing with a group of objects. For example, ask the child for "one spoon" from a group of toys which include two spoons, one cup and one plate. Give verbal and non-verbal cues as necessary.
4. Refer to 1.123 (Understands concept of one, Activity #4).
5. Ask the child to pass out one napkin, one cup, and one snack to each person.
6. Ask the child to take one napkin, one cup, one snack.
7. Ask the child to take one musical instrument out of the box.
8. Ask the child to take one toy out of a group of them.

1.136 MATCHES SHAPES—CIRCLE, TRIANGLE, SQUARE (TOYS) (26-30 mo.)

The child identifies two shapes which are exactly alike.

A. Provide the child with experiences in discriminating shapes (start with circles, but adapt activities using squares, then triangles). Talk about the shapes as you do the following:
 1. Start with the circle and look for it in the environment. Mention and point out the circular shape of things whenever appropriate such as round crackers, tomato slices, round soaps, puddles, balloons, coins, jar covers, the moon.
 2. Trace circular shapes with your hands and fingers.
 3. Walk on large circles on marked pavement.
 4. Put circles up to decorate the room and use stick-on circles on the toy box or bath tub so they will be noticed or discussed many times during the day.
 5. Make snacks using round crackers. Make cookies with Dad or Mom.
 6. Look at picture books about shapes.
 7. Draw a "secret circle" in the child's palm.
 8. Play with puzzles involving shapes. Formboards, picture puzzles, and parquetry may be used, depending on the child's ability.
 9. Place toy circles in the child's wading pool. Let the child find all the circles and put them in a jar. This can be a fun water activity for him.
 10. Paste circles made out of cardboard, construction paper, tissue, foil, stickers, jar covers for a circle collage.
 11. Give each child a paper bag or cloth bag with dif-
ferent objects and toy circles. Tell the children to look into their bags and find all the circles. Have them put the circles into a circular can in the middle of the group.

B. Experiences in Matching Shapes:
 1. Use two pairs of shapes. Make the first pair large, round and yellow; the second pair small, triangular and blue. Show the child the circle, let him hold it. Then show the child a tray on which you have placed the other circle and one triangle. Ask the child to point out to you the same shape or to pick up the same shape. Should the child attempt to pick up the incorrect shape, guide his hand to the correct one. Let him look at the two shapes in his hand and say, "Same, the shapes are the same." Try again.
 2. When the child can do activity #1, change the pairs of shapes. Use a large pair of red circles and an equally large pair of white triangles. Follow the same procedure.
 3. Use a pair of large yellow circles and a pair of small yellow triangles.
 4. Use a pair of large red circles and a pair of equally large red triangles.
 5. Increase the choices to one out of three.

1.137 MATCHES COLORS—BLACK, WHITE (26-29 mo.)

The child identifies objects of the same color and at least one object that is identical to the other objects except for its color.

A. Discriminate Colors:
 1. Refer to 1.70 (Shows understanding of color and size).
B. Matches Colors:
 1. Use three objects to teach matching. Use a pair of black objects and one white object or a pair of white objects and a black object. When the child can successfully match two colors, use objects with primary colors, such as a pair of white objects and a *red* object, white and blue, back and yellow, yellow and blue, etc.
 2. Use of containers for matching skills.
  a. Place a container in front of the child. As the child watches place one white cube in the container. Give her another white cube and ask her to place it with the cube of the same color. Repeat this with the black cubes and another container. Take them all out.
  b. Let the child place a white cube into the container. Show her another white cube and one black cube. Ask her to put the cube of the same color into the container.
  c. Let the child place a white cube into one container and a black cube into another container. (If necessary, the containers may be colored

black or white to match the color of the cubes as an added aid in discrimination. Later, they should be neutral in color.)

3. Use colored cars (objects). Show the child a car (i.e., red) and tell him the color. Let him hold and examine the car while you pick two more cars (one red, the other blue). Show the child the two cars and ask him to pick the car which is identical in color to the one in his hand. Let the child play with the cars before continuing the activity with other colors or going on to another activity.

4. Paste circles of different colors on separate sheets of paper. Match colored objects (shapes, toys, clothes) to each color. Start with two circles and later add more.

5. Use a checker board and have the child match red and black tokens to appropriate squares. Do not overwhelm the child with all the checkers at one time; start with a few and if the child wishes to continue, give her more.

6. Give each child a different colored bucket. Let them look for plastic eggs (or cubes, or toys) which are the same color as their bucket. The eggs should be "hidden" in a small area of the room where the children search. This is not a race or a contest. There should be no one winner.

1.138 KNOWS OWN SEX OR SEX OF OTHERS (26-33 mo.)

Children enjoy imitating the different people they know at this age. They make no discrimination of sex roles, although they are aware of sex differences. Girls' "trying on" traditional male roles, and boys' playing with dolls or dressing up in Mom's clothes should be accepted as a natural part of play and growing up.

1. Talk to the child about being a girl (or boy). Say, "Sarah is a girl," or "This belongs to a girl, yes, it is Sarah's ball." Name other familiar people who are of the same sex as the child. Say "Mom is a girl, sister Joan is a girl, your friend Kitty is a girl, and Sarah is a girl."

2. Mention the child's sex when doing other activities which involve people or pictures of people. Say, "That is a man, you are a boy."

3. Play games in groups with all the girls doing something and all the boys doing something else.

4. A child, especially one with a baby sister or brother, may ask about the sibling's penis or vagina while watching the baby being bathed or diapered. This is a natural time to say, "That is Carl's penis, Carl is a boy just like you," or "You are a girl, all girls have vaginas." The proper term for the genitals should always be used, as you do so with other body parts. However at this age sex differentiations is rarely made according to genital parts. The child usually attends first to clothing, hair, or name. It will be awhile before the child will understand enough to discriminate as adults do.

1.139 MATCHES IDENTICAL SIMPLE PICTURES OF OBJECTS (27-30 mo.)

The child identifies from a group of three pictures of objects, the two which are the same.

1. General Suggestions for Matching.
   a. Use pictures which are exact duplicates.
   b. Use pictures of simple familiar objects.
   c. Use pairs of pictures which are equally attractive.

2. Use recent identical photographs of the child (duplicated to make a pair) and a photograph of another person who is familiar to the child. Have the child match the pictures of herself. (Do the same with other members of the family.)

3. Use playing cards for children. Show the child pairs of pictures and have him indicate if the pictures are identical. Place each identical pair in a line in front of the child.

4. Give the child one picture card of a matched pair. Place the matching card in front of him along with a different picture card. Have the child pick out or point to the matching picture of the matched pair.

5. Use animal rummy cards, lotto games, pictures cut out from magazines, xeroxed pictures and have the child match the pictures.

1.140 LISTENS TO STORIES (27-30 mo.)

1. Choose story books with the following characteristics:
   a. Stories which are short and have only a few words on each page.
   b. Stories which have many large, colorful, uncomplicated pictures.
   c. Stories which have a simple plot and a sequence of events.
   d. Stories with topics which are relevant to young children and their concerns.

2. Suggestions for storytelling with or without a book:
   a. Use many gestures.
   b. Use intonation and inflection to set the mood; accent certain concepts and expected events; express feelings, etc.
   c. Know your story and use short, clear sentences.
   d. Be flexible. Every page need not be read.
   e. Consider the child's attention span. Do not read too slow or fast or ask too many questions.
   f. Pick stories you tell the child.

3. Tell the child stories about herself which describe the events of that day.

4. Tell the child stories you know or have created using aids, such as pictures or objects whenever appropriate.

5. Use storybooks as an aid. Rather than reading the story verbatim, use your own words. Read only the simplest of storybooks word for word.

6. Go to the library and select storybooks "together." The child may choose a book too difficult for her, but let her "borrow" it and you borrow others.

7. Encourage the child to listen to children's stories and to nursery rhymes on the phonograph or tape recorder with the accompanying books and pictures.
8. Make up stories about the child. Tell stories using the child's name. Children love to hear fantastic adventures about themselves.

1.141 UNDERSTANDS MANY ACTION VERBS (27-30 mo.)

The child shows understanding of action verbs by doing them on request or by pointing to pictures describing the action verbs.

1. Talk to the child describing his activities and your own.
2. Give the child simple directions and help him with them. Talk about the actions. Examples are: sit, stand, walk, run, jump, eat, talk, laugh, clap, smile, look, find, get, color, paint, come, go, drink, play.
3. Refer to 1.132 (Selects pictures involving action words).
4. Refer to 1.142 (Identifies objects with their use) for activities in which action words can be used.

1.142 IDENTIFIES OBJECTS WITH THEIR USE (28-34 mo.)

The child points to the correct object when the function of the object is described.

1. Explain why we do things.
   a. Bath time: "Your hands and feet are so dirty, let's take a bath!"
   b. Mealtime: "You must be very hungry, look at all the rice you're eating! What do we do when we are hungry? Yes, we eat our food!"
   c. Dressing or undressing: "Oh, it is so cold! Let's put on your pretty pink sweater."
   d. Bedtime: "Mom is very tired, I need to sleep."
2. Encourage the child to let you know by gestures or words what objects are needed for common activities. For example, ask the child what he needs to brush his teeth.
3. Play sorting games with everyday objects; use five pieces of clothing and five fruits. Ask the child to give you all the things to eat or all the things to wear.
4. Use an appropriate puzzle. Help the child complete it by describing the functions of the puzzle pieces. For example, "The dog needs something to hear with, let's put his ear here."
5. Use lotto games. When holding up the card (crayon) say, "Who has the crayon, the crayon is for coloring pictures." After the child or children can play quite well, do not show the picture but say, "I have something to color pictures with." Add more description about use if necessary.

1.143 IDENTIFIES BODY PARTS WITH THEIR FUNCTION (28-34 mo.)

The child indicates with word or gesture the appropriate functions of body parts.

1. Talk, show, play games to teach the appropriate function of different body parts.
   a. Eyes—to look at things or see things;
   b. Nose—to smell things;
   c. Mouth—to talk, sing, and eat;
   d. Ears—to listen to things;
   e. Hands—to do things;
   f. Feet—to walk, run, kick;
   g. Teeth—to bite and chew.
2. Look at action pictures and describe what the person or animal is doing. Imitate the action and point out the body part being used.
3. Use dolls to do imaginative play and suggest some things for the doll to do, such as listening for the phone. See whether the child turns the doll's ear toward the play phone.
4. There is no one "right" answer to the function of body parts. For example, eyes can close, wink as well as see. Ears can be for washing or hanging glasses onto. Feet are to be tickled. The child who suggests these functions is not "wrong" but should learn the specific function as well as the other things a body part can do.

1.144 MATCHES PRIMARY COLORS (29-33 mo.)

Refer to 1.137 (Matches colors—black, white).

1.145 MATCHES SIMILAR PICTURES OF OBJECTS (30-36 mo.)

The child identifies different pictures of the same object.

1. Use photographs, Christmas cards, postcards, greeting cards (birthday, get-well, thank you) or magazine pictures mounted on index cards for games which involve matching similar pictures.
2. Refer to 1.139 (Matches identical simple pictures of objects). Replace identical cards with similar pictures of a subject (e.g., pictures of houses, dogs, cars).
3. Give each child a picture of a particular object (houses, dogs, balls). Prepare a stack of cards with similar pictures of the objects. Show a card and ask who has the matching card. Go through the entire stack (make sure the child has an equivalent number of cards).
4. Give each child a picture of a particular object. Next give each child a stack of magazine pictures (most of which match her cards). The child must select the matching pictures from the stack. She then pastes the pictures into a book or on to a large piece of paper to make a collage.
5. Find pictures or models of two or three houses. Place the picture of an object in front of each house. Give the child a stack of similar pictures to match to each of these pictures. Use about two to three pictures to be placed in

front of each house. The child can pretend to be the mailman delivering postcards to the people in the houses.

1.146 SORTS SHAPES—CIRCLE, TRIANGLE, SQUARE (TOYS) (30-36 mo.)

The child groups objects by their shapes.

1. Place a circle in a container and a triangle in another container and set them in front of the child. Give the child a circle and ask him to put it in the container with the same shape. Continue until the child has placed three circles and three triangles in the correct container.
2. Do activity #1 except give all six shapes at once for the child to sort and place in the correct containers.
3. Vary the game and make it harder as the child progresses.
   a. Increase the number of containers.
   b. Give the child three shapes to sort.
   c. Vary the material—buttons, plastic pieces, poker chips.
4. Refer to 1.136 (Matches shapes—circle, triangle, square [toys]). Modify the sorting activities.

1.147 COMPLETES THREE—FOUR PIECE PUZZLE (30-36 mo.)

The child completes a puzzle of an object, person or animal with three to four related pieces.

1. Choosing puzzles with two to three unrelated pieces.
   a. Choose puzzles which have pieces of whole objects rather than a part of a whole.
   b. Choose puzzles which have pieces with different, distinctive shapes, such as a bird, a dog, and a train rather than an apple, the sun and an orange.
   c. Choose puzzles with a few large pieces.
   d. Choose puzzles with favorite, familiar objects.
   e. Add small and large knobs, if necessary. Refer to 1.71 (Place round piece in formboard; Activity #5.c.).
2. Progress to puzzles with three to four related pieces after the above mentioned single piece puzzles are successfully completed. Refer to 1.71 (Place round piece in formboard) for teaching suggestions.
3. Give the child time to play and practice his skills without adult attention.
4. Give the child assistance, if needed.
   a. Color code the pieces, for example, paint the red bird's place red.
   b. Use a book stand to tilt the puzzle.

1.148 STACKS RINGS IN CORRECT ORDER (30-36 mo.)

The child independently stacks rings in correct order on the ring stand. The child may make self corrections as he proceeds.

1. Start with a ring stack with a graded stand.

    a. Help the child feel the gradation of the stand by moving his hands from the top ring down.
    b. Place the two largest rings in front of the child. Ask him to pick the larger of the two and place it on the peg.
    c. Add another ring and encourage the child to pick the largest (proceed until all rings are stacked).
    d. Let the child feel the entire ring stack after all the rings are stacked. Talk about how the rings grow bigger or smaller when you move your hands from the bottom to the top.
    e. State the color of the ring the child should stack if he needs additional assistance.
    f. Make available three, four, then all the rings for the child to choose from and stack.
2. Use a ring stack with a uniform stand so the centers of the rings are uniform in size.

1.149 POINTS TO LARGER OR SMALLER OF TWO SPOONS (30-36 mo.)

1. Refer to 2.76 (Uses size words).
2. Create games using identical objects. While playing, ask the child to point to or give to you the larger or smaller of two objects.
   a. Ask the child to "feed" her dolls with the large or the small baby bottle.
   b. Let the child paint with small and large brushes.
   c. Make jello for dessert with the child. Ask him to stir the jello with the big spoon.

1.150 UNDERSTANDS CONCEPT OF TWO (30-36 mo.)

The child gives you on request two objects from a group of objects.

1. Point out, talk about, and let the child experience the concept of two in everyday activities:
   a. Body parts—wash two hands.
   b. Dressing—two sandals for two feet, two ribbons, two flowers.
   c. Foods—two carrots, two pieces of meat left.
   d. Outdoor trips—lady with two children, two balloons, two buses.
2. Accent the concept of two in familiar fun activities.
   a. Match two colors, two shapes, two objects.
   b. Color or draw two dots, two circles, two lines.
   c. Do two puzzles, put away two toys.
   d. Make two balls, cakes, cookies out of playdough.
   e. Pass two clothes pins at a time, throw two handfuls of grass into the trashcan.
3. When the child has two of something, ask her for them. Say, "Give me two crayons." Encourage the child to count with you as she gives the crayons to you. Thank her and give them right back. Begin to include pairs of different things from which to choose.

4. Ask the child to take two, give you two or touch two objects out of a group of objects.
5. Have the child imitate one or two claps, one or two beats on the drum. Count aloud "one" or "one, two" as you make the sound.

1.151 IDENTIFIES FAMILIAR OBJECTS BY TOUCH (30-36 mo.)

The child selects on request a familiar object without looking at it.

1. Encourage the child to touch various textures in the environment. Let the child play outdoors and feel the differences in playing on the grass, on a mat, in the sand, on cement porches, in dirt.
2. Talk about the texture of things the child plays with— (furry stuffed bunny, smooth ball, hard block).
3. Give the child different textures to fell: smooth plastic, rough towel, sticky tape, soft feather, a damp sponge. Use the adjectives, such as "smooth," "rough" while he is touching an object.
4. Help the child crumple newspaper, tinfoil, leaves, tissue paper. Talk about the different textures and sounds of each item when crumpled.
5. Let the child put his hands into a jar of macaroni, beans, or rice. Discuss the different textures; compare them with the cooked version.
6. Cut a hole out in opposite sides of a box. Make the holes large enough for your hands to fit through it. Show the child a toy car and place it in the box. Encourage the child to put his hands in, find the car and bring it out. Do the same with another object such as an orange.
   a. Place an object in the box. Let the child touch it and guess what it is. If the child is non-verbal, ask, "Is it an orange?" Let him indicate the answer with a gesture.
   b. Put two objects in the box and let the child feel them. Ask the child for one of the objects.
7. Use a sturdy cloth bag and let the child help you place two different objects such as a shoe and a ball in the bag. Shake the bag and ask the child to find the shoe without looking into the bag. He can use one hand or both hands. Change the objects and/or add one or two more objects when the child can do more.

1.152 ENJOYS BEING READ TO AND LOOKS AT BOOKS INDEPENDENTLY (30-36 mo.)

1. Give the child many experiences with books—thumbing through picture books; being read to by another; pointing out details, identifying pictures in books; being allowed to hold a book and turn the pages while being read it; being encouraged to contribute to a story being read to him by answering questions, such as "What's happening here?" or "What do you see?"
2. Provide the child with a selection of picture books—

simple animal stories; nursery rhymes; familiar objects or people (e.g. Sesame Street characters, Winnie the Pooh); a favorite toy or animal; holiday books (Christmas, Halloween).
3. Teach the child the proper care of books (no tearing or scribbling, returning to proper place). Visit a library and let the child select her own books with or without assistance. If child needs assistance in selecting a book choose two or three books and have her select a book from your choices. (Selecting books from a great variety can be overwhelming.)
4. Look at books with your child and read simple stories. Name pictures and encourage her to imitate.
5. Read a picture story to your child. Go over the pictures with him telling you what happened.
6. Use books and stories in which the child is familiar with the sequence. Ask what will happen next.

1.153 PLAYS HOUSE (30-36 mo.)

The child is capable of longer, more elaborate make-believe activities involving more than imitative actions. The child pretends to "be" Mom, Dad, the mailperson, doing what they do, talking as they do. Dressing up becomes fun. The child still needs adult assistance and modeling.

1. Suggested equipment and materials for playing house, office, etc.:
   a. Cardtable with a blanket draped over it.
   b. Small cardboard boxes (cars, trains, buses).
   c. Large T.V. and refrigerator cardboard boxes (to be filled with sand, foam pieces or other materials and used like a sandbox).
   d. Doll houses.
   e. Sandbox with dishes, shovels, cooking utensils.
   f. Tricycles and wagons.
   g. Child size lawn tools (rakes, lawnmowers).
   h. Child size brooms, mops, carpet sweepers.
   i. Child size carpentry tools (screwdrivers, saws, hammers).
   j. Wooden, plastic or cardboard toy furniture (sinks, stoves, potty chairs, refrigerator, beds).
   k. Dolls and doll carriages.
   l. Men's and women's clothing (aprons, shoes, silk slips, hats, gloves, ties).
   m. Newspaper, magazines, leis, necklaces, bracelets, watches, cameras.
2. Play with the children at first, gradually withdraw.

1.154 POINTS TO SIX BODY PARTS ON PICTURE OF A DOLL (30-36 mo.)

1. Refer to 1.91 (Identifies one body part).
2. Make an outline of the child with crayon and a large sheet of paper. Add and color in features. Hang the drawing in the child's room. Occasionally talk about it and use it to identify body parts, eyes, nose, fingers, navel, toes, etc.

3. Do lots of holiday activities involving pasting together body parts to make animals and people like the Easter Bunny or Santa Claus. Look for ideas in holiday magazines.

4. Cut out children's faces from magazines. Make a booklet. Discuss the differences and similarities of the children's hair, eyes, mouths, legs, clothes.

5. Draw pictures of people in the sand or dirt. Name the body parts as you add them in. Let the child do some and you add others.

1.155 UNDERSTANDS MORE ADJECTIVES (30-33 mo.)

The child shows understanding of more adjectives by labeling or more frequently, by picking out the object or feature described.

1. Describe the child's activities and your activities. Describe objects; discuss hot, cold; big, little; happy, sad; loud, soft; light, heavy; long and short. Show items with these characteristics to the child. Help him experience them through sight, touch, smell, sound.

2. Look through magazines and identify different objects by their physical characteristics.

3. Give directions involving adjectives. "Get the big one."

4. Refer to 2.76 (Uses size words).

5. Use playdough and change its form while you describe what you are doing. "This is flat. I will roll it up and make it round."

6. Refer to 1.70 (Shows understanding of color and size) for additional activities involving color and size.

1.156 SORTS COLORS AND POINTS TO SEVERAL COLORS WHEN NAMED (33 mo. and above)

The child groups three to five objects of the same color, using objects which are identical except for color.

A. Sorts Colors.
1. Refer to 1.108 (Sorts Objects).
2. Let the child sort colored marbles into milk cartons.
3. Let the child place pegs of the same color in one section of the pegboard.
4. Structure the child's environment to provide opportunities for sorting activities. For example, mark in red toys which belong on a top shelf and mark in blue toys which belong on a bottom shelf. Paint the top shelf red and the bottom shelf blue. The child will be matching and sorting colors when he puts his toys away.
5. Let the child make paper chains for the Christmas tree. Let him cut the strips, *sort* the strips by color into piles, then paste the loops.

B. Identified Colors.
1. Refer to 1.70 (Shows understanding of color and size).

2. Start with one color. Use the child's favorite color or the color of the child's favorite toy. Teach the child the primary colors.

3. Do art activities with emphasis on the color you are teaching the child. Refer to 1.99 (Uses playdough and paints).

4. Play a game of identifying objects in the environment which are the same color as the color you are teaching.

5. Color with the child. Occasionally ask the child to give you a specific crayon. See if the child can give you the correct color crayon.

6. Reinforce the child's close approximations of names of colors, such as "wed" for red, "bue" for blue. Do not stop to correct the child or ask him to repeat the words correctly. Praise the child's understanding of the concept and his ability to name a color correctly.

1.157 IDENTIFIES LONGER STICK (33 mo. and above)

The child picks the longer stick (two to three inches longer) out of a choice of two.

1. Teach the child the concept of "longer" using available materials for comparison, such as arms, legs, sticks, rulers, rope, watering hose. Use the word as the child feels the "longness" of things.

2. Let the child feel long lines made from a variety of materials.
   a. Playdough.
   b. Rug pieces.
   c. Thick yarn and string.
   d. Rope.
   e. Blocks.
   f. Cloth.
   g. Paper rolls.
   h. Sandpaper strips.
   i. Ribbon.

3. Place two identical objects which differ in length in front of the child. One object should be half the size of the other. Encourage the child to feel the longer object by running her hand or fingers from left to right along its length. Ask the child to give you the longer object.

4. Place two sticks (parallel to each other) in front of the child. Ask the child to give you the longer stick. If the child cannot do this, do more of activity #3. Vary the positional cues for the longer stick.

1.158 BEGINS TO PICK LONGER OF TWO LINES (33-36 mo.)

1. Compare long and short balloon strings and kite strings with the child when appropriate.

2. Compare long and short lines with the child.
   a. Make long and short boundry lines out of tape to kick balls over, throw balls to, etc.

   b. Point out the lines the child made when scribbling with crayons, felt pens, paint brushes, chalk. You might make a short line and ask the child to draw a long line next to it.

   c. Make long and short lines in the sand with fingers and sticks.

3. Draw two lines on paper or on a chalkboard and ask the child to identify the longer line.

4. Place two flat objects, such as tape, ribbons, yarn, string, in front of the child or tape the objects to the wall. Ask the child which one is longer.

1.159 UNDERSTANDS ALL COMMON VERBS, MOST COMMON ADJECTIVES (33-36 mo.)

The child understands almost all verbs and adjectives commonly used. He may ask when he does not understand. This is a continuation of development in understanding verbs and adjectives.

1. Refer to 1.141 (Understands many action verbs) and 1.155 (Understands more adjectives).

2. Look through magazines and identify objects which are "hot" or "big." Cut and paste to make a picture book for the child.

3. Use adverbs and the child will begin to use them, such as "He is running fast!", "The dog barked happily," "That is a very pretty one."

NOTE: Each child is unique and may master skills at a rate and age different from other children. The age references in this Guide are approximations. You should not be concerned if your child does not display skills exactly within the specified age ranges. See the Introduction for additional clarification.

2.01 CRY IS MONOTONOUS, NASAL, ONE BREATH LONG (0-1½ mo.)

The child's cry is a total response seen throughout the body as well as heard at birth and during the first month. At first the cry is undifferentiated and is not modified by mouth-opening and closing.

1. Attend to the child's cries and try to fulfill her needs.
2. Attend to the child's sounds even if she does not really cry. A whimper can be a cue to you and an interaction you can reinforce.
3. Refer to 5.08 (Stops unexplained crying).

2.02 CRIES WHEN HUNGRY OR UNCOMFORTABLE (0-1 mo.)

The child's cry is her first form of communication. It is imperative to attend to the child's cries to help her develop a pattern of interaction. The child learns her sounds are useful and have meaning to others.

1. Try to discover why the child is crying. Is she hungry? Does she need to be burped? Diapers wet? Is she cold? Tired?
2. Remedy the problem and comfort the child by quiet talking, handling, or rocking.
3. Refer to 5.08 (Stops unexplained crying).

2.03 MAKES COMFORT SOUNDS–REFLEXIVE VOCAL (0-2½ mo.)

A child who is feeling good, makes comfort sounds. These sounds are usually accidental, the result of changes in tension of the muscles used for speech. Some of the sounds are those used in the English language like "k," "mm," "aaah" or "nnn."

1. Listen for the child's random sounds. Talk to her in response to her sounds.
2. Imitate her sounds.
3. Smile, coo and talk to the child as you feed, bathe, clothe or care for her in other ways.
4. Refer to 5.01 (Enjoys and needs a great deal of physical contact and tactile stimulation).

2.04 MAKES SUCKING SOUNDS (½-3 mo.)

A child, who is feeling comfortable and relaxed may make sucking sounds. These sounds are usually reflexive, the result of changes in tension of the muscles used for sucking.

1. Allow plenty of time for feeding so you and the child are relaxed and comfortable.
2. Look at the child as you feed her. Make lip smacking sounds as you present food to her.
3. Imitate her sounds. Tell her how much you like her and her sounds.
4. Refer to 6.01 (Opens and closes mouth in response to

food stimulus) and 6.02 (Coordinates sucking, swallowing and breathing).

2.05 CRY VARIES IN PITCH, LENGTH AND VOLUME TO INDICATE NEEDS SUCH AS HUNGER, PAIN (1-5 mo.)

The child's only way to obtain attention is by crying. Respond to her crying by meeting her needs. The child learns her sounds are useful and have meaning to others. The child should not be allowed to cry for long periods of time unattended. Try to find out why the child is unhappy. Many parents can recognize the child's problem by the way she is crying.

See Introduction (footnote 2).

2.06 LAUGHS (1½-4 mo.)

The child chuckles or laughs out loud in response to an environmental stimulus instead of cooing or smiling to show her pleasure.

1. Refer to 5.07 (Responds with smile when socially approached), and 5.09 (Vocalizes in response to adult talk and smile) for preskill activities since laughing comes after social smiling and vocalizing.
2. Play with your child:
   a. Make funny noises.
   b. Tickle him gently.
   c. Bounce him gently.
   d. Laugh and chuckle.
   e. Play simple "peek" games behind your hands.

2.07 COOS OPEN VOWELS (AAH), CLOSED VOWELS (EE), DIPHTHONGS (OY AS IN BOY) (2-7 mo.)

The child's developmental pattern in the production of vowel sounds starts from the simple vowel sounds to the complex diphthongs. The open vowel sounds are the first and easiest sounds requiring the opening of the mouth with vocalization and no rounding of the lips. The closed vowel sounds follow and the mouth is not as wide open. Diphthongs are vowels which go from one sound to another.

1. Play vocal games using open and closed vowel sounds as well as diphthongs. Say "ahh" to the child and wait for the child to respond. Then say "ooo" or "eee." Give the child time to respond by cooing or smiling.
2. Make diphthongs for the child when he is looking at your face. Say, "Ahh-eee." Change slowly from one sound to another. Exaggerate your lip movements. Do this to hold the child's interest and attention.
3. Imitate the vowel sounds the child makes.
4. Use your fingers to gently open and close the child's mouth or lips slightly while the child is vocalizing. Do

2.0 EXPRESSIVE LANGUAGE

this slowly. The slight movement will change the sounds he is making.

5. Use gentle vibration on the chest while the child is lying in supine to change his sounds a little. Use one hand to vibrate up and down. Place your other hand on the child. Put your vibrating hand on top of your other hand. For example, to vibrate with your left hand, your right hand will be on the child's chest. Put your left hand on top of your right hand. Little pressure is needed. Be sure to vibrate only while the child is exhaling. Change your speed of vibration to change the sound, shaking your vibrating hand faster or slower. Vocalize "ah" as you do this to encourage the child to vocalize. Many children are fascinated by this and will continue vocalizing. You can try this with a child who is fussing if you are sure he is not hungry or hurt.

6. Refer to 5.07 (Responds with smile when socially approached).

7. Do not continue any expressive language activities if the activity is not enjoyable for you and the child.

2.08 DISASSOCIATES VOCALIZATIONS FROM BODILY MOVEMENT (2-3 mo.)

The child no longer vocalizes primarily in conjunction with body movements. He separates his vocalization from his body movement. The child begins to lie quietly and vocalize, cooing or laughing in response to stimulation.

1. Encourage the child to vocalize when he is lying quietly. Coo to the child.

2. Talk quietly. Be careful not to overstimulate the child with quick movements, bouncing or tickling.

3. Move the child's hands slowly as you vocalize. Place the child's hands on your face as you talk quietly.

4. Sing to the child while rocking or holding him. Look at him and wait for him to vocalize.

2.09 CRIES MORE RHYTHMICALLY WITH MOUTH OPENING AND CLOSING (2½-4½ mo.)

The child modifies his cry by rhythmically opening and closing his mouth at a very early age. This is a normal developmental stage which occurs with maturation. Listen for changes in the child's cry. These changes show an increase in coordination of the muscles involved in respiration and phonation.

See Introduction (footnote 2).

2.10 SQUEALS (2½-5½ mo.)

The child produces loud, sudden bursts of vowel sounds when excited.

1. Encourage squealing by delighting the child. Squealing is a sound which expresses the child's delight, happiness, and excitement.

2. Tickle the child gently to elicit squeals.

3. Play a game by creeping your fingers toward the child.

4. Make funny faces or sounds.

5. Imitate the child's squealing sounds to let him know you like them.

6. Move the child up and down rapidly in the air. The excitement of this activity often delights the child.

2.11 RESPONDS TO SOUND STIMULATION OR SPEECH BY VOCALIZING (3-6 mo.)

The child vocalizes in response to sound and continues an interchange of sounds.

1. Coo to the child. Make inviting sounds to draw the child's attention.

2. Sing to the child. It does not matter whether you can carry a tune or not or whether you know the words.

3. Hum to the child.

4. Entertain the child by snapping your fingers, clicking your tongue, clapping your hands, tapping your fingers.

5. Use squeak toys, spoon clappers, jingle bells, cans or containers with interesting rattles to interest the child. Make a sound and wait for the child to "ask" for it again.

2.12 LAUGHS WHEN HEAD IS COVERED WITH A CLOTH (3½-4½ mo.)

Not every child goes through this stage. The child who does enjoy this stage laughs with delight when his head is briefly covered with a cloth.

1. Let the child's head remain covered for a few seconds when dressing or undressing him. Respond with delight and surprise as the child's face reappears. Caress the child with a gentle rub on his stomach, a kiss, or with gentle blowing on his cheek.

2. Use a soft diaper, extra shirt or wash cloth and brush the cloth across the child's face so he can feel the moving air. Gently drop the cloth over his head. Express pleasure and laughter as he reappears from under the cloth.

3. Use a handiwipe, paper or light cloth. Place the cloth between your face and the child's so your face is gradually hidden from the child's view. Smile and play with the child until your face is completely hidden. Pause before removing the cloth. Appropriate verbalizations such as "I'm going to hide Mommy," and "Here's Mommy," should be used.

4. Use a tissue and drape it over the child's face. Play "Peek-a-boo" by peeking under the tissue and around the sides or by blowing it off. Talk to the child with phrases, such as "Where's baby?" "I see you," "Amber, where are you?"

5. Use another diaper or handy cloth to cover the child's face when changing her diaper. Keep talking so the child knows you are still there. Remove the cover quickly and let her see your smiling face. The commonly used phrases

are "Where's Mclinda? (pause) There you are!" or "Where's baby?" Maintaining physical contact with the child while her head is covered is reassuring for her.

2.13 BABBLES CONSONANT CHAINS "BABA-BABA" (4-6½ mo.)

The child discovers his voice and all the funny sounds he can produce as his coordination of lips, tongue and jaw improves. In his fascination he produces and repeats sounds in long strings, such as "bababbaba," and later the couplet "baba." He also uses sounds other than "baba." If the child fails to babble or decreases his babbling it is a warning sign suggesting possible hearing problems.

1. Respond with pleasure to the child's sounds. Smile, repeat his sounds, pay attention to him.
2. Do not disturb the child when he is making happy babbling sounds in his crib. If you interrupt his play, he will probably stop his sound making to listen to you.
3. Encourage the infant to imitate your babbling by playfully producing the sounds you have heard him make.
4. Facilitate babbling of "b" or "m" sounds by gently closing and opening the child's lips while he is vocalizing. Make the sounds with him at times while you do this.
5. If the child does not babble or he decreases the amount and variety of babbling, make sure his hearing is all right. Ask his doctor to refer him to an audiologist.

2.14 VOCALIZES ATTITUDES OTHER THAN CRYING—JOY, DISPLEASURE (5-6 mo.)

The child indicates her feelings with voice quality, tone and inflection. She is not limited to crying or laughing.

1. Acknowledge and respond appropriately to the child's sounds. Prompt reaction to the child's sounds will help her discover its usefulness and will provide an incentive for the child to make new sounds.
2. Imitate the happy, joyful sounds of the child.
3. Let the child hear voices with special intonations, such as happy, sad, angry voices. Avoid the very strong negative inflections which can frighten the child.
4. Use facial expressions and gestures with your vocalizations to help the child understand various attitudes being expressed, such as a stern look when giving a warning, smiling broadly when expressing joy. End with positive intonations as much as possible.

2.15 REACTS TO MUSIC BY COOING (5-6 mo.)

Infants coo, a melodic, soft vowel sound, when happy or contended. All infants do not react to music by cooing.

1. Provide soft music in the child's environment, e.g., early in the morning when the child first awakens, in the after-noon at the beginning of nap time, in the evening when bathing the child or preparing the child for bed.
2. Hum or sing quiet songs as you rock your child or as you work around the house.
3. Sing nursery songs and perform single movements. Help the child make the movements with you, e.g., rocking forward and back to "Row, Row, Row Your Boat," moving hands and fingers overhead to "Twinkle, Twinkle Little Star."
4. Sing to the child. Hum to the child. Sing all your favorite songs. A good singing voice is not required.
5. Move the child to the rhythm of the music while you vocalize.
6. Listen to the radio or play records on the player with the child for short periods of time. Sing or hum along. Caution: If you play the radio or record player for long periods of time, the child may block out the sound and not respond to it at all.
7. Enjoy all types of music with your child.

2.16 LOOKS AND VOCALIZES TO OWN NAME (5-7 mo.)

The child looks for the speaker and often coos when she hears her name.

1. Use the child's name when you talk to her. Use a consistent name at least 75 per cent of the time. Avoid confusing your child with several names, such as "Sweetie," "Honey," "Baby."
2. Call the child's name to attract her attention. Use her name when you play games, such as "Peek-a-boo." Cover the child's face and ask, "Where's Mary?" When you "find" her say, "There's Mary" or "I found Mary!"
3. Call the child's name first and attract her attention before you begin to play with her.
4. Call the child's name when she is playing. Reward her if she attempts localization and makes any vocalizations after you speak or call her name.
5. Call the child from different directions when her back is turned toward you. Give her a big smile when she turns.
6. Gently say the child's name when awakening her. Reward any vocalizations the child makes in response to her name.
7. Sit in front of a mirror with the child. Say the child's name and point to her. Say your name and point to yourself.
8. Attract the child's attention with a squeak toy or funny noise. Call the child's name, then make the funny noise and call the child's name again.
9. Call the child's name while dressing, feeding or bathing her. When she looks at you entertain her with a funny face.

2.17 BABBLES DOUBLE CONSONANTS "BABA" (5-8 mo.)

The child produces "couplets" of double syllables instead of long chains as coordination of lips, tongue and jaw improves. Occasionally, parents interpret these couplets as meaningful words.

1. Imitate the child's babbling by producing only double consonant sounds.
2. Use double consonant words, such as "mama," "dada," "byebye," "oh-oh."
3. Refer to 2.13 (Babbles consonant chains "Bababa.").

2.18 BABBLES TO PEOPLE (5½-6½ mo.)

The child participants in conversation using babbling sounds. The child or the adult may start this interchange.

1. Repeat back to the child the sounds he makes. Make a big game of it. Note what sounds he makes. The first vowel sounds are generally the "oo," "ah," "ee" and "uh" sounds. The first consonant sounds are generally the "b," "m" and "d" sounds. Babbling activity incorporates these sounds in isolation and also short vowel-consonant combinations, such as "ba-ba," "ma-ma," "da-da."
2. Encourage any spontaneous vocalizations by patting her affectionately and repeating her sounds. Be sure she can see your face when you talk to her.
3. Use varying intonations and inflections because the child picks these up sooner than words. Reward any babbling activities by talking to the child in different melody patterns.
4. Name the object for the child if the babbling appears object oriented.
5. Talk to the child and allow him time to respond vocally. Take the time to talk to him in a pleasant, friendly voice after he responds.
6. The abrupt cessation of babbling activity at this time or in the months to follow may be a sign of hearing dysfunction. Babbling activity ceases because of a lack of feedback to the child's hearing system. Ask his doctor to refer him to an audiologist.

2.19 WAVES OR RESPONDS TO BYE-BYE
(6-9 mo.)

The child moves her hand for bye-bye in stages, first with help, then in imitation and later, on request or spontaneously.

1. Say "Bye-bye" and wave to people when they leave you. This includes Mommy, Daddy, brothers and sisters, friends, relatives and even the family pets. Let the child observe you. Encourage her to participate.
2. Say "Bye-bye" when you leave people or places. Let the child observe you. Encourage her to participate.
3. Help the child wave by moving his hand.
4. Show the child pictures of people driving off in cars. Let the child wave "bye-bye" to them. Use simple, realistic pictures.
5. If the child waves "bye-bye" before it is time to go, she may be telling you she wants to leave. Acknowledge her actions, if it seems likely.
6. Avoid repeatedly telling the child to say "Bye-bye." Some children find they get more attention by not responding since people will keep encouraging them to wave "bye-bye." Be sure you give the child more attention when she responds than when she does not.

2.20 SAYS "DADA" OR "MAMA," NONSPECIFIC-
ALLY (6½-11½ mo.)

The child often says "dada" and "mama" as the first sounds he produces. As parents respond to and encourage these sounds, they become useful and meaningful to the child.

1. Respond with delight to the child's sounds. If father hears "dada" he should respond with delight, e.g., "Oh, did you call me?" "Here's Daddy." If possible, he should go to the child and play a game or talk to the child.
2. Respond to the child's sounds of "mama" and "dada" by referring specifically to mother or father, e.g., "Mama's at work, Daddy is here." Repeat the child's sounds and use them meaningfully.
3. Use "mama" or "daddy" when playing "Peek-a-boo."
4. Refer to 2.17 (Babbles double consonants "Baba") and continue the activities.

2.21 SHOUTS FOR ATTENTION (6½-8 mo.)

The child uses his voice to attract attention when he learns that adults will respond to his sounds.

1. Respond to the child's sounds. This is extremely important. It is his attempt to control his environment. Make it rewarding for the child to vocalize.
2. Ignore the child when he flails his arms and legs to attract attention. Wait until he vocalizes. Respond immediately after he vocalizes so he understands the connection between his vocalizing and the attention he is receiving. Be judicious about ignoring the child.
3. Play a game similar to "Peek-a-boo." Let the child call, then appear for a brief play period (up to 15 seconds), then disappear from the child's sight until he calls again.

2.22 PRODUCES THESE SOUNDS FREQUENTLY
IN BABBLING: B, M, P, D, T, N, G, K, W, H,
F, V, TH, S, Z, L, R (7-15 mo.)

The child generally makes all these sounds in vocal play. Letter sounds are listed in the sequence in which they usually appear.
The first consonant sounds are often bilabials, sounds produced by using both lips, "m," "b," "p." These sounds may be

heard in conjunction with feeding, the "lip smacking" sounds. The "d" and "t" sounds may also be heard during feeding time. The rest of the sounds generally appear in the order given. The more difficult sounds, requiring more precise movements will develop as oral musculature coordination improves. You will probably hear at some time during the child's babbling, all the sounds that appear in your expressive language. This does not mean these sounds are immediately used in talking since precise coordination is required to change quickly from one sound to another to make a word. The same pattern of development of sounds produced in babbling, such as "b" before "sh," will be heard later in the development of consistent articulation of words, such as "boy" before "shoe."

2.23 VOCALIZES IN INTERJECTIONAL MANNER (7½-9 mo.)

The child produces noises which sound like exclamations.

1. Use a variety of inflections when talking to the child. Be sure to use them appropriately.
2. Reinforce the child's exclamatory vocalizations by imitating the sounds and responding in an exciting manner to the stimulus, "Oh! Look! Here comes the kitty!"
3. Use "uh-oh" and "oops" and "wow" as you play with the child.
4. Refer to 2.21 (Shouts for attention) and continue the activities.

2.24 BABBLES WITH INFLECTION SIMILAR TO ADULT SPEECH (7½-12 mo.)

The child is tuning in to the specific patterns, the intonations and the melody of his language. This is an extremely important stage of development. The child's babbling sometimes sounds like adult sentences, e.g., the accent may be placed on final syllables which makes a sentence sound like a question.

1. Speak to the child with extra emphasis on patterns such as:
   a. Question inflections—"Do you want to eat?"
   b. Descriptive inflections—"That's a soft rug."
   c. Interjections—"Oh! Look! That's a pretty baby!"
2. Use appropriate and exaggerated inflections when playing games, such as:
   a. "Row Row Row Your Boat."
   b. "Peek-a-Boo."
   c. "Pat-a-Cake."
   d. "This Little Piggy." (on toes)
3. Sing songs as you dress, diaper, or bathe the child such as:
   a. "Old MacDonald."
   b. "This is the Way We Wash Our Clothes." (adapt to activity)
   c. "Hickory Dickory Dock."
4. Play a game of imitation with the sounds the child makes

e.g., "Okay?" "Okay." "Okay!" "O . . . kay." Do the same patterns with "oh." Later, make the sound first and wait for the child to imitate you before you change your inflection. Articulation is not important.
5. Refer to 2.23 (Vocalizes in interjectional manner) and continue the activities.

2.25 BABBLES SINGLE CONSONANT "BA" (8-12 mo.)

The child begins to break strings of the consonant sounds down, to produce only single consonant sounds. Encourage this development.

1. Continue to imitate the babbled sounds produced by the child.
2. Encourage the child to imitate your sounds by playfully producing sounds you have heard him make.
3. Use single syllables. Repeat only the single consonant sound when the child produces strings of sounds.
4. Play "Peek-a-boo" games to encourage the production of a single consonant sound, saying "boo" or "ba" when the child or adult is "found."

2.26 SHOWS UNDERSTANDING OF WORDS BY APPROPRIATE BEHAVIOR OR GESTURE (9-14 mo.)

The child's responses and simple gestures show his understanding of common language experiences.

1. Refer to 1.56 (Responds to simple verbal requests) and continue the activities.
2. Give directions, such as "Let's put your pants on, give me your foot." See if the child extends her foot out to you. Let the child respond to your voice only. If she does not, accompany your directions with gestures, e.g., "Foot, where's (child's name) foot. Here's your foot! Give me your foot."
3. Provide many opportunities for the child to show what she understands.
   a. Say "Where's Daddy?" when Dad is within the child's visual field.
   b. Ask, "Where's your bottle?"
   c. Say, "Let's go bye-bye." Does the child look toward the door, her sweater, the car? Does she wave?
   d. Play "Peek-a-boo" or "I'm going to get your nose!" Does the child laugh and squeal in anticipation?
   e. Say, "Want up?" before picking the child up. Does she reach up to you with her hands?
   f. "No-No," "Come here," "Give a kiss" are phrases children often respond to with gestures or with behavioral changes.
4. Refer to 6.29 (Cooperates with dressing by extending arm or leg) and continue the activities.
5. Refer to 1.48 (Listens selectively to familiar words) and continue the activities.

2.0 EXPRESSIVE LANGUAGE

2.27 BABBLES IN RESPONSE TO HUMAN VOICE (11-15 mo.)

The child replies to vocal stimulation with a collection of babbling sounds, partial words and intonation patterns. The child attempts to "communicate" with melody and intonation patterns sounding like sentences. The child's sound making is directed to the person talking to him.

1. Respond with chatter and reinforce the child's interpersonal attempts at social verbalization. Continue using extra emphasis on inflections, rhythm and melody of the speech sounds.
2. Be sure to allow time for the child to vocalize after you talk to him.
3. Talk to the child about his experiences and his activities.
4. Refer to 2.18 (Babbles to people) and continue the activities.

2.28 BABBLES MONOLOGUE WHEN LEFT ALONE (11-12 mo.)

The child enjoys hearing herself and playing with sounds she can make.

1. Do not disturb the child when he is making happy babbling sounds in his crib. If you interrupt his play, he will probably stop his sound making to listen to you.
2. Provide the child with interesting objects to look at and play with. These can be toys made for babies or household objects which can be just as fascinating to a child. Brightly printed cloth, mobiles, cups, spoons, several keys on a ring help keep the child happy and interested. This is when he is most apt to babble.
3. Talk, sing or hum to yourself as you work around the home so the child can hear you.

2.29 SAYS "DADA" OR "MAMA," SPECIFICALLY (11-14 mo.)

The child's babbling until this point is usually non-directed. The child begins to direct his babbling sounds of "da-da" and "ma-ma" specifically to his parents around this time because the parent responds and reinforces these sounds.

1. Make sure you name yourself "Da-da," or "Daddy," "Ma-ma" or "Mommy" when you greet the child, when you pick the child up or when you call him.
2. Reward the child's correct use of a name, if he usually calls both parents or all people "Dada." Use the name of the other parent and/or people to help the child understand that each name is for a specific person.
3. Respond quickly when you are correctly named. Give the child lots of praise for being correct!
4. Show the child pictures of familiar people. Label the pictures. Encourage the child to point to whom you name and to say the names. Use large clear pictures the child can touch.

2.30 REPEATS SOUNDS OR GESTURES IF LAUGHED AT (11-12½ mo.)

The child repeats an activity which brought attention from others. This is a specific repetition, not done by chance, and occasionally the child adds embellishments to amuse an audience.

1. The child learns how to gain our attention in a positive way and uses it to keep our attention. This playful interaction is a great time to encourage the imitation of actions, sounds, and the names of objects. Do not overuse this time if the child is no longer interested. Applaud the child's activities; the child will undoubtedly have several other "acts" for you.
   a. Playing "Peek-a-Boo."
   b. Playing "Pat-a-Cake."
   c. Kissing his parents or a favorite toy.
   d. Stacking blocks.
   e. Dropping toys.
   f. Imitating your sounds.
   g. Carrying on a "conversation" with you by babbling.
   h. Dancing or moving to music.
   i. Vocalizing to music.
   j. Saying words repetitively.
   k. Waving bye-bye.
2. Refer to 5.50 (Enjoys being center of attention in family group).

2.31 SPEECH MAY PLATEAU AS CHILD LEARNS TO WALK (11½-15 mo.)

The child, when concentrating his energies in mastering the task of walking, appears to plateau or even regress in his expressive language skills. As the child gains confidence in walking, he "regains" his language skills.

See Introduction (footnote 2).

2.32 UNABLE TO TALK WHILE WALKING (11½-15 mo.)

The child must concentrate when learning a skill. He may not be successful if he puts his energies into two activities at once. As the child becomes more competent in walking and talking, he begins to do both at the same time. This is closely related to 2.31 (Speech may plateau as child learns to walk).

See Introduction (footnote 2).

2.33 OMITS FINAL AND SOME INITIAL CONSONANTS (12-17 mo.)

The child is often inarticulate during his initial months of experimentation with his newly acquired speech ability. He often omits or distorts the initial and final consonant sounds in words and short phrases. Articulation, as a fine motor skill, requires maturation and practice.

1. Do not be concerned or worried if the child's words are difficult to understand. You can probably recognize the words by context.
2. Do not correct the child directly. Provide a good model for the word or phrase that is being mispronounced, e.g., if the infants says "poon" for "spoon" say, "That's right, that's a spoon."
3. Continue to talk to the child by naming objects in his environment, by describing his activities and your activities.
4. Do not yield to the temptation to say the word the way the child does, even if it sounds cute. The child thinks he is saying it correctly and may be confused if you mispronounce the word.

2.34 BABBLES INTRICATE INFLECTION (12-18 mo.)

The child babbles many sounds using inflection patterns heard in adult speech. He makes statements, scolds, asks questions, tells stories, all without words, but with eloquent inflection, pitch and rhythm.

1. Refer to 2.24 (Babbles with inflection similar to adult speech) and continue the activities.
2. Play with inflection patterns and encourage him to imitate. Use single words and short phrases. Say, "Hello. Hello!" or "Come here. Come here? Come here!"
3. Demonstrate different inflections as you "scold" the dog, beckon to the child, "worry" out loud about dinner or question what is happening. Encourage the child to vocalize in response to you.
4. Respond appropriately to the child's inflections. If he sounds like he is scolding, say, "Oh, you are scolding me. You want me to come now!"
5. Avoid interrupting the child's sound making when he is entertaining himself.

2.35 EXPERIMENTS WITH COMMUNICATION— NOT FRUSTRATED WHEN NOT UNDER- STOOD (12-17½ mo.)

The child experiments with his new sounds, words and short phrases. His "talking" is often non-directed and seems more like a game or an experiment to him.

The child carries on a monologue "talking" to people, animals and inanimate objects. The child seldom shows concern or frustration when there is a lack of feedback or a reply. However, adults should continue to reply in the most appropriate way possible.

See Introduction (footnote 2).

2.36 USES SINGLE WORD SENTENCES (12-14 mo.)

The child's first words are utterances which have articulation qualities like the adult's pronunciation of the word, are recognizable even to a stranger and are used meaningfully.

1. Remember the child must understand or have receptive vocabulary before he begins to talk. Be sure to provide him with a considerable amount of language background by talking to him in meaningful ways.
2. Interpret the child's utterance for him. His single word can have a variety of meanings, e.g., "Mama" can mean:
   a. "That's mama."
   b. "Where's mama?"
   c. "Help!"
   d. "Look!"
   Listen and respond appropriately. Enlarge on his sentence, e.g., say:
   a. "Yes, that's mama."
   b. "Here's mama."
   c. "Need help? Can't you reach your ball?"
   d. "I see you. That's pretty clever!"
3. Expand on the child's one word sentence. Depending on the situation you may expand "eat" to "You want to eat?" "Yes, the man is eating," or "Yes, Mommy wants to eat, too."
4. Do not expect perfect articulation. Model correct pronunciation. If the child says "doddie" you might say "Yes, that's a doggie. That's big doggie."
5. Refer to 2.37 (Uses expressive vocabulary 1-3 words).

2.37 USES EXPRESSIVE VOCABULARY ONE- THREE WORDS (12-15 mo.)

The child may expressively have about one to three words she uses correctly and may imitate many more words. In a linguistic sense, expressive maturity is not generally based on quantity, but on the quality of expression.

1. Use repetition constantly describing objects in as many different ways as possible. A ball can be a green ball, a red ball, a big red ball, a soft ball. Once the child knows a word, add the adjectives, verbs, and adverbs which enhance the child's total understanding of the object. It is estimated that a child is exposed to five hundred to six hundred repetitions of a word before he reproduces it.
2. Do not correct misarticulations. Model the correct pronunciation. Many children do not articulate correctly at this developmental stage.
3. Avoid *continually* asking, "What's this?" or "What's that?" when looking at pictures or books. Say "Oh, look!" Describe the object, name the object, explain its function, repeat the object's name. The child will tell you what an object is when he is ready and physically able to tell you.
4. For the older child with oral motor problems, it may be desirable to develop nonverbal skills, such as a communication board or sign language. This is appropriate when a child's receptive language skills surpass his expressive language skills. Consult a speech pathologist.

2.38 VOCALIZES OR GESTURES SPONTANEOUSLY TO INDICATE NEEDS (12-19 mo.)

The child vocalizes words or sounds to attract attention and uses gestures to help get his message across to others. Some common gestures are: nod of the head for "Yes," twist of the wrist for "All gone," and wave of the hand for "Bye."

1. Use gestures and words which are natural and meaningful to your culture to communicate with your child. Can you gesture "Come here," "Okay," "Cold," "Hot," "Don't know," "Silly"?
2. Respond to all of the child's attempts to communicate. This is how he learns the power of communication.
3. Encourage the child to call your name instead of only using a gesture. Do not overanticipate wants and needs.

2.39 GREETS WITH VERBAL CUES (12-15 mo.)

The child is greeted verbally by an adult, without the use of gesture. The child responds with a wave and later with a verbal "Hi."

1. Model "Hi" and "Bye" for the child. Practice these words in a natural context. Avoid using "Hi" and "Bye" inappropriately, when no one is coming or going.
2. Wave "Bye, bye" or "Hi" and say the words to cars or buses on the street, animals you pass on walks, the child's own toys when they are being brought out or put away. Take advantage of all opportunities to use "Hi" and "Bye, bye."
3. Say "Hi" or "Bye, bye" every time you greet someone, modeling appropriate inflection of the greeting according to the situation.
4. Encourage other people to look at the child and say "Hi" or "Bye, bye."
5. Do not discourage the child from saying "Hi" to everyone they pass on the street or in the supermarket. Many people will respond. If the child is disappointed by those who do not respond, give a simple explanation and distract the child, e.g., "He's busy buying groceries like we are. Let's look for the apples."
6. Use hand puppets to play a "Hi" and "Bye" game similar to "Peek-a-Boo." Let the puppet say "Hi" to everyone and everything. Then, let it "talk" about leaving and call out "good-bye" as it disappears. Encourage the child to say "Hi" and "Bye-bye" to the puppet.
7. Play a similar game using yourself or a sibling as the speaker. The speaker stands behind a door. Let someone knock on the door or call the speaker by name. The speaker opens the door, says "Hi" to everyone, then "Bye, bye" as she disappears behind the door. Eventually the child may like to be the speaker (with your help).

2.40 USES EXCLAMATORY EXPRESSIONS— "OH-OH," "NO-NO" (12½-14½ mo.)

The child begins to use the expressions "oh," "uh-oh," "no-no" appropriately.

1. Model the correct moment to say "oh" or to show surprise or happiness to the child, e.g., when you are:
   a. Opening a package.
   b. Playing with a toy that surprises, such as a jack-in-the-box.
   c. Looking through books.
   d. Finding a hidden object.
2. Use the phrase "No-no" when the child approaches a dangerous spot, such as a hot stove. Encourage the child to imitate you. Ask, "Do you touch that? No-no!" Even though a child says "No-no" as she approaches a hot stove, or as she reaches to pull kitty's hair, it does not mean she will not touch the stove or pull the kitty's hair. It just shows she is cognizant of the meaning and the appropriateness of the phrases.
3. Use "uh-oh" when a toy drops to the floor or when mother spills milk or when the blocks are about to fall.

2.41 SAYS "NO" MEANINGFULLY (13-15 mo.)

The child says "No" appropriately, often accompanied by a head shake or by turning away.

1. Label the child's response for him when he gestures "No" by turning his head. Say to him, "You are telling me 'No'!"
2. Abide by the child's statement, if at all possible, when he tells you "No." This helps the child realize the power and usefulness of speaking. Acknowledge his statement, if it is not possible to go along with it by saying, "I understand you said 'No,' but this time we must do it anyway."
3. Provide opportunities for the child to use "No." Let him make simple decisions. Ask the child, "Do you want to go outside?" "Do you want more peas?" Stop, during a favorite activity and ask, "Should I put the bubbles away?" If the child does not respond, put them away, at least until you hear a protest you can label as "No." Avoid giving the child a choice if you are not willing to abide by his decision.
4. Refer to 5.39 (Displays independent behavior: is difficult to discipline the "No" stage).

2.42 NAMES ONE OR TWO FAMILIAR OBJECTS (13-18 mo.)

The child names familiar objects spontaneously or on request.

1. Tell the child the names of familiar objects as she plays with or uses them, such as car, ball, bottle, spoon, shoe. Use the names frequently.
2. Encourage the child to imitate names of familiar objects. Praise all of his attempts. Do not expect perfect articulation.

3. Play a game using familiar objects. Hold up two objects and say, "Do you want the car or the ball?" Encourage the child to imitate or name spontaneously the one he wants, in addition to his gestured response. If the child does not want to verbally respond, do not make an issue of it or withhold the toy as "punishment." Model the correct response, such as "Ball, Sara wants the ball."
4. Read picture books together. Encourage the child to imitate or spontaneously name familiar objects. Choose books with realistic pictures and with only one or two objects to a page.
5. Concentrate on two or three familiar objects whose initial sounds the child can already pronounce. If he can say "da-da," teach "dog" or "doll." If he says "ba-ba," teach "bottle," "bath" or "ball." Read a book with these pictures in it every day. Name the objects over and over.

2.43 ATTEMPTS TO SING SOUNDS TO MUSIC (13-16 mo.)

The child does not sing sounds on key. The child's first effort to sing is actually "talking" (or yelling) to music.

1. Sing songs with your child as you bathe, dress or tuck her into bed. Encourage and reward any sounds or body movements.
2. Play children's records or find music on the radio the child enjoys. Listen together and sing along with the music. Make up motions to go with the songs.
3. Let the child do little dances or body movements together with the sounds and with the attempts at musical imitation.
4. Use instruments (clackers, sticks, rattles) to stimulate interest.
5. Sing a few songs that have repetitive verses. Very, very familiar (and short) songs are the most imitated.
6. Whistle, hum or sing a tune with nonsense syllables, e.g., "ba-ba" or "da-di-da."
7. Sing favorite songs, such as "Happy Birthday," "Jingle Bells," "Row Row Row Your Boat," "Twinkle Twinkle Little Star."

2.44 USES VOICE IN CONJUNCTION WITH POINTING OR GESTURING (14-20 mo.)

The child indicates his needs and wants by vocalizing along with pointing or gesturing.

1. Do not over-anticipate the child's needs and wants. Let her communicate her need by gesturing and voicing.
2. Respond to the child's attempts to communicate. When she reaches toward your glass of lemonade and says "kaka," say "Krissy wants some? Krissy wants a drink? Okay, here, you may have Mommy's."
3. Be sure to look and talk about what the object or event is about which the child is pointing and vocalizing. When you talk about things the child is interested in you can increase the child's receptive language. When she points

out the window and says "ah!" say, "What do you see? Do you see that big doggie? That's Brian's doggie. Remember when you pet him at Brian's house?"
4. Let the child hold a "magic stick" or another object in both hands while he talks to encourage increased vocalization and decreased pointing. Another suggestion is to let the child talk to you on the telephone.
5. The child's hearing should be checked if he is overusing gestures and seldom using his voice. Some hearing impaired children develop elaborate gesture systems.

2.45 USES TEN–FIFTEEN WORDS SPONTANE-OUSLY (15-17½ mo.)

The child uses ten to fifteen words spontaneously to express herself.

1. Refer to 2.37 (Uses expressive vocabulary one-three words).
2. Remember that language develops from what is most important and close to the child.
   a. The child learns family member names first, followed by frequently seen friends and neighbors.
   b. Objects used daily, such as a diaper and a cup are named before objects less frequently seen, such as his stroller or toothbrush.
   c. Refer to 1.91 (Identifies one body part) for the order in which body parts are learned.
   d. Names for clothing, toys, household objects and animals follow the same pattern of the familiar being spoken first and the less familiar later on.
3. Refer to 1.69 (Reacts to various sensations such as extremes in temperature and taste).
4. Avoid asking the child to say things. If he does not respond after one or two invitations, do not ask again. Otherwise, this may provide more attention to the child and reward him for not talking rather than for talking.
5. Interpret early words with "rich interpretation." This means "Mama" can mean many things from "Where is Mama?" to "You are Mama."
6. Early words may include nouns such as Mama, doggie, bottle; verbs such as come, go; adjectives, such as hot, pretty; and even prepositions such as up.

2.46 VOCALIZES WISHES AND NEEDS AT THE TABLE: NAMES DESIRED ITEMS (15-17½ mo.)

The child asks for milk or a cookie spontaneously. Word approximations, such as "mi" or "coo ie" may be used.

1. Do not over anticipate the child's needs. Give the child the desire to communicate her needs. If she really wants a cookie she will vocalize although it may be with a cry or shout at first. Be careful not to carry this too far and overly frustrate the child.
2. The child must know the names of objects at the table to ask for them. Label things for him. Ask what he wants.

Give him a choice, "Do you want this apple or milk?"
3. Be willing to accept an approximation of a word at first; accuracy will come later.
4. Do not make an issue over asking for food.
5. Refer to 6.30 (May refuse foods—appetite decreases).

2.47 MAKES SOUNDS IN BABBLING, BUT OFTEN SUBSTITUTES THOSE SOUNDS IN WORDS (15½-21 mo.)

The child makes sounds in babbling but does not use the sounds correctly yet in words. He may say "sh" in babbling but substitutes "t" for "sh" when he says "shoe." It is easier for him to produce strings of the same sounds than to make the rapid changes required for articulation in words.

1. Repeat correctly the words the child uses so he hears and sees a good model.
2. Encourage the child to imitate the words you say. Make up nonsense words, e.g., "boo boo" and "goo boo." Repeat them playfully. This should be a fun, enjoyable game.
3. Be patient. "Perfect" articulation takes years to develop.
4. Do not ask the child to repeat the words "correctly" or tell him he is saying them "wrong."
5. Do not encourage the child to repeat the incorrect sounds by commenting on their being "cute" or by asking him to "perform" for friends.
6. Sing songs using sounds instead of words.
7. Imitate environmental sounds, such as "ch ch ch" or "t t t."

2.48 JABBERS TUNEFULLY AT PLAY (17-19 mo.)

The child discovers the value of talking. He begins to talk to get and maintain an adult's attention, to see if speech continues to be useful in controlling his environment, to practice his new skill, and to enjoy the sound of his own voice.

1. Describe what you are doing to provide the child a model.
2. Let the child talk. Encourage him by responding positively. If the child talks to get and maintain your attention, pay attention to him. If he is talking for the pure enjoyment of listening to his own voice, do not interrupt him.
3. Continue to model sentence structure and articulation by talking to the child and by repeating his sentences and word approximations correctly.
4. Continue to play, making environmental sounds. It is a good way to practice new sounds the child can use later in articulation.

2.49 ECHOES PROMINENT OR LAST WORD SPOKEN (17-19 mo.)

The child usually imitates the last spoken word as a clue to help him remember directions. Do not overreact because you do not want to encourage the echoing of all speech so that the child fails to use spontaneous speech. Usually the imitation of the last word spoken is done by a child as a clue to him for remembering directions.

See Introduction (footnote 2).

2.50 USES EXPRESSIVE VOCABULARY OF FIFTEEN—TWENTY WORDS (17½-20½ mo.)

The child uses fifteen to twenty words spontaneously to express himself.

1. Refer to 2.45 (Uses ten to fifteen words spontaneously).
2. Name body parts while bathing the child. Play games when the child can identify a few body parts. Wash the places the child can identify, model by naming them, then ask, "Where shall I wash now?" Encourage the child to verbalize as she points. Repeat this activity using a rubber doll.
3. Refer to 1.106 (Enjoys nursery rhymes, nonsense rhymes, fingerplays, poetry).
4. Play with playdough, paints, sand and water and naming the actions and objects used. Squish, pinch, poke and roll the playdough. Smell it. Cut it with a cookie cutter. Splash with water. Wash the dishes together. Blow on the water. Watch a paper towel soak up liquid. Use lots of verbs and adjectives to talk about the activity you are doing together.
5. Use self talk when the child is with you. Self talk is describing your activity as you do something "I'm washing the dishes. First wash a spoon. Here's another spoon. What's this? A glass."
6. Use parallel talk with the child. Describe his activities as he does something. "You are playing with the blocks. Stack them up. Here comes another. Boom. It fell down."

2.51 USES JARGON WITH GOOD INFLECTION AND RATE (18-22 mo.)

The child's use of jargon, the meaningless repetition of consonant sounds using speech inflection patterns, is a natural development. Jargon is most often heard when the child is in solitary play. He is practicing the sounds, inflection and fluency of speech. The child may use a few understandable words within his jargon. Some children do not go through a prolonged jargon stage. Do not worry if he progresses directly to speech. Also, do not imitate jargon. If we imitate or respond as if we understand, the child may begin to think it has meaning to us.

See Introduction (footnote 2).

2.52 USES OWN NAME TO REFER TO SELF (18-24 mo.)

The child gives her first name when asked or uses her first name spontaneously.

1. Use the child's name as you talk to her during daily activities, such as bathing, dressing, eating, playing.
2. Model for the child. When she says "Water" say, "Heather wants water." When she says "Up" say, "Heather wants up."
3. Ask questions and help with the answer by modeling. "Who is my little girl?" "Who wants water?" "Who wants up?" If she does not answer for her "Heather does!"
4. If the child says, "Heather is hungry," you as model can reply, "Are you hungry? So am I," or "I'm hungry too." The child is not expected to use "I" at this time in development, but the receptive exercise is valuable.

2.53 IMITATES ENVIRONMENTAL SOUNDS (18-21 mo.)

The child imitates environmental sounds in play. These may be animal, nature or machine sounds.

1. Point out environmental sounds to the child. Identify and imitate them. Include, waves at the shore, dogs barking, children playing, a ball bouncing, the toilet flushing.
2. Make a tape of environmental sounds together with the child. Play the tape back and discuss and imitate the sounds.
3. Tape the sounds of dogs, cats, cows, sheep, horses, pigs and birds. Animal sounds are often favorites. Some libraries have children's records of animal sounds.
4. Play "garage" with cars and trucks making engine sounds as well as the sounds of sirens and horns.
5. Talk about the weather on a windy day and make wind sounds. How about the sounds of a rainy day?

2.54 IMITATES TWO WORD PHRASES (18-21 mo.)

The child says simple two word phrases in imitation. This usually begins when the child has an expressive vocabulary of twenty to thirty words.

1. Encourage the child to imitate by modeling phrases. Encourage and listen for phrases, such as "Big boy," "Go bye bye," "Mommy's car," "My doggie," "Daddy come."
2. Say short phrases playfully for the child to imitate, the same way you said words and inflection patterns earlier. Expand on what the child says. When the child says "Car," say "Yes, a *big* car!" Wait for imitation.
3. Use combinations of single words that the child already uses. If the child says "Me," "Car," and "Go," then "Me go" or "Go car" should be easy for the child to begin two word imitations.
4. Do not expect perfect articulations. Praise all attempts to imitate.

2.55 ATTEMPTS TO SING SONGS WITH WORDS (18-23 mo.)

The child attempts to sing with or without others, using a few words. The child may be off key and use the same words over and over.

1. Expose the child to simple songs. Sing to him. Play children's records for him. Repeat the words.
2. Simple tunes and lyrics with refrains are learned most quickly.
3. Learn a few finger plays, such as "Pat-a-Cake" or "This Little Piggy," and teach them to the child.
4. Car rides can be made more exciting if the whole family joins in the singing. Let the child fill in words or phrases at times. A fun and easy song to start with is "Old MacDonald had a farm."
5. Refer to 2.43 (Attempts to sing sounds to music), and 1.106 (Enjoys nursery rhymes, nonsense rhymes, fingerplays, poetry).

2.56 NAMES TWO PICTURES (19-21½ mo.)

The child labels two different pictures spontaneously or when asked, "What is this?"

1. Refer to 1.92 (Recognizes and points to four animal pictures).
2. Refer to 1.60 (Enjoys looking at pictures in books).
3. Look at pictures everywhere in the everyday environment. Take turns asking and answering "What's this?" Look at:
   a. Pictures in magazines, catalogs, junk mail.
   b. Pictures on cereal boxes, clothing, wallpaper, sheets or blankets.
   c. Pictures in family photo albums. Family members and pets are favorites.
   d. Posters and murals in stores, banks, libraries.
   e. Books, commercial and homemade scrapbooks.
4. Think of the words the child uses. Can you find pictures of those words? Make a scrapbook.

2.57 USES TWO—WORD SENTENCES (20½-24 mo.)

The child begins to form short two-word phrases and sentences as she expands her vocabulary of single words to twenty or thirty words.

1. Expand the child's single words sentences. If the child says "Cookie," say "You want more cookie? More Cookie?" "More" is a good word to encourage here because it can be used meaningfully with many words and is easy to say, e.g., "More cookie," "More juice," "More bubbles," "More play."
2. Model three- and four-word sentences, just as you previously modeled two-word phrases when the child spoke only single words.
3. At this stage, the child is rapidly absorbing and retaining

on a receptive level the myriad of prepositions, pronouns, adjectives, helping verbs. Although the child will not use them until later, it is essential to provide a richness to the short phrases the child is using at this time.

4. Continue using parallel talk and self talk with the child.
5. Refer to 2.54 (Imitates two word phrases) and continue the activities.

2.58 USES NOUNS, VERBS, MODIFIERS (20½-24 mo.)

The child will use different part of speech, such as nouns, verbs (especially action verbs) and modifiers (such as adjectives) as his expressive vocabulary increases.

1. Expose the child to different parts of speech. Discuss the happenings in the child's environment. "Johnny is eating his lunch. He is eating," "Oh, that's a dirty shirt! Let's wash it," "Look at the funny kitty. She's playing."
2. Use familiar picture books and point to a boy eating, a big dog, a girl running, a sleepy baby. Many magazines have suitable pictures for this activity.
3. Refer to 1.91 (Identifies one body part) and 2.50 (Uses expressive vocabulary of 15-20 words) for additional activities which include the use of nouns, verbs and modifiers.

2.59 TELLS EXPERIENCES USING JARGON AND WORDS (21-24 mo.)

The child's jargon peaks and begins to decline and you will probably hear more words within the jargon. The child will try to tell experiences, filling in with jargon when he does not have the words to use.

1. Refer to 2.51 (Uses jargon with good inflection and rate).
2. Respond to the child's use of meaningful words by imitating them or responding appropriately.
3. Listen carefully to what the child is saying. Allow him sufficient time to complete his statement. Be very interested, even if you do not understand.
4. Repeat the words you understand by saying, "You saw the *what*?" "There was a big dog?" Encourage the child to continue or tell more.

2.60 USES INTELLIGIBLE WORDS ABOUT 65 PERCENT OF THE TIME (21½-24 mo.)

The child speaks in words that can be understood, although he may not articulate them properly. Articulation skills and intelligibility improve as the child's fine motor skills develop. If the child is not intelligible 65 percent of the time at this stage and there is no physical disability involving the articulators (tongue, lips, jaw, soft palate) the causes may be:
   a. General delayed development, including fine motor skills.
   b. Hearing loss or previous hearing loss which was present while the child was beginning to talk. Even a mild temporary hearing loss associated with an ear infection can affect articulation development.
   c. Lack of good speech models.
   d. Idiopathic. This means no one really knows the cause.

1. The child's hearing should be tested if he is not producing words recognizable by a stranger.
2. Work on general fine motor skills if they are delayed.
3. Continue playful babbling of sounds, the imitation of nonsense words and rhymes.
4. Encourage the child to look at your lips as you speak. Women may wear very bright lipstick.
5. Sing songs with sound repetitions. Sound repetitions can be found in most speech improvement books and child's rhyming books.
6. Play a game of imitation, make faces, speech sound and gestures. Making faces and gestures helps to keep this activity a game.
7. Make a scrap book of pictures you and the child can name together. Choose pictures with sounds the child can make in babbling or can imitate easily.

2.61 NAMES THREE PICTURES (21½-24 mo.)

The child labels three different pictures spontaneously or when asked "What is this?"

1. Refer to 2.56 (Names two pictures).
2. Encourage the child to name pictures he has drawn.

2.62 USES ELABORATE JARGON (22-24 mo.)

The child usually peaks at this developmental stage in his use of jargon. You will probably note a decrease in jargon as he learns to express himself in words and phrases.

See Introduction (footnote 2).

2.63 IMITATES FOUR WORD PHRASES (22-24 mo.)

The child repeats simple four-word sentences immediately after you say them, such as "Amber's cat and dog," "Boy running to Mom," "Don't do that Kitty," "Give me more juice."

1. Praise all attempts to imitate.
2. Teach simple finger plays and songs with repetitious lyrics.
3. Repeat nursery rhymes for the child. Read or tell simple stories with repetitions of lines as in *Good Night Moon* by M. W. Brown, *Green Eggs and Ham* or *Feet, Feet, Feet* by Dr. Seuss. Include old favorites which contain repetitious phrases, such as *Goldilocks and the Three Bears, The Three Little Pigs,* and *The Gingerbread Man.*
4. Encourage the child to talk to his doll. Suggest directions he could use, such as "Time to sleep baby."
5. Let the child give messages to his parents or siblings,

"Tell Mommy, I need help," "Tell Daddy, Give me a kiss," "Tell Brian 'It's time for dinner.'"

2.64 SINGS PHRASES OF SONGS (23-27 mo.)

The child sings phrases of songs. She attempts to follow a tune, but may be off key.

1. Expose the child to simple songs. Sing to him. Play children's records for him. Repeat the words.
2. Use simple tunes and lyrics with refrains since these are learned most quickly. Often the child's first song is "Happy Birthday." Others are "Jingle Bells," "Mary Had a Little Lamb," "Row, Row, Row Your Boat," "Twinkle, Twinkle Little Star," "This is the Way We Wash Our Clothes," "Old MacDonald Had a Farm."
3. Sing songs with the child and let her fill in the significant phrases.
4. Use pictures and gestures to help the child remember the words.

2.65 PRODUCES THE FOLLOWING SOUNDS CLEARLY: P, B, M, K, G, W, H, N, T, D (24-27½ mo.)

The child produces these sounds in words, especially at the beginning of words. The child may not use these sounds all the time.

1. Encourage vocal play with these sounds through games. Pretend to be a cowgirl with a herd of mooing cows, let the child whoosh like the wind, or play "Pop goes the weasel."
2. Model words with these sounds so the child hears and sees a good model.
3. Repeat a word clearly. Encourage, do not pressure the child into imitating a word he mispronounces. If the child is not interested in imitating words or sounds respect her feelings, give her a caress and do something different.
4. The child's hearing should be checked if he does not produce many consonant sounds in words. The child may have a mild hearing problem, perhaps left over from a cold or ear infection. A temporary, mild to moderate hearing loss at an early age can have an adverse effect on the child's articulation development.
5. Refer to 2.60 (Uses intelligible words about 65 percent of the time).

2.66 USES PRONOUNS (24-30 mo.)

The child uses pronouns spontaneously instead of her name. Usually the first pronouns are self-centered (me, mine) or used in commands ("You come!").

1. Use pronouns to describe actions as they occur. Talk

about familiar things, "He's watching TV," or "She's sleeping." Ask about the actions in pictures, such as, "What is the boy doing? He is eating." Use gestures at first, if necessary.
2. Play the "Mine" game. When the child playfully claims something as "mine," you playfully say "mine" claiming it is yours. This kind of game can include "you," "his" or "hers." Dolls and puppets can model this game.
3. If the child uses a short phrase or single words without a pronoun, model for the child by repeating what he has said but include the pronoun, e.g., "Want cookie," can be changed to "I want cookie."
4. If pronouns are used incorrectly, model the correct use in self talk. Encourage, but do not pressure the child to imitate. If the child says, "Me want cookie," say, "Oh, you want a cookie? Okay, I want a cookie too." Modeling instead of correcting is important because the child is not criticized and his repeated hearing of correct models will eventually bring about the desired effect.
5. Model the use of pronouns instead of using your name when talking to the child. Although at one developmental stage it was appropriate to say, "Mommy wants to read Amber a book," for pronoun emphasis you might say, "I want to read you a book."

2.67 USES THREE WORD SENTENCES (24-30 mo.)

The child develops three word sentences first in imitation. He begins to use longer sentences as he develops the ideas and thoughts he wants to share, as well as a larger repertoire of words.

1. Use simple sentence structures part of the time, not all the time. It is important to expose the child to more complex structures too.
2. Give the child your full attention when he is trying to tell you something. This is often difficult in busy families so it may be helpful to schedule fifteen minutes to spend listening and talking with your child as you do something quiet together.
3. Note that early three word sentences involve the child's wants and needs. The grammatical structure of these sentences may be immature and some consonant sounds may be missing, especially in the middle and at the end of a word. Examples of early three word sentences: "Me want truck," "Give me cookie."
4. Refer to 2.57 (Uses two-word sentences), and 2.63 (Imitates four word phrases).

2.68 USES PAST TENSE (24-30 mo.)

The child begins to use past tense as she tells her experiences. She may over regulate the verbs by using "ed" incorrectly, e.g., "runned." This over regulation shows she is learning and using grammatical rules automatically.

1. Talk to the child about past activities. Encourage the

child to tell what he did yesterday, last night, or some other time in the past.

2. Model for the child the use of past tense by relating stories from the past. Use short, simple sentences, e.g., "Yesterday we went to the store. We bought new shoes for Larry." You may also repeat the child's sentences correctly so he hears a good model.

3. Encourage appropriate modeling in the family. If the child understands the past tense, that is, responds to statements and questions using the past tense appropriately, but does not verbalize the past tense spontaneously, perhaps there is a lack of models. This can be the influence of a local dialect in some areas.

4. Be sure to use the future tense as well as the past tense when talking to the child. Talk about a special event before and during the event and afterwards discuss the event again.

2.69 USES EXPRESSIVE VOCABULARY OF FIFTY OR MORE WORDS (24-30½ mo.)

The child uses fifty or more words spontaneously to express his ideas and thoughts. These words include nouns, verbs, pronouns and adjectives.

1. Continue to model and expand the child's verbalizations. The child's use of short sentences indicates a growing linguistic competence. It is essential to model increased sentence structure.

2. Enjoy and accept the child's experimentation with language and the errors that are sure to be made. Do not imitate the errors but model correct usage.

3. Listen to the child. Meaningful use of language is of utmost importance, not rote naming or rote imitation of phrases.

4. Keep a list of the words and phrases the child uses. Add to it daily. At home, the refrigerator door is a good place to keep the list.

5. Refer to 2.58 (Uses nouns, verbs, modifiers).

2.70 NAMES FIVE PICTURES (24-29 mo.)

The child labels five different pictures spontaneously or when asked "What is this?"

1. Draw pictures for the child. See if he can guess what you have drawn. Draw pictures of objects he can name, such as ball, car, tree, house, flower, boy, girl, ice cream cone.

2. Refer to 2.56 (Names two pictures) and 1.92 (Recognizes and points to four animal pictures).

2.71 IMITATES SPONTANEOUSLY OR REQUESTS NEW WORDS (24-27 mo.)

The child imitates words he has heard others use or asks for new words by saying "What's this?" or even "How do you say it?"

1. Encourage the imitation of words just as you have encouraged other imitations of actions and sounds. Praise and reward all attempts at imitation.

2. Answer the child whenever he asks, "What's this?" even if he repeatedly asks and your patience is running low.

3. Turn his question "What's this?" around and let the child answer. Say, "You tell me, What's this?" Take turns asking and answering.

4. Provide many experiences to stimulate language. Go for walks, visit friends, go to the store, gas station, library or zoo. Talk about the experience before, during and after the activity.

2.72 EXPERIMENTS WITH COMMUNICATION— FRUSTRATED WHEN NOT UNDERSTOOD (24-28½ mo.)

The child becomes frustrated and may even cry when he cannot express verbally his wants and needs. A little frustration provides the motivation to develop better language skills, but too much hinders development.

1. Encourage the child to use gestures and to show you what he means. Label verbally for him what he tells you non-verbally.

2. Provide enough time and opportunity for the child to express himself.

3. Combine a "wh" word with the part of the child's message you understand. Say, "You ate what?" "You saw a what?" "What about Daddy?" "The dog did what?" This shows you are listening and she is at least partially successful in her communication.

4. Take advantage of the context and the situation to help you interpret the child's meaning.

2.73 RELATES EXPERIENCES USING SHORT SENTENCES (24-34 mo.)

The child uses short sentences to tell about experiences in the recent past. This may be completely spontaneous or may require a question and/or encouragement to tell more.

1. Read a picture story with the child. Go over the pictures and let her tell you what happened in the story.

2. Ask the child about an activity she just completed. If the child just finished taking a bath, ask her what she did in the bathroom. Ask specific questions about immediate events; do not ask vague questions about activities which, to the child, happened a long time ago. Later when the child can recall more experiences with details, you can ask general questions such as "What did you do yesterday?"

3. Give the child as much direction and information as he needs to help him recall and tell you his experiences when you ask about them. For example, instead of "What did you do?: you might ask, "What did you do with Mother at the park?" Remember this is not a test of memory, but

an encouragement to relate fun experiences. If the child hesitates, feels shy or has forgotten, help him remember.

4. Ask the child about experiences you know in some detail. You can help the child when she needs some hints to remember things and you can participate in the conversation. You are remembering an activity together.

5. Let someone else ask the child about something you and the child did together and have already discussed.

6. Probe for more detail after the child has finished telling her experience. If the child says, "I went to the zoo yesterday," you can say, "Tell me about the animals you saw." This will lead to a further statement by the child you can expand on in a similar manner.

7. Use questions the child can answer. Ask questions about sounds, smells, colors, numbers, sequence of events.

8. Play "telephone call" and use this activity to extract details of previous events for fun. Ask questions such as, "Did you like the park?" or "Tell me more about the aquarium."

9. Mother and Dad can model for the child by relating their experiences to him.

10. Using family photograph albums for remembering and talking about experiences together can be fun. Souvenirs of outings can also help a child relate her experience.

2.74 ANSWERS QUESTIONS (24-36 mo.)

The child answers simple questions about his experiences. He may not answer a question if he considers it redundant or if the listener does not need further information.

1. Ask appropriate questions about the child's life. If you do not get an immediate response, wait before asking again. Be sure the child is paying attention. Do not force the issue by demanding a response. We cannot make a child talk and we want to avoid giving more attention for not talking than for talking. On the other hand, avoid asking questions if you do not have the time to wait for an answer or do not really expect an answer.

2. Ask questions which require a choice since they are easier than open-ended questions, such as, "Do you want juice or milk?" rather than "What do you want to drink?" Short answer questions are easier, too.

3. Ask the child questions such as:
   a. What do you want to wear? Your jacket or your sweater?
   b. Where is your new book?
   c. What did you do at school? Grandma's? Billy's house? What did you play with? Who did you play with?
   d. How did you hurt your knee?
   e. What's the matter?

4. Model for the child if the child has difficulty answering questions. Use self talk. "What do I want to wear, my jacket or my sweater? My sweater. I want to wear my sweater."

5. Ask the child what will happen next as you read a favorite story together.

2.75 FORMULATES NEGATIVE REASONING (24-36 mo.)

The child disagrees with an adult over something she knows. She indicates either with gesture or verbally she understands what "not" means.

1. Ask the child his name or say, "Your name is Bruce." Then ask the child, "Are you Toney?" Laugh and shake your head, say, "No, not Toney, you are Bruce; your name is Bruce." Use favorite toys and question their ownership say, "This is my ball." The child should respond "No, mine!" Reply, "Yes, you are right, not my ball, it is Bruce's ball."

2. Show the child a spoon. Ask him what it is. Show him a shoe, ask him what it is. Show him a shoe, ask him if it is a spoon. Say, "This is *not* a spoon." Tell him the correct name, "This is a shoe." Use other *familiar* objects.

3. Point to a familiar object such as a ball and tell the child a false name, "Look at the book." See if the child will try to correct you. If not, say, "This is *not* a book, it is a ball."

4. As a child plays with two familiar objects, such as a cup and a doll, ask the child to give you the toy or object that is not a cup. Reinforce the correct response with "Yes, this is *not* a cup, this is a doll." Should the child give you the incorrect object, name what the child has given you and say, "This is a cup, give me the one that is not a cup—the doll, the doll is not a cup."

5. Play sorting games. Prepare a pile of three same-colored spoons, a ball, a thread spool, and a block. Pick up a spoon and ask the child, "What is this?" Then pick up the ball and ask, "Is this a spoon?" If the child does not respond appropriately, say, "No this *is not* a spoon. This is a ball. Let's put it here," and place the ball in a separate pile from the spoon. Instruct the child to place the spoons in one pile and the objects which are not spoons in another pile.

2.76 USES SIZE WORDS (25-30 mo.)

The child must understand the meaning of size words before he can use them. The child is likely to ask for "the big one" (cookie, glass, paper) first when he does understand. Since the size is relative, you may wish to present both big and little concepts simultaneously.

1. Use size words appropriately when the opportunity arises to contrast two identical or very similar, familiar objects, toys, etc. Let the intonation of your voice emphasize a concept, such as "Big."

2. Take a walk with the child through the neighborhood and point out and emphasize the big things you see. Point out the things that are very big, bigger than the child. Use hand gestures, in addition to your voice to aid in the description of the "big house." Allow the child to contrast her size to the big tree by going under it, looking up and touching the trunk and leaves.

Another time emphasize the small things in the environment.

3. Do some simple imaginative play with the child using her whole body and emphasizing a concept such as "Big."
   a. Make your body small, curling up, then make it big standing up and stretching your body. Let the child imitate.
   b. Let the child observe the plants she planted grow. Pretend to be seeds. Curl up as the seeds and grow standing up and spreading the arms.
   c. Let the child watch a balloon become larger as you blow it. Let your hands pretend to cup the small balloon and as you blow, the hands spread wider and wider apart.
   d. Use a hand or foot pump to blow up plastic balls and animals.
   e. Gather several children to hold hands and play games such as "Ring Around the Rosie." Make a very small circle, everyone close in, then a big circle, everyone step backwards, and play the game again.
4. Aid and encourage the child to use big and small toys and common household objects.
   a. Use playdough to pound and stretch and make big cookies or roll small ones.
   b. Use crayon or chalk to make big, long lines and large circles, and small short lines and tiny circles.
5. Use balls or red circles or anything identical except for size. Ask the child to give you the big ball or the "Big one." Cues should be used when needed and gradually withdrawn, such as:
   a. Holding out one's hand near the big ball.
   b. Looking at the big ball.
   c. Nodding at the big ball.
   d. Intentionally mentioning the color of the big ball, if it is different.
6. For the blind child, use the same objects for the first week. Give her the big one to feel, then the little one. Then say, "Here's the big one," and let her explore and accustom herself to its size. *Remember size is relative, so the difference in size should be very apparent.*
7. Ask the child which of two objects (identical, except for size) she wants.
8. Use finger plays which demonstrate size, "Here's a ball and here's a ball. A great big ball I see. Shall we count them? One, two, three."
9. Tell a story about a big dog with a big bark and little dog with a little bark. Alternate the sound of the bark and ask the child which dog barked.
10. Use a big chair, a big box, a little chair and a little box. Ask one child to sit on the big chair. Ask another child to join the first child. Let both get off the chair. Next, let a child sit on a small chair and let another child try to join him. Talk about it. Repeat the sequence using boxes, wastebaskets or circles drawn on the floor.

2.77 USES PLURALS (27-36 mo.)

The child uses plurals, often over-regulating at first. The child says, "books," "blocks," "shoes," but also "feets" and "mens."

1. Use plurals to discuss objects in the environment. Use the singular form, too.
2. Use the *Sesame Street* record with the song "I have two eyes." Sing with the child and point to his own body parts or use the large poster which comes with the record.
3. Play with blocks. Tell the child, "Give me one block," then "Give me two blocks." Ask the child how many blocks he wants.
4. Discuss the people in the house. Perhaps there are one girl and three boys or one child and four adults.
5. Talk about pets, "We have one cat, and the neighbors have two dogs."
6. Refer to activities in the Cognitive section, "Understands concept of one" (24-30 mo.) and "Understands concept of two" (30-36 mo.)
7. Look at picture books. Find "a baby," "lots of babies," "pretty flowers," etc. Catalogs are good for labeling with plurals.

2.78 REFERS TO SELF USING PRONOUN (27-30 mo.)

The child uses "I" or "me" consistently instead of his name. If the child becomes a little confused on the use of me and you, be patient and provide models for him to hear.

1. Refer to yourself, using "I" and "me," and to the child as "you." Use pronouns in your speech as you talk to other people.
2. Use self-talk during play to describe your activity. Use plenty of "I's" and "me's."
3. Use imaginative play with dolls, toys and animals; puppets work especially well. Let them "talk":
   a. Say, "Who wants a cookie?" Let the doll "answer" in another voice, "Me! Me!"
   b. If the doggy is in the kitchen with you and the child, "ask" the dog, "What do you want?" Answer for the dog in another voice, "I want my supper!"
4. Use story books to model use of pronouns. Find stories with lots of simple conversations between people.
5. Refer to 2.66 (Uses pronouns).

2.79 PRODUCES SOUNDS CORRECTLY AT BEGINNING OF WORDS (27½-32 mo.)

The child produces most consonant sounds correctly at the beginning of words. Some sounds, such as "s," "z," "sh," "ch," "r," "l," may still be distorted or another sound substituted for them. Correct sound production requires a great deal of fine motor coordination of the lips, tongue, jaw and soft palate. It is especially difficult to change rapidly from one consonant sound to another. This is one reason why initial sounds are produced first, and middle and final sounds are omitted.

1. Encourage the child to use words that begin with the easier sounds, "b," "p," "m," "t," "d," "k," "g." Talk about "ball," "baby," "Mommy," "Daddy," "bottle," "doggie," "diaper," "cookie."
2. Praise all attempts to use words.
3. Repeat correctly the words the child says so he hears a good model.
4. Use a variety of picture books and locate pictures which require the sounds mentioned in item number one.
5. Make a scrapbook of easy to say pictures.
6. Refer to 2.60 (Uses intelligible words about 65 percent of the time) and 2.65 (Produces the following sounds clearly: P, B, M, K, G, W, H, N, T, D).
7. Do not pressure the child to repeat sounds "correctly" and do not tell him his sounds are "wrong." He will do the best he can if you model only correct sounds. To pressure the child to speak more clearly, more than he is able to, may result in his becoming hesitant to talk.
8. Consult a speech pathologist for help with articulation problems.

2.80 VERBALIZES ONE PREPOSITION (28-33 mo.)

The child must understand prepositions before she can use them verbally.

1. Teach receptive understanding of prepositions by helping the child become aware of her position in relation to other objects. Say, "Come, get *in* bed," "Stand *beside* Mommy," "You're going *up* the slide, then you will go *down*." Next the child learns how to find and place objects in relation to other objects. Say, "Your ball is *under* the table," "I think I saw your shoes *next to* the television," "Put your shirt *into* the laundry box," "Put the box *next to* the chair."
2. Play follow the leader. Go *under* the table, *around* the chair, *through* the door and back.
3. Give directions involving prepositions. Use gestures and demonstrations. Later, omit the gestures and demonstrations.
4. Tell the child where to find and place things, e.g., "*in* the closet," "*in* the toy box," "*under* the table," "*next* to the television."
5. Make a train with double rows of chairs. At the signal "Go" everybody takes a seat or finds a new one. Ask "Who is *in front of* Mary?" "Who is *beside* Mary?" To answer these questions correctly the child must understand the prepositions. Later ask, "Where is Mary? Where am I?" To answer these questions correctly the child must use the prepositions expressively.
6. Ask where objects are and answer for the child if he seems unsure. "Where are my shoes? Oh, *under* the table." "Where is Daddy? *In* the kitchen." Sometimes, giving a choice may help. "Where is the milk, *on* the table or *in* the refrigerator?" Allow time for the child to answer. Let him know he has helped you.

7. Sort objects into a box and a can with the child. Take turns giving directions saying where each object goes, "Take one *out*" or "Put one *in*."
8. Talk about placing things *in* the cart, *in* the bag, *in* the car while doing the grocery shopping. At home take things out of the car and out of the bag. Ask the child where to place them next.
9. Talk about taking things *in* and *out* of the sink, washer, dryer, closet, suitcase.
10. Talk about turning the light, the water, the television and the record player *on* and *off*.

2.81 FRUSTRATED IF NOT UNDERSTOOD— UTTERANCES HAVE COMMUNICATIVE INTENT (28½-36 mo.)

The child attempts to communicate his ideas and thoughts rather than his simple needs or wants. When he is not understood, he may become very frustrated, cry or become very angry or simply say, "Never mind" or "Forget it" as he gives up.

1. If you do not understand the child, try one of these things:
   a. Repeat a word you *do* understand saying, "You saw what?" or "You ate the what?"
   b. Ask the child to show you what she wants.
   c. Take advantage of any clues in the environment. If the child runs to you after you hear a siren go by and if she is pointing to the window, she is probably telling you about the fire trucks she saw. Ask her, "Did you see the fire truck?"
   d. Avoid telling the child, "I can't understand you" or "Don't talk until you can talk better." Instead say, "You sound excited," or "Wow, my ears must be sleeping. Tell me that again!"
   e. If the child is talking very fast, slow down your own rate and she will probably slow down her rate.

2.82 REPLACES JARGON WITH SENTENCES (29-31 mo.)

The child's use of jargon decreases and finally disappears as this expressive vocabulary and linguistic competence increase.

1. Encourage words and phrases by repeating them and responding to them with pleasure.
2. Do not imitate jargon.
3. Provide the child with experiences she can talk about and give her many opportunities to talk about her experiences.
4. Refer to 2.76 (Uses size words).

2.83 NAMES EIGHT OR MORE PICTURES (29-36 mo.)

2.0 EXPRESSIVE LANGUAGE

The child labels eight or more familiar pictures spontaneously or when asked, "What is this?"

1. Refer to 2.56 (Names two pictures), 2.61 (Names three pictures), 2.70 (Names five pictures).
2. Refer to 1.60 (Enjoys looking at pictures in books), and 1.92 (Recognizes and points to four animal pictures).

2.84 REPEATS WORDS AND SOUNDS (29-36 mo.)

The child repeats words or sounds automatically when he is happy or excited. Do not ask him to stop, repeat, or slow down. Sometimes this non-fluency is labelled "stuttering." Actually it is part of a normal pattern as the child develops proficiency with more complicated grammatical structures and vocabulary. It is most often seen during emotional periods, including stress, but also when the child is tired or not feeling well. Do not require speech at these times; be a careful, patient listener. If you are worried about this, talk to a speech pathologist.

See Introduction (footnote 2).

2.85 TALKS INTELLIGENTLY TO SELF (29½-36 mo.)

The child talks intelligently to herself as she develops vocabulary and ease in talking. She talks to her toys and describes her own play.

1. Let the child hear you talk to yourself as you describe what you are doing.
2. Allow him uninterrupted time to play by himself and to use his imagination to entertain himself. Refer to 1.130 (Shows interest in sounds of objects) and 1.153 (Uses locomotion to regain object and resumes play).
3. Model ways of talking to yourself when you play with the child, e.g., talk to the gas station man when playing with cars. Let two cars carry on a brief "dialogue."
4. Try to be unobtrusive with your attention. Some children will not talk to themselves if they feel an adult is listening or watching them, especially if the adult is amused. If you interrupt a child at play and she seems embarrassed about her talking, try to be matter-of-fact. Do not comment on her verbal play.

2.86 USES MOST BASIC GRAMMATICAL STRUCTURES (30-36 mo.)

The child has learned the basic rules for grammar structure and can manipulate them to suit his needs. Listen carefully and you will hear the following structures:

1. Possessive: I am writing Daddy's name.
2. Negative: I am *not*.
3. Interrogative: Is he sleeping?
4. "Wh" question: *What* is that?
5. Contraction: *He's* watching.
6. Imperative: "Go, right now!"

7. Auxiliary "be": He is going.
8. Past "to do": I *did* read a book.
9. Adjective: I have a *black* dog.
10. Pronoun: *I* was very angry.
11. Conjunction: Peter is here *and* you are there.
12. Infinitive Complement: I want *to play*.
    a. Model all structures and especially ones which the child seldom uses. Examples:
       1. Conjunctions: I ate my cookie and I drank my juice. Sandra is here but Peter is absent. You want to paint and Mary wants to color.
       2. Past "to do" (Model this with another adult).
          A: Why don't you wash your hands?
          B: I *did* wash my hands.
          A: Go draw a picture.
          B: I *did* one already.
    b. Write a story together. Let the child tell a story from pictures. Write as the child talks, modeling and expanding the sentences. Read the story with the child.
    c. Refer to 2.76 (Uses size words).

2.87 OVER REGULATES AND SYSTEMIZES PLURALS AND VERBS (FOOTS, DOED) (30-36 mo.)

The child's language is delightful at this stage. This is a natural development that gives us "half shut moons" and excited shouts of "I doed it!" Enjoy it. The child learns the exceptions simply by listening to the speech models around him. You can help his learning by correctly repeating his utterances, providing a good model. His over-regulation shows he is learning and applying automatically the grammatical structures of our language.

See Introduction (footnote 2).

2.88 VOCALIZES FOR ALL NEEDS (30-31½ mo.)

The child has vocabulary and linguistic system adequate to indicate his needs verbally rather than through gesture.

1. Give the child the opportunity and the desire to talk by not over-anticipating his needs. When he does verbalize a request be sure to acknowledge and respond to it.
2. Avoid pressuring the child for speech since this often results in the child not talking at all. He discovers he can receive more attention for not talking. This can happen for example, when mother tells her child to say, "Bye-bye" to auntie. The first time, the child says "Bye-bye" immediately and that is it. The second time, he does not say "Bye-bye" and the mother and auntie both fuss over him, coaxing and teasing him to say "Bye-bye" and they give him a lot of attention.
3. "Misunderstand" a child's gestures occasionally to encourage verbalization. When he hands his empty cup to you say, "Yes it is empty," and hand it back even though you suspect he wants more juice. Let him vocalize to indicate juice or "more." Use this judiciously; be very careful not to overdo it.

4. Ask questions which require more than a "yes-no" response or other simple gesture. Give a choice of response. "Do you want the big one or the little one?"

5. Be sure to allow plenty of time for the child to respond verbally.

2.89 GIVES FULL NAME ON REQUEST (30-33 mo.)

The child gives her first and last name on request.

1. Teach the child her full name. Use it playfully as you care for her.
2. Talk to the child about the full names of Daddy, Mommy, Grandmother, a friend.
3. Ask him his full name. If he gives just his first name ask, "Johnny who?" Let him show off to relatives and friends telling them his full name, if he enjoys it and can be successful. Praise his efforts and do not demand perfect articulation.
4. Make up stories using the child's full name.
5. Show the child her full name as you write it when labeling her clothes, art work, and other belongings.
6. Ask the child if she is "Mary Tanaka," using an incorrect last name. Repeat with several incorrect names playfully, finally using her correct name or asking the child to say her name correctly for you.

2.90 PARTICIPATES IN STORYTELLING (30-36 mo.)

The child helps to tell a familiar story by adding words and comments, and by anticipating the events in the story. He may correct the adult if the adult omits details.

1. Tell stories from picture books in your own words. This is often more satisfactory than reading stories with long paragraphs to a child who is anxious to see the next page. By telling the story in your own words, it is possible to match the length of the story to the child's attention span and it is easier to encourage the child to help tell the story.
2. Be sure to tell favorite stories, such as *The Three Bears, The Three Little Pigs, Little Red Riding Hood, The House That Jack Built, The Gingerbread Man.*
3. Visit the local library and ask the librarian to help you pick out stories suitable to the child's interests.
4. Wait for the child to add words and phrases in stories he has heard several times or in stories which have repetitious sections. Say, "Little baby . . . bear said . . . Who's been eating *my* . . ." Later you can wait for the child to fill in whole phrases and sentences.
5. Take turns telling the story on different pages in a story book.
6. Make up stories from magazine pictures. Ask "Who is in the picture?" "What is happening?"
7. Encourage the child to tell stories using the pictures he has made.

8. Invite the child to tell a story while you illustrate it or write it down so he can illustrate. (Remember, a story may consist of only one or two sentences.)
9. Start to tell a story about an activity the child has been involved in. Allow plenty of opportunity for the child to finish the story. "Bobby and I went somewhere special today. We went to the . . . zoo. We saw lots of animals. Remember the bear? Can you tell Daddy what the bear was doing?"

2.91 RECITES A FEW NURSERY RHYMES (30-36 mo.)

The child recites a short nursery rhyme with a minimum of verbal or gesture prompting from an adult.

1. Refer to 1.106 (Enjoys nursery rhymes, nonsense rhymes, fingerplays, poetry).
2. Choose a familiar favorite rhyme that can be depicted by pictures and gestures.
   a. Let the child start to participate by adding the right word when you pause.
      Sample:
      "Hey diddle, diddle,
      The (pause)_____ and the fiddle.
      The cow jumped over the (pause) _____."
      Use pictures or stuffed animals and objects to provide as many clues as possible.
   b. Play act the rhyme or part of the rhyme.
      Sample:
      "Humpty Dumpty sat on a wall,
      Humpty Dumpty had a great (pause) _____ ."
      The children can be on a low stool and pretend to fall to the floor. Later, they can begin to accompany their actions with words.
3. Allow the child to tell you or "read to you" nursery rhyme pictures and stories.
4. Repeat nursery rhymes many, many times.
5. Sing nursery rhymes together.

2.92 USES EXPRESSIVE VOCABULARY OF 200 OR MORE WORDS (30½-35 mo.)

The child's expressive vocabulary follows his receptive vocabulary development. He uses two hundred or more different words expressively and understands even more.

1. Continue talking to the child. Describe what he is doing. Describe what you are doing. Tell him what happened yesterday and what will happen tomorrow. Tell him stories. Take him places and talk about his experiences.
2. Give your child the opportunity and the desire to talk by not over anticipating his needs. At the same time, avoid pressuring the child for perfect speech by constantly correcting him. Many children react to this kind of pressure by not talking.

2.93 VERBALIZES TWO PREPOSITIONS (33-35½ mo.)

The child uses two different prepositions spontaneously.

1. Be sure the child understands prepositions before expecting her to use them. Refer to 2.80 (Verbalizes one preposition) and continue those activities.
2. Place a large blanket on the floor and let the child hide under it. Sing a song, such as "Where is Peter?" and let the child say, "Under here," at the appropriate time.
3. Use umbrellas on a rainy day to go from one place to another. Say, "Stay *under* the umbrella or you'll get wet."
4. Build an obstacle course that goes *under, around, through, behind,* and *beside.* Let the child go on the course and talk about where he is and what he is doing.
5. Sing and play "Humpty Dumpty." At the appropriate time, everyone falls *in front of* the chairs.
6. Play "Hide-and-seek." Let the child tell you where he hid.
7. Play "Hide-and-seek" with an object. Take turns hiding a favorite toy. Let the child guess where the toy is hidden.
8. Let the child ride tricycles between two lines. Ask the child "Where are you going?"
9. Take turns giving directions of where to stand. Suggestions are, "Stand *under* the light," "*In front of* the window," "*Between* Mary and Jimmy," "*In front of* me." Ask the child, "where are you standing?"

2.94 BEGINS TO RESPOND TO OPPOSITE ANALOGIES (33-36 mo.)

The child gives the opposite of a word when the word is presented in a sentence or as a question, e.g., The stove is hot and the refrigerator is _____; The refrigerator is not hot, it is _____.

1. Start with concept pairs the child knows. Use them in sentences and in situations which help give meaning.
   a. At the zoo:
      (1) The peanut is small and the elephant is big.
   b. At the beach:
      (1) You are wet and your towel is dry.
      (2) That sand is wet but this sand is dry.
   c. In the kitchen:
      (1) The ice cream is cold and the cocoa is hot.
   d. At the store:
      (1) We are coming and they are going.
2. Begin to verbally pair opposites in appropriate situations.
   a. Up and down:
      (1) Let the child stand up and squat down to songs and rhymes.
      (2) Let the child ride a seesaw and a swing verbalizing his position in space.
   b. Open and close:
      (1) Use appropriate doors, gates, toys.
      (2) Sing songs, use fingerplays, read stories which involve the concept.
   c. Wet and dry:
      (1) Make appropriate comparisons when bathing, washing clothes, swimming.
      (2) Compare wet and dry objects, such as leaves, newspapers, towels, soap.
   d. Big and small.
   e. On and off:
      (1) Use everyday objects such as switches on lights, flashlights, television, oven.
      (2) Place things on and off boxes, chairs, tables.
   f. In and out.
   g. Stop and go.
   h. Fast and slow.
   i. Hot and cold.
   j. Soft and loud.
   k. Come and go.
   l. In front of and behind.
   m. First and last.

2.95 REPEATS FIVE WORD SENTENCES (33½-36 mo.)

The child mimics a few five word sentences and begins to use them spontaneously in conversations.

1. Stress the intonation, melody, and word order of the longer sentences. Add adjectives and prepositions; stress action words, e.g., The little dog is running.
2. Use pictures to set the scene, e.g., show a picture of a cat eating. Ask the child to express his thoughts or feelings *first,* then model a longer, more linguistically complex sentence and describe the scene to the child.
3. Avoid methodical imitation tasks and repetition. The attention span and the individual limits of the child should be considered.
4. Tell stories which contain repetitive lines, such as in *The Gingerbread Man, Henny Penny, The Three Bears.* Take turns telling parts of the stories.
5. Refer to 2.76 (Participates in storytelling), 2.86 (Uses size words), 2.90 (Uses most basic grammatical structures).

2.96 RELATES EXPERIENCES MORE FREQUENTLY USING SHORT SENTENCES (34 mo. and above)

The child uses short sentences to tell about past experiences as well as plans for the near future. This may be completely spontaneous or may require a question and prompting to tell more.

1. Refer to 2.73 (Answers questions), and 2.74 (Relates experiences using short sentences).
2. Ask questions which require more than a "yes-no" response. "What did you have for lunch?" requires more than "Did you have milk or soda?" which requires more than "Did you drink milk?"
3. Be sure to allow time for your child to tell you his experiences.

4. Let the child do interesting things she can talk about. Several days before a special trip or outing, talk with the child about the upcoming event. Encourage her to tell others about the adventure to come. Use a calendar to help the child understand when something will happen. Events to look forward to may include holidays, birthdays, camping trips, visits to and from relatives, visits to special places, such as a museum or a circus.

2.97 ASKS QUESTIONS BEGINNING WITH "WHAT," "WHERE," "WHEN" (34½ mo. and above)

The child asks questions using "What," "Where," and "When" in addition to asking questions by intonation.

1. Model by asking appropriate simple purposeful questions: "What do you have in your hands?" "What is that noise I hear?" "What do I smell?" "Where are you?" "Where is your tricycle?" "When is Aunt Lucile coming?" "When did you get up?"
2. If the child uses gestures to indicate she wants to know what something is, say, "What is that? That is an elephant."
3. Say the complete sentence for the child when the child begins to verbalize and ask implied "Where" questions with one word. The child may say, "Dog?" and mean, "Where's the dog?" Answer with "Where is the dog, Jimmy? The dog is in the house."
4. Ask aloud "Where" questions when the child is nearby, e.g., while looking for something, say, "Where is my book? Where did I put it? Is it in this drawer? No, it's not there! That's not where I put it! Where is my book? Oh? Here it is, on the table, that's where!"
5. Respond positively when the child begins to ask "When" questions. Be as specific as possible in your answers to the child, e.g., if the child asks, "When see Sara?" respond with, "We will see Sara tomorrow. Tomorrow is when you put on your pajamas and go to sleep and wake up, that's tomorrow." Or "We will see Sara after Carl and Mom go to the store." Do not simply reply, "Later" or "Wait."
6. Answer the child's questions when she begins to verbally ask, "What? What's this?" or "Where Daddy?" Do not expect perfect grammar or articulation. Do not tell the child to ask you in a complete sentence.

2.98 USES INTELLIGIBLE WORDS ABOUT EIGHTY PERCENT OF THE TIME (35 mo. and above)

The child speaks in words that can be understood, although he may not articulate them properly. Articulation skills and intelligibility improve as the child's fine motor skills develop.

If the child is not intelligible 80 percent of the time by this age and there is no physical disability involving the articulators (tongue, lips, jaw, soft palate) the causes may be:
a. *General delayed development, including fine motor skills.*
b. *Hearing loss or previous hearing loss which was present while the child was beginning to talk. Even a mild, temporary hearing loss associated with an ear infection can affect articulation development.*
c. *Lack of good speech models.*
d. *Idiopathic. This means no one really knows the cause.*

1. Refer to 2.60 (Uses intelligible words about 65 percent of the time) and 2.79 (Produces sounds correctly at beginning of words).
2. Do not expect perfect articulation. Although the child's speech is intelligible almost all the time, the child still articulates some words and sounds. Provide a good model by saying these words and sounds correctly, but do not pressure the child to repeat them.

2.99 USES EXPRESSIVE VOCABULARY OF 300-1,000 WORDS (35 mo. and above)

The child's linguistic maturity by now should be developed to the point of decreasing percentages of nouns and increasing percentages of adjectives, adverbs, verbs, and other words that indicate linguistic growth.

The variability of impressive vocabulary length at age three is great, depending upon the amount of exposure to verbal input, the environmental factors of family, amount and type of interaction with peers, amount of materials and exploration, and physical and mental development.

The receptive vocabulary is normally many times the expressive vocabulary; the child should understand much more than she expressively displays. Emphasis should be placed on using the receptive abilities of the child to develop the expressive talents. Considerable dysfluencies still exist with the temendous growth of vocabulary and "rules" and experimentation; be patient and model correct responses without formal correction; keep the learning experience a happy one. Keep speech and language learning positive!

1. Continue to provide opportunities for the child to expand his language skills. Take the child to the zoo, library, store, dentist, farmer's market, museum. Discuss the things you see, hear and smell.
2. Watch educational television programs with the child and discuss the program.
3. Go to the library story hour for preschoolers. Let the child borrow books he can enjoy at home.
4. Let the child assist you at home. Make cookies or soup together, wash the car, sort the laundry, wash the dishes. Discuss what you are doing and why.
5. Ask the child "thinking" questions, such as "Why do we go shopping?" "Why do you wash your hands?" "Why do you sleep?"
6. Refer to 2.73 (Relates experiences using short sentences) and 2.76 (Uses size words).

2.0 EXPRESSIVE LANGUAGE

2.100 VERBALIZES THREE PREPOSITIONS
(35½ mo. and above)

The child uses three different prepositions spontaneously.

1. Work on the more difficult prepositions for receptive language, such as *into, through, inside, over,* while continuing to provide opportunities to use the easier prepositions expressively.
2. Refer to 2.80 (Verbalizes one preposition) and 2.93 (Verbalizes two prepositions).

3.01 NECK RIGHTING REACTIONS (0-2 mo.)

This reaction occurs in order to keep the head in proper alignment with the trunk. When the head is turned to one side, the body follows by rolling over. This reaction eventually helps the child learn to roll and assume the handknee position.

1. Position yourself above the child's head with the child in supine. Place your hands on each side of the child's head. Gently lift the head so the chin touches the chest, then rotate the head to one side. The child's shoulder should follow, then the trunk and finally the hips. Turn the child in both directions.
2. If the body does not turn, maintain the turn of the head with one hand, and use the other hand to turn the child's shoulders in the same direction. The shoulders should then be followed by the trunk and the hips.
3. Talk or sing to the child during these activities.
4. Note: Handling should be done cautiously and under the supervision of a physical or occupational therapist.

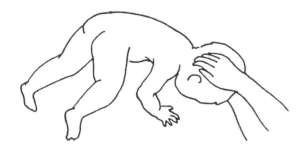

3.02 TURNS HEAD TO BOTH SIDES IN SUPINE (0-2 mo.)

The child tends to keep the head on the side rather than in mid-line at this stage. It is important that the child turn to both sides to avoid muscle tightness or flattening of the head on one side.

1. Alternate the position of toys and mobiles in the crib so the child will look to different sides to see them.
2. Sit on one side and shake a rattle and talk to the child so he will look at the source of sound. Move to the other side and repeat. If the child does not turn his head do it for him.
3. Change the child's position in the crib. Alternate every other day, with the head first at one end, then at the other end.
4. Approach the child from different sides when picking him up.
5. Change the position of the light (sunlight or lamp) from one side of the crib to the other periodically; one week on the right side, the next week on the left.
6. Carry the child alternately on right and left shoulders, allowing him to look from each side.
7. Feed the child on alternate sides; first cradle on the right

arm, then the left arm.
8. Lay the child on his back. Lift his hips a little and roll him to one side and wait for his head to follow. Return to the middle, then turn him to the other side.

3.03 LIFTS HEAD IN PRONE (0-2 mo.)

The child should briefly raise his head off the support when lying on his stomach. The head must be in mid-line, not turned to the side.

1. Lay the child on his stomach with a pillow or rolled towel under his chest. This will encourage him to lift his head.
2. Place the child on his stomach. Grasp his shoulders from behind. Gently lift his shoulders up. This will encourage him to lift his head.
3. Place the child on his stomach. Gently extend his arms over head and lift slightly. This will encourage his next extensors to work and help the child lift his head.
4. Lay the child on an adult's stomach and chest. The adult should talk to him, sing, and smile to encourage him to lift his head.
5. Shake a rattle or musical toy over the child's head to encourage him to look up.

3.04 HOLDS HEAD UP 45 DEGREES IN PRONE (0-2½ mo.)

The child's head should come up high enough to form about a 45° angle to his base of support when placed in prone position. The child's face should be forward in mid-line.

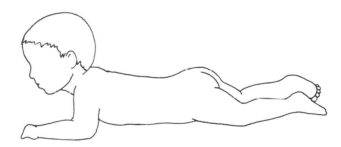

1. Refer to 3.03 (Lifts head in prone, Activities #1-5).
2. Place the child in the proper position as illustrated. Encourage her head to come higher by shaking a noisy toy a little above her line of vision so she will raise her head to see it.
3. Stroke down the neck extensors lightly and rapidly to encourage head lifting.
4. Raise the child's head to a 45° position so she can experience the position. Be sure that the face is forward, not turned to either side.
5. For the cerebral palsied child, if there is tightness pulling the head and shoulders forward, move the child gently from side to side at the shoulders until the tightness diminishes.

3.05 HOLDS HEAD TO ONE SIDE IN PRONE
(0-2 mo.)

The child's head should naturally turn to either side when placed face down on his stomach. If the head should stay in mid-line there is danger of suffocation.

1. Rotate the child's head to both sides about twice a day, but do not force it.
2. If the child tends to prefer one side strongly encourage him to turn to the other side by placing him in the crib such that the noise and activity or a light in the room will attract his attention to the non-favored side.
3. Place toys and mobiles for him to look at on the non-favored side.
4. Lower the child to a mat face down. Someone else shake a rattle to one side to get him to turn his head as he approaches the surface. If necessary rotate his head passively to look for the noise.

3.06 LIFTS HEAD WHEN HELD AT SHOULDER
(0-1 mo.)

The child will momentarily lift her head when held upright at an adult's shoulder.

1. Allow the child's head to be unsupported except for your shoulder. One hand can be held a short distance behind the head to prevent it from falling too far backwards after it has been lifted.
2. Hold the child at one shoulder for awhile, then the other shoulder. This will encourage her to turn her head in a different direction when she looks for your face and voice.
3. Hold the child sitting on your lap with your hands supporting her at the shoulders. Gently tilt her to the right side and wait for her head to come back to a straight position. Repeat the same movements to the other side.
4. Using position #3 above, tilt the child's body slightly forward and wait for her head to come up. Then tilt her slightly backwards and again wait for the righting to occur. Do not tilt the child too far off center if there is difficulty in getting her head back up. Move her only as much as you think she can recover.
5. Encourage head lifting by having someone stand behind you talking to her, smiling at her, or shaking a rattle to attract her attention.

3.07 HOLDS HEAD UP 90 DEGREES IN PRONE
(1-3 mo.)

The child's head should come up high enough to form a 90 degree angle to his base of support, when placed in prone position.

1. Refer to 3.03 (Lifts head in prone, Activities #1-5).

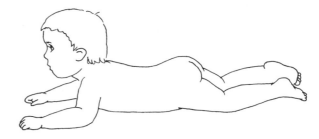

2. Refer to 3.04 (Holds head up 45 degrees in prone, Activities #2, 3 and 5).
3. Raise the child's head to a 90 degree position so he can experience the position. Be sure the face is forward, not turned to either side.
4. Rock the child from side to side in this 90 degree position and help him shift his weight from one arm to the other.

3.08 HOLDS HEAD IN SAME PLANE AS BODY WHEN HELD IN VENTRAL SUSPENSION
(1½-2½ mo.)

The child's head should be held at the same level as the body (the legs will hang down) when the child is held horizontally in mid-air.

1. Show a bright toy or light to the child while he is being held in the air with his face toward the floor. If he does not look up, stroke the back of his neck and gently lift his head to see the toy or light.
2. Hold the child around his trunk in a horizontal position with his face down. Walk him around the room pretending he's an airplane or bird. Encourage him to look out a window, at pictures on a wall, etc.
3. Use sounds of a rattle or a musical toy to encourage him to look up.
4. Begin with the child suspended vertically. Wait until he is visually attracted to something and then gradually move him to a horizontal position while his eyes stay on the object.

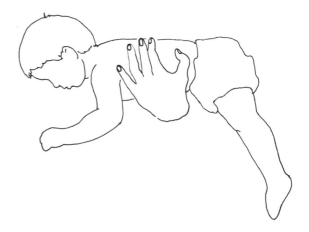

5. Attract the child's attention with Mother's voice and face as these are often most interesting to her.
6. Refer to 4.03 (Regards colorful object for few seconds) for suggested objects to present.

3.09 EXTENDS BOTH LEGS (1½-2½ mo.)

The child is now moving out of a totally flexed posture into one of more extension. Check to see if the child's legs stay almost flat on the table when lying in supine and prone.

1. Place the child in prone. If the legs automatically come up under the body in a flexed position, slowly pull them out into extension while gently rubbing over the buttocks area, rocking the hips from side to side.
2. Lay the child in supine. Push the legs gently toward the chest. Release the pressure and gently guide the legs back until they are straight and down flat on the table.
3. If the child holds her legs straight in supine place your hand on the child's feet and push gently upward toward the hips. Push to offer resistance and increase strength. Do not push hard enough to make them bend. If they do bend, hold them straight with your hand over the child's knees.
4. Encourage the child to push with both legs against "Thumper," a rabbit face strung across the crib which jingles when kicked.
5. Bend the child's hips when he lies in supine. Next straighten his knees. Rock him a little from side to side in this position, while pushing gently down on his heels.

3.10 ROLLS SIDE TO SUPINE (1½-2 mo.)

The child can turn to lie on his back when placed in a side-lying position.

1. Lay the child on his side periodically to play with a toy. Remove the toy and show the child how to return to his back by gently moving back his shoulder or hip. Place a small pillow or towel next to the child's back to help him stay in a side-lying position.
2. Move a toy or mobile across the child's line of vision and then over his head. Encourage the child to follow the toy until he rolls over. Be sure the child rolls to both sides whenever doing this activity.
3. Place the child inside a large carpeted cylinder in side-lying position. Move the cylinder slightly to start the rolling movement to supine.
4. Place the child in side-lying on a towel. Lift one edge of the towel to start the rolling movement to supine.

3.11 KICKS RECIPROCALLY (1½-2½ mo.)

The child, when excited, will kick her legs up and down in an alternating fashion, while lying in supine.

1. Move the child's legs up and down alternately in a slow, easy rhythmical manner while singing a song. One leg bends at the hip and knee, while the other leg is straightened at the hip and knee.
2. Place brightly colored straps around the child's ankles. Have the child's head slightly elevated so she can see the movement and talk about her feet and legs.
3. Place bells on the ankles to jingle during movement.
4. For a child with hypertonic muscles, do this exercise on a beach ball. First relax his trunk, arms and legs by gentle rotational movements on the ball. After the child is relaxed, try any of the above mentioned activities.
5. Reinforce any voluntary kicking movements with smiles, praise and/or touching.
6. For a child with some kicking skills, hang things in her crib to kick, e.g., the large rabbit "Thumper" which can be strung across the crib.

3.12 EXTENSOR THRUST INHIBITED (2-4 mo.)

The reflex is normally present during the first two months of life, but it begins to diminish by now and becomes integrated into other more functional activities. With the child lying in supine and the legs held loosely flexed to the chest, scratch the sole of one foot. If the leg extends strongly, the extensor thrust is present. If the leg stays flexed, the response is inhibited.

1. Place the child on his back with a pillow or towel under his head and hips. Flex the hips and knees to his chest. Firmly press the soles of his feet with your hand, but do not allow hip and knee extension. Progress to lighter pressure.
2. Start with firm pressure then use different textures to stimulate the feet, e.g., toweling, hard plastic, cotton balls, scratchy dish cleaners, fur, sandpaper.
3. Stimulate the feet while the child is in different positions, e.g., side-lying, supported sitting.
4. Lay the child on his back on a large beach ball. Flex the hips and knees and gently rock the hips from side to side. Let go and let the child enjoy the rocking movement. If the legs begin to extend, prevent the movement. Rock again to relax.
5. If the legs or trunk begin to thrust into extension, gently rotate the hips until relaxation occurs.

3.13 FLEXOR WITHDRAWAL INHIBITED (2-4 mo.)

This reflex is normally present during the first two months of life, but it begins to diminish by now and becomes integrated into other more functional activities. With the child lying in supine position, scratch the bottom of his foot with a fingernail.

If the leg forcefully pulls into flexion, the flexor withdrawal reflex is present. If there is a mild removal of the foot, but not the entire leg, the reflex is inhibited. If the child always withdraws his feet when stimulated, he should be desensitized to touch to be able to proceed with weight bearing skills in the future.

1. Press gently against the bottoms of the child's feet while his legs are extended in supine. Prevent withdrawal by holding the knees down.
2. Stimulate the child's foot while he is in different positions, e.g., side-lying, prone, supported sitting.
3. Start with firm pressure then gradually proceed to a lighter touch. This procedure should neither hurt nor tickle.
4. Put on a glove at first if your hand is not tolerated.
5. Add different textures as the child shows added tolerance, e.g., terrycloth, cotton balls, furry material, sponge, scratchy dish cleaners, sandpaper. Talk to the child about how the different materials feel to him, e.g., soft, rough.
6. Bend the hips and knees (in supine) so the feet rest firmly on the mat. Press down on the knees to promote weight bearing on the feet.

3.14 ASSUMES WITHDRAWAL POSITION (2-3½ mo.)

When the child is lying in supine, observe to see if a position of total flexion of arms and legs is sometimes assumed.

1. Put a small pillow under the child's head and one under his hips while he lies in supine. Flex the hips and knees to his chest and tap them gently. Slowly let go and encourage the child to maintain the position.
2. Place a small pillow under the child's head and one under his hips while he lies in supine. Fold the child's arms across his chest and hold them briefly. Try to let go, while encouraging the child to maintain this position.
3. Place a pillow behind the child's back to keep him in a side-lying position. Bend his hips and knees to his chest. Provide toys to play with while he is in this position.
4. Place the child on his back. Fold his arms across his chest and bend his hips and knees. Rock him gently in this position. Encourage the child to hold the position briefly when you take your hands away. Sing a slow rocking song during the movement.
5. Tickle, stroke, kiss or blow on the child's stomach to help elicit abdominal contractions.
6. Place the child in a hammock or on a blanket which is arranged so the child is in the totally flexed position. Swing him gently forward and back, side to side, and rotate him in a large circle.

3.15 HOLDS CHEST UP IN PRONE—WEIGHT ON FOREARMS (2-4 mo.)

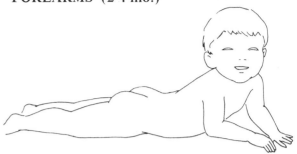

Place the child on her stomach. See if the head and chest are lifted with some weight on the forearms. This is sometimes referred to as the "puppy position."

1. Lay the child on a wedge to promote weight bearing on her forearms. Give her a musical toy to watch and to hear.
2. Roll a towel and place it under her arms as she lies on her stomach. Place toys in front of her to look at and/or to listen to while she holds this position.
3. Help the child lift her head and chest while pulling up on her shoulders. Place a musical toy in front of her to watch. Position her hands flat and fingers straight by stroking on the back of her hands. Once in this position, gently shift the child's weight from one arm to the other in easy rocking movements.
4. Press down lightly on the shoulders while the child is in "puppy position." Pressure should help the child bear weight on the arms and should not make the child collapse.
5. For the older delayed child: When this position can be held independently, have her alternately reach for objects in front, up to the side and back.
6. Place the child on her stomach on a large beach ball. Bend the lower legs up at the knees and keep the hips flat. Rock the ball to be sure the child is relaxed. Then encourage her to hold her head and chest up to look at a mobile suspended in front.
7. Make activity #3 more difficult by lifting the child's pelvis and legs so most of her weight will be on her arms.
8. If the child's shoulders are elevated and the neck hyperextended in puppy position, gently raise the head into mid-position by placing your hands on each side of the child's head and lifting.

3.16 ROTATES AND EXTENDS HEAD (2-3 mo.)

Place the child in prone position. Observe to see if the child can lift his head into extension and then turn it to both sides.

1. Present toys to the sides and overhead so the child will move his head to find them.
2. Place the child on his stomach in a location near family members so he will move his head around to follow people moving.
3. Move a push toy in front of him to encourage following

with his eyes.

4. If the child does not actively turn his head to the side once the head is extended, hold the head with two hands and guide it first to one side then to the other.

5. If the child shows preference to turn only to one side, concentrate activities and passive movements to the unused side. The child can also be positioned so interesting objects are on the unused side.

3.17 ROLLS PRONE TO SUPINE (2-5 mo.)

Rolling should be accomplished by moving the head, the shoulders and the hips separately rather than the body moving as one piece. The child should demonstrate the roll two or three times to be sure it was purposeful rather than accidental.

1. Position the child's arm out of the way, either straight up overhead or down by the side, on the side toward which he is moving.

2. Position an adult at each end of a long towel or blanket. The child is in prone on one end of the blanket. This edge of the blanket is slowly raised so the child will roll down to the other end. The adult at the other end lifts that end of the blanket so the child will roll back. Do not use this exercise if the child arches his back, head and legs during the roll.

3. Place the child on a slight incline so he will have a hill to roll down. Start the child in prone.

4. Roll by using the shoulder to lead. One arm should be up over the child's head. Pull the opposite shoulder back. The child will assist by moving his head, trunk, and legs when he feels his arm moving. Repeat, using the other arm and helping the child roll to the opposite side.

5. Roll by using the leg to lead. Bend one hip and one knee up; the other is held straight. Gently turn the bent leg to the opposite side of the body. The child's trunk, arms, and head should follow. Repeat using the other leg.

6. Move a toy or mobile across the child's line of vision and over his head to encourage him to follow it and roll over.

7. Place the child in prone inside a hollow cylinder made of an old flour container or several inner tubes glued together. Roll the cylinder and the child will roll inside it.

3.18 HOLDS HEAD BEYOND PLANE OF BODY WHEN HELD IN VENTRAL SUSPENSION (2½-3½ mo.)

The head should be higher than the level of the body when the child is held horizontally in mid-air. The hips may come up into some extension.

1. Refer to 3.08 (Holds head in same plane as body when held in ventral suspension).

2. Lay the child prone on a table. Her head should be forward over the side of the table and supported by an adult's hand. Gradually remove the supporting hand and encourage the child to lift her head. The legs and trunk

should be well supported with the adult's other hand.

3. Place the child on her stomach in a hammock or net swing with her entire body supported, except for her head. Swing her gently forward and back and side to side.

4. Begin with the child vertically suspended. When she is watching an interesting toy or face, move her trunk gradually to the horizontal position while encouraging her to keep her eyes on the toy or face.

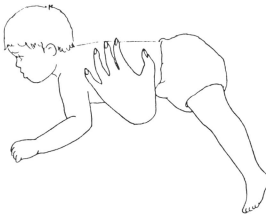

3.19 ASYMMETRICAL TONIC NECK REFLEX INHIBITED (3-5 mo.)

This reflex is normally present during the first three months of life, but it begins to diminish now and becomes integrated into other more functional activities.

The asymmetrical tonic neck reflex (ATNR) is also called the "fencer position." When the head is turned to the right, the right arm extends and the left arms flexes. The legs are sometimes also affected; the right leg flexes and the left leg extends. When the head is turned to the left the extremities move in the opposite direction.

1. Place the child in side-lying. This position encourages the arms to come together in mid-line. Provide toys to play with while the child is in this position.

2. Lay the child in supine. Help the head stay in mid-line and prevent it from turning by using a small neck pillow. Bring the arms together and cross them over the chest. Rock the child gently in this position. If arm tension

feels diminished, gently let go to see if the child can maintain this flexed position.

3. Place the child in supported sitting. Offer toys in mid-line for play to encourage the child to keep his head centered.

4. Place the child on his back with his head in mid-line looking at an adult's face. Play games moving his arms out to the side, forward in front of his face, and overhead. Move both arms at the same time and in the same direction. Sing songs to make it fun.

5. Lay the child in supine. Help the head stay in mid-line and prevent it from turning. Flex the child's hips and knees to his chest and tap them gently. Try to let go. Encourage the child to maintain the position.

6. Encourage symmetry (sameness) of limb positions while the child is at rest and during movement.

3.20 HOLDS HEAD IN LINE WITH BODY WHEN PULLED TO SITTING (3-6½ mo.)

Raise the child from supine to a sitting by slowly pulling the child's hands. The child should lift her head and hold it steady as soon as her head leaves the floor.

1. Start with the child in sitting on your lap or on the floor facing you. Hold her at the shoulders and slowly lower her backwards on a diagonal. Both shoulders should be pushed up toward the ears. This helps "set" the head so it does not fall back. If the head starts to fall, immediately bring the child forward. Do not let the child lose the head control. Lower the child to a wedge or incline at first, then progress by going all the way down to the floor.

2. Lower the child straight back instead of on a diagonal after activity #1 is successfully completed.

3. Work on head control as the child is pulled up after activity #2 is successfully completed. Start the child on an incline and pull her forward holding her shoulders. When she can do this, lay her flat on the floor and start the pull up.

4. Pull the child up from the floor providing support at the elbows.

5. Pull the child up providing support at the hands.

6. Pull the child so her shoulders are barely off the floor. Wait for her to lift her head.

7. Pull the child up to sitting using her arms or hands after every diaper change.

8. Lie on your back with the child lying supine on your stomach. (The child's head is toward your feet.) Perform a sit-up and the child will lie back; when you lie back, pull the child to sitting.

9. Talk to the child and/or use a noisy toy to encourage her to lift her head as she is pulled up.

10. For the older child, try sit ups using a mop stick. The child holds the stick with both hands. The adult holds the child's knees down and pulls up on the mop stick

pulling the child into sitting.

11. Bend the child's knees up so her feet are flat on the floor. Secure them with one hand and use the other hand to help her pull to sitting.

12. Reduce the help you give the child as her skill develops. Let the child lift her head and pull on your hands.

13. Sit the child on a table with her legs over the edge. Hold her hands out to the side and ask her to pretend she is a flying bird. Tilt her to one side and encourage her to straighten up. Tilt her to the other side, then on diagonal and straight back. As the child improves, tilt her farther off balance so it becomes more difficult for her to right herself.

14. For the older delayed child: Place a small toy or yarn ball under her chin and tell her not to let the toy fall. She should keep the ball under her chin as you pull her to sitting.

3.21 HOLDS HEAD STEADY IN SUPPORTED SITTING (3-5 mo.)

The head should maintain a steady position without bobbing forward or to the side when the child is held in an upright position.

1. Refer to 3.06 (Lifts head when held at shoulder.)

2. Hold the child at your shoulder. Walk around the house pointing to pictures on the walls. Point out flowers and trees in the yard.

3. Hold the child in sitting on your lap or on the floor. Support his trunk with your hands. Place an attractive moving toy at eye level for the child to watch. Place the toy on a low table if the child is sitting on the floor.

4. Use a downward gentle pressure on the head when the top of the head is in an upright position. This will stimulate the contraction of all the neck muscles.

5. Carry the child in a backpack which supports the trunk of the child and allows for free head movement.

3.22 SITS WITH SLIGHT SUPPORT (3-5 mo.)

The child should maintain a sitting position with a small amount of support at the lower back.

1. Use a chair which supports the child sufficiently to maintain a good sitting posture. Do not provide more support than the child needs. Consult with a physical or occupational therapist. Some examples of useful chairs include:
   a. Triangle chairs.
   b. Floor sitters.
   c. Infant seats.
   d. Roller chairs.
   e. Car safety seats.
   f. Swimming rings (inflatable).
   g. Standard pre-school chair with a footrest added if necessary.

2. Provide seat belts when more stability is needed. Place

seatbelts across the hips, not around the trunk or waist.

3. Provide more stability for the trunk of the child by placing a tray or table in front of the chair. This will give the hands and arms something to push against. The child can also play with appropriate toys on the table while sitting.

4. Make a chair for a young child by cutting and folding a cardboard box to fit the child's dimensions. Cover it with bright contact paper to make it attractive.

5. Place the child in a sitting position at the beach or in a sandbox. Cover the child's legs and trunk with enough sand to sufficiently support him. Gradually brush the sand away giving the child less support and requiring more trunk control. Note: Do not put sand on the child if he is lying down. The weight of the sand on the chest can be too heavy.

3.23 BEARS SOME WEIGHT ON LEGS (3-5 mo.)

The child should take some weight on her legs, as opposed to letting the knees collapse into flexion when held in a standing position. Be sure the feet are flat, the legs slightly apart and the knees slightly bent when working on the following activities:

1. Caution: Weight bearing activities for children with cerebral palsy should be carefully controlled to avoid setting off undesirable extension patterns. Bouncing activities on the feet should be avoided.

2. Place the child in supine. Bend the hips and knees and place the feet flat on the mat. Press down on the knees so the weight is on the feet.

3. Place the child standing in a jump seat (baby bouncer, Jolly Jumper).

4. Hold the child's trunk, not his hands or arms, when lifting him to an upright position.

5. Strengthen the legs for standing by having the child lie on his back in front of a wall and push against the wall using both feet.

6. Place the child in standing on a prone board for table activities.

7. Use a standing table for eating or for fine motor activities.

8. Bounce the child in standing to music.

9. Kneel in front of a mirror. Place the child in standing and hold him against your body for support. Hold his knees straight if necessary.

10. Stand the child on her feet when going in and out of the bathtub.

11. Stand the child on different textures: soft, hard, rough, smooth.

12. Lay the child on her back on a beach ball. Hold her under the arms and gently lower her to the floor so she can put her feet down and bear some weight on her legs. Rock her from side to side to shift her weight from one leg to the other.

13. Repeat activity #12 with the child on her stomach.

14. Support the child at the hips in standing. Push down gently toward the floor to help increase her stability.

3.24 MORO REFLEX INHIBITED (4-5 mo.)

This reflex is normally present during the first four months of life, but it begins to diminish by now and becomes integrated into other more functional activities. It is elicited by a sudden loud noise or a sudden change of head position. The arms extend rapidly and then circle back into flexion as if to cling. If this reflex remains strong after four months, it seriously impairs continued motor development throwing the child off balance in upright positions.

1. Hold and cuddle the child in a flexed position. Make a loud sound. Do not allow the child's arms to move in response to it. Talk to the child softly and reassure him.

2. Increase ordinary household noises gradually so the child can build a tolerance for sounds and for normal activity.

3. Point out the source of the sound to the child, so he can begin to associate the sound with its source.

4. When moving the child into different positions in which the Moro reflex may occur, try to prevent this reflex by not allowing head or arm extension.

5. The Moro reflex diminishes as the child's head control improves. Refer to 3.21 (Holds head steady in supported sitting).

3.25 PROTECTIVE EXTENSION OF ARMS AND LEGS DOWNWARD (4-6 mo.)

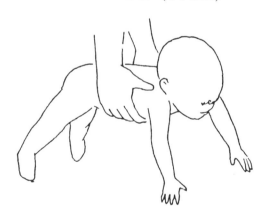

The child is held in the air by the trunk face down. Rapid movement toward the floor should elicit arm and leg extension as the child readies to protect himself against a fall.

1. Place the child over a twelve to fourteen inch ball or a roll with her arms up over her head. Gently move her forward on the ball and then quickly move the child so her hands will touch the floor to brace herself and protect her head.

2. Move the child's arms down if she does not bring them naturally over the ball. Help her with the feeling of bearing weight on her arms by holding her elbows straight and moving her body weight forward over the extended arms. The fingers and wrist should be extended.

3. Move the child more rapidly on the ball as protective extension improves.

4. Provide a large toy or picture to look at to make the ball rolling a fun activity. Do not place a toy on the floor for the child to pick up as this promotes the wrong type of hand pattern.
5. Place the child over a wastepaper basket covered with a pad and roll the child forward.
6. Demonstrate the activity with another child if the child is apprehensive.
7. Play airplane by moving the child around the room in a horizontal position. Aim the child toward the floor so his arms will come down when you "land."
8. Provide something interesting for the child's hands and feet to touch as he comes down. "Land" in sand, grass, water, on a carpet or on linoleum. Landing on a large squeaky toy or picture may be fun as long as the child does not attempt to pick it up.

3.26 BEARS WEIGHT ON HANDS IN PRONE (4-6 mo.)

A child placed in the prone position should lift his head and chest and should support his weight on his hands with his elbows extended. This is sometimes called the "extended puppy position."

1. Use a wedge. Lay the child on his stomach over the wedge. Encourage him to push up on his hands. Blow soap bubbles for him to watch.
2. Place the child over a rolled towel. Encourage elbow extension by attracting his attention to a playing music box directly overhead.
3. Lay the child in prone, bearing weight on his forearm. Gently pull up at his shoulders to help him extend his arms and shift the weight to his hands. Rock him from side to side. Sing a rhythmical song and rock to the tune.
4. Hold a favorite toy high over the child's head so he can see it only by pushing up on his hands.
5. Lay the child prone over your lap with his arms on the floor on one side and his legs on the other side. Provide toys for him to look at while he bears weight on both hands. Keep the child's arms forward and his hips flat.
6. Sit the child on your lap. Help the child straighten his arms out in front and touch a wall, a book, or some large object. His hands should be flat. He can bear a little weight on his hands, if forward pressure is given at the shoulders.

3.27 EXTENDS HEAD, BACK AND HIPS WHEN HELD IN VENTRAL SUSPENSION (4-6 mo.)

The child's head should be raised above the level of the body, the back should be held straight and the hips should be extended at the same level as the back when the child is held in mid-air around the trunk.

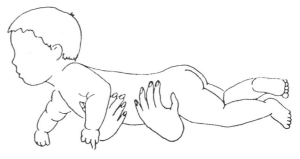

1. Refer to 3.08 (Holds head in same plane as body when held in ventral suspension).
2. Place the child in prone in a hammock or net swing with the hammock supporting the child only under her abdomen. Swing gently side to side and forward and back.
3. Stroke lightly along the entire spine from the head down to stimulate contraction of the muscles.
4. For the cerebral palsied child with increased extensor muscle tone, this skill should not be encouraged.
5. For a child hypotonia, rapid bouncing on your arms and the singing of a peppy tune may help encourage the child to lift his head, trunk and legs.

3.28 ROLLS SUPINE TO SIDE (4-5½ mo.)

Rolling should be accomplished by moving the head, the shoulders and the hips separately rather than the body moving as one piece. The child should demonstrate the roll two or three times to be sure it was purposeful rather than accidental.

1. Refer to 3.17 (Rolls prone to supine, Activity #2-7).
2. Place the child in supine. Shake a noisy toy to one side to attract his attention. Encourage him to roll to it. Give a little help if necessary.
3. Take one leg and place it across the body with the foot flat and the hip and knee bent. Rock the child a little going forward and back over the foot. Repeat on the opposite side using the other leg.
4. Take one arm to the opposite side of the child and let him feel different textures/toys: fluffy, rough, smooth, hard. Repeat on the other side.

3.29 SITS MOMENTARILY LEANING ON HANDS (4½-5½ mo.)

Place the child in a sitting position. The child's trunk naturally flexes forward. Place the child's hands on the floor or on his knees and let go cautiously. The child should hold this position one to two seconds.

1. Place pillows around the child for support. Gradually remove the pillow support when the child has his weight on his hands and seems steady.
2. Sit the child between your legs with his hands bearing weight on your legs and with his back supported by your abdomen. Move the child forward and lessen the back support as he improves.
3. Let the child sit with his arms supported on a small pillow in front of him.
4. Place the child's hands on his knees. Hold his elbows straight and push down on the shoulders to encourage him to bear a little weight on his hands. Tap on the back of his upper arm to encourage him to straighten his elbows.
5. If extensor spasticity is present, when the child starts to topple backwards, help him to move forward by stroking the front of his neck or stomach or by holding his shoulders or shirt to prevent a fall. Try not to push him from the back or the head.
6. If the child has hypotonia, encourage straightening of the back by bouncing him gently on his bottom while in sitting.

3.30 DEMONSTRATES BALANCE REACTIONS IN PRONE (5-6 mo.)

Place the child on a surface which can be tilted. The child's head, trunk, and extremities act to prevent a fall by moving in a direction opposite to the tilt.

1. Lay the child in prone on a blanket. Hold the blanket taut (two to four adults are required for this activity) and tilt the child from side to side.
2. Place the child in prone on a large beach ball and rock to the side.
3. Place the child in prone on a vestibular board. Rock from side to side and forward and back.

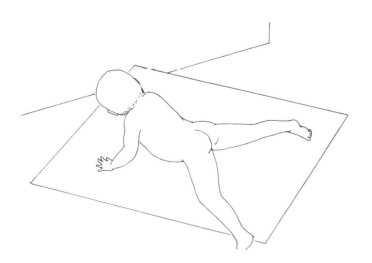

4. Let Father go on his hands and knees. Place the child in prone on Father's back. Dad gently tilts to the left and to the right. The child should hold on and right herself. Someone else should be present for safety.
5. Place the child in prone on a water bed. Tilt the child from side to side by pushing down on each side of the water bed. A water bed for an infant can be made by filling a plastic garbage bag with water.
6. Place the child in prone on his father's stomach. Father then proceeds as in activity #4.

3.31 CIRCULAR PIVOTING IN PRONE (5-6 mo.)

The child moves in circles on his stomach although he is unable to crawl forward or back.

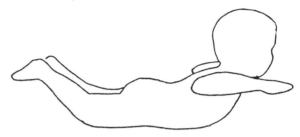

1. Refer to 3.27 (Extends head, back and hips when held in ventral suspension) for activities to develop the extended position.
2. Place a toy slightly out of the child's reach so he has to pivot for it. Move it a little further away after some play time. Use a smooth surface to reduce the friction for the child.
3. Place the child on a crawligator or on a board with castors. Teach the child how to push it with his arms and legs so he can go to the side to retrieve a toy.
4. Make a game of crawling around the child as he lies on the floor in prone. This may encourage him to pivot around to follow your movements.

3.32 MOVES HEAD ACTIVELY IN SUPPORTED SITTING (5-6 mo.)

The child should be able to turn her head in all directions maintaining good control when sitting with good trunk support.

1. Place the child in supported sitting in an infant seat or in the corner of a sofa. Help the child to play with toys on either side and encourage him to look at them.
2. Let the child observe as the adults work around the house. A child in a seated position can watch Mother wash clothes or cook dinner. Her movements and her discussion with the child on what she is doing should encourage the child to follow her with his eyes and head.
3. Place the child in a well supported sitting position in a high chair. Use a seatbelt around the hips and make sure the feet are supported. Place pillows at the sides if trunk control is poor. Use the high chair tray for toys or books. A suction toy is good if the child cannot hold

3.0 GROSS MOTOR

toys yet or tends to drop or throw them.

4. Sit the child in a corner of the room where she will be supported by two walls. Provide toys to play with while the child is in this position.

5. Hold the child in sitting. Tilt her to one side and wait for her head to raise. Tilt her to the other side and repeat the activity. Pull down on the shoulder opposite to the head tilt if assistance is needed.

3.33 HOLDS HEAD ERECT WHEN LEANING FORWARD (5-6 mo.)

The child is placed in a sitting position and given trunk support. The child's head should be fully erect.

1. Place the child in supported sitting. Encourage the child to hold her head up by stroking the back of her neck and lifting a toy overhead for her to look at.

2. Sit in front of a mirror with the child. Call attention to the child in the mirror. She must keep her head up to see herself.

3. Refer to 3.32 (Moves head actively in supported sitting) for additional activities.

3.34 SITS INDEPENDENTLY INDEFINITELY BUT MAY USE HANDS (5-8 mo.)

Place the child in a sitting position. Withdraw your support when the child is well balanced, with or without using his hands. The child should maintain this position for at least five minutes.

1. Vary the child's sitting positions. Let the child sit with his legs extended in front of him, to one side or crossed in front. Discourage the child from sitting on or between his feet. The child can place his hands on the floor in front of him to help him maintain his balance.

2. For the older delayed child: Let him practice sitting with his arms behind him, bearing weight on them while watching television.

3. Place the child in a straddle position over a roll. His feet should be flat on the floor, his back should be erect and

the child's hands should be on the roll or on his own legs. Play horsey, pretending to gallop and singing a cowboy song.

4. Rock the child from side to side in the above straddle position as his balance improves.

5. Offer the child a toy in such a way that he must balance on one hand to accept it. Vary the position from which the toy is offered (i.e., from each side, far in front, over head) so the child will move slightly off balance to retrieve it.

6. Help the child keep his back straight in sitting by using one or more of the following activities:
   a. Tap and rub the base of the child's spine.
   b. Bounce him gently in the sitting position.
   c. Tap the shoulders back to discourage back rounding and internal rotation of the shoulders.
   d. Stroke the center of the back gently and rapidly.

7. For the child with hypertonicity, try to reduce the tone by lifting the arms at the sides and rotating the trunk slowly. Place the child's hands down on the mat on one side when the tightness decreases. Repeat the activity and place the child's hands on the mat on the other side.

3.35 RAISES HIPS PUSHING WITH FEET IN SUPINE (5-6½ mo.)

Place the child in supine with hips and knees flexed and feet held flat on the floor. Encourage her to lift her hips by patting the child's bottom.

1. Caution: Do not do this activity if a child has extensor spasticity.

2. Help the child lift her hips by rubbing her buttocks to encourage extension. The tactile stimulation of the buttocks helps the muscles to contract.

3. Hold the child's legs together if they should fall to the sides. Gradually encourage the child to keep her legs together, without assistance.

4. Play a bridge game with the child by running a car or truck underneath her as she lifts her hips.

5. Encourage the child to raise her hips as you change her diaper.

3.36 BEARS ALMOST ALL WEIGHT ON LEGS (5-6 mo.)

Place the child in standing position. Cautiously remove your support. The child should be able to hold most of his weight and require help mainly for balance.

1. Hold the child facing you on your lap. Support his trunk against you and encourage him to bear weight on his legs as he stands on your thighs.

2. Lie on your back and make a game of having the child stand on your stomach or chest. Provide support at the trunk. As the child improves, change support to the

shoulders, then the arms, then the hands.

3. Place a low mirror on the wall. Hold the child in standing to look at himself in the mirror. Talk about his body parts.
4. Hold the trunk rather than the hands or arms when lifting the child to an upright position.
5. Support the child at the hips in standing and push down gently toward the floor to help increase his stability.
6. Be sure the child's feet are flat, legs slightly apart, and knees slightly bent.
7. Let the child stand on different textures—soft, hard, rough, smooth.
8. Encourage the child to "dance" to music. Help him stand and sway on his feet.
9. Caution: Weight bearing activities for children with cerebral palsy should be carefully controlled to avoid setting off undesirable movement patterns. Bouncing activities on the feet should be avoided. Consult with a physical therapist.

3.37 LIFTS HEAD AND ASSISTS WHEN PULLED TO SITTING (5½-7½ mo.)

Place the child in the supine position. Hold the child's hands and pull him slowly up to sitting. The child should bring up his head and pull actively against your grip with his hands.

1. Refer to 3.20 (Holds head in line with body when pulled to sitting, Activities #1-14).
2. Repeat the items above only do not initiate the pull up until the child's head is off the floor.
3. Reduce gradually the amount of pull you are giving. Let the child actively take over by pulling himself on your hands.

3.38 ROLLS SUPINE TO PRONE (5½-7½ mo.)

Rolling should be accomplished by moving the head, the shoulders and hips separately rather than all at the same time. The child should demonstrate the roll two or three times to be certain it was purposeful rather than accidental.

1. Refer to 3.17 (Rolls prone to supine, Activities #2-6).
2. For the child with hypertonicity, bend the hips and knees and rock gently side to side. When the hypertonicity decreases, help him roll over.
3. Place the child in supine. Lift the child's head forward. Turn it gently to one side and wait for the arms, trunk, and legs to follow. Repeat on the opposite side. Try this in front of a mirror.
4. Place the child in supine. Place a toy or yourself to one side and slightly above the child's head so he must roll over completely to see you or the toy.
5. Let the child remove his arm from underneath himself after he rolls over. If he has difficulty, help him minimally by lifting the shoulder where the arm is stuck; the arm should come forward.

6. Place the child on a slight incline so he has a hill to roll down. Start the child in supine.
7. Place the child in supine inside a large hollow cylinder. Roll the cylinder and the child rolls inside it. The cylinder may be lined with a variety of textures. Place the child in the cylinder with a minimum of clothing, if this is tolerable to the child.
8. Roll the child on a large ball by moving his legs in one direction and allowing the ball to move in the opposite direction as the child rolls.

3.39 BODY RIGHTING ON BODY REACTION (6-8 mo.)

Turn the child's head to one side while in supine. The child should roll over segmentally with the shoulders turning first, followed by the pelvis, then the legs. The child should not roll stiffly as one piece.

1. Refer to 3.17 (Rolls prone to supine).
2. Refer to 3.38 (Rolls supine to prone).
3. Place the child in supine on a large treatment ball. Bend her legs up to the chest. Move her legs side to side while the shoulders remain motionless. This helps achieve trunk flexibility if there is stiffness present. Follow this relaxation activity with a specific activity, such as having the child roll across the ball.

3.40 DEMONSTRATES BALANCE REACTIONS IN SUPINE (6-7 mo.)

Place the child on a surface which can be tilted. The child's head, trunk, and extremities act to prevent a fall by moving in a direction opposite to the tilt.

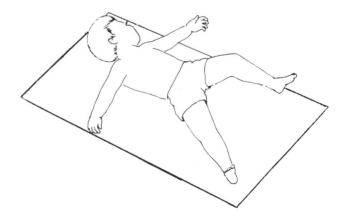

1. Lay the child in supine on a blanket. Hold the blanket

taut and gently tilt from side to side. Do not move the blanket so far that the child rolls over.

2. Place the child in supine on a large beach ball. Follow the directions of activity #1.

3. Make or purchase a rocking board, which is a flat board, with a curved base. Place the child in supine and rock from side to side.

4. Let Father go on his hands and knees. Place the child in supine on Father's back. Dad gently tilts the child from side to side. Someone else should be present for safety.

5. Place the child in supine on a water bed. Tilt the child from side to side to side by pushing down on each side of the water bed. A water bed for an infant can be made by filling a plastic garbage bag with water.

3.41 PROTECTIVE EXTENSION OF ARMS TO SIDE AND FRONT (6-8 mo.)

Place the child in a sitting position. Push her off balance suddenly toward the front or side. The child should protect herself from a fall to the side by extending one arm and catching her weight. She should protect herself from a fall to the front by extending both arms and catching her weight.

A. To the Side
1. Push the child gently to one side when she is sitting. Help her bear weight on one arm. Hold her in this position briefly. Repeat on the other side. Do this activity with the child in different sitting positions: long-leg, cross-leg or side-sitting.

2. Place the child in sitting. Sing a song and encourage the child to sway her body from side to side. As the child moves to one side, let her touch one hand down to the floor. Repeat on other side as she sways.

3. Push the child gently to the side while still holding onto the opposite arm. If her hand does not come down to catch herself, place it on the floor for her and help her bear weight as in activity #1. Repeat on the opposite side.

4. Push the child off balance more rapidly when she has accomplished activity #3. Push her to one side and then the other. If her arm does not come out, help

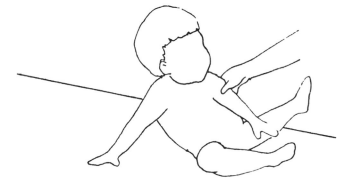

her. Let the child push you off balance.

5. Place the child on a vestibular board. Encourage her to catch herself by extending her arm as you quickly tilt the board to one side.

6. Place the child in side-sitting, with both arms to one side and the legs together on the other side. Push the child to the side so the hands must come down, and catch her weight. Repeat after reversing the side of the arms and legs.

B. To the Front
1. Place the child in sitting. Let the child look at a book or toy. Encourage her to bear weight on her arms which should be in front of her. Push down gently at the shoulders to straighten her arms.

2. Sit the child upright without bearing weight on her hands. Push her forward so she must catch herself. Do not allow her to fall. If she does not place her arms forward, help her. Let her push you over.

3. Roll the child forward over a bolster or a small ball. Help her place her arms down. Move more rapidly as she develops more confidence.

3.42 LIFTS HEAD IN SUPINE (6-8 mo.)

Observe the child as she lies in the supine position to see if head flexion occurs. Place a toy on her chest to help encourage head lifting.

1. Stroke over the muscles on the front of the neck with your fingers to give the child the sensation of what you want. Follow this by lifting the child's head several times.

2. Place the child in supine on an incline for back support. Encourage the child to lift her head. Gradually lessen the slope until the child is flat on the floor and can lift her head.

3. Place a toy or book with an interesting picture on the child's chest. Encourage him to lift his head to look at the picture or toy.

4. Talk to the child while he lies on his back. Smile, move your head from side to side or nod. Slowly move your face towards the child's toes so he follows with his eyes and lifts his head. Do this activity with favorite toys and rattles.

5. Call the child by name when approaching her before you pick her up so she must lift her head to see you and localize the voice calling her name.

6. Add tactile stimulation to the above activity. Rub the child's stomach to encourage her to see what and where she is being touched as well as to see your face as you call her name.

7. Refer to 3.37 (Lifts head and assists when pulled to sitting).

8. Place the child in supine. Hold the child at his shoulders. Use short, quick pulls to help the muscles around his neck begin to lift the head.

3.43 HOLDS WEIGHT ON ONE HAND IN PRONE (6-7½ mo.)

Place the child in the prone position and offer a toy. The child should be able to hold weight on one hand and take the toy with the other hand.

1. Place the child in prone with his weight supported on two hands as he looks at a book on a book stand. Offer the child a toy or a goody high enough in front so he must lift one hand and reach forward to get it. Repeat with the other hand reaching.
2. Offer toys or goodies from one side, then the other side.
3. Hang a balloon or mobile overhead for the child to reach.
4. Let the child lie in front of a mirror. Encourage the child to touch his face in the mirror.
5. For the older delayed child: Place him in prone and ask him to point out body parts on a doll.

3.44 GETS TO SITTING WITHOUT ASSISTANCE (6-10 mo.)

Observe to see if the child can sit up independently from either a prone or a supine position, using any method.

1. Place the child in side-lying with her knees bent to the chest. Place your hand under the child's side, but assist only if necessary. Encourage the child or gradually help her bear her own weight on her forearms. Her weight should shift to her hands as she comes up. Her hands should move closer to her body until she is upright in side-sitting. She should use both forearms and hands to push herself into sitting. Do this side-lying to sitting activity from both sides.
2. Lay the child in prone. Pull up at the child's shoulders so she comes up on extended arms. Place your hands on the child's hips and pull her back with both legs to the side. The child should end in side-sitting.
3. If the child is in supine help her roll to the side and start the activity as described in #1.

3.45 BEARS LARGE FRACTION OF WEIGHT ON LEGS AND BOUNCES (6-7 mo.)

Place the child in supported standing and observe any bouncing movements of the legs.

1. Bounce the child up and down in a standing position so the knees bend.
2. Let the child jump in a "jolly jumper."
3. Play lively music. Show the child how to bounce up and down to the music while holding an adult's hands.
4. Vary the bouncing activity by using a water bed, an old rubber tire, a thin board supported on both ends, a bed, an old mattress, or a child-size trampoline.
5. Lift the child to the upright position by holding the trunk, not the hands or arms.
6. Caution: Weight bearing activities for children with

cerebral palsy should be carefully controlled to avoid setting off undesirable movement patterns. Bouncing activities on feet should be avoided. Consult with a physical therapist.

3.46 STANDS, HOLDING ON (6-10½ mo.)

Place the child in standing position at a railing he can hold. Let go cautiously and the child should be able to hold the position. When working on the following activities always be sure the feet are flat on the floor and the knees are apart and slightly bent.

1. Sit in a chair. Let the child stand between your legs facing you and holding onto your legs. Babble to each other, tell nursery rhymes, or sing songs
2. Sit on the floor. Place the child in a straddle position over your leg. Support the child holding his trunk. Play "horsey" by bouncing him up and down on your knee, then stop to let him bear weight.
3. Stand the child with his back supported by a corner wall. Place a stool or small chair in front of him to hold onto. Place an interesting book or toy on the chair.
4. Hold the child's knees straight and support his back while the child holds on to a couch or low table. The child should lean forward and maintain his balance by resting on his arms. Let the child look at a book or toy.
5. Hold the child's legs straight and support his back while he holds on to furniture with his hands.
6. Hold the child at the trunk while he holds on to furniture with his hands.
7. Hold the child at the hips only, while he holds on to furniture with his hands.
8. Decrease your hold gradually when the child is standing and holding on to the furniture.
9. Provide at first a small railing for the child to hold on to, such as a crib or playpen railing, for this is easier for the child to grip than a large piece of furniture which has no gripping surface.
10. Take the child on walks or to the zoo. Pause at different places where the child can stand and hold on to a railing while you point to and name animals or other objects.
11. Move the child slightly to one side to shift his weight a little to one leg. Move him to the other side to shift weight again.
12. Caution: Remain by the child during these activities to prevent falls. The child cannot sit down from this position without assistance.

3.47 PULLS TO STANDING AT FURNITURE (6-10 mo.)

The child holds onto furniture and pulls himself up to a standing position without assistance from an adult. The child pulls himself to standing using his arms, primarily. The legs may straighten at the same time or may straighten one at a time.

3.0 GROSS MOTOR

1. Place the child on his knees beside Mother. Encourage him to climb up to Mommy's lap. Mother should help by holding his hands and helping the child pull to standing. The child should be rewarded with a hug and a chance to be with Mommy for awhile.
2. Stack two large firm pillows and place a toy on top. Encourage the child to pull to standing to obtain the toy.
3. Place a favorite toy on a low table or chair. Assist the child to his knees while he holds onto the furniture. Move the toy far enough away so the child must stand to reach it.
4. Begin with the child squatting in front of you. Hold his knees apart and be sure his feet are flat on the floor. Rock him forward and ask him to stand up. Someone else may help at first by holding his hands. Give assistance by straightening his knees. The child then raises his trunk and head. Do this in front of a mirror or near a mobile he can touch once he is standing.
5. Refer to 3.67 (Stands by lifting one foot) for a more mature standing pattern description.
6. Remain by the child during these activities to prevent falls. The child cannot sit down from this position without assistance.

3.48 BRINGS ONE KNEE FORWARD BESIDE TRUNK IN PRONE (6-8 mo.)

Lift the child's hip slightly on one side and watch for natural hip and knee flexion of the same side. The abdomen should remain flat on the floor. Observe the child in play to see if this occurs naturally.

1. Place the child in prone. Lift his hip so the hip and knee on that side bends. If the leg remains extended, gently rock the hips from side to side until the legs relax. Lift the hip on one side again and help the child bend his knee.
2. Lay the child in prone and let him play with a toy. Place his hip and knee to one side in flexion. Help him maintain this position in a relaxed manner while he is attending to the toy.
3. Repeat the above activities for both legs.
4. Note: Encourage the child if he begins to crawl forward during the activities above.

3.49 CRAWLS BACKWARD (7-8 mo.)

Observe to see if the child moves backward on his abdomen by pushing with his arms.
The child may do this spontaneously as he experiments with movement. Teaching should be confined to the more functional forward movements.

3.50 DEMONSTRATES BALANCE REACTIONS ON HANDS AND KNEES (8-9 mo.)

Place the child on his hands and knees on a surface which can be tilted. The child's head, trunk and extremities act to prevent a fall by moving in a direction opposite to the tilt.

1. Place the child in the hand-knee position. Move the child off balance by gently pushing him to each side. Push at the shoulders or hips.
2. Let the child assume the hand-knee position on Father's back. Guard the child while Dad gently tilts his back from side to side.
3. Place the child on a large ball or a large firm bolster in the hand-knee position. Rock side to side, forward and back.
4. Place the child in the hand-knee position on a vestibular board. Rock the child slowly at first then more rapidly as the child improves in balance.
5. Place the child in the hand-knee position on a waterbed. Tilt and rock the bed.

3.51 SITS WITHOUT HAND SUPPORT FOR TEN MINUTES (8-9 mo.)

Place the child in sitting position. Give the child activities which will occupy her hands so they will not be used for support.

1. Play ball with the child while she sits unsupported.
2. Place the child in sitting. Let the child play with a Busy Box hung on the wall at her level.
3. Let the child hold large objects which require two hands, e.g., a large ball, balloon or doll.
4. Hold a toy overhead so the child must reach up with her arms.
5. Play pat-a-cake.
6. Let the child play two-handed musical instruments, e.g., a tambourine, triangle or rhythm sticks.
7. For the older delayed child: Place small toys on one side of his body with a can or box on the other side. The child must reach for a toy on one side and turn to the opposite side to place it into the box.
8. Let the child sit on a small box with her feet supported on the floor. Do any of the above activities.
9. Let the child sit astride a narrow seat with her feet on the floor and legs apart. Let her look at books or identify body parts in a mirror.
10. Use a table and chair for activities if the child's back is very rounded and her head is held forward. Be sure the child's hips and knees are at 90° in a seat. Be sure the chair provides for back extension. Use a footstool, if necessary, to support the feet.
11. Encourage the child to keep her back straight in sitting by using one or more of the following activities:
    a. Tap and rub the base of the spine.
    b. Bounce the child gently in the sitting position.
    c. Tap the shoulders back.

d. Stroke the center of the back, gently and rapidly.

3.52 CRAWLS FORWARD (8-9½ mo.)

Place the child in the prone position. The child should be able to move forward on his abdomen by pulling with his arms and pushing alternately with his legs. The child may go backwards by pushing with his arms during his first attempts to crawl. Continue to present toys in front of the child. Show him how to use his legs to crawl forward.

1. Place the child in prone. Encourage the child to explore his environment by providing a lot of time on the floor.
2. Place a toy one to two feet in front of the child as he lies in prone. Lift one hip and help the child bend the hip and the knee on that side. Place your hand on the bottom of his foot. Rub his hip with your other hand and gently move him forward at the hip until his leg straightens. Repeat on the opposite side. Continue this activity until he reaches the toy. Let him play with the toy before repeating this activity. The child should be on a smooth or slippery surface with a shirt and long pants on to reduce friction and make movement easier for him.
3. Repeat activity #2, but wait for the child to push against your hand and straighten his leg.
4. Repeat activity #2 on a carpet for resistance and to make the child work a little harder.
5. Repeat activity #2 encouraging coordinated arm movements. The sequence movement should be: right arm, left leg, left arm, right leg.
6. Increase crawling distance by gradually moving a toy farther away or by giving the child a rolling toy which moves when the child plays with it.
7. Provide a crawligater or a scooter board with wheels to help the child crawl.
8. Let the child crawl through a box, under a chair or table, through a tunnel, to a mirror or to his parents.

3.53 MAKES STEPPING MOVEMENTS (8-10 mo.)

The child spontaneously makes walking type movements when held in standing.

1. Hold the child in standing. Ask another child or adult to make stepping movements without moving forward. Encourage the child to imitate this "marching."
2. Move the child's legs passively up and down.
3. Let the child stand on your feet. "March" using exaggerated up and down leg movements.
4. Encourage the child to "march" to music.
5. Encourage the child to "walk" across the room to another adult or to a favorite toy while someone supports his trunk.
6. Hold the child's shoulders. Rotate one shoulder forward, wait for a step, then rotate the opposite shoulder forward.

3. 54 ASSUMES HAND–KNEE POSITION (8-9 mo.)

Observe to see if the child can independently assume the hand-knee position with his abdomen off the floor.

1. Place the child over a firm pillow or blanket roll to accustom him to the hand-knee position. Support should be thick enough to allow the child's arms to fully extend. Let him watch a musical or moving toy.
2. Extend a towel from the child's hips to his chest to support him in a hand-knee position.
3. Place the child in prone. Pull the child's hips up so his knees will bend. The child's hands should be on the floor with his elbows as straight as possible. Hold the child at his hips to control his movements.
4. Place the child in the hand-knee position. Rock the child forward and back and from side to side.
5. Place the child in the hand-knee position. Encourage him to lift one hand for a toy and bear weight on the other hand. Repeat with the other hand. Provide support if he begins to lose his balance.
6. Encourage the child to hit a ball with one hand while in the hand-knee position.

3.55 DEMONSTRATES BALANCE REACTIONS IN SITTING (9-10 mo.)

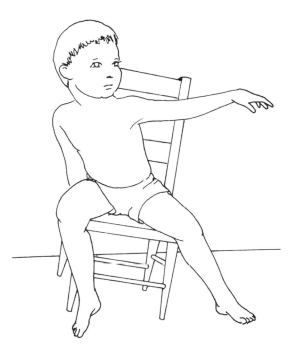

Place the child in sitting position on a surface which can be tilted. The child's head, trunk and extremities act to prevent a fall by moving in a direction opposite to the tilt.

1. Let the child sit in a hammock made of a towel. Swing the child side to side and forward and back.
2. Use a canvas swing which provides good trunk support.

3. Place the child in sitting on a ball or a firm bolster. Rock the child from side to side to encourage balancing. Hold the child at her trunk. As her balance improves, move to holding at her hips and finally give only minimal support at her legs.

4. Let the child sit on a rocking horse. Help her bounce up and down and rock forward and back.

5. Use a variety of swings: a swing with a back and sides, a swing without a back, a large swinging platform, a swinging bolster.

6. Place the child in sitting on Dad's back. Hold the child at her hips. Ask Dad to rock back and forth and from side to side.

7. Sit the child straddling a roll (or a small stool with no back). Encourage the child to reach across her body to pick up a small toy. Have her bring the toy back and place it in a can.

8. Let the child throw bean bags into a container in front of her. Use the straddle position in activity #7.

9. Let the child straddle an adult's leg. Let the child pick up a large block from the floor, move it to the other side, and build a tower.

10. Let the child sit on your knee, facing you. Support her at the trunk or hips, if necessary. Bounce her up and down to the rhythm of a song or nursery rhyme.

11. Sit the child on a waterbed. Tilt and rock the bed to require balancing reactions.

12. Place the child seated on a large ball, bolster or vestibular board which can be tilted from side to side and forward and back.

3.56 PROTECTIVE EXTENSION OF ARMS TO BACK (9-11 mo.)

Place the child in a sitting position. Push her suddenly backwards. The child should protect herself from a fall by catching her weight on one arm.

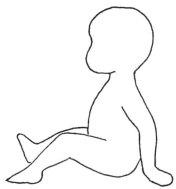

1. Let the child listen to music while sitting with both hands behind her. Encourage her to lean back on her hands. Rock the child from side to side in rhythm to the music so the child's weight shifts from one arm to the other.

2. If the child has difficulty with activity #1, place her hand behind her back flat on the floor. Help him bear weight on his arm by pushing down gently on his shoul-

ders. Repeat on the other side.

3. Tilt the child gently off balance backwards. Encourage the child to catch herself on one hand to prevent a fall. Hold the child by the opposite arm so a real fall will not occur. Make it a game: "Do not let me push you."

4. Place the child on a vestibular board. Tip the board quickly backwards. The child should place her hands behind her to protect herself from a "fall."

3.57 GOES FROM SITTING TO PRONE (9-10 mo.)

Place the child in a sitting position. Observe to see if the child can independently lower himself onto the floor into prone.

1. Assist the child from sitting to prone. Place the child's legs to one side. Gradually lower the child to a side-lying position. Encourage him to keep his hands on the floor.

2. Use a very soft surface at first, such as a bed or soft carpet, so the child will not injure himself if he moves too rapidly.

3. Play an adapted version of "Ring Around the Rosie . . . we all *lie* down." Incorporate one or two more children for this game.

4. Place toys just out of the child's reach so he must change his position into prone to move closer and obtain the toys.

3.58 LOWERS TO SITTING FROM FURNITURE (9-10 mo.)

Place the child in standing position by a piece of furniture. Remove your support and see if the child can independently lower herself safely into a sitting position. Compared to a fall, this is a slower, more controlled movement.

1. Assist the child from standing to sitting by lowering her in a squat position and then to sitting.

2. Assist the child from standing to sitting by placing one of her knees down, then the other knee. Help her sit back on her heels.

3. Let the child retrieve a toy on the floor when the activity is completed.

4. Arrange large pillows behind the child to sit back on when she is lowering herself without assistance. Remove the pillows gradually until the child can safely lower herself all the way to the floor.

3.59 CREEPS ON HANDS AND KNEES (9-11 mo.)

The child moves forward on hands and knees with his abdomen off the ground. The child uses a reciprocal pattern which is movement of opposite hands and knees: right hand, left knee, left hand, right knee.

1. Place the child in a hand-knee position. Rock the child from side to side to encourage him to shift his weight

from one arm to the other.

2. Offer a toy to one side so the child must lift his hand to obtain it. Repeat on the other side.

3. Encourage the child to move in this pattern: right hand, left knee, left hand, right knee.

4. Let the child retrieve a favorite toy placed nearby. Vary the distance of the toy depending on the child's ability.

5. Flick lightly under the child's fingers to encourage extension during creeping.

6. Wrap a towel around the child's waist to hold and support him as he creeps.

7. Use a creeper or craligator to support the child's abdomen. Teach the movement pattern described in activity #3.

8. Let the child creep through boxes fitted together like a maze or through a cloth "tunnel."

9. Use a sheet or blanket to make a tent over a small table or two chairs for the child to play under. Place some toys in the tent and encourage the child to creep in.

10. Make a ramp out of wood or use an ironing board propped up on a stool. Encourage the child to creep up the ramp to a toy. Turn the child around and let him creep down.

11. Help the child creep towards the television to help you turn it on for a favorite show.

12. Hold the child's ankles while he creeps. Provide a little resistance to make creeping more difficult which increases the child's strength.

13. If the child moves both legs together, gently hold one ankle to let him know he should move only one at a time. Switch ankles as he moves along.

14. For the older child who understands color matching, place a red ribbon on the right wrist and the left knee, a green ribbon on the left wrist and the right knee. Ask the child to move the matching colors in sequence, e.g., "red hand, red foot; green hand, green foot."

3.60 STANDS MOMENTARILY (9½-11 mo.)

Place the child in standing position. Hold the child from behind and gradually decrease your support until the child briefly stands alone.

1. Let the child stand with her back supported against a corner.
   a. Let her hold a large toy which requires two hands.
   b. Encourage her to dance to music.
   c. Give her a ball to throw for this moves her briefly away from the support of the wall.
   d. Hold her knees straight if she tries to sit.

2. Practice independent standing balance by holding the child from behind and briefly letting go. Continue talking to the child so she is sure you are there.

3. Place the child in standing at a low stool or coffee table. Ask her to imitate you as you lift your hands away briefly from the support.

4. Tie a cloth belt around the child's chest under the arms. Support the child in standing by holding the belt and as

balance gets better lessen the support.

5. Sit on the floor with one knee bent up. Place the child standing astride and partly supported by your raised thigh. Lower your thigh so the child is no longer supported and slowly withdraw hand support. Play a game such as "pat-a-cake" with the child.

3.61 WALKS HOLDING ON TO FURNITURE (9½-13 mo.)

The child is unsupported by an adult and takes a few steps holding the furniture for support.

1. Place the child in standing at furniture or at a playpen railing. Encourage him to take steps to the side by placing a toy slightly out of reach, Let the child play with the toy for a while, then move it slightly out of reach again.

2. Place two chairs next to each other. Encourage the child to walk from one chair to the other. Move the chairs further apart as the child becomes more competent.

3. Vary the places where the child can walk, such as holding onto a bookshelf, a window sill, or a small fence at a park.

4. Help the child walk toward a picture or busy box hanging on the wall while holding onto the wall for support.

3.62 EXTENDS HEAD, BACK, HIPS AND LEGS IN VENTRAL SUSPENSION (10-11 mo.)

The child's head, back, hips and legs are held extended when the child is held in mid-air around the trunk.

1. Refer to 3.27 (Extends head, back and hips when held in ventral suspension, Activities #1-3).

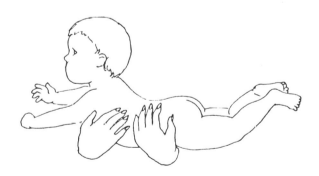

2. Suspend the child in the air by holding her around her trunk. Very rapidly lower and lift the child in an attempt to generate excitement which may elicit extension of head, back, hips and legs.

3. Let an adult lie on his back. Place the child in prone on the adult's legs. The adult holds the child's hands which are stretched out to the side. The adult lowers and raises his legs rapidly in an attempt to elicit extension of head, back hips and legs.

3.63 PIVOTS IN SITTING—TWISTS TO PICK UP OBJECTS (10-11 mo.)

The child can move in a circle in the sitting position.

1. Place the child in sitting. Give her objects to place in and out of a container. Place the container in front of her and the objects toward the back or side so she must twist to pick up the objects.
2. Place toys out of the child's reach so she must turn around a little for them. Gradually move the toys further away to the side so she must pivot completely to obtain them. Help her, if necessary.
3. Ask Mother or Father to sit behind the child and talk to her. Encourage her to turn around to see them. Praise her and play a fun game after she turns.

3.64 CREEPS ON HANDS AND FEET (10-12 mo.)

The child has both feet and both hands on the floor with arms and legs extended. The child "walks" forward in this position. This is also known as "plantigrade creeping" or "bear walking."

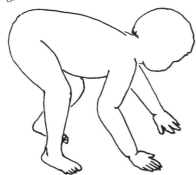

1. In this position let the child play a game of peeking under his legs at a sibling, Mom or Dad. Demonstrate for him and ask him to imitate.
2. Help the child make a "bridge" with his body by bending forward and placing his hands on the ground. Move a truck under the "bridge" or over the "bridge" along the child's arched body.
3. Place a toy directly in front or to one side of the child's arm when he is in the position illustrated. The child uses one hand to retrieve the toy and maintains his weight on three extremities.
4. Rock the child forward and back and from side to side in the illustrated position. This requires shifting the child's weight bearing from one foot and hand to the other foot and hand.
5. Place a toy where the child must move forward a few steps to retrieve it.

3.65 WALKS WITH BOTH HANDS HELD (10-12 mo.)

The child can walk forward three or four steps when an adult holds both of the child's hands.

1. Show the child how to walk while pushing a chair or a weighted box.
2. Help the child walk with a rollator or walker. The walker should not have a seat in it.
3. Let the child stand on an adult's feet and "walk," facing forward. The adult should hold both of the child's hands.
4. Let the child practice walking by holding the child's two hands at his own shoulder height (do not hold his hands over his head).
5. Let the child practice walking by holding the child's two hands down by his sides.
6. Let the child walk by pushing a doll carriage or a wagon with a secure handle.
7. Let the child walk by pushing an infant walker. The child should stand outside the walker rather than inside. If there is a seat, remove it.
8. Help the child walk with two sticks for support. One stick is held in each hand, out at the side. The child's arms are rotated out with thumbs up. The adult provides stability by holding the sticks and helping the child sequence the movements.
9. Reduce your support to only one hand and walk by the child's side as his balance improves.
10. Provide different motivations for the child to walk, such as pull toys on a string, especially those which make a noise, bells on the child's shoes or favorite toys on any assistive devices.
11. Push down on the child's shoulders or hips to increase the child's stability. Encourage the child to walk in this position without having his hands held.
12. Hold the child at his hips or shoulders. Rotate one shoulder or hip forward and shift the child's weight to one side to encourage walking.

3.66 STOOPS AND RECOVERS (10½-14 mo.)

The child bends down from a standing position and regains standing without need for support.

1. Let the child sit on a stool and bend forward for a toy or musical instrument.
2. Play a game of bowing with the child, e.g., bowing to greet family members, bowing after the child performs.
3. Encourage the child to bend down slightly from a standing position, to touch a tall toy such as a big stuffed animal or an inflatable toy.
4. Ask the child to stand. Place a small object six inches in front of his feet. Encourage the child to stoop into a squatting position to pick up the object. Do not let the child sit down on the floor to recover the object.
5. Play ball and ask the child to pick up the ball by bend-

ing over. Use a large ball at first so the child does not have to bend so far. Gradually reduce the size of the ball until the child must stoop quite far to retrieve it.

6. Ask the child to pick up a toy or object and bring it to you. The child may enjoy picking up a scrap of paper to throw in the wastebasket.

3.67 STANDS BY LIFTING ONE FOOT (11-12 mo.)

The child rises to a standing position by pulling himself to kneeling, lifting one foot, and finally standing up. The child will be holding onto something for support.

1. Place the child in a half-kneeling position (one knee on the floor, the opposite foot forward a few inches and flat on the floor). Rock the child forward and back in this position. Switch legs and repeat.

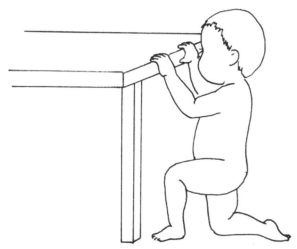

2. Place the child in sitting. Turn the child and tilt him to one side so both hands reach out to the floor. He can now move onto hands and knees. From hands and knees, he should pull to kneeling using a low table or chair. Help him place one foot forward so he can stand up with weight on that foot. Prepare a toy for him to play with once he is in standing.
3. Place the child in a half-kneeling position whenever he pulls up to standing at furniture. This helps him understand the separate use of his legs.
4. Encourage the child to stand up in a play pen or crib to play with a toy purposely attached to the top.
5. Encourage the child to pull up at a window sill to look at birds or plants outside.
6. Let the child reach for toys and books placed at "pull up" level on a shelf.

3.68 STANDS A FEW SECONDS (11-13 mo.)

Place the child in a standing position. Remove your support. The child should remain standing two to three seconds.

1. Let the child play in standing with a busy box. Position the busy box at the appropriate height.
2. Help the child stand by an aquarium and feed the fish.
3. Encourage the child to "dance" to music. Let him imitate you.
4. Place the child before a mirror which is far enough away that he cannot lean or hold on to it. Encourage him to look at himself. Praise his standing ability.
5. Count as the child stands so he can note the passage of time. Show him an egg timer or a toy version of one. He should stand until the sand reaches the bottom. (Be sure to begin with the sand almost at the bottom.)

3.69 ASSUMES AND MAINTAINS KNEELING (11-13 mo.)

Kneeling is a position in which full body weight is supported on the knees. (The child should not sit on her feet; her hips should be extended.) Observe to see if the child can move from a sitting to a kneeling position without using any support.

1. Place the child facing you with her hands on your shoulders. Provide support at the hips to help the child assume the kneeling position. Once in kneeling, give some downward pressure at the hips. Rock from side to side.
2. Help the child to practice kneeling by using the arm of a chair or sofa as support. The child may kneel at the arm and play with a toy or look at a book.
3. Place the child on her knees. Provide support by holding her shoulders and hips. Gradually let go and let her maintain the position by herself.
4. Place the child in knee sitting on the floor. Hold a toy just out of her reach above her head. Encourage her to lift up on her knees to reach for the toy.
5. Make the task of activity #4 more difficult by holding the toy or goody so high the child must reach up with her arm(s) for it.

3.70 WALKS WITH ONE HAND HELD (11-13 mo.)

The child walks five to six steps while an adult holds one hand.

1. Let the child push a small chair, stool, or doll carriage on a smooth surface.
2. Help the child walk with the use of sticks for support. He should hold one stick in each hand out to the sides and move them opposite to his feet, right, stick, left foot, left stick, right foot.
3. Let the child walk with you holding onto a towel or diaper tied around his waist for support. Gradually reduce your support as the child's balance improves.
4. Let the child walk holding one end of a ruler with an adult holding the other end.
5. Give the child objects to carry to family members while an adult holds her hand.

3.0 GROSS MOTOR

6. Encourage the child to walk as much as possible. Avoid the urge to carry him. Allow enough time so the child can walk to places such as from the car to the house or from a play area to a table.

3.71 STANDS ALONE WELL (11½-14 mo.)

Place the child in standing position and remove support. The child should remain standing at least ten seconds.

1. Place the child in a standing table for practice.
2. Let the child stand between parallel bars. Offer him a toy. The child momentarily stands without support as he reaches for the toy.
3. Encourage the child to stand at an easel to finger paint.
4. Plan some activities for the child to do in standing during music or storytelling time in a classroom group session.
5. For the older delayed child: Have him stand and throw balls or bean bags into a box or large pan.
6. Place the child in standing at a low table to do fine motor activities, such as scribbling with crayons.
7. Place the child in standing in a small hole at the beach. Support him by surrounding his legs with sand. Gradually brush the sand away and encourage him to stay up.

3.72 WALKS ALONE TWO TO THREE STEPS (11½-13½ mo.)

The child walks independently without support, using two to three unsteady steps.

1. It is unnecessary to buy special support shoes unless your doctor advises otherwise. The child's bare feet are his best support. Use soft soled shoes if he must be protected from the cold or from rough surfaces. The feet are more likely to develop strength if they can move freely.
2. Help the child walk with support provided at his shoulders so his hands are free.
   a. Place a strap around the child's chest so you can support him with the strap instead of his hands.
   b. Support the child below his shoulders. Gradually decrease your assistance.
   c. For the child with hypotonia, e.g., Down's Syndrome, help increase stability by providing some downward pressure on the shoulders.
3. Place the child between two chairs (or adults) and encourage two to three independent steps. Gradually increase the distance the child must walk.
4. Let the child hold onto the furniture. Encourage two or more steps to another piece of furniture to obtain a favorite toy or bottle.
5. Hold the child's hand when going to the car or table. Release his hand and encourage him to take the last two to three steps by himself.

3.73 DEMONSTRATES BALANCE REACTIONS IN KNEELING (12-15 mo.)

Place the child in kneeling position on a surface which can be tilted. (The child should not sit on his feet; his hips should be extended.) The child's head, trunk and extremities act to keep the body upright by moving in a direction opposite to the tilt.

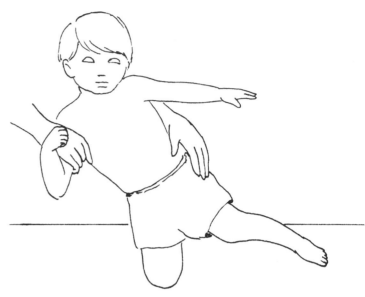

1. Place the child on the floor in kneeling. Rock the child from side to side to music.
2. Play games in kneeling which require weight transfer from one knee to the other, e.g., throwing a ball or bean bag into a container.
3. Use a rocking or vestibular board as a "boat." The child can pretend to be a fisherman kneeling on the boat. Talk about the "waves" as the "boat" tips.

3.74 FALLS BY SITTING (12-14 mo.)

Place the child in standing position. The child moves to the floor by letting go of her support and sitting down.

1. Show the child how to lower herself from standing. Help her release her hold on furniture or your hand and sit down. Help her gently through the motions going slowly at first to avoid a frightening experience.
2. Let the child walk with a strap around her chest. Help lower her to sitting by holding the strap.
3. Use a soft place for the child to practice sitting down such as on a mattress, on a waterbed, or on lots of pillows.
4. Laugh and clap as the child lands on the floor so she feels it is fun.
5. Model the activity for the child by holding on to a piece of furniture, releasing your hold, and falling down into a sitting position.
6. Laugh or say "uh oh" cheerfully as the child falls so she

may laugh too. If you look worried, she may cry. Comfort her if she cries, but do not react as if you expected her to cry.

3.75 STANDS FROM SUPINE BY TURNING ON ALL FOURS (12½-15 mo.)

The child should be able to assume a hands-feet position then rise to a standing position without support.

1. Let the child rise to standing by holding onto a stool. Help him come straight up into standing when he is standing with his hands on the stool, by pulling back on the shoulders.
2. Assist the child into standing by holding on to a towel or strap tied around his chest under his arms.
3. Place the child in the hand-knees position and help him push up into the hand-feet position. He then gradually rises to standing. Provide balance assistance as needed.
4. Encourage the child to stand and touch a mobile suspended in the middle of a room where there is no support for the child to hold onto.
5. Let the child stand up to touch a flower or leaf on a low branch of a tree.
6. Caution: The child's heels should remain flat on the floor or ground. Otherwise, hold them down at the ankles as he stands up.

3.76 WALKS BACKWARDS (12½-21 mo.)

The child independently walks in a backward direction for six feet without support.

1. Hold the child's hips from behind and help him walk backwards.
2. Walk backwards and have the child imitate you.
3. Place a chase game. Pretend to chase the child as he walks backwards.
4. Let the child walk backwards and pull a noisy toy. He can watch the toy move by walking backwards.
5. Refer to 3.79 (Walks without support). Perform these activities backwards.
6. Let the child walk on a strip of textured material, e.g., carpet, foam, plastic packing goods.
7. Walk backwards between two lines drawn on cement or in the sand and encourage the child to imitate you.
8. Place two ropes as boundaries on the grass. Let the child walk between the ropes.
9. Face the child and hold her hands. Move together forward and backward to music.
10. Place the child's feet on yours and walk backwards.
11. Let the child "help" you move a heavy object (table, large box). She should walk backwards "pulling" the object while you push forward on the other side.

3.77 THROWS BALL UNDERHAND IN SITTING (13-16 mo.)

The child throws the ball forward by positioning the arm down at his side with the palm of the hand up.

1. Let the child roll balls of varying sizes. Start with a large ball he rolls with both hands. Decrease the size of the balls until the child rolls a ball small enough to hold in one hand.
2. Use rolled up socks, bean bags, crumpled paper balls, yarn balls or balloons as variations in activity #1.
3. Vary the child's sitting positions as he throws the ball: on the floor in tailor (crossed legs) position, with legs to the side and with legs straight out in front, on a low stool, in a child size chair.
4. Let the child throw a ball to an adult using an underhand throw. First model the throw, then move the child's arm through the proper movements.
5. For the older delayed child with imitation skills: Let him imitate your actions with a ball. Sit facing each other. Move the ball under your knees, behind your back, and overhead. Use the underhand throw when appropriate. Then allow the child to start and you imitate him.
6. Let the child throw a ball into containers using an underhand throw. Start with a large container. Gradually decrease the size of the container to make it harder. The child should remain close to the container to insure success.
7. Increase the difficulty of the above tasks by moving the child further away from the container.
8. Be sure the child tries each activity with both left and right hands.
9. Repeat the activities #1 to #7 in standing.
10. Let the child roll a ball and knock down lightweight objects, such as milk cartons, empty plastic bottles or the cardboard centers from paper rolls.
11. Let the child throw balls under a low table or stool and through a hula loop or large barrel.
12. Vary the types of balls to provide interest. Use rubber, plastic, vinyl, sponge, cloth, tennis, tactile or contoured balls.

3.78 CREEPS OR HITCHES UPSTAIRS (13½-15 mo.)

Creeping means moving on hands and knees (some children may use hands and feet). Hitching means moving while in a sitting position.

1. Let the child practice creeping up inclines.
2. Let the child creep up a low curb or a very small step.
3. Place a "goody" on the second step. Help the child move through proper creeping movements as he moves up the steps. (Right hand, left knee, left hand, right knee).
4. Teach the child to come down the steps feet first while still on his hands and knees.
5. Make a lot set of stairs using small stools or cardboard

3.0 GROSS MOTOR

93

boxes for the child to practice on.
6. Make steps using large pillows if the child has a tendency to call off balance.
7. Show the child how to go upstairs sitting backwards (hitching).
8. Caution: The child may try this task frequently as he gains confidence. Use a gate to guard the stairs so the child practices only when supervised.

3.79 WALKS WITHOUT SUPPORT (13-15 mo.)

The child walks most of the time for long distances and seldom falls down. No support is necessary. (Some children quite normally start to walk as early as nine months or as late as eighteen months.)

A. The child walks short distances, but creeping is still the primary method of locomotion. The typical walking pattern begins with the feet turned out and spread wide apart. The child's arms are held out to the sides for balance. The child lacks stability and walks stiffly with a side to side tipping motion.
   1. Let the child pull toys which makes noises, e.g., quacking ducks on a string.
   2. Provide push toys with long handles, such as toy lawnmowers or corn poppers.
   3. Refer to 2.32 (Unable to talk while walking).
B. Walking becomes the primary method of locomotion.
   1. Let the child walk in bare feet on different textures, such as grass, gravel, sand, concrete, carpet, linoleum, uneven ground.
   2. Ask the child to do little errands for you, such as bringing a diaper or throwing away a piece of paper.
   3. Help the child walk up and down inclines, such as a hill, a wide board placed on a low stool, a sand dune.

3.80 WALKS SIDEWAYS (14-15 mo.)

The child moves sideways without support; the feet are not expected to cross over.

1. Let the child hold onto furniture. Show her how to move sideways to get a toy. Her feet should not cross over.
2. Place the child's feet on your feet. Hold her hands and move sideways to the right and to the left. Use music or rhythm.
3. Stand facing the child and hold both of her hands. Tell her to follow what you do. Step to the side moving to the left and to the right.
4. Make a corridor so narrow the child can only fit by walking sideways.
5. Place a long carpet strip on the floor on which the child walks sideways. Show the child how sliding the feet sideways at the beach makes a track in the sand.
6. Hold the child at the hips or the shoulders. Move her to one side and her feet will follow. Move slowly, be sure her feet do not cross over. Move in both directions.

7. Increase the difficulty of activities #1 to #7 by teaching the child to cross the feet when walking sideways. Hold the child's hands and show her how to move one foot in front of the other. Move with the child in both directions.
8. Teach the child to place one foot behind the other and move sidewards to the left and right.
9. Form a circle with several children and move sideways to music or play "Ring around the Rosie."

3.81 RUNS—HURRIED WALK (14-18 mo.)

The child is technically walking rapidly, one foot is on the ground at all times. The body is held stiffly upright and the eyes are fixed on the ground.

1. Hold the child's hands and help him "run" or walk fast.
2. Play a game of chasing the child or having him chase you.
3. Find a slight incline for the child to walk down; a slope will encourage running.
4. Let the child chase a wind-up toy.
5. Let the child throw a ball then run after it.
6. Encourage the child to chase the birds at the zoo.
7. Caution: Do not encourage running if the rapid movements tend to cause exaggeration of abnormal movement patterns. Consult with a physical therapist.

3.82 BENDS OVER AND LOOKS THROUGH LEGS (14½-15½ mo.)

The child's knees are slightly bent as she looks backwards between the legs.

1. Refer to 3.64 (Creeps on hands and feet).
2. Place a low box or stool in front of the child for her to put her hands on. This makes it easier for a child having difficulty getting her hands all the way to the floor.
3. Shift the child's weight forward and back and from side to side while in this position.
4. Make a new version of "Peek-a-Boo." Turn your back to

the child. Slowly bend over and look at her through your legs. Say, "I see you" or make some exclamation of surprise. The child may want to imitate you.

5. Assist the child with her balance, if necessary. Tell her everything is upside down as she looks and enjoys the experience of this position.

6. Encourage two children to play this game and look at each other between their legs.

7. Let the child see how she looks by positioning herself in front of a mirror.

8. End the game by helping the child do a somersault or forward roll.

3.83 DEMONSTRATES BALANCE REACTIONS IN STANDING (15-18 mo.)

Place the child in standing position on a surface which can be tilted. The child's head, trunk and extremities act to prevent a fall by moving in a direction opposite to the tilt.

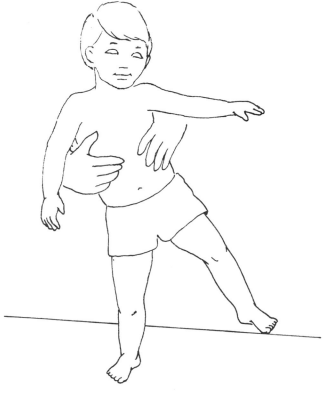

1. Place the child in standing and gently rock her from side to side so she shifts her weight onto each leg. Do this to music for fun and rhythm.

2. Stand the child on a vestibular board which rocks from side to side. The child can pretend to be surfing as you slowly move the board.

3. Help the child stand on Dad's back with Mother nearby for safety. Ask Dad to rock from side to side.

4. Place the child in standing on a waterbed. Her movements alone will require balancing reactions.

3.84 WALKS INTO LARGE BALL WHILE TRYING TO KICK IT (15-18 mo.)

The child kicks a ball by walking toward the ball and moving it forward by bumping his leg or body into it.

1. Seat the child so his feet cannot touch the floor and can swing freely. Demonstrate kicking a large ball from a sitting position. Encourage the child to kick the ball. Move his legs for him if necessary. Gradually decrease the size of the ball.

2. Put light weights on the child's ankles when kicking in sitting.

3. Ask the child to kick the ball into a box or at milk carton "bowling pins" in sitting.

4. Let the child use a large beach ball in standing. Encourage the child to move the ball forward by walking up to it and hitting it with his body.

5. Help the child kick a large ball with one foot. Help the child balance on one foot and swing the other foot.

6. Be sure the child practices with alternate feet in all activities.

3.85 THROWS BALL FORWARD (15-18 mo.)

The child is in standing position and throws the ball in any manner, underhand or overhand.

1. Refer to 3.77 (Throws ball underhand in sitting) for preliminary activities and a variety of ideas for targets to aim at.

2. Let the child throw the ball in supported standing. An adult holds the child under the arms, at the trunk, or hips and encourages the child to throw the ball.

3. Decrease assistance by providing a table the child may hold with one hand. The child may stand with his back supported by a wall or a piece of furniture.

4. Increase the difficulty of the task by asking the child to throw toward the sides instead of forward.

3.86 WALKS WITH ASSISTANCE ON EIGHT INCH BOARD (15-17 mo.)

The child walks at least three feet on an eight-inch wide plank raised one to two inches from the floor with someone holding her hand.

1. Add textures to the walking board for interest. The child feels them with his bare feet. Add noises the child can activate as he walks along the board.

2. Let the child walk with one foot on the board and one foot off the board.

3. Assist the child to walk with both feet on the board and with both hands held. Gradually reduce assistance holding only one hand.

4. Place the board within a set of parallel bars so the child may hold onto the bars.

5. Show the child how to walk on the board using two long sticks as supports.
6. Ask the child to walk sideways with both hands held by an adult. The feet should slide and meet but should not cross.
7. Use a strap around the child's waist to assist and support the child. This leaves the child's hands free for balancing.
8. Place a toy or "goody" at the end of the board as an incentive to walk.
9. Place the board in front of a mirror so the child can see what she is doing.
10. Place cut out foot prints along the board as a guide for the child. Do not expect the child to keep his feet exactly on the prints.

3.87 PULLS TOY BEHIND WHILE WALKING (15-18 mo.)

The child walks independently and holds the string of a pull toy. Children learn to push before they learn to pull.

1. Begin with pushing activities, such as pushing a toy lawnmower, a popper or the child's own stroller.
2. Give the child the string attached to a toy. Encourage him to pull the toy as he walks. A noisy toy is helpful so he can hear it even if he cannot see it.
3. Make a pull toy by tying several shoe boxes together. Place objects in the boxes to make noise as the child pulls the toy.
4. Let the child walk on a wide walking board and pull a toy along side the board.
5. Let the child pull the toy on a walk up an incline, through a narrow space or around a line in a circle.
6. Provide commercial pull toys, such as trunks, animals, trains, wagons, cars.
7. Place the child in a small wagon or on a "sit on" pull toy and take him for a ride.
8. Let the child place a favorite doll or stuffed animal on a pull toy and take it for a ride.
9. If the child has difficulty with grasp, attach a large bead, peg or ring at the end of the string of the pull toy. Another variation is to make a loop "handle" at the end of the string.

3.88 THROWS BALL OVERHAND LANDING WITHIN THREE FEET OF TARGET (16-22 mo.)

The child is in standing position and throws by bringing his hand up beside his head. The ball should travel for a distance of three feet and land within three feet of the target.

1. Let the child throw bean bags into a box in sitting. Teach him to throw overhand by passively taking him through the movement.
2. Vary the objects thrown overhand: crumpled paper balls, round sponges, small balls. (Do not let the child throw inappropriate toys, such as blocks or items with other functions.)

3. Let the child throw a ball underhand first to accustom himself to throwing in standing.
4. Help the child practice an overhand throw in standing by playing different types of ball games. Roll the ball to him when returning it.
5. Provide interesting targets, such as plastic bowling pins, milk cartons, pillows, large boxes, containers of various types, a colorful wall picture, an inflatable toy which rebounds after being hit. Let the child throw from close range to be successful, then gradually move the targets further away.
6. Let the child throw small shells or pebbles into the water and enjoy the splash and ripples.
7. Let the child enjoy a pillow fight on your bed with small throw pillows.
8. Let the child throw plastic balls into a wading pool or a big water-filled tub outdoors.
9. Caution: For the child with tightness in the shoulders and arms, try to reduce the tightness by rotating the upper trunk and shoulders before attempting the above activities. Consult with a physical or occupational therapist.

3.89 STANDS ON ONE FOOT WITH HELP (16-17 mo.)

The child can lift up one foot and balance on the other when supported.

1. If the child has involvement of the legs, the adult may have to carefully control the leg which is supporting the body weight. The heel should be flat on the floor and the knee slightly bent. Provide assistance by holding up the non-weight bearing leg.
2. Assist the child in stepping over low obstacles, such as four yardsticks placed in a line or between the rungs of a ladder placed on the floor.
3. Let the child hold your shoulder as she attempts to place her feet into her pants.
4. Place the child in standing at a table to look at a book or while doing fine motor or art activities. Let the child place one foot on a low stool. This shifts most of her weight to the opposite side of her body. Repeat with the other foot. Be sure the child is not leaning forward but is bearing weight on the extended leg.
5. Position yourself behind the child and hold the child's leg up for her with one hand. Support her with your other hand so she can experience the position. Rock to music in this manner. Repeat on the opposite leg.
6. Reduce gradually the amount of help you give the child. Slowly release her hand and hold only her leg up.
7. Hold the child's hand, but release your hold on her leg. Do this activity by standing with her and asking her to imitate your action.
8. Perform in front of a mirror so the child can observe the activity.
9. Place the child in standing on one foot. Rock the child from side to side to music with decreasing support.
   a. Provide support at the trunk.

b. Decrease support by holding only the hips. Place the child's hands on your shoulders.

c. Hold the child's two hands.

d. Stand and hold only one hand.

3.90 WALKS UPSTAIRS WITH ONE HAND HELD (17-19 mo.)

The child walks upstairs by placing one foot up and then moving the other foot up onto the same step.

1. Hold both of the child's hands and help her step up onto a small curb.

2. Use low child-size stairs rather than standard stairs. If none are available, a set can be made using graduated stools or sturdy cardboard boxes. The child should begin learning to walk upstairs with these to make it easier.

3. Discourage the child from using alternating feet for this is a more advanced skill.

4. Let the child hold a wall or railing with one hand while you hold the child's other hand. The child should be encouraged to gradually hold only the adult's hand.

5. Include stairs as part of an obstacle course for fun with a small group of children.

6. Use stairs or small stools around the house or classroom, sinks, toilets, or high counters.

3.91 CARRIES LARGE TOY WHILE WALKING (17-18½ mo.)

The child carries a large object with one or both hands without assistance.

1. Give the child a small toy or object to carry in one hand until he balances well enough to walk without using both arms out at his sides.

2. Let the child carry a large toy. It should not obstruct his view.

3. Let the child carry his teddy bear and put it to bed.

4. Ask the child to take a large ball outside.

5. Suggest that the child take a pillow to Daddy for his head.

6. Encourage him to help Mommy empty the trash by carrying a small wastebasket.

7. Let the child help with the groceries by taking large lightweight items from the bag to an adult waiting at the cupboard.

8. Let the child help clear the table of unbreakable items and take them to the appropriate place in the kitchen.

3.92 PUSHES AND PULLS LARGE TOYS OR BOXES AROUND THE FLOOR (17-18½ mo.)

The child performs this activity independently without assistance.

1. Let the child push: a chair, a stool, a toy chest, a large inflated toy, or a large wastebasket.

2. Show the child how to push a large cardboard box around the room. Make the activity purposeful, such as collecting and placing in the box colored plastic eggs hidden around the room at Easter time.

3. Let the child place a stuffed animal or doll in a box and take it for a ride.

4. Increase the difficulty to push or pull by placing in the box a heavy object, such as wooden blocks, toys, a 5 lb. bag of sugar or flour.

5. Show the child how to push a sturdy box, stool or chair to a toy shelf and climb onto the box to retrieve an out-of-reach toy.

6. Show the child how to pull the box by holding the edge and walking in front of it. Encourage him to switch hands by switching sides.

7. Make a hole in the box to use as a handle or pass a rope through small holes to give the child a handle to pull.

3.93 WALKS INDEPENDENTLY ON EIGHT INCH BOARD (17½-19½ mo.)

The board is eight inches wide, six feet long, and one to two inches off the floor. The child walks the entire length without assistance.

1. Place the walking board in front of a mirror so the child sees herself as she moves forward.

2. Place a goody the child can eat or a favorite toy, such as a Tyke Bike the child can ride at the end of the board.

3. Include the walking board as part of an obstacle course with tunnels, slides, stairs.

4. Raise the walking board six inches off the ground by placing it on two low stools.

5. Elevate one end of the board to create an incline.

6. Place bean bags or small toys at intervals for the child to step over.

7. Place a special treat in the middle of the board such as food, a whistle, a balloon, so the child must reach down to retrieve it and then recover to continue to the end.

8. Let the child carry a large ball or stuffed toy when walking on the board.

9. Let the child hold a wand with blunt or rounded edges in both hands when walking on the board.

10. Offer a bag or purse filled with heavy objects to carry to the end of the board.

11. Let the child walk sideways on the board using a sliding step; later crossing one foot over the other.

12. Help the child walk backwards with support, later without assistance.

13. Find a sidewalk curb in a safe area with little traffic and supervise as the child walks on it.

3.0 GROSS MOTOR

3.94 TRIES TO STAND ON TWO INCH BALANCE BEAM (17½-18½ mo.)

The board is two inches wide, six to eight feet long, well supported on each end and three to four inches off the ground. Demonstrate standing on the balance beam. Ask the child to try. He should step up on it with only one foot, without holding onto any support.

1. Let the child explore the two-inch balance board placed in his play environment.
2. Let the child watch you stand on the board. He may imitate you.
3. Help the child stand on the board. Hold his hands and play a game in which he steps up on one side and down the other.
4. Place the board near a wall or railing to provide the initial support the child may need.

3.95 BACKS INTO SMALL CHAIR OR SLIDES SIDEWAYS (17½-19 mo.)

Use a small child size chair. The child approaches the chair from the front or the side and sits on it without assistance.

1. Let the child explore the chair. The child may climb forward on it, then turn around and sit down.
2. Help the child seat herself on a low bench.
3. Place the chair against a wall when the child is first learning to seat herself. This will prevent the chair from tipping over backwards.
4. Place a child size chair at an angle by a table and place a small footstool in front of the chair. Let the child hold onto the table. Show her how to place one foot on the stool, then push back onto the chair.
5. Let the child stand, without a stool with her back at the side of the chair. Help her place one hand on the table and one on the seat of the chair. After she sits down on the chair, she pushes herself around to face forward.
6. Let the child practice seating himself whenever he uses his chair to eat or play. Try not to hurry and lift him into the chair. Let him seat himself independently.

3.96 KICKS BALL FORWARD (18-24½ mo.)

The child in standing position kicks a ball with one foot without assistance.

1. If standing is difficult, kicking the ball may be taught in sitting.
2. Help the child kick a large ball.
3. Let the child imitate you kicking a large ball.
4. Let the child kick smaller balls. Decrease the size of the balls, gradually progressing down to the size of a tennis ball.
5. Draw a line on the cement outside or place tape down on the floor inside. Let the child stand two feet away and kick the ball over the line. Gradually move the child farther back.

6. Show the child how to kick into a large box. Gradually use smaller boxes.
7. Arrange for the child to play kickball with an adult or another child.
8. Be sure the child practices kicking with alternate feet.
9. Put light weights on the child's ankles when kicking.
10. Let the child kick a heavy ball, using the above games.
11. Suspend a large ball from the ceiling two to three inches above the ground. Let the child kick the ball.
12. Help the child kick over empty milk cartons. Place noisy or heavy objects inside the milk cartons for variety.
13. Hang a sheet or blanket up. Let the child kick the ball so it rolls under and behind the sheet.
14. Encourage the child to kick a ball through a short, wide tunnel or under a low bench.

3.97 THROWS BALL INTO A BOX (18-20 mo.)

The child in standing position throws a ball into a box placed one foot away.

1. Refer to 3.85 (Throws ball forward) if the child needs assistance in standing.
2. Let the child throw a variety of balls, balls of different sizes or textures, balls which squeak or contain bells.
3. Let the child throw other appropriate objects such as bean bags, crumpled paper, or balloons.
4. Vary the containers the ball is thrown into, e.g., a wastepaper basket, a dishpan, a large cooking pot, a laundry basket.
5. Adapt holiday activities, toss plastic eggs into an Easter basket, toss non-breakable Christmas ornaments into a large stocking.
6. Make the task more difficult by gradually increasing the distance between the child and the box.
7. Increase the difficulty of the task by placing the box to the side of the child rather than directly in front of him. Let the child throw the ball from both sides.

3.98 MOVES ON "RIDE ON" TOYS WITHOUT PEDALS (18-24 mo.)

The child can propel a wheeled vehicle forward without assistance.

1. Use a toy, such as a Tyke Bike, coaster wagon or any toy with wheels, which the child can sit on and move by pushing with his feet.
2. Show the child how to kick both legs to push himself backward.
3. Show the child how to pull with both legs to go forward.
4. Show the child how to move forward by moving one leg at a time. This is a pre-skill for a tricycle.
5. Increase the child's leg strength by adding resistance. Strap weights to the toy, let another child ride if there is room, move through carpet, grass or sand, or hold the toy back a little as the child moves.
6. If the child lacks balance in sitting, this activity can be

good for the legs. A back extension can be built on the seat and a safety belt added.

3.99 RUNS FAIRLY WELL (18-24 mo.)

Running is an activity in which neither foot is touching the ground during one phase of the movement. The child is well balanced, his arms and legs alternate smoothly.

1. Hold the child's hand and help him move in a fast walk. Play a game chasing a pet dog or sibling.
2. Play a chase game challenging the child to catch you (let him succeed). Then you try to catch the child.
3. Let the child run down a slight incline or hill to help increase speed.
4. Let the child chase a wind-up toy car.
5. Plan races with two or three children and provide a treat for each child, such as a special toy or a food treat.
6. Designate two spots at opposite ends of a room for the child to run to and touch. The child starts at one spot, runs to touch the other spot, such as a picture on the wall and returns to the starting place. This pattern may be hard to learn. Do not criticize the child if he does not complete the activity.
7. Let the child run on different surfaces in bare feet such as grass, cement, carpet, title.
8. Let the child run in sand. Show him what fun it is to look back and see the footprints left behind. Start on firm wet sand and move to the more difficult soft, dry sand.

3.100 CLIMBS FORWARD ON ADULT CHAIR, TURNS AROUND AND SITS (18-21 mo.)

The child accomplishes this activity without assistance.

1. Let the child use a stool to help her climb onto an upholstered armchair. Place a favorite toy on the chair as an incentive. Assist her as much as necessary at first.
2. Decrease your help gradually and let the child climb onto the chair by herself.
3. Help the child climb onto a straight chair without arms as her climbing and balance skills improve.
4. Encourage the child to climb up and sit on the chair to read a book, look out the window, or listen to a record.

3.101 WALKS DOWNSTAIRS WITH ONE HAND HELD (19-21 mo.)

The child walks downstairs by placing one foot down and then moving the other foot onto the same step. (Alternating feet is a more advanced skill.)

1. Hold both of the child's hands and help her step down a small curb. Progress to holding only one hand.
2. Choose low stairs when beginning to help the child go down a series of steps. If no stairs are available, a set can be made with graduated stools or cardboard boxes.
3. Discourage the child from using alternating feet. Let the child place two feet on a step.
4. Walk down the stairs in front of the child facing him. Hold both of his hands. As he gains confidence move to the side and let the child hold the wall or railing with one hand while you hold his other hand.
5. Encourage the child to gradually hold only your hand. Go slowly enough so he has time to balance as he moves.
6. Include stairs as part of an obstacle course for fun.
7. Adapt the bathroom sink to the child's height by placing a small set of stairs in front of it.

3.102 PICKS UP TOY FROM FLOOR WITHOUT FALLING (19-24 mo.)

The child can squat down or bend over and pick up a toy and maintain sufficient balance to stand up again.

1. Note: Child with tight heelcords may need help keeping the heels flat on the floor during this activity.
2. Let the child be a "jack-in-the-box." The child stoops down to be small and then pops up quickly and "grows" tall.
3. Place a small toy which the child likes on the floor. Walk to it and show her how to pick up the toy by squatting down for it. It is important to keep the back straight.
4. Help the child squat down to the floor to pick up a toy. She may need help in bending her knees and in balancing as she squats down.
5. Play a game by setting blocks around the room. Let the child pick up the blocks and place them in a wagon she pulls behind.
6. Ask the child to pick leaves off the lawn. Let her carry a small bag to place the leaves in.

3.103 SQUATS IN PLAY (20-21 mo.)

The child has sufficient balance to play on the floor for several minutes in a squatting position.

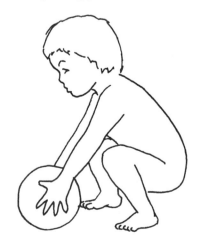

1. Place the child on an adult's lap. The child should be in the squat position with feet flat, hips and knees bent. Let the child hold onto the adult's arms. The adult can sing songs and recite nursery rhymes in this face to face position.
2. Place the child in a squat position with her feet flat on the floor, her hips and knees bent and her back straight. Support her by holding both knees and resting her back against your legs. In this position, rock her from side to side and forward and back.
3. Decrease your support gradually so the child must balance independently. Engage her interest in her toys or books placed on the floor in front of her as she balances.
4. Play a game "Up up up—Down down down." Help the child stand up and reach high with her arms, then go down to a squatting position.
5. Note: This is a good exercise for heel cord stretching, if necessary. Place the child in squat position. Help her rock forward, keeping her heels flat. When she is balanced and relaxed in the squat position, help the child stand up. Use your hands to place pressure on the knees to straighten them. The child's head and trunk should remain bent forward.

3.104 STANDS FROM SUPINE BY ROLLING TO SIDE (20-22 mo.)

The child is in supine position. The child rolls to the side and sits up, using the hands for support. The child then stands up without assistance or holding onto a support.

1. Refer to 3.44 (Gets to sitting without assistance, Activity #1).
2. Refer to 3.75 (Stands from supine by turning on all fours, Activities #1-6).
3. Play games requiring the child to move from supine to standing. Help her move correctly when necessary.
   a. The child pretends she is sleeping then must get up to: shut the window, close the door, let out the cat, get a drink of water.
   b. The child, while in supine picks up objects from the floor, e.g., cars, blocks, animals, and stands up to put them into a "garage," container or "house."

3.105 WALKS A FEW STEPS WITH ONE FOOT ON TWO INCH BALANCE BEAM (20½-21½ mo.)

The child walks with one foot on the balance beam. The other foot is on the floor. The child receives no assistance.

1. Help the child walk on a curb with one foot and the other foot off.
2. Show the child how to walk with one foot on the grass and the other foot on the sidewalk.
3. Show the child how to walk on the balance beam with one foot on and the other foot off the beam. Encourage him to imitate you.
4. Assist the child by holding one hand.

5. Use a balance beam as part of an obstacle course.

3.106 WALKS UPSTAIRS HOLDING RAIL—BOTH FEET ON STEP (22-24 mo.)

The child's feet do not yet alternate. The child receives no adult assistance.

1. Start with low steps and a railing the child's height, if possible. Place a toy on the second or third step for the child to retrieve. If the stars are narrow enough the child may first hold onto both rails.
2. Encourage the child to walk up the stairs face forward with one hand on one rail, rather than sideways with both hands on one rail. Let him carry an object in one hand, such as a small bucket, to prevent his using that hand for support.
3. Use stairs as part of an obstacle course for fun.
4. Place pictures on the stairs for the child to step on. Discuss the picture "steps" with the child. Be sure the pictures are securely fastened with no loose edges.
5. Paint the stairs different colors for discussion.
6. Let the child climb the stairs to a sliding board. The slide is the incentive for the climbing activity.
7. Make modified stairs to assist the child up and down a sink or toilet.
8. Stand behind the child when he is climbing up long flights of stairs to protect him from a fall.
9. Encourage the hesitant child to step up to the next stair by placing a small squeak toy he can retrieve as an incentive.

3.107 JUMPS IN PLACE BOTH FEET (22-30 mo.)

The child jumps up with both feet lifting off the ground at the same time.

1. Play bouncing games to music in which the child must bend and straighten her knees. This leads to the jumping movement.
2. Help the child jump by lifting her up in the air with your hands under her arms or around her chest.
3. Jump and encourage the child to imitate.
4. Use an old mattress, a child size trampoline or inner tube for bouncing and jumping games.
5. Let the child jump and hit an object suspended from the ceiling, such as a balloon, a vinyl beach ball or a dangling toy.
6. Let the child jump into a circle, e.g., a hula hoop or a circle made of masking tape.
7. Hold hands with the child and jump, singing "Here Comes Peter Cottontail." Pretend you are bunnies.
8. Let the child place his feet on yours as you jump.
9. Let the child jump to you from a high place. She will tend to fall forward first.
10. Pretend you and the child are kangaroos. Hold hands and jump around the room.
11. Jump off very low objects, such as a walking board. The

child will step off at first. Encourage her to use both feet while you hold her hands.

12. Caution: Do not encourage jumping if the activity causes exaggeration of abnormal movement patterns. Consult with a physical therapist.

3.108 GOES UP AND DOWN SLIDE (23-26 mo.)

The child climbs a ladder and goes down the slide independently.

1. Let the child practice climbing using a rail on both sides.
2. Use a small indoor-type ladder and slide. Help the child place her feet on the ladder rungs. Encourage her to hold onto the sides. The child may require special assistance to move her from standing to sitting at the top of the slide.
3. Begin with a ladder having flat steps before introducing the round rung type of ladder.
4. Include a slide in an obstacle course. Let other children participate as models.
5. Let the child explore the slide at her own pace and watch others at first. Do not force her to slide down if she is frightened.
6. Help the child slide down, going slowly at first. If she clings too tightly to the sides, hold her hands as you slide down with her. Reassure her that you will catch her at the bottom if she is willing to slide down independently.
7. Vary the activity by letting the child slide down on her abdomen with her arms over her head, by crawling up the slide to the top, or by going backwards down the ladder from top to bottom.
8. Encourage the parents to allow the child to climb a ladder at home with close supervision.

3.109 STANDS ON TIPTOES (23-25½ mo.)

The child comes up on her toes either spontaneously or on request.

1. Caution: This activity should be discouraged for the cerebral palsied child with extensor spasticity in the legs.
2. Place the child in prone on a large therapy ball. Lower her legs so just her toes touch the floor. Bounce her repeatedly on her toes. Do not let her heels touch the floor.
3. Let the child stand on tip toes to retrieve an object slightly out of reach, such as a towel on a towel rack.
4. Let the child reach for snack foods on a kitchen countertop.
5. Hang an attractive object just out of the child's reach. Encourage her to reach for it holding a wall for support as she rises on tip-toes.
6. Tape an object or a picture to the wall. The child must stand on tip-toe to touch it.
7. Suspend a balloon from the ceiling at such a height the child must tiptoe to hit it.

3.110 WALKS WITH LEGS CLOSER TOGETHER (23-25 mo.)

The child previously walked with legs apart (abducted). The child can now balance better so he can bring his legs closer together (adducted) for a smoother gait.

1. Place strips of masking tape fifteen inches apart on the floor. Ask the child to walk between the strips to remove a toy at the other end. Gradually make the walkway smaller by placing the strips closer together.
2. Use a plank of wood about twelve inches wide and one inch thick for the child to walk on. Wood can be covered with different textured materials, such as corduroy, sandpaper, terrycloth, velvet, sponge, nylon netting. Make the task interesting by placing squeakers under the material.
3. Draw lines with chalk on a sidewalk and let the child walk between the lines.
4. Create a narrow corridor with cardboard boxes and let the child walk through.
5. Note: Hypotonic children with widely abducted legs have sometimes been helped by sleeping in pajamas with the inside seams of the pant legs sewn together.
6. Attach strip of material about ten inches long between the pant legs for a short time while the child is walking. When this is tolerated it can gradually be shortened until it is about two to three inches.

3.111 CATCHES LARGE BALL (24-26 mo.)

The child in standing position catches a ball at least twelve inches in diameter.

1. Place the child in standing and blow bubbles toward her. Let her pop the bubbles or catch them on a bubble blower of her own.
2. Place the child in sitting either on the floor or in a small chair where she does not have to work for balance. Throw a large balloon for her to catch.
3. Ask another adult to help move the child's hands to catch the balloon providing the experience of success. It may help to also remind her to keep watching the balloon as it approaches.
4. Place the child in standing to catch the balloon after she is successful in sitting.
5. Use a large ball and repeat activities #2, 3, and 4.
6. Refer to 3.77 (Throws ball underhand in sitting, Activities #1-11) for ideas on throwing activities which can be followed by playing catch.
7. Throw the ball off to one side to require more balancing from the child. Do this activity after the child can catch the ball thrown directly to her.

3.112 RIDES TRICYCLE (24-30 mo.)

The child moves forward on a tricycle sometimes using the pedals, sometimes with his feet on the ground. The child pushes the tricycle with his feet on the ground to turn corners.

3.0 GROSS MOTOR

1. Help the child practice alternate bending and straightening of the legs while lying on his back. Move his legs for him and then ask the child to move. Sing a rhythmical bicycling type song, such as "Daisy Daisy."
2. Use a Tyke Bike without pedals. Encourage the child to push with one foot then the other.
3. Allow the child to sit on a tricycle and first push with his feet on the ground. Hold his feet on the pedals and show him how to pedal the tricycle forward.
4. Strap his feet to the pedals. Help the child move one foot at a time by pushing one knee then the other.
5. Add a wooden extension to the pedal, if the child cannot reach the pedals. Include a strap if the child needs help keeping feet on the pedal.
6. Encourage the child to climb onto the tricycle by himself while you supervise. He may get on either from the back or the side, holding the handlebars and lifting first one foot on, then the other foot. If the child climbs on from the back, he stands on the back rim before getting onto the seat.
7. If sitting balance is not fully established, tricycle riding can be a useful skill because of the mobility it allows. Seat extensions for back support can be purchased or made. A seat belt can be added for safety.

3.113 IMITATES SIMPLE BILATERAL MOVEMENTS OF LIMBS, HEAD AND TRUNK (24-36 mo.)

The child should be able to imitate the movements she sees another make: up and down, front to back, and sideways. The arms should be able to cross in front of the body.

1. Demonstrate a movement the child should imitate. Let the child face you. Move the child's body or extremities if she does not imitate.
2. Use movements from the following games:
    a. Simple Simon says, "Bring your head down, bring your head up."
    b. "Windmill." Make circles with both arms.
    c. "Touch Toes." Lift arms high above head, bend over and touch toes.
    d. "Tree." Lift arms above head, bend trunk to one side then the other, as if waving in the breeze.
    e. "Bicycle." In supine, move legs up and down.
    f. "Open/Close." In supine, keep legs flat down on the floor, extend each leg toward the side to open and bring them together to shut.
    g. "Bird." Wave both arms up and down.
    h. "Hug yourself." Extend arms and hold opposite sides of body.
3. Adapt the song "Hokey Pokey" to play with your child. "Put your arms up, put your arms down."
4. Incorporate movements of limbs, head and trunk during simple pretend games from stories or nursery rhymes.
5. Use simple rhythms in activities, such as patting both knees once, then twice; stamping in sequence one foot then the other.

3.114 WALKS UPSTAIRS ALONE–BOTH FEET ON STEP (24-25½ mo.)

The child walks upstairs without assistance from an adult or a railing. The feet do not yet alternate.

1. Refer to 3.106 (Walks upstairs holding rail–both feet on step, Activities #1-7) let the child experiment without an available railing for support.
2. Hold the child's shirt or pants until he gains confidence, if reassurance is necessary.
3. Play a mountain climbing game and sing "The bear went over the mountain."
4. Pretend you and the child are on an elevator in a department store. With each new step you take, call out a floor number and identify the "stop" saying. "Women's clothing," "Furniture," "Hardware," "Stationary," or "Children's toys."

3.115 WALKS DOWNSTAIRS HOLDING RAIL– BOTH FEET ON STEP (24-26 mo.)

The child's feet do not yet alternate. The child receives no adult assistance.

1. Let the child first practice on a small curb holding someone's hand.
2. Let the child practice walking down child-size steps using a railing her height, if possible.
3. Encourage the child to watch where she is going so her feet do not overshoot the step.
4. Place a toy at the bottom of several stairs as an incentive for the child.
5. Practice on adult size stairs. If the railing is too high for the child's reach encourage her to place her hand on the wall.
6. Walk backwards in front of the child to protect her from a fall as she walks down a long flight of stairs.
7. Place pictures on the stairs for the child to step on or cover the stairs with colored paper. Be sure the pictures or paper are securely fastened with no loose edges.
8. Use stairs as part of an obstacle course for fun.
9. Make modified stairs to assist the child up and down to a sink or toilet.

3.116 JUMPS A DISTANCE OF EIGHT INCHES TO FOURTEEN INCHES (24-30 mo.)

The child jumps forward with both feet lifting off the floor at the same time and landing at the same time.

1. Place two lines of colored tape on the floor about two inches apart. Show the child how to jump over them. Gradually increase the distance between tapes.
2. Place a strap around the child's chest if he is fearful. Hold the strap in front as reassurance to the child that you will catch him.
3. Let the child pretend a long roll of paper about two feet

wide is a "river" to jump over. If he jumps over, he will not get his feet "wet."

4. Cut circles and squares or cut out animal shapes. Let the child stand on one and jump onto another.
5. Help the child jump over a small ditch or mud puddle.
6. Make ridges or draw lines in the sand at the beach for the child to jump over.
7. Look for cracks in cement sidewalks to provide jumping boundaries.
8. Pretend to be hopping bunnies and do the bunny hop to music.
9. Shine a flashlight on the floor and ask the child to jump into the light. Increase the distance the child jumps.
10. Caution: These activities may not be good for a child with increased extensor muscle tone. Check with a physical therapist.

3.117 JUMPS FROM BOTTOM STEP (24-26½ mo.)

The child jumps without adult assistance from a seven-inch step using both feet at the same time.

1. Show the child how to jump from a low curb. Exaggerate the knee bending so the child can easily observe you. Explain your movements to the child.
2. Encourage the child to imitate you or another child. Hold the child's hands as he jumps to help him feel secure.
3. If knee bending is difficult for the child, help him bend his knees and push off. Let another adult provide security and hold his hands.
4. Let the child jump in place in other settings to practice this skill.
5. Help the child gradually progress in his jumping abilities until he can jump from a seven-inch step without assistance.

3.118 RUNS— STOPS WITHOUT HOLDING AND AVOIDS OBSTACLES (24-30 mo.)

The child performs this activity independently and without falling.

1. Place an obstacle in the child's path when she runs from one spot to another. Let her run toward the obstacle, then show her how to run around it.
2. Place a large obstacle between two adults. Encourage the child to run from one adult to the other, avoiding the obstacle.
3. Create an obstacle course by placing boxes and cans twelve inches apart in patterns. The child runs from one end of the obstacle course to the other without touching one can or carton. As the child improves, place the obstacles closer together.
4. Use a tree as a good natural obstacle to avoid when running outside.
5. Play a game of running to a wall and stopping right in front of the wall without touching it.
6. Make traffic light signals, using red, yellow and green paper. Hold up the green "go" paper and encourage the child to run fast. Hold up the yellow "slow" paper and encourage the child to run slowly. Hold up the red "stop" paper and encourage the child to stop running when she sees the red paper.
7. Teach the child to stop immediately when she hears the command to "stop." This is an important safety measure in the event she runs into a street or toward anything dangerous.

3.119 WALKS ON LINE IN GENERAL DIRECTION (24-26 mo.)

Draw a ten-foot line on the floor. Demonstrate by walking on it. Ask the child to imitate you. The child should walk in the same direction as the line, but need not keep his feet on the line.

1. Draw a permanent line on a shower curtain for use when needed. The curtain can be easily rolled up and put away. Lay a piece of red tape on the carpet or linoleum in the house.
2. Place a favorite toy or goody at the end of the line as a reward for the child.
3. Use natural lines outdoors, such as cracks in sidewalks, deserted parking lots with the markings for car spaces.
4. Include walking a line as part of an obstacle course for fun.
5. Draw footsteps on a line for the child to place his feet in as he walks.

3.120 WALKS BETWEEN PARALLEL LINES EIGHT INCHES APART (24-30 mo.)

Place two ten-foot lines on the floor eight inches apart. Demonstrate by walking between the lines. Ask the child to imitate you. He should walk the entire distance.

1. Use milk cartons, blocks, rope, stools to create two obvious lines. Let the child walk in the path created by the two lines.
2. Create a variety of parallel lines:
   a. Use ink to draw lines on a shower curtain.
   b. Use chalk to draw lines on cement.
   c. Use colored tape to make lines on linoleum or a carpet.
   d. Make lines in sand.
3. Vary the activities as the child walks between the lines.
   a. Place different shapes to step on such as circles, squares, triangles.
   b. Place squeaky toys at intervals.
   c. Use different textures to step on.
   d. Let several children play choo-choo train and walk between the lines holding each other's shoulders.
   e. Tape little boxes or adult shoes onto the child's feet.

Let the child pretend he is wearing snow shoes or skis.

3.121 STANDS ON TWO INCH BALANCE BEAM WITH BOTH FEET (24½-26 mo.)

Demonstrate by standing on the balance beam. Ask the child to imitate you. The child should stand on the beam with both feet for two to three seconds.

1. Show the child how to face the balance beam and step up on it with both feet perpendicular to the beam. Let the child experiment.
2. Assist the child by holding his hands as he steps up. Let the child balance independently by releasing his hands once he is on the beam.
3. Show the child how to stand on the beam with both feet pointed parallel to the beam, i.e., one foot in front of the other.
4. Assist the child when he is assuming the above position. Release the child's hands, if possible.
5. Play a game using the height of the child. Let him stand on the balance beam to increase his height. The adult kneels beside the beam to assist the child and allows the child to tower over.

3.122 IMITATES ONE FOOT STANDING (24-30 mo.)

The adult demonstrates the one foot standing position and the child should imitate without assistance.

1. Blow bubbles near the ground and let the child step on the bubbles with one foot.
2. Show the child how much fun it is to step on the cellophane bumps found in packing material.
3. Provide commercial toys operated by a small bulb which can be stepped on rather than hand operated, such as a dump truck.
4. Help the child hold one foot up in standing. Practice in front of a mirror so the child can see himself.
5. Encourage the child to imitate a sibling standing on one foot.
6. Sing songs and help the child rock back and forth to the music while he is standing on one foot.
7. Show a picture of a stork (often found in baby ads) or a flamingo standing on one foot.
8. Show a picture of another child standing one one foot. Ask the child to imitate.
9. Be sure the child uses each foot in the above activities.
10. Be sure the leg supporting the body weight is straight with the knee slightly bent and the heel flat on the ground.
11. Let the child place one foot on a skate board and move it around. This requires balancing on the weight bearing leg. Use each foot.

3.123 WALKS DOWNSTAIRS ALONE—BOTH FEET ON STEP (25½-27 mo.)

The child walks downstairs without assistance from an adult or a railing. The feet, however, do not yet alternate.

1. Refer to 3.115 (Walks downstairs holding railing—both feet on step, Activities #1-9). Eliminate the use of the railings.
2. Refer to 3.114 (Walks upstairs alone—both feet on step, Activities #2-4). Use the activities by reversing upstairs for downstairs.

3.124 WALKS ON TIP—TOES A FEW STEPS (25½-30 mo.)

The child stands on tip-toes without assistance and takes two to three steps forward. (The child's knees and hips should be straight.)

1. Refer to 3.109 (Stands on tip toe, Activities #1-4).
2. Encourage the child to walk on tip-toe to music.
3. Demonstrate by walking on tip-toe for the child. Assist her by holding her hands over her head and lifting gently to give the child the feeling of rising.
4. Play "So Big." Show the child how she becomes taller by standing on her tip-toes. The adult remains on his knees and the child should observe how she is almost as tall.
5. Let several children tip toe together in a line or in a circle.
6. Show the child a picture of a ballet dancer dancing on her toes. Ask the child to imitate.
7. Play a game by being very quiet while the child's dolls are sleeping. Tip toe and whisper. Contrast this activity by being noisy and stamping your feet.

3.125 JUMPS BACKWARDS (27-29 mo.)

The child jumps backwards with both feet lifting off the floor at the same time and landing at the same time.

1. Refer to 3.116 (Jumps a distance of eight inches to fourteen inches, Activities #1-10). Ask the child to perform these activities backwards.

3.126 ATTEMPTS STEP ON TWO INCH BALANCE BEAM (27½-28½ mo.)

Demonstrate by walking on the balance beam. Ask the child to imitate you. The child should have both feet on the beam and should attempt to walk forward.

1. Demonstrate by walking on a balance beam with arms outstretched for balance. Pretend you are a tight rope walker.
2. Help the child perform this activity by holding his hands out in the same manner.

3. Decrease the support you provide the child as he stands on the beam by moving your hands to his shoulders, freeing his arms for balancing.
4. Include a balance beam as part of an obstacle course.
5. Let the child pretend the beam is a bridge over a mud puddle. If he steps off, his foot gets "wet."
6. Help the child walk on narrow ridges in other settings, such as a narrow low wall, bleacher seats in a stadium, curbs, railroad ties.
7. Show the child how to slide his feet along the board, rather than taking alternating steps.
8. Demonstrate alternating steps as the child's balance improves.

3.127 WALKS BACKWARD TEN FEET (28-29½ mo.)

The child performs this activity without assistance.

1. Set up a walkway ten feet long:
   a. In the sand.
   b. Using carpet pieces or interesting textured material.
   c. Marked by chalk on cement.
   d. Marked by colored tape on tile floor.
   e. Marked by a rope on grass.
   f. On a long roll of plastic where footprints or small pictures can be pasted or painted.
2. Tell the child you are going to walk backwards down the path to a special treat:
   a. A dip in the pool or ocean.
   b. A ride on a swing or see saw.
   c. A favorite toy, e.g., a car or Tyke Bike.
   d. A favorite activity, e.g., art or eating.
3. Help the child walk backward on the course by holding one hand.
4. Take two children on the course holding one hand of each child.
5. Encourage the children to walk the course for a short distance. Gradually lengthen the distance.
6. Let the child pull a toy or pull a wagon with a doll placed in it along the course.
7. Ask the child to use different steps, e.g., walking backwards, shuffling or using a slide step.
8. Let several children pretend to be a train and stand in a line. They can move forward and backward to music with train sounds.

3.128 JUMPS SIDEWARDS (29-32 mo.)

The child jumps sidewards with both feet lifting off the floor at the same time and landing at the same time.

1. Refer to 3.116 (Jumps a distance of eight to fourteen inches, Activities #1-10). Ask the child to perform these activities sidewards.

3.129 JUMPS ON TRAMPOLINE WITH ADULT HOLDING HANDS (29-31 mo.)

The child's feet should lift off the trampoline surface at the same time.

1. Be sure an adult stays on a large trampoline with the child to demonstrate and to assist the child.
2. Stand on the ground and hold the child's hands or let the child hold a railing if using a child-size trampoline.
3. Substitute an old mattress or inner tube if trampolines are unavailable.
4. Encourage the child to bend her knees and push off with her toes in jumping.
5. Let the child start in sitting on the trampoline when adult assistance is withdrawn. The child progresses to hands and knees, kneeling, and finally standing.
6. Caution: Do not encourage this activity if it causes an exaggeration of abnormal movement patterns. Consult with a physical therapist.

3.130 ALTERNATES STEPS PART WAY ON TWO INCH BALANCE BEAM (30-32 mo.)

The child should take at least two alternating steps on the balance beam.

1. Refer to 3.126 (Attempts step on two inch balance beam).
2. Show the child how to move sideways across the beam.
3. Ask the child to walk backwards on the balance beam as her skill increases.

3.131 WALKS UPSTAIRS ALTERNATING FEET (30-34 mo.)

The child walks up regular size stairs without using a railing or the assistance of an adult. One foot is placed on each step alternating with the other foot.

1. Demonstrate the method of alternating feet with only one foot on each step. Watch and work with the child through the movements so he has a feel of the task.
2. Start with low steps and a railing the child's height, if possible. Place a toy on the second or third step for the child to retrieve. If stairs are narrow enough the child may first hold onto both rails.
3. Use stairs as part of an obstacle course for fun. Expect alternating feet on the walk upstairs.
4. Place pictures on the stairs for the child to look at.
5. Paint the stairs with bright colors or cover them with colored paper. Be sure the paper is securely fastened with no loose edges.
6. Prepare a prize at the end of the climb for the child.
7. Make modified stairs to assist the child up and down a sink or toilet.
8. Place cut out footprints in an alternating pattern on the stairs. Encourage the child to place her feet on them as

she walks up.
9. Play "giant steps" up the stairs. Exaggerate your own alternating feet.

3.132 JUMPS OVER STRING TWO TO EIGHT INCHES HIGH (30-36 mo.)

The child jumps with both feet together. The child should be able to jump two inches high by age thirty months and about eight inches high by age thirty-six months.

1. Place a long thin object on the ground for the child to jump over, such as a rope, yardstick, or mop handle.
2. Tie a brightly colored string with bells on it one inch above the ground. Suspend the string from two small stools, rungs of two chairs, two dowels hammered into the ground, or across two small shovels stuck in the sand at the beach.
3. Show the child how to jump over the string. Assist his initial attempts by holding his hands. If he misses, the bells will ring and signal the error to him.
4. Move the string higher gradually as the child improves.
5. Use a yardstick or dowel in place of the string. If it falls, the mistake is obvious to the child.
6. Begin this activity in a carpeted or sandy area so the child will not be injured by falls.
7. Show the child how to bend his knees as he lands to stop his movement.

3.133 HOPS ON ONE FOOT (30-36 mo.)

The child hops on one foot and hops forward.

1. Hold the child's hand as she learns to hop. Hop with her. Pretend you are kangaroos with sore feet hopping to the doctor for help.
2. Refer to 3.116 (Jumps a distance of eight inches to fourteen inches, Activities #1-10). Do not worry about increasing the distance.
3. Be sure to repeat the activities using both feet.

3.134 JUMPS A DISTANCE OF FOURTEEN INCHES TO TWENTY-FOUR INCHES (30-34½ mo.)

1. Refer to 3.116 (Jumps a distance of eight inches to fourteen inches).

3.135 STANDS FROM SUPINE USING A SIT—UP (30-33 mo.)

The child is in supine position. The child sits up by curling the body forward and using the hands for support. The child stands up without assistance or holding on to a support.

1. Teach the child this style of sitting up by holding her hands and helping her come forward.
2. Hold the child's legs down as she sits up to make it easier. Remind her to push down with her hands on the floor.
3. For the Cerebral Palsied child this activity may not be helpful. The preferable pattern would be 3.104 (Stands from supine by rolling to side). Check with a physical therapist.

3.136 STANDS ON ONE FOOT ONE SECOND TO FIVE SECONDS (30-36 mo.)

A child holds this position for one to three seconds without help. The time is increased to five seconds by age thirty-six months.

1. Step through the rungs of a ladder placed on the floor or grass:
   a. Use music as the child steps through the ladder. Use music with a slow beat. Increase to a faster tempo as the child's stepping abilities improve.
   b. Use a ladder as part of an obstacle course or let it become a challenging path to the sandbox or swing.
2. Sing "London Bridge" with two children standing and holding their clasped hands high. The children pass under the "Bridge." Sing "London Bridge" is "on the ground" with two children squatting and holding extended arms straight in front of them. The children step into and over the arms of the "Bridge."
3. Rock the child forward and backward to music holding the child's right hand and the left leg bent at the knee. (The adult stands behind the child.) Reverse the hand and foot:
   a. Rock the child from side to side in the position as above.
   b. Move the child in a circular pattern to music in the position as above.
4. Encourage the child to lift his foot for three seconds.
   a. Standing between two chairs and holding onto both chairs.
   b. Standing between chairs and holding with only one hand.
5. Ask the child to imitate you standing on one foot. Make a game of counting how long the child can hold his foot up. Repeat, using the other foot.
6. Let the child slip one foot at a time into a large shoe, boot, or slipper.
7. Let the child hold onto the adult with one hand or lean against a wall when putting on pants.
8. Ask the child to stand and to pick up small objects, such as marbles using his toes. Let the child place the objects in a low dish or box cover. Gradually make the container smaller and place it up higher.

3.137 WALKS ON TIPTOES TEN FEET (30-36 mo.)

The child completes the skill without assistance. Hips and knees should be straight.

1. Encourage the child to walk on tip toe to music.
2. Let several children tiptoe together in a line or in a circle. Let the children pretend to be very quiet.
3. Use a ten foot strip of material with textures, such as carpet, foam, sandpaper, plastic bumpy packaging material. Encourage the child to walk tiptoe on the strip as far as he can. He should gradually tiptoe the whole length.
4. Place small squeaky noisemakers under the material at intervals so the child will receive auditory reinforcement as he tiptoes.
5. Play games on tiptoe, such as "Ring Around the Rosie" or "London Bridge."
6. Suggest walking tiptoe in different surroundings, e.g., on grass, on sand, on cement, on a wide wooden plank.
7. Let the child pretend to be a ballet dancer.

3.138 KEEPS FEET ON LINE FOR TEN FEET (30-32 mo.)

The child walks on a line drawn ten feet long. She should not step off at all.

1. Refer to 3.119 (Walks on line in general direction).
2. Let a few children hold hands. Let each child have his own line to follow. Let all the children walk the lines together. Praise everyone's effort.
3. Place bean bags at one end of the line. Let the child carry the bean bags to the other end to place into a container.

3.139 USES PEDALS ON TRICYCLE ALTERNATELY (32-36 mo.)

The child propels and steers a tricycle without assistance.

1. Decrease your assistance when the child has learned to pedal the tricycle with foot straps.
2. Tap the child's higher knee and say "push." Continue in an alternating fashion by repeating on the other knee.
3. Remove the foot straps and let the child practice pedaling. The child may experience difficulty at first because the feet may slide off the sides, front or back of the pedals. Remind the child to hold the feet on correctly.
4. Teach the child how to steer. The child with involvement on one side of the body may have particular difficulty with this and must be encouraged to keep both hands on the handles.
5. Let two children play "follow the leader" on their tricycles.
6. Let the child ride a tricycle on an obstacle course pedaling around, under, over or through different items in a maze.

7. Let the child ride a tricycle on different textures such as carpet, grass, rocky area, gravel, sand. Discuss the relative ease and difficulty of the various riding surfaces.

3.140 WALKS DOWNSTAIRS ALTERNATING FEET (34 mo. and above)

The child walks down regular size stairs without using a railing or the assistance of an adult. One foot is placed on each step alternating with the other foot.

1. Demonstrate the method of alternating feet with only one foot on each step. Physically take the child through the movements so she becomes accustomed to the feel of the task.
2. Refer to 3.115 (Walks downstairs holding rail—both feet on step). Activities can be repeated with alternating feet.

3.141 CLIMBS JUNGLE GYMS AND LADDERS (34½-36 mo.)

Playing on jungle gyms encourages total body coordination, development of an understanding of body positions in space, music strengthening and the understanding of spatial relationships.

1. Caution: An adult should always be nearby; a fall could be serious.
2. Let the child begin the activity on easier climbing equipment, such as a ladder with flat steps or an indoor-outdoor gym.
3. Teach the child the importance of holding onto the ladder rather than depending on an adult for support.
4. Let the child play under and around a large jungle-gym first, familiarizing himself with it.
5. Let the child climb with barefeet. Barefeet tend to slip less and are more reliable than hard sole shoes, rubber slippers or sandals.
6. Show the child how to climb up one rung at a time so the feet will not overshoot the rung.
7. Assist the child, initially, in climbing down since it is more difficult than climbing up.
8. Show the child how to hang suspended in the air holding onto a low rung.
9. Help the child drop to the ground by holding onto him as he lets go. Let him drop down on his own when he feels confident.

3.142 CATCHES EIGHT INCH BALL (35+ mo.)

The child in standing position catches a ball at least eight inches in diameter.

1. Let the child first catch the eight inch ball in sitting. Aim the ball directly at her so she catches it easily in her lap.
2. Proceed to catching activities in standing.

3.0 GROSS MOTOR

3. Use a variety of objects for the child to catch, such as nerf balls, bean bags, yarn balls.
4. Throw the ball off to one side to require further balancing from the child.

3.143 JUMPS A DISTANCE OF 24 INCHES TO 34 INCHES (34½-36 mo.)

1. Refer to 3.116 (Jumps a distance of eight inches to fourteen inches).

3.144 AVOIDS OBSTACLES IN PATH (34½-36 mo.)

The child does not fall or bump into obstacles in his way.

1. Place a large obstacle such as a stack of pillows, a large box, a chair, or a stool, between two adults. Encourage the child to walk or run from one adult to the other. If she has difficulty walking or running around the obstacle, hold her hands and help her.
2. Take the child to a park to run around, avoiding trees and bushes.
3. Create an obstacle course indoors, by using pillows, stools, small tables. For the outdoor obstacle course, use potted plants, a wheelbarrow, boxes, barrels, old tires.
4. Mark an obvious path with two boundaries using long ropes, chairs or boxes side by side. The path should be narrow enough so an object in the path must be consciously avoided.
5. Point out the obstacle to the child and suggest ways to avoid them. The child may have to go over, around, under and through some obstacles.

3.145 RUNS ON TOES (34½-36 mo.)

The child runs on toes without assistance in a smooth, easy manner.

1. Demonstrate running on toes to the child. Ask her to run with you as you hold her hand.
2. Play soft bouncy music. Let the child alternate between regular running and running on tip-toe. Use children's records which include special types of music for this activity.
3. Run on different textures, such as linoleum, carpet, cement, grass, sand.
4. Make straight lines and circles using tape on the floor or chalk on cement. Let the child run on tiptoe following the lines.
5. Encourage several children to run together on tiptoe from a starting to an ending point.
6. Pretend to be birds extending arms out for wings and running on tiptoes.
7. Tell a simple story for the children to act out. Use different forms of locomotion, such as creeping, walking

and running on toes.
8. Ask the child to run up a steep hill on tiptoes.
9. For the cerebral palsied child, this activity may be harmful. Check with a physical therapist.

3.146 MAKES SHARP TURNS AROUND CORNERS WHEN RUNNING (34½-36 mo.)

The child turns easily when running without losing balance or falling down.

1. Plan circle games where the children run holding hands to get the feeling of turning gradual corners, e.g., "Ring Around the Rosie."
2. Create an obstacle course using boxes, barrels, chairs, plastic bottles, tires and let the child run around them. Arrange the course so sharp turns must be made.
3. Let the child chase you around the outside of the house or around a corner inside the house.
4. Play "London Bridge." Let two children stand and hold hands high to make a bridge. Let the children run in a circle and pass under the bridge.
5. Play baseball; set up four bases in a playground. Let the children run from base to base carrying a ball.
6. Let the child run from one wall to the opposite wall in a room and back again.
7. Draw zig-zag lines in sand or on cement with chalk. Let the child run with an adult along the line from beginning to end, holding hands at first.

4.01 REGARDS COLORFUL OBJECT MOMENTARILY (0-1 mo.)

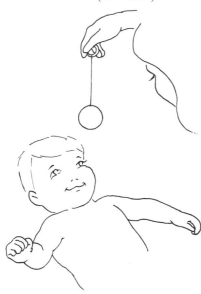

The child regards, glances or looks at a colorful object for one second.

1. Use objects of bright colors, such as red or sharp contrasting colors, such as red and yellow.
2. Present a colorful object about eight inches from the child's eyes, at chest level and to the side he is facing. Move the object slowly before him, encouraging him to look at the object.
3. Cradle the child in the feeding position, then present the object for regard. Do this if he does not regard a colorful object while in supine.
4. Use a colorful object with auditory stimulus, such as rattles with different sounds, a noise maker, a bell, or a musical toy.
5. Present a bright, colorful object or toy, such as a red rubber ball, a red yarn ball, a large red ring dangling from a string, a piece of red and yellow or black and white striped cloth.
6. Position your face in front of the child about eight inches away at chest level. Talk to him quietly, smiling and nodding your head. Refer to 5.02 (Regards face).
7. Place a colorful mobile, with or without music, on the crib at least eight inches away at the child's chest level.
8. For the visually handicapped child:
   a. Use bright colors, such as red, or sharp contrasting colors such as black and white or red and white.
   b. Use a red rimmed flashlight. Do not shine it directly in the child's eyes. Shine above or below the eyes about eight inches away at chest level.

4.02 MOVES ARMS SYMMETRICALLY (0-2 mo.)

The child moves his arms together with random movements to the sides. The whole body may respond to a stimulus.

1. Talk or sing to the child in face to face position. Refer to 5.02 (Regards face).
2. Present a colorful toy or rattle about eight inches from the child's eyes at chest level. This is a comfortable distance for the child to look at a toy. The child may then be stimulated to move his arms in excitement.
3. For the older delayed child:
   a. Position the child's arms symmetrically and move them together as you talk to him.
   b. Place wrist bands with bells on both the child's wrists. The sounds of the bells produced by the child when he moves his arms may encourage him to move his arms to produce more sounds. The wrist bands may be made with fabric or elastic.

4.03 REGARDS COLORFUL OBJECT FOR FEW SECONDS (½-2½ mo.)

The child looks at a colorful object for four to five seconds.

1. Position the child in supine, side-lying, carried in your arms, or in an infant seat.
2. Present the stimulus to the side the child is facing about eight inches away from the bridge of his nose and slightly below his eye level.
3. If the child has not developed a prolonged regard of four to five seconds, approach the child when he just awakens from his sleep or a nap and is in a drowsy state; present a colorful object or other stimulus as suggested in 4.01 (Regards colorful object momentarily).
4. Present the following objects to encourage prolonged regard. Choose two or three objects which may be most attractive to the child:
   a. For the disinterested child, use bright, sharp contrasting colors to make it exciting such as red and yellow.
   b. For the visually handicapped child, use sharp contrasting colors such as black and white or red and white.
   c. Use curved lines or concentric circles such as a bull's-eye design of contrasting colors (adapted from Robert L. Fantz, "Visual Perception From Birth As Shown By Pattern Selectivity," Annals of the New York Academy of Sciences, 118, 1965, pp. 793-814).
   d. Use a checkerboard design of contrasting colors (adapted from Fantz, "Pattern Selectivity," pp. 793-814).
   e. Use bright colorful objects such as a red ball, a shiny object, or a piece of wide striped cloth of contrasting colors.
   f. Present faces such as a magazine picture of a human face, a simple drawing of a happy face or a picture of a face with disarranged features (adapted from Fantz, "Pattern Selectivity," pp. 793-814).
   g. Use any figure drawn with ten or more angles (adapted from Maurice Hershenson, Harry Munsinger and William Kessen, "Preference for Shapes of Intermediate Variability in the Newborn Human," Science, 147, 5 Feb. 1965, pp. 630-631).
   h. Try a large picture with many small parts.

4.0 FINE MOTOR

i. Consider figures or designs with strong background, foreground contrast.

j. Caution: Once prolonged regard has been established, the use of the above patterns should be discontinued. Instead, concentrate on eye contact for beginning social interaction. Refer to 5.04 (Establishes eye contact).

4.04 FOLLOWS WITH EYES MOVING PERSON WHILE IN SUPINE (½-1½ mo.)

The child follows a moving person with his eyes while lying on his back. The child may stop following a moving person with his eyes while in supine after three to four months of age.

1. Place the child in supine. Talk to him as you approach him or as you move about the room.
2. Keep the child nearby within easy view while you are moving about doing your chores.
3. Stay near the child then gradually move away while facing him, and then return. Talk to him or attract his attention by other means, e.g., wear a bright scarf or hat.

4.05 STARES AND GAZES (1-2 mo.)

The child looks at an object or person for a prolonged period of time.

1. Talk or sing to the child in a soothing manner while feeding, bathing or in face-to-face position.
2. Respond to any eye contact by nodding your head, smiling, talking to the child, and stroking his stomach.
3. Let the child look at bright, colorful objects or toys.
4. Use mobiles, with and without auditory stimulus.
5. Call the child's attention to blinking Christmas tree lights.
6. Use colorful, printed crib sheets, bumpers, blankets.
7. Attach a mirror or a stainless steel cookie sheet to the side of the crib or playpen. Tape or cushion sharp edges. Position the child in side-lying. If necessary, use a rolled blanket placed against his back to help him maintain side-lying.

4.06 FOLLOWS WITH EYES TO MIDLINE (1-3 mo.)

The child visually tracks an object from the side he is facing to the midline.

1. Place your face in front of the child about eight inches away at chest level. When the child looks at you, move your face toward the child's midline. Use facial expressions and vocalizations to keep him looking at and following your face. Repeat this activity without vocalization when the child seems ready.
2. Alert the child while in supine with an object about eight inches away at chest level. Move the object from one side to the midline. Repeat from the other side.

a. Use a bright, colorful object with or without sound.
b. Use a penlight or flashlight with a red shield and move the light from side to center about eight inches away from his face. Do not shine it directly into his eyes but slightly above or below the eyes.
c. Use a dangling object such as a red ball, a red plastic ring, or a shiny round gold pendant.

4.07 BRINGS HANDS TO MIDLINE IN SUPINE (1-3½ mo.)

The child brings his hands to the middle of his body while lying on his back.

1. Place your hands on the child's shoulders. Bring her shoulders forward, holding her upper arms and encouraging her hands to come toward the midline.
2. Help the child feel and pat her chest with both hands.
3. Place the child's hands in front of her where she can see them. Refer to 1.11 (Inspects own hands).
4. Bring the child's hands to midline and rub them together. If necessary, guide her arms from behind the child or in face-to-face position, bring her hands together.
5. Pat the child's hands together repetitively, singing songs, e.g., "Pat-a-cake." Refer to 5.26 (Cooperates in games).
6. Let the child explore your face with her hands while in supine.
7. Encourage the child to bring her hands to her mouth.
8. For the older delayed child:
   a. Place the child in side-lying and bring her hands together for her if she is unable to bring her hands together while in supine.
   b. Should the child pull her arms into flexion when you hold or touch her hands, hold the child's arms or wrists to assist her in bringing her hands to midline.

4.08 ACTIVATES ARMS ON SIGHT OF TOY (1-3 mo.)

The child moves his arms about when he sees a toy.

1. Present a bright, colorful toy with or without auditory stimulation, such as a rattle, a red ring, a mobile, a stuffed animal, a squeeze toy or a wind up toy.
2. Touch his hand or hands with the toy. Bring the toy within the child's visual field to encourage arm activation.
3. Move his arms if necessary.
4. Bounce him gently on your lap as he looks at the toy.

4.09 BLINKS AT SUDDEN VISUAL STIMULUS (2-3 mo.)

The child blinks when an object is suddenly brought close to his eyes.

1. Lower a yarn ball quickly toward the child's eyes.

2. Flash a penlight at the child's eyes quickly, only for an instant.
3. Turn the light on in a darkened room.
4. Turn the light on when the child awakens from a nap or sleep.
5. Tap the child's eyelids carefully and gently with your index finger, if he fails to blink at a direct visual threat.

4.10 FOLLOWS WITH EYES PAST MIDLINE (2-3 mo.)

The child visually tracks an object past the midline.

1. Move a visual stimulus about eight inches from the child's face going from one side to the other.
2. Shake or move the object to attract the child's attention if she loses the object past midline. If using a penlight, do not shine it directly into her eyes but slightly above or below her eyes.
3. String toys, such as colored rings or colorful sewing spools across the crib or playpen. Move the toys from the midline to one side, then the other when the child is in supine.
4. Move your face from the child's midline to one side, then the other.
5. Use a hand puppet, moving it across the child's midline.

4.11 FOLLOWS WITH EYES DOWNWARD (2-3 mo.)

The child visually tracks an object downward, but often inconsistently.

1. Place the child in supine. Bring the stimulus downward toward his chest and within his visual field. Keep the object about eight inches from his face. The visual stimulus may be a dangling ball or ring, a bright rattle, or a penlight.
2. Hold the child in front of you. Raise him slightly above your head and encourage him to look at your face with a downward gaze.
3. Approach the child from the foot of his crib so he must look for you with a downward gaze.
4. Move a flashlight downward on the wall or ceiling and let the child visually track the light.

4.12 INDWELLING THUMB NO LONGER PRESENT (2-3 mo.)

The child's thumb is no longer held in his hand.

1. Shake the child's hand gently if his hand is fisted with thumb indwelling.
2. Tap or stroke the back side of the child's fingers and thumb.
3. Bring the child's hands together at midline and rub them together.
4. Open the child's hand by bringing his fingers and thumb out gently.
5. Let the child grasp your finger or a rattle with a comfortably sized handle, placing his thumb and fingers around your finger or the rattle.
6. For the older delayed child:
   a. Let him bear weight on his open hand with his thumb and fingers extended while in prone, on hands and knees, or in sitting. Refer to 3.43 (Holds weight on one hand in prone), 3.54 (Assumes hand-knee position).
   b. Let him grasp the handle of a musical or percussion-type instrument.
   c. Let him grasp the handles of a rolling pin with the thumbs out and his hand around the handle. Let him roll out play dough or clay. Let him press down or bear weight on the dough with open hands.
   d. Let him grasp and pull play dough or clay with both hands. Let him roll out the dough between his hands or on the table.
   e. Let him make thumb prints on the dough. (Theraplast, a putty for hand exercises, can be used instead of play dough or clay).
   f. Let him grasp cones to stack and unstack. Offer empty cone-shaped thread spools.
   g. Let him feel different textures, such as fabric, sand, uncooked beans, uncooked macaroni.

4.13 GRASPS TOY ACTIVELY (2-4 mo.)

The child maintains grasp of an object placed near or in his hand.

1. Touch the child's palm side of the hand with a thin handled rattle. Place it in his hand to encourage grasp. Assist in maintaining grasp for short periods if necessary by placing a fisted hand over his.
2. Place your finger in the child's hand and let him grasp it.
3. Let the child grasp safe, comfortably shaped objects, such as small squeeze toys, teething rings, small toys or rattles.

4.14 LOOKS FROM ONE OBJECT TO ANOTHER (2½-3½ mo.)

The child looks briefly at one object then another object when both are held within his visual field.

1. Place one object or toy in front of the child. Place a second object about eight inches away from the first

object. Remove one and draw the child's attention to the remaining object. Reintroduce the first object.

2. Place one object or toy with auditory stimulation to one side of the child, then introduce the second object with a different auditory stimulation on the other side. Alternate the different sounds and encourage the child to respond by looking at one object then the other.
3. Wave a bright colored scarf, then wave another scarf in front of the child.

4.15 KEEPS HANDS OPEN FIFTY PERCENT OF THE TIME (2½-3½ mo.)

The child's hands are open and not fisted about half the time.

1. Tap or stroke the back of the child's hand, if her hands are usually fisted.
2. Open the child's hand by bringing his fingers and thumb out gently.
3. Rub or pat the child's hands together, or pat her hand on your hand.
4. Let her feel her own body (chest, stomach, head, arms, legs), or your face and body.
5. Refer to 4.25 (Keeps hands open most of the time) for additional activities.

4.16 REACHES TOWARD TOY WITHOUT GRASPING (2½-4½ mo.)

This is a beginning reach in which the arms move generally toward a visual stimulus.

1. Touch the child's hand with an object then move it away. Place the object close enough to the child so he succeeds in touching it even with a slight reach.
2. Leave safe toys in the crib placing them close enough to the child to encourage reaching.
3. Let the child reach toward your face and let him touch you.
4. Encourage the child to reach toward a dangling toy or safe objects strung across the crib. Hang these objects low enough so the child can be successful.
5. Encourage the child to reach toward his bottle.
6. Encourage reaching by blowing soap bubbles or dangling a beach ball from the ceiling.

4.17 FOLLOWS WITH EYES 180 DEGREES (3-5 mo.)

The child visually tracks an object 180 degrees.

1. Bring a visual stimulus into the child's line of vision about eight inches from his face. Move it slowly in a 180 degree arc from one side to the other.
2. Move the object from above his head and down toward his toes.

3. Talk to him or make sounds as you move your face in front of the child.

4.18 FOLLOWS WITH EYES, MOVING OBJECT IN SUPPORTED SITTING (3-4½ mo.)

The child visually tracks a moving object while held in a sitting position or placed in a seat.

1. Let the child look at a mobile while in supported sitting.
2. Roll a ball very slowly on a table in front of the child or pull a toy slowly across the table. Encourage the child to watch the object; tap the table by the toy, if necessary.
3. Seat the child where he can watch you move about. Talk to him while you do your chores.
4. Wear a bright or crazy hat or tie a bright balloon on your wrist and move about in front of him.
5. Use hand puppets or stuffed animals and provide movement and animation.
6. Blow soap bubbles across or away from the child.

4.19 FOLLOWS WITH EYES UPWARD (3-4 mo.)

The child visually tracks an object upward.

1. Place the child in supine. Let the child track a bright colored toy, a rattle or a penlight held above his head within his visual field.
2. Move your face slowly above the child's face to encourage him to track upward.
3. Talk, smile and nod your head to encourage the child to look up at you during breast or bottle feeding.
4. Approach the child from the head of the crib and encourage him to look for you with an upward gaze. Call his name or tap the crib headboard.
5. Move a flashlight upward on the wall or ceiling. Make interesting "shadow pictures" with your hands.

4.20 GRASP REFLEX INHIBITED (3-4 mo.)

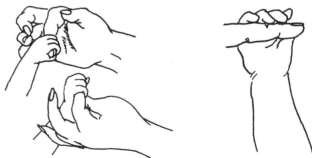

The child's grasp reflex is a response which occurs when pressure or stimulation is applied to the palm; the fingers close into a tight grasp. This reflex begins to diminish from about three months of age.

1. Provide the child with a toy he can comfortably grasp.

2. Let the child grasp hard toys and soft toys.
3. Let the child feel different textures with open hands, such as toweling, burlap, flannel, velvet.

4.21 CLASPS HANDS (3½-5 mo.)

The child brings his hands to midline and grasps his own hands.

1. Help the child to look at his hands. Refer to 1.11 (Inspects own hands).
2. Bring the child's shoulders forward. Hold the child's forearms and bring his hands to midline. Maintain his hands together for short periods of time. Refer to 4.07 (Brings hands to midline in supine).
3. Rub the child's hands together and assist in maintaining clasped hands if necessary.
4. Place the child in supine, in side-lying or in supported sitting and encourage the child to clasp his hands.
5. For the older delayed child who has difficulty bringing his hands to midline: Position him in side-lying; this may facilitate his bringing his hands together.

4.22 USES ULNAR PALMAR GRASP (3½-4½ mo.)

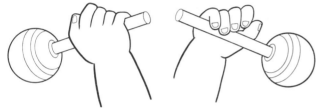

The child grasps an object which is placed in his hand. He uses an ulnar palmar grasp, that is, he grasps the object with the ring finger and little finger against his palm.

1. Let the child grasp small toys which fit comfortably into his hand such as rattles with comfortably long, thin handles, teething rings, safe, non-toxic toys.
2. Let the child grasp your finger from the ulnar side of his hand.
3. Let the child grasp a cone shaped toy with the small end of the cone on the ulnar side of the hand.

4.23 LOOKS WITH HEAD IN MIDLINE (4-5 mo.)

The child prefers to look at an object in supine with his head usually held at midline. The limbs are symmetrical in posture and the asymmetrical tonic neck reflex is inhibited.

1. Refer to 3.19 (Asymmetrical tonic neck reflex inhibited).
2. Place your face about eight inches away from the child's face. Smile, nod, and talk to him with his head at midline.
3. Place a mobile above the child at chest level.
4. Hang or dangle safe toys for the child at midline.
5. Flash a light for the child to look at with his head in midline.

6. For the older delayed child:
   a. Place a foam pillow under the child's head to position his head in slight flexion, if he tends to hyperextend his head.
   b. Use a cut-out neck pillow, if the child is unable to keep his head in midline.
   c. Position the child's arms symmetrically on his chest or to the sides, if necessary.

4.24 FOLLOWS WITH EYES WITHOUT HEAD MOVEMENT (4-6 mo.)

The child visually tracts an object within his visual field without turning his head.

1. Present a visual stimulus while the child is in supine and move it slowly within his visual field. Encourage the child to follow the object with his eyes without moving his head.
2. Move the object slowly in horizontal, vertical, and circular movements within the child's visual field as the child maintains his head in midline. Gently hold the child's head stationary, if necessary, to encourage eye and head separation movements unless this angers the child.

4.25 KEEPS HANDS OPEN MOST OF THE TIME (4-8 mo.)

The child's hands are relaxed and remains open most of the time.

1. Refer to 4.15 (Keeps hands open fifty percent of the time).
2. Let the child feel different textures, such as a texture ball or uncooked beans in a large box.
3. Let the child hold or carry objects which require both hands, such as large blocks made with small milk cartons or a large ball.
4. Let the child tap a drum with open hands.
5. For the older delayed child:
   a. Position the child in side-lying, in prone or in sitting and encourage keeping hands open.
   b. Position the child over a roll or bolster, wedge, or vinyl ball in prone and roll him forward encouraging weight-bearing on his open hands. The above activities (#1 through 4) can be used while the child is in this position.

4.26 REACHES FOR OBJECT BILATERALLY (4-5 mo.)

The child uses both hands to reach for an object.

1. Place your face on the child's stomach and rub his stomach with your face. Encourage him to reach for your head with both hands.
2. Place your face close to the child. Encourage him to reach for your face with both hands.

4.0 FINE MOTOR

3. Place a milk bottle or a toy within the child's reach at midline and encourage him to reach with both hands.
4. Place the child in supine and encourage him to reach bilaterally toward a suspended ball, dangling toy or cradle gym.
5. Offer the child two toys. Touch each of his hands simultaneously with the toys and bring them within his reach.
6. Offer both of your hands to the child before lifting him and encourage him to reach toward you. Refer to 5.21 (Lifts arms to mother).
7. Use floating toys during the child's bath to encourage bilateral reach.
8. For the older delayed child who is unable to reach with both hands: Bring his arms forward from the shoulders.

4.27 REACHES FOR TOY FOLLOWED BY MOMENTARY GRASP (4-5 mo.)

The child reaches and maintains grasp of an object momentarily.

1. Hold the child facing you and allow her to reach, touch and grasp your face.
2. Let the child reach, touch and grasp her bottle.
3. Place safe toys within reach of the child to encourage reach and grasp.
4. Let the child reach and grasp for toys during his bath.
5. For the older delayed child who needs assistance: Guide her arm in the reaching motion and direct her reach to touch and grasp a toy.
6. Offer toys with different textures, shapes, sizes and mounds, such as a yarn ball, a rattle, a teething ring, or a bean bag.

4.28 USES PALMAR GRASP (4-5 mo.)

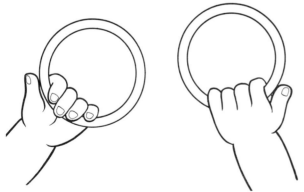

The child grasps an object against the palm without use of the thumb.

1. Let the child grasp small toys, such as a block, a spool, a squeeze toy, a teething ring, a bean bag, a peg, a spoon, a teething biscuit, a slice of hard toast.
2. Position the child in supported sitting, in prone with weight on forearms, in side-lying or in supine.
3. For the older delayed child:

a. Position him in prone over a roll or a wedge, in side-lying or in sitting. If the child is sitting on the floor, use a low bench for a table.
b. Let the child grasp the handle of a musical percussion instrument.
c. Let the child grasp a toy hammer or a xylophone stick.
d. Let the child grasp a rolling pin to roll out dough.

4.29 REACHES AND GRASPS OBJECT (4½-5½ mo.)

The child reaches and maintains grasp of an object.

1. Refer to 4.27 (Reaches for toy followed by momentary grasp).
2. Touch the child's hand with an object to encourage reach and grasp.
3. Hold out your hands invitingly to the child to encourage him to reach for you and grasp your hands before you lift him up.
4. Place safe toys within the child's reach to encourage reach and grasp.
5. Offer the child a teething biscuit or safe toys to grasp and mouth.
6. For the older delayed child: Offer him finger foods as well as toys to grasp.

4.30 USES RADIAL PALMAR GRASP (4½-6 mo.)

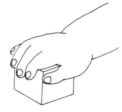

The child uses a radial palmar grasp, that is, he grasps an object with his thumb, index and middle fingers against his palm.

1. Provide the child with objects she can grasp with one hand.
2. Offer the toy toward the index finger side of the child's hand.
3. Place a cube or block in a box or container to encourage the child to grasp with the index and middle fingers side of the hand.
4. For the older delayed child: Let her squeeze play dough or theraplast (exercise putty) with the index and middle fingers side of the hand.

4.31 REGARDS TINY OBJECT (4½-5½ mo.)

The child looks at an object the size of a pellet raisin.

1. Place a tiny object in front of the child and encourage him to look at the object by tapping near it, by moving it, or by pointing to it.
2. Place a tiny object on the child's tray, a table, or in a bowl. A contrasting background color may help the child see the object better.

3. Place a small bell in a container and shake it to get his attention.
4. Show him small buttons on your clothing or details on a stuffed animal.
5. Caution: Be sure the child does not put unsafe objects into his mouth.

4.32 LOOKS AT DISTANT OBJECTS (5-6 mo.)

The child shows visual interest in objects at a distance.

1. Place a musical mobile at the end of the crib.
2. Call the child from a distance, e.g., before entering her room, call or wave to get her attention.
3. Turn the ceiling light or lamp on and off.
4. Hang simple, colorful pictures on the wall.
5. Roll a colorful ball past or away from the child. Use a ball with auditory or visual stimuli.
6. Face the child holding a bright toy or object. Move backward to increase the distance between you and the child.
7. Use puppets, stuffed animals, simple colorful pictures or toys to encourage visual interest at a distance.
8. Point out a passing dog, cat, car, bicycle, etc.
9. String colorful balloons and hang them at a short distance from the child.
10. Take the child shopping or to the zoo and point out things of interest.

4.33 DROPS OBJECT (5-6 mo.)

The child drops an object rather than purposefully releasing it.

1. Offer the child toys to grasp, such as a rattle, a teething ring, a diaper. Do not be upset if he drops it.
2. Let the child splash water in the bath.
3. Let the child grasp an ice cube; he may drop it because it feels so cold.
4. For the older delayed child:
   a. Flex the child's wrist, applying slight pressure on the back of the hand so the fingers extend and the object is dropped. Accidental dropping must precede purposeful release.
   b. Hold the child's wrist and gently shake his hand to help him drop the object, or tap, rub, or stroke the back of his hand to encourage hand opening.

4.34 RECOVERS OBJECT (5-6 mo.)

The child picks up an object he dropped if it is within easy reach.

1. Shake the dropped toy or object to provide a visual or auditory cue to encourage the child to recover the toy.
2. Place the child's hand over the toy to help her recover it, if necessary. Teach her that she can help herself.

4.35 RETAINS SMALL OBJECT IN EACH HAND (5-6 mo.)

The child holds a small object in each hand simultaneously for a short period of time.

1. Offer the child a small object for each hand to grasp. Offer the objects one at a time.
2. Use narrow handled rattles, small rubber toys, teething biscuits, cut out sponge shapes or pegs. The two objects do not have to be exactly the same.
3. Assist the child in maintaining grasp of the objects if necessary. Pay special attention to the hand holding the first object; the child is most likely to forget this one.
4. Let the child grasp your index fingers in each of his hands and pull him to sitting from supine.

4.36 WATCHES ADULT SCRIBBLE (5½-7 mo.)

The child watches while you scribble on paper.

1. Use black or red crayon or felt pen to scribble, make simple strokes, draw a circle, or make a face on a large white piece of paper.
2. Scribble on a chalk board.
3. Do finger painting or brush painting. Let the child join you in any way he wishes.
4. Position the paper on a table or flat surface. Place the paper upright on a book stand or wall at eye level, if the child has difficulty looking down at the table surface.

4.37 REACHES FOR OBJECT UNILATERALLY (5½-7 mo.)

The child reaches for an object with one arm. Unilateral reaching may occur with either arm at this age.

1. Position the child in supine or in sitting and offer him a toy directly or place it within easy reach.
2. Encourage the child to reach with one arm and then with the other. Touch the child's hand with the toy, if necessary, to encourage reaching.
3. Position the child in side-lying and place a toy within his reach. Repeat in side-lying on the other side.
4. Position the child in prone with his weight on his forearms and encourage the child to bear weight on one arm and reach with the other arm.
5. For the older delayed child: Position him in prone on a prone board, wedge, or roll and let the child reach for a toy with one arm.

4.38 TRANSFERS OBJECT (5½-7 mo.)

The child grasps an object with one hand then transfers the object to the other hand.

1. Let the child hold a long-handled toy horizontally with

two hands. Bring the toy to a vertical position until the child releases the toy with one hand and maintains grasp of the toy with the other hand.

2. Let the child grasp an object with one hand, then help her transfer the same object to the other hand, if necessary.

3. Let the child grasp the object with one hand then offer a second object to the same hand. Help her transfer the first object, if necessary, then encourage her to grasp the second object.

4. Make a small ball of masking tape and let the child grasp the ball. Encourage her to pull the tape ball off with the other hand.

5. Place a picture sticker on the palm of the child's hand and encourage her to pull it off with the other hand.

4.39 BANGS OBJECT ON TABLE (5½-7 mo.)

The child bangs an object on the table or any hard surface during play.

1. Let the child imitate you tapping or banging your hands on the table.

2. Seat the child on a high chair with a tray or on the floor with a low table. Let him grasp a block, spoon, or other small toy to bang on the table. Let him imitate your banging or help him bang by moving his arms, if necessary. Enjoy making the noise together.

4.40 ATTEMPTS TO SECURE TINY OBJECT (5½-7 mo.)

The child makes attempts to grasp a pellet-sized object; the child is not necessarily successful in securing it.

1. Place a tiny object such as tiny colored bear, a bean, a bell or a raisin on the table. Move or tap beside the object to encourage the child to attempt to grasp it.

2. Place a tiny object in a shallow box or bowl and shake the container so the child will make the attempt to secure the object.

3. Wear a necklace made with one small bead on a string. Encourage the child to attempt to secure the bead.

4. For the older delayed child: Offer small bits of finger foods to encourage the child to make the attempt to grasp. Refer to 6.24 (Chews food with munching pattern), Activity #11, for suggested finger foods.

4.41 MANIPULATES TOY ACTIVELY WITH WRIST MOVEMENTS (6-8 mo.)

The child grasps, explores and manipulates a toy with active rotary wrist movements.

1. Encourage the child to look at the toy or object he is grasping. If necessary, bring his arms forward and guide his hands so he looks at the object and turns his wrists

to look at or to manipulate the toy.

2. Let the child grasp a toy which is easy to hold and which provides enjoyable visual, auditory, and tactile stimuli to turn and handle the toy.

3. Encourage hand-to-mouth exploration with finger foods, safe toys and objects.

4. Use colorful wrists bands with bells sewn on to encourage active wrist movements.

5. Let the child play with a bell which has a handle to grasp. A small dinner bell is ideal for this purpose.

4.42 REACHES AND GRASPS OBJECT WITH EXTENDED ELBOW (7-8½ mo.)

The child reaches directly with extended elbow and grasps an object.

1. Suspend a vinyl ball from the ceiling or doorway at a height where the child must extend his arm to reach it. He can be positioned in supine, in side-lying, or in sitting.

2. Let the child knock over a tower of blocks built at arm's length from him.

3. Let the child reach for soap bubbles or balloons.

4. Touch the child's hand or hands with a toy and hand it to him within reaching distance. Also encourage reaching across the midline.

5. Let the child reach for your face.

6. Wear a small loop or a necklace of pop beads around your neck and let him reach and grasp for it with elbows extended.

7. Let the child look in the mirror and encourage him to reach and touch the mirror.

8. Let the child reach and grasp his bottle, finger foods, spoon, or cup.

9. Position the child in prone with weight on forearms or hands or in hand-knee position. Refer to 3.15 (Holds chest up in prone weight on forearms) and 3.26 (Bears weight on hands in prone). Place the toy slightly out of reach to encourage weight shifting on one arm and extended reach with the other arm.

10. Position the child in prone over a large vinyl beach ball or a roll. Move the child forward holding his hips or legs and let him reach with extended elbow and grasp a toy placed on the floor.

11. Position the child in prone over a wedge or roll and let him reach for toys on the floor with extended elbow.

12. Position the child in sitting. Offer objects for extended reach above his head, to his side, or toward his back. To encourage trunk rotation in sitting, place or offer a toy to one side and let the child turn his trunk to reach for the toy. Repeat on other side.

4.43 USES RADIAL DIGITAL GRASP (7-9 mo.)

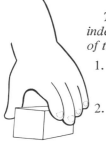

The child grasps an object with the thumb, index and middle fingers without the use of the palm.

1. Let the child grasp a block, peg, or other toy which encourages the use of his thumb, index and middle fingers.
2. Place the object in a cup, muffin tin or egg carton to encourage radial digital grasp.
3. Offer objects or finger foods at the thumb side of the hand.
4. For the older delayed child:
   a. Let him grasp and pull at play dough with his thumb and fingers.
   b. Let him use small castanets or clappers with his thumb and fingers.
   c. Let him use hand puppets, moving his thumb and fingers.

4.44 RAKES TINY OBJECT (7-8 mo.)

The child grasps at a pallet sized object such as a raisin by using a raking motion. The child flexes the fingers toward the palm without using the thumb.

1. Refer to 4.40 (Attempts to secure tiny object).
2. Encourage the child to grasp small objects placed on a surface within easy reach. Use a bell, a bean, dry cereal.
3. Position the child in prone with weight on his forearms, in side-lying or in sitting.
4. Caution: Be sure the child does not put small, unsafe objects into his mouth.

4.45 USES INFERIOR PINCHER GRASP (7½-10 mo.)

The child grasps a small object with his index finger and thumb. The thumb is positioned at the lateral or lower part of the index finger.

1. Offer the child small or thin objects to grasp, such as half-inch cubes, pegs, sticks, bells; also try tiny objects, such as raisins, dry cereal, finger foods.
2. Place the object on the table surface for the child to grasp.
3. Place the object in a bowl or small container to encourage thumb and index finger grasp.
4. For the older delayed child:
   a. Let him pinch and pull play dough or theraplast with his thumb and index finger.

b. Let him attempt to turn the knob of a wind up toy or turn the knob of the radio.

4.46 BANGS TWO CUBES HELD IN HANDS (8½-12 mo.)

The child grasps a one-inch cube in each hand and hits them together.

1. Let the child hold a cube in each hand and imitate you banging the cubes on the table. Then let him imitate you banging the cubes together.
2. Place your hands over the child's and bang the cubes together with him if he does not imitate your motions. Encourage him to try the activity by himself.
3. Let him bang together two small cans or two percussion instruments with handles such as cymbals or maracas.

4.47 REMOVES PEGS FROM PEGBOARD (8½-10 mo.)

The child removes previously placed pegs from the pegboard.

1. Use large pegs three-fourths of an inch. Let the child imitate removing the pegs if she does not do it spontaneously. Assist her if necessary. Encourage her to take them "all out."
2. Place large crayons, felt pens, or unsharpened pencils in an empty juice can and let the child take the objects out.
3. Make holes in a shoe box. Place unsharpened pencils or felt pens into the holes and let the child remove them.
4. Place something tiny under the peg on the pegboard, so the child sees it when she removes the peg.

4.48 TAKES OBJECTS OUT OF CONTAINER (9-11 mo.)

The child empties or removes objects from a container by dumping it over or by taking out the objects one by one.

1. Let the child take objects out of a container in imitation of you.
2. Fill the container with a little water or sand. Let the child empty the container by dumping the water or sand out of the container.
3. Use containers, such as boxes, cans, pots, pans, buckets, milk cartons, waste baskets, clothespin bags, purses, paper sacks, cups, bowls, bottles.
4. Use items to fill the container, such as blocks, spools, bean bags, pop beads, clothespins, poker chips, uncooked beans, macaroni, rice, sand, water.

4.0 FINE MOTOR

4.49 EXTENDS WRIST (9-10 mo.)

The child extends his wrist during play or during the manipulation of objects.

1. Encourage the child to wave bye-bye.
2. Position a toy above the child's wrist level to encourage wrist extension.
3. Place textured pictures on the wall which the child can feel with fingers and wrist extended.
4. Finger paint by placing the paper on the table, slant board or wall.
5. Let the child press down on a squeeze toy.
6. Let the child push against a large ball.
7. For the older delayed child:
   a. Let him turn pages in a book. Place the book on a flat surface or on a slanted bookstand.
   b. Let him press down on play dough with his hand or roll out the play dough with a rolling pin.
   c. Let him bear weight on his hands with wrist and fingers extended. Position him in prone with weight on his hands and with elbows extended, in hands and knees position, in side sitting with one hand flat and to the side, and long let sitting with hands flat toward the back.
   d. Position the child in prone over a wedge, roll or large ball and let the child bear weight on his hands with wrist and fingers extended.

4.50 RELEASES OBJECT VOLUNTARILY (9-11 mo.)

The child releases an object in a controlled, purposeful and intentional manner.

1. Let the child squeeze wet sponges, squeeze toys, or play dough to give her the feeling of controlled grasp and release.
2. Let the child grasp and release objects repetitively, taking out or putting objects into a container. Use a can so a sound is produced when an object is released and dropped.
3. Let the child grasp and release sand, grass, beans, bean bags.
4. Ask her to give you the object she is holding or exchange an item with her. Do not keep her "present," but let her keep yours.
5. Let the child roll a ball. Refer to 5.46 (Plays ball cooperatively).
6. For the older delayed child who is unable to release objects:
   a. Flex her wrist and apply slight pressure on the back of the hand so the fingers extend and the object is released.
   b. Tap, rub, stroke the back of her hand to encourage

hand opening to release the object.
c. Let the child stack large blocks or rings, do simple puzzles with knobs or use the pegboard.

4.51 POKES WITH INDEX FINGER (9-12 mo.)

The child isolates his index finger to poke or feel objects.

1. Place pieces of different fabrics on the bottom of egg carton sections and let the child feel these varied textures with his index finger. Show him how to poke his finger into the egg carton.
2. Place marble-sized play dough into egg carton sections and let the child poke or press down with his index finger.
3. Use a chinese checkerboard or pegboard and let the child use his index finger to poke or touch each hole.
4. Let the child find a tiny object in thick carpeting by poking with his index finger.
5. Let the child poke play dough or clay, making index finger impressions.
6. Let him finger paint and encourage him to use his index finger.
7. Encourage him to poke his index finger into the play phone dial.
8. Let the child play with push-button toys, such as the "busy box" or "surprise box."
9. Let the child press piano keys with his index finger.
10. Let the child press the door bell and the elevator button.

4.52 USES NEAT PINCER GRASP (10-12 mo.)

The child grasps a tiny object the size of a raisin with precise thumb and index finger opposition.

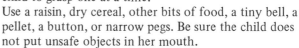

1. Place a tiny object on the table or any surface for the child to grasp one at a time. Use a raisin, dry cereal, other bits of food, a tiny bell, a pellet, a button, or narrow pegs. Be sure the child does not put unsafe objects in her mouth.
2. Use tiny objects which do not easily roll away when the child tries to grasp them.
3. Place a tiny object in a cup or egg carton cup to encourage the child to grasp the object with his thumb and index finger.
4. Place a short, colorful piece of string on the carpet, on the table, or even on the child where she can easily see and reach for it by grasping with her thumb and index finger.
5. Provide bits of food at snack time to encourage finger feeding as well as neat pincer grasp.
6. For the older delayed child:
   a. Let her make a collage using various items, such as shells, sticks, macaroni, beads, twigs, leaves, string.
   b. Let the child pinch and pull play dough with her thumb and index fingertips.

c. Let the child pinch clothes pins. Let her remove the pins placed on the rim of a can. Let her drop them into the can. Then let her pinch and place the pins on the rim of the can herself. Tactfully provide assistance, if necessary.

4.53 TRIES TO IMITATE SCRIBBLE (10½-12 mo.)

The child holds the crayon and makes contact with the paper in imitation but does not necessarily make marks on the paper.

1. Use a large crayon, tap on the paper and make scribble marks. Encourage the child to imitate you.
2. Assist the child, if necessary, to make contact with the crayon and paper.
3. Tape the paper to the table to prevent the paper from slipping or moving.
4. Let the child use chalk and a chalkboard.
5. Let the child use a felt pen or a primary sized pencil. Saw the pencil in half if the new pencils are too long. Be sure the pencil point is not sharp.
6. Let the child do other activities to encourage scribbling, such as finger painting, sponge painting, brush painting.

4.54 USES BOTH HANDS FREELY; MAY SHOW PREFERENCE FOR ONE (11-13 mo.)

The child uses either or both hands during play. The child may show a preference for one hand; do not insist upon one hand over the other. Do not worry if there is no preference for sometime.

1. Position or offer toys at midline and let the child use either hand.
2. Offer a toy to one hand and then to the other hand and encourage the child to grasp the toy.
3. Place some blocks to either side of the child. Let the child put the blocks into a can placed at midline.
4. Let the child play with toys large enough to require the use of both hands.
5. Let the child play with toys which require pulling or pushing.
6. For the hemiplegic child, encourage the child to use both arms and hands. Encourage the use of the involved arm and hand as an assister.

4.55 GRASPS CRAYON ADAPTIVELY (11-12 mo.)

The child grasps the crayon and positions one end of the crayon toward the paper.

1. Place a large crayon on the table in front of the child so he can grasp the crayon according to his hand preference.
2. Encourage the child to grasp the crayon and help him adjust the crayon in his hand, if necessary.
3. Let the child use a large crayon, a felt pen, or chalk.
4. Tape the paper down on the table, if necessary, and encourage the child to mark the paper or scribble by imitation.
5. Let the child use a stick or a wooden spoon to poke, to make strokes in the sand (wet or dry).
6. For the older delayed child:
   a. Build up the crayon by wrapping a thin layer of foam with masking tape for the child with poor grasp.
   b. Let the child use crayons which are large enough to fit into his whole hand. These can be made by melting old used crayons and pouring them to set and cool in aluminum ice cube trays, muffin tins or small paper cups. Cut the crayons to desired size.

4.56 PUTS OBJECTS INTO CONTAINER (11-12 mo.)

The child puts objects or toys into a large container.

1. Let the child put objects into a container in imitation.
2. Let the child put objects into an empty can so she hears the object drop into the can, or use a large transparent container so the child sees the objects drop into the container.
3. Use other containers such as boxes, pots, pans, buckets, milk cartons, waste baskets, large bowls, paper sacks, or purses.
4. Use objects such as blocks, spools, bean bags, pop beads, clothes pins, poker chips, uncooked beans, macaroni.
5. Refer to 4.50 (Releases object voluntarily) if the child has difficulty releasing the object into the container.

4.57 SUPINATES FOREARM (11-12 mo.)

The child actively supinates his forearm, that is, he turns his forearm over so the palm is facing up. The child reaches and grasps for an object with forearm in mid-supination, that is, the forearm is positioned with the thumb side of the hand up.

1. Encourage the child to do "Pat-a-Cake" by clapping hands together with his forearm in mid-supination.
2. Offer the child toys with handles pointing toward him

to encourage reaching and grasping the toy with forearm in mid-supination.

3. Shake hands with the child with forearms in mid-supination.

4. Let the child imitate gestures, such as "Come, Come," "All good!" to encourage supination and pronation movements.

5. Let the child imitate gestures to songs such as "Twinkle, Twinkle Little Star," "Open, Shut Them."

6. Let the child use musical percussion instruments with handles and other toys with handles, such as a toy hammer or xylophone stick.

7. Let the child use the play telephone, bringing the phone to his ear.

8. Let the child hit a drum or tamborine positioned to the side so he hits it with his forearm in mid-supination.

9. Place the child in supine. Let the child reach for his legs, ankles, or feet with forearms in mid-supination.

10. Encourage supination by allowing the child to reach forward with his arms when he wants to be picked up.

4.58 PLACES ONE BLOCK ON TOP OF ANOTHER WITHOUT BALANCING (11-12 mo.)

The child puts one block on top of another without releasing the second block, or without accurately balancing the second block on the first (as in a tower). (A block is about one and a half inches square; a cube is one inch square.)

1. Let the child imitate your placing one block on top of the other. Tap the second block on the first block, if necessary, to gain his attention.

2. Use larger blocks if the child has difficulty placing a one-inch block on top of the other. Let the child use both hands to handle larger blocks.

3. Make larger blocks with milk cartons. Beans or sand may be put into the blocks for sound or added weight. Also use boxes, food containers, paperback books for the child to place on top of another.

4.59 MARKS PAPER WITH CRAYON (12-13 mo.)

The child makes contact with the crayon on the paper and makes visible marks on the paper.

1. Refer to 4.53 (Tries to imitate scribble) and 4.55 (Grasps crayon adaptively).

2. Tap the paper with the crayon and encourage the child to imitate you.

3. Make simple strokes on the paper and encourage the child to imitate you.

4. Let the child do finger painting or brush painting.

5. Tape the paper to the table, if necessary, to prevent the paper from slipping or moving.

6. Let the child use a chalk, a marking pen.

4.60 PUTS THREE OR MORE OBJECTS INTO CONTAINER (12-13 mo.)

The child consecutively puts three or more objects or cubes into a container the size of a cup or bowl. He may need some encouragement to complete the task.

1. Give the child three or more cubes and encourage him to put them consecutively into a cup or a small container the size of a cup. Demonstrate, if necessary.

2. Give the child small toys, spools or stringing beads to put into a container the size of a cup or bowl.

3. Encourage the child to put small toy cars into a box.

4. Let the child use a transparent container to put objects in so he can see the objects.

4.61 BUILDS TOWER USING TWO CUBES (12-16 mo.)

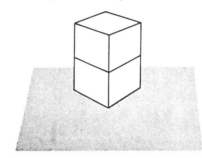

The child places a one-inch cube on top of another cube and releases it. The cube is balanced on top of the other cube to build a tower of two cubes.

1. Seat the child at a table or on the floor at a low table. Give the child two cubes.

2. Demonstrate building a tower of two cubes. Tap the first cube on the table to get his attention, if necessary, and place the second cube on the first. Give simple verbal directions. Use two different colored cubes for contrast.

3. Use larger blocks, if the child has difficulty with coordination or with the concept of building a tower.

4. Use other materials for building a tower, such as cigar boxes, tissue boxes, small cereal boxes, large square pieces of wood, square sponges, square plastic food containers, cottage cheese containers, cans. Milk cartons can be cut to make square blocks. Fill the carton partially with sand or uncooked beans to weight them.

4.62 PLACES ONE ROUND PEG IN PEGBOARD (12-15 mo.)

The child puts at least one round peg (three fourths-inch in diameter) into the pegboard.

1. Refer to 1.63 (Puts cylinders in matching hole in container).

2. Let the child place at least one peg in the pegboard. Assist her if necessary. Hand her the peg so she holds the top of the peg if she has difficulty with placing the bag in the hole. She may place and remove the peg repetitively. This is normal.

3. Let the child use peg-like toys, such as the *Fisher Price Little People* toys.

4. Use a shoe box and make holes on the cover. Use dowels, large unsharpened pencils, hair rollers, felt pens, or adding machine paper rolls, and let the child place them in the holes.

5. Position the pegboard on a table top. Use a slanted upright book stand if the child has difficulty looking downward.

4.63 POINTS WITH INDEX FINGER (12-16 mo.)

The child isolates his index finger to point.

1. Identify objects, people, pictures by pointing with you index finger.
2. Encourage the child to imitate your pointing. Help him point to himself, to you, to facial features, to parts of the body.
3. Respond when the child tries to get your attention by gesturing or pointing or requests something by pointing.
4. Let the child feel texture books with his index finger.
5. Refer to 4.51 (Pokes with index finger).
6. Refer to 1.73 (Understands pointing).
7. For the older delayed child:
    a. Accept the child's way of pointing, e.g., with his whole hand, if he is unable to isolate his index finger to point.
    b. Let him use a pointer such as a pencil with an eraser tip. Build up the handle of the pointer if the child has poor grasp.
    c. Let him use a head band with a pointer attached, if the child has better head control than hand control.
    d. Let him point with his eyes, by positioning objects where he can look pointedly at the object to identify it.

4.64 INVERTS SMALL CONTAINER TO OBTAIN TINY OBJECT AFTER DEMONSTRATION (12½-18 mo.)

Give the child a small container with a tiny object in it to see if he will spontaneously invert the container to obtain the object. The opening of the container should be about 5/8 to 3/4-inch so the child cannot put his hand into it.

1. Place a raisin, a pellet, dry cereal, a colorful bead, or a bell in a clear small container so the object can be easily seen. Encourage the child to obtain the object by inverting the container. Demonstrate, if necessary.
2. Use a pill container or a small bottle with a narrow neck so the child cannot put her whole hand into the container to remove the object.
3. For the older delayed child:
    a. Let the child use a small can, such as a tomato paste can or an empty film container and place in it a cube, a one-inch bead or a Ping-Pong ball. Show him how to turn the container over so the object falls out.
    b. Let the child invert an hourglass type of toy so the

beads or sand flows from one end of the glass to the other.

4.65 SCRIBBLES SPONTANEOUSLY (13-18 mo.)

The child grasps a crayon and scribbles spontaneously without assistance.

1. Provide paper and crayons. Say, "Write," or "Color." If the child does not grasp the crayon and scribble spontaneously, encourage her to imitate you after a demonstration. Assist her, if necessary.
2. Use various kinds of paper, such as construction paper, newsprint, scratch paper, newspaper, wrapping paper, butcher paper. A roll of paper can be conveniently stored and can be used as needed in different lengths.
3. Use various kinds of markers, such as crayons, pencils, felt markets, chalk, paintbrushes, finger paints.
4. Position the paper on the floor, on the table, on the wall, on an easel, or use a chalkboard.
5. Use a paintbrush and water. The child can "paint" with water on a cemented area or on a chalkboard.
6. Place typing paper over a patterned or textured material, such as an embossed Christmas card, a woven place mat, textured floor covering, or a brick, and let the child stroke or scribble on the paper with a crayon or pencil. The design or the pattern will show through the paper.
7. Let the child scribble to music, using different rhythms and sounds. Stop or start the music for the older child.
8. Let the child scribble on the plastic sheet of a "magic slate."

4.66 INVERTS SMALL CONTAINER SPONTANE-OUSLY TO OBTAIN TINY OBJECT (13½-19 mo.)

The child turns the container over spontaneously to obtain the tiny object without a demonstration. The opening of the container should be about 5/8-inch to 3/4-inch in diameter so the child cannot put his hand into it.

1. Refer to 4.64 (Inverts small container to obtain tiny object after demonstration).
2. Use a pill container or a small bottle with a narrow neck so the child cannot put her whole hand into the container to remove the object.
3. Put a raisin, a pellet, dry cereal, a colorful bead or a bell into a clear small container so the object can be easily seen. Encourage the child to obtain the object.

4.67 PUTS MANY OBJECTS INTO CONTAINER WITHOUT REMOVING ANY (14-15 mo.)

The child puts at least eight objects into a container without removing any in the process.

4.0 FINE MOTOR

1. Start with a few objects (two or three). Increase the number of objects as the child puts more objects into the container without removing any. Encourage the child to, "Put them all in."
2. Hand the child another object quickly to put into the container, if she starts to remove an object from the container.
3. Use cans, boxes, paper or cloth bags, bowls, pots or large hats as containers.
4. Use a large container with a small opening so the child cannot put her hand into the container to remove the objects.
5. Use a can with a lid such as a coffee can. The child can help place the lid on the can after she puts all the objects into the container. Tape the sharp rim of the coffee can.
6. Let her pour all the objects out and repeat the activity if she seems to enjoy it.

4.68 USES BOTH HANDS IN MIDLINE—ONE HOLDS, OTHER MANIPULATES (16-18 mo.)

The child holds the object or toy at midline. One hand holds the toy while the other manipulates, explores, or feels the toy.

1. Let the child squeeze a wet sponge, one hand holding the sponge and the other hand squeezing it.
2. Let the child hold a pinqheel with one hand while the other hand moves it.
3. Let the child place a hand puppet on his other hand.
4. Let the child stack and remove rings with one hand while the other holds the base.
5. Let the child hold a container or bag of food with one hand and with the other hand take out the objects or food. Ask him to give you something from the container, or let him feed the animals or pidgeons at the zoo.
6. Let the child use a musical instrument, such as a drum, a tambourine or a triangle, which requires the use of both hands, one hand holding while the other manipulates.
7. Let the child peel a banana, holding it with one hand and peeling it with the other.
8. Let the child pound pegs, hammering with one hand and stabilizing the toy with the other hand.
9. Let the child hold the paper down on the table with one hand and scribble with the other hand.
10. Let the child play in the sand. Let him scoop, stir, pour with one hand and hold the container with the other hand.
11. Let the child help with bathing a doll or himself, soaping the washcloth, soaping himself or soaping the doll with one hand.
12. For the older delayed child:
    a. Let the child remove the paper wrapper from a juice bar or a popsicle, holding the stick with one hand and removing the wrapper with the other.
    b. Let the child do stirring activities, holding the bowl with one hand and stirring with the other; stirring

sand or dirt with water; stirring while making pudding with cold milk; stirring a bowl of packing foam, un-cooked macaroni or beans.
13. For the hemiplegic child: Encourage awareness of the affected side by letting the child do bilateral activities, using the affected side as the assisting or stabilizing hand.

4.69 BUILDS TOWER USING THREE CUBES (16–18 mo.)

The child balances three one-inch cubes one on top of the other.

1. Refer to 4.61 (Builds tower using two cubes).
2. Build a tower of three cubes and let the child imitate you.
3. Encourage the child to build three cubes after he is suc-cessful with two cubes.

4.70 PLACES SIX ROUND PEGS IN PEGBOARD (16-19 mo.)

The child places at least six round pegs (three-fourths-inch in diameter) in the pegboard without removing any in the process. Urge the child to keep going and "Put them all in."

1. Refer to 4.62 (Places one round peg in pegboard).
2. Offer the child at least six round pegs, one at a time, to put into the pegboard. Increase the number of pegs if the child is successful.

4.71 IMITATES VERTICAL STROKE (18-24 mo.)

The child observes while you draw a vertical stroke and he imitates it with your vertical stroke in view. The child's stroke is acceptable if the line is drawn within thirty degrees.

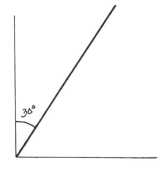

1. Use a dark crayon on white paper. Sit next to the child at the table. Tape the paper down, if necessary.
2. Make a vertical stroke on the paper. Encourage the child to imitate the vertical stroke on the same paper to the right or below your stroke. Assist as necessary.
3. Give the child simple verbal directions, e.g., saying "Down" while stroking downward.
4. Let the child imitate you raising your arm and making a gross downward stroke in the air. Draw a vertical stroke on a chalkboard or on paper placed on the wall or easel.
5. Let the child fingerpaint and imitate a vertical stroke with his hand or finger on the paper.
6. Let the child make vertical strokes in wet or dry sand. Wet sand will give more resistance. Let him use his finger, a stick, or a pencil.

7. Let the child stroke on flattened clay or play dough using a stick or pencil.
8. Let the child feel and follow with his finger or crayon a vertical line made of a half inch strip of sandpaper glued to cardboard.
9. Refer to 4.65 (Scribbles spontaneously) for suggested materials to use.
10. For the older delayed child:
    a. Make a wide vertical stroke and let him mark over the stroke. Let him imitate the stroke. Repeat.
    b. Let the child connect broken lines of a vertical stroke.
    c. Let the child connect a top dot to a bottom dot to make a vertical stroke.

4.72 BUILDS TOWER USING FOUR CUBES (18-22 mo.)

1. Refer to 4.61 (Builds tower using two cubes).
2. Build a tower of four cubes and the child imitate you.
3. Encourage the child to build a tower of four cubes after he is successful with three cubes.

4.73 IMITATES CIRCULAR SCRIBBLE (20-24 mo.)

The child observes while you scribble continuous circles and he imitates it with your scribble in view.

1. Scribble a continuous circle on paper saying, "Make a round circle," or "Go around and around," or "Draw a round ball."
2. Let the child imitate you. Tape the paper down if necessary.
3. Let the child draw circles in the air using gross arm movements. Then let him draw circles on the chalkboard of paper on the wall or easel.
4. Let the child draw circles while finger painting.
5. Let the child draw circles in wet or dry sand with his finger or a stick.
6. Let the child help you stir a bowl of sand or uncooked rice.

4.74 STRINGS ONE ONE-INCH BEAD (20-23 mo.)

The child strings at least one one-inch bead with a heavy corded string.

1. Demonstrate bead stringing to the child using *Playschool Jumbo Wood Beads.*
2. Allow the child to briefly experiment through trial and error. Keep attempts short. Assist as necessary.
3. Let the child hold the end of the string in the fingers of one hand and the bead in the fingers of the other hand.
4. Let the child pass the tip of the string through the hold of the bead or bring the bead to the string. Watch that

she does not attempt to move both the string and the bead together at the same time.
5. Reinforce one to two inches of the tip of the string with masking tape, if necessary, or reinforce the string with metal shoelace tips.
6. Use plastic tubing for "string."
7. For the older delayed child:
    a. Let the child pass large wooden or plastic circles or blocks with holes through a dowel.
    b. Let the child string one-inch wide paper rolls using plastic tubing for "string."

4.75 IMITATES HORIZONTAL STROKE (21-24 mo.)

The child observes while you make a horizontal stroke and he imitates it with your horizontal stroke in view.

1. Make a horizontal stroke from the left to the right of the paper and say to the child, "Across" or "This way."
2. Encourage the child to imitate on the same paper below or to the right of your stroke. Assist the child, if necessary.
3. Let the child stroke in the air, in the sand, on play dough, on sandpaper, or with paint.
4. Let the child move an object from his left to his right using either his hand or a stick.
5. Let the child hit a suspended beach ball, using his hand or a stick, moving his arm from left to right.
6. For the older delayed child:
    a. Make a wide horizontal stroke and let him mark over the stroke. Let him imitate the stroke by drawing next to it. Repeat.
    b. Let the child connect broken lines of a horizontal stroke.
    c. Let the child connect dots to make a horizontal line.

4.76 FOLDS PAPER IMITATIVELY, NOT PRECISELY (21-24 mo.)

The child folds the paper over once in imitation. He does not fold it exactly or precisely.

1. Let the child turn pages of a book or magazine one at a time.
2. Let the child imitate you when you fold diapers, small wash cloths, or the newspaper, or napkins.
3. Fold a paper in half. Encourage the child to imitate with his piece of paper. Precision should not be required at this age.
4. Assist, if necessary. It may be easier to assist from behind the child.
5. Wrap a flat object, such as a card, a small note pad or ruler by folding the paper over to wrap the object. Let the child imitate you.
6. Put an object into a small paper bag and fold the ends of the bag over once and let the child imitate you.

4.0 FINE MOTOR

4.77 BUILDS TOWER USING SIX CUBES (22-24 mo.)

1. Refer to 4.61 (Builds tower using two cubes).
2. Build a tower of six cubes and let the child imitate you.
3. Encourage the child to build a tower of six cubes after he is successful with five cubes.
4. Offer more cubes, if he has successfully built a tower of six cubes.

4.78 HOLDS CRAYON WITH THUMB AND FINGERS (23-25 mo.)

The child holds a crayon with her thumb and fingers, rather than in a fisted hand.

1. Place the paper on the table and tape it down, if necessary.
2. Place the crayon on the table in front of the child and let her pick it up. She may have a preferred hand, but do not insist she use a particular hand.
3. The child can grasp the crayon in her thumb and fingers with her forearm in pronation or palm down position.
4. Place the crayon on the table and turn its writing point toward the child's little finger. Let the child pick the crayon up with her thumb and fingers, palm down. She then adjusts the crayon, turning her fingers so the point of the crayon is in position to make contact with the paper.
5. Position the child's hand with her little finger resting on the table. Place the crayon between her thumb and fingers.
6. Use large crayons, at first, because they are easier to grasp than the smaller crayons.

4.79 IMITATES THREE BLOCK TRAIN USING CUBES (23-26 mo.)

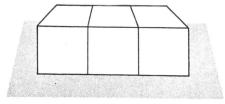

The child observes you making a train using three cubes (one-inch square) and successfully aligns them horizontally with your model in view.

1. Use three cubes and line them in a row to make a three block train. Push the cubes across the table. Encourage the child to imitate with his blocks.
2. Use larger blocks or milk cartons if the child has difficulty with cubes.
3. Make a circus train using empty boxes and place small animals or little toy people in them. Push the train and make train sounds.

4.80 STRINGS THREE ONE-INCH BEADS (23-25 mo.)

1. Refer to 4.74 (Strings one one-inch bead).
2. Offer beads one at a time.
3. Use *Playschool Jumbo Wood Beads.* Let the child begin by stringing the shorter beads which are easier to string than the longer beads.

4.81 SNIPS WITH SCISSORS (23-25 mo.)

The child cuts with the scissors, taking one snip at a time rather than doing continuous cutting.

1. Let the child use small kitchen tongs to pick up objects and to practice opening and closing motions.
2. Let the child use a child sized scissors with rounded tips.
3. Demonstrate by placing your finger and thumb through the handles.
4. Position the scissors with the finger holes one above the other. Position the child's forearm in mid-supination, that is, thumb up. Let the child place his thumb through the top hole and his middle finger through the bottom hole. If his fingers are small, place his index and middle fingers in the bottom hole. The child will adjust his fingers as he gains experience.
5. Let the child open and close the scissors. Assist as necessary by placing your hand over his hand.
6. Let the child snip narrow strips of paper and use it for fringe in art work.
7. The different types of scissors which are available for children are a scissors with reinforced rubber coating on the handle grips, a scissors with double handle grips for your hand as well as the child's hand, a left-handed scissors, a scissors for a prosthetic hook. Use these different types of child's scissors appropriately as required.

4.82 IMITATES A CROSS (24-36 mo.)

The child observes while you draw a cross and he imitates it with your cross in view.

1. Refer to 4.71 (Imitates vertical stroke) and 4.75 (Imitates horizontal stroke).
2. Draw a vertical stroke first and say, "Down." Next, draw a horizontal stroke from left to right and say, "Across," to make a cross.

3. Let the child imitate and draw below your cross on the same paper. Repeat and assist as necessary.
4. For the older delayed child:
   a. Let the child imitate a cross with gross arm movements in the air.
   b. Let the child make strokes in wet or dry sand, or on the chalkboard.
   c. Let the child make a cross with sticks, placing the first stick vertically then the second horizontally across the first stick.

4.83 MAKES FIRST DESIGNS OR SPONTANE-OUS FORMS (24–35 mo.)

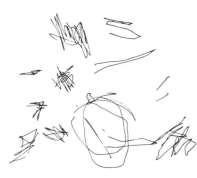

The child begins to make definite and controlled strokes which appear to be spontaneous designs or forms. He is beginning to manipulate the crayon with his thumb and fingers and therefore make smaller, more controlled forms or marks.

1. Offer paper and crayon, marker or pencil. Allow the child to use the materials spontaneously.
2. Ask the child to draw a picture.
3. Let the child scribble or imitate the writing movements of an adult.
4. Let the child pretend she is writing a letter, making a shopping list, or drawing a detailed picture.
5. Let the child finger paint or brush paint.

4.84 PUTS TINY OBJECT INTO SMALL CON-TAINER (24-30 mo.)

The child puts a tiny object such as a pellet or raisin into a small bottle with a 5/8–3/4-inch opening.

1. Demonstrate picking up a tiny object and putting it into a small clear bottle.
2. Let the child grasp a tiny object, such as a raisin, bell, or bead and let him drop it into the bottle.
3. For the older delayed child:
   a. Let the child put a larger object into a larger container, such as a cube into a baby food jar.
   b. Let the child drop a tiny object through a funnel placed in the opening of a small container.

4.85 FOLDS PAPER IN HALF (24-30 mo.)

The child folds a piece of paper in half and creases it without crumpling the paper.

1. Sit next to the child and demonstrate folding the paper

in half by bringing the bottom of the paper to the top and creasing it.
2. Ask the child to fold his paper. Assist him as necessary.
3. Crease the paper in half for the child if necessary. Let the child "fold" the paper on the crease and press down on the fold.
4. Let the child help you fold napkins, wash cloths, newspapers.
5. Refer to 4.76 (Folds paper imitatively but not precisely).
6. Mark the top edge of the paper and the bottom underside of the paper with a felt pen. Let the child bring the bottom marked line to the top marked line. Let the child fold the paper in hald and press down on the fold.
7. Place a thin book which is half the size of the paper on the paper. Let the child bring the bottom end of the paper up to cover the book and in this way, fold the paper in half.

4.86 COPIES A CIRCLE (25-36 mo.)

The child copies or reproduces a circle from a model without observing a demonstration.

1. Place the model above the child's paper and ask him to draw one just like it.
2. Draw a circle and let the child imitate, if he has difficulty copying a circle.
3. Refer to 4.73 (Imitates circular scribble).
4. Give simple verbal directions along with the motions, such as "Around and stop," or "Make a circle or a ball."
5. Give assistance as to the direction of the stroke, e.g., "This way," circling your arm toward the left. Let the child use gross arm movements and make a circle in the air.
6. For the older delayed child, plan activities which give him concepts of a circle, such as:
   a. Playing with a ball or feeling the shape of a ball.
   b. Sitting in a circle or walking on a marked circle.
   c. Playing with a hula hoop encircling him or encouraging him to sit in it, roll it, feel it or throw bean bags into it.
   d. Stirring or mixing motions with a spoon.
   e. Winding a ball of yarn or string on a large spool.

4.87 BUILDS TOWER USING EIGHT CUBES (28-31 mo.)

The child successfully builds a tower of at least eight cubes.

1. Refer to 4.61 (Builds tower using two cubes).
2. Offer the child more cubes as he successfully builds a tower.
3. Seat the child at the table or on the floor with a low table, or if he prefers, let him stand at the table.

4.0 FINE MOTOR

4.88 SNIPS ON LINE USING SCISSORS
(28-35 mo.)

The child cuts with one snipping movement at a time on a drawn line.

1. Refer to 4.81 (Snips with scissors).
2. Draw vertical lines one to two inches apart on a half-inch strip of paper. Let the child snip the paper off cutting on the vertical line.
3. Use a thick marking pen and draw short vertical lines about one to two inches apart along the edge of a paper. Let the child snip each line with one snip and make a fringe.
4. Let the child snip on a line drawn across the page.
5. Give the child comfortably sized paper which he can easily grasp while cutting.
6. Let the child place his arms or hands on the table while he uses the scissors.

4.89 HOLDS PENCIL WITH THUMB AND FINGERS—ADULT-LIKE GRASP
(29-31 mo.)

The child holds a pencil with his thumb and fingers in an adult-like grasp.

1. Let the child use a primary pencil which is wider in diameter than a regular pencil. It will be easier for him to grasp than a regular pencil.
2. Let the child hold a spoon for self feeding with his thumb and fingers in an adult-like grasp, with forearm supination or the palm up position.
3. Refer to 4.78 (Holds crayon with thumb and fingers).

4.90 PLACES SIX SQUARE PEGS IN PEGBOARD
(29-31 mo.)

The child places at least six square pegs (about 5/8 inch) in the pegboard.

1. Offer the child six pegs to place in the pegboard. Increase the number of pegs as she successfully puts the six pegs into the pegboard.
2. For the older delayed child: Let her place square pegs or blocks in the matching square hole on the lid of a coffee can. Outline the square hole with colored masking tape for emphasis.

4.91 IMITATES THREE BLOCK BRIDGE USING CUBES (31 mo. and above).

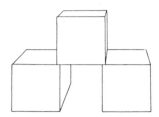

The child builds a bridge using three cubes (one-inch) and builds a three block bridge after a demonstration and with the model in view.

1. Let the child watch you build a bridge with three cubes. Place two cubes enough apart to balance a third cube.
2. Leave this model in view and give the child three cubes. Ask him to build a three block bridge. Assist as necessary.
3. For the older delayed child:
   a. Use large wooden blocks, blocks made of milk cartons, or boxes to build a three block bridge.
   b. Play a variation of "London Bridge." Use huge blocks to build a bridge. Or build a bridge using two chairs with a board across the chairs. Let the child crawl under the "bridge."

4.92 BUILDS TOWER USING NINE CUBES
(32-36 mo.)

The child builds a tower using nine cubes (one-inch square).

1. Offer the child additional cubes if he successfully builds a tower of nine cubes.
2. Refer to 4.61 (Builds tower using two cubes).

4.93 STRINGS ONE-HALF-INCH BEADS
(33½ mo. and above)

1. Let the child string half-inch beads to make a necklace. Square beads may be easier to grasp, at first, than the round beads.
2. Let the child string large uncooked macaroni to make a necklace. Macaroni can be dipped in paint or food coloring.
3. Make a Hawaiian lei by stringing cut-out paper flowers. The hole in the center of the flower may be made with a small hole puncher. String cut straws (half-inch to one-inch in length) in between the flowers.
4. Refer to 4.74 (Strings one one-inch bead).

5.01 ENJOYS AND NEEDS A GREAT DEAL OF PHYSICAL CONTACT AND TACTILE STIMULATION (0-3 mo.)

1. The child often attempts to establish contact with a warm, mothering figure (whether mother, father or other primary caretaker) by crying. Be sure to satisfy the child's hunger and tactile needs together.
2. Do not prop the bottle. Cuddle the child while she is eating.
3. Adjust your posture so the child feels safe and secure. Be sure the child feels neither smothered nor in danger of falling. Experiment with different positions. At this developmental stage the child has a strong need for security when held.
   a. Watch for startle responses. Hold the child more firmly if they occur.
   b. The child may need to be swaddled. Wrap her firmly, but not tightly, in cloth or blankets. Swaddling is useless unless the arms and legs are immobilized. Swaddle between birth and three months only. Discontinue if this is resisted. Use swaddling only when necessary to provide security for the child.
4. Adult body tension is easily transmitted to a young child. Caretakers should be relaxed, calm, confident.
5. A child may prefer frolic-type handling, stroking, tickling, kissing. Active cuddling or hugging may be resisted because it is experienced as a restraint. No child should resist *all* physical contact. Resistance this strong is a warning signal; refer the child for psychological or medical consultation.
6. If the child seems to be struggling and rejects all cuddling, he may be uncomfortable. Readjust your arms and the child's position. If there is muscle hypertonicity, seek physical therapy consultation.
7. Cuddle, hold, rock, walk, stroke, and pet the child as much as possible. No amount of cuddling is too much at this age. Active stimulation, such as tickling, bouncing, must be done in moderation. The child tries easily and should be allowed to withdraw from periods of active play.

5.02 REGARDS FACE (0-1 mo.)

The child momentarily and solemnly stares at the face of the person interacting with him.

1. Place the child in supine or in supported sitting. Bend over the child with your face eight to ten inches away and at his chest level. Nod your head, talk quietly and smile while gently stroking his stomach.
2. Touch and hold the child frequently. Position the child so he can see your face when feeding him by bottle. Occasionally, talk, smile, and nod to him.
3. Pick up a crying child and hold him up so he can see your face or hold him over your shoulder to stimulate visual regard of the environment. Frequent soothing for cries in this manner visually stimulates the young child.

4. Wait until the child is in a drowsy state, eyelids droopy and beginning to close, then lean over the child, nod your head, and talk until he exhibits regard. If the child does not regard your face and instead just cries, discontinue or postpone this activity until a later time. Do not attempt this if you really want the child to sleep.
5. Hold the child cradled in a feeding position, but do not let him feed or suck. Smile, nod, and talk to him. Do not use this activity if it frustrates or angers the child.
6. Play with the child. Early, solemn regard is the foundation for innumerable skills such as social smile and play, visual exploration, recognition of mother and fear of strangers. This is the earliest learning experience. Do not neglect development at this time.
7. All of the activities in 4.01 (Regards colorful object momentarily) and 4.03 (Regards colorful object for few seconds) are appropriate for helping facial regard as well.

5.03 SMILES REFLEXIVELY (0-1½ mo.)

The child's smiles are fleeting and rare at this time. They do not occur consistently.

1. Talk, nod, and smile while stroking the child's cheek at one side of his mouth. This may elicit reflexive smiling. If this elicits a rooting reflex and frustrates the child, discontinue the activity.
2. Do enjoyable physical activities and movements, such as gentle bouncing, jiggling, clapping hands, tickling.
3. Touch and handle the child as much as possible. Make physical contact pleasant. Refer to 5.01 (Enjoys and needs much holding, physical contact, tactile stimulation).
4. Talk to the child. Speak quietly; speak in paragraphs; do not use single words for now. The child usually prefers quiet, normally high-pitched female voices at this time. For this reason, the first smiles are often directed at the mother. If the child startles to the sound of an adult voice, perhaps the speech she hears is too abrupt.
5. Remember, a child needs quiet times, too. Noise can be too much or too constant for the child to tolerate.

5.04 ESTABLISHES EYE CONTACT (0-2 mo.)

The child looks at the adult in the eye fairly consistently when approached.

A. Consistent active gaze aversion, an important indication of disruption in young infancy, can be caused by overstimulation or the wrong kinds of stimulation.
   1. Cut down on the quantity of social stimulation. Talk very quietly and handle the child gently; do not force a response. Provide only one stimulus at a time. Watch for tiredness. Notice when the child is ready to play and is wakeful, alert, and in a good mood. Follow the child's lead.
   2. Continue to make an effort to reach the child socially and interact with him a few times a day. Do not allow withdrawal into complete self-absorp-

tion. Even if the child does not cry for or seek attention, give him social attention anyway. Refer to 5.03 (Smiles reflexively).

3. If the child always looks away and rejects eye contact, try following his face with your face and "catching" his eyes with yours even momentarily. Smile and praise the child if you are successful.

4. Experiment by covering the child's face with a blanket or cloth. Position yourself so your face is the only thing the child sees when the cloth is removed. Pull the cloth off or let the child pull it off if he can. Say, "Boo," and move a little closer to his face. Do not continue this activity if it scares the child.

5. If a child avoids eye contact, he may also resist physical contact. If so, apply firm pressure rather than gentle stroking. Firm pressure may be more easily accepted than a "tickly" gentle stroke. Gentle stroking can result in startle responses from the child. "Cue" him that contact is imminent by first speaking softly to him and then touching an extremity, his arm or leg. This helps the child become less hypersensitive to touch, begin to tolerate or even enjoy adult company, and perhaps calm down enough to accept eye contact. Refer to 5.05 (Molds and relaxes body when held, cuddles) for additional suggestions.

6. Try to achieve eye contact by lifting the child above your head and smiling up at him. Do not continue this activity if it frightens him.

7. Refer to 5.02 (Regards face), 4.03 (Regards colorful object for few seconds), 4.06 (Follows with eyes to midline), and 4.04 (Follows with eyes moving person while in supine).

8. A child who refuses both eye contact and physical contact consistently and seems physically normal should be referred for professional (psychological, psychiatric, neurological) consultation.

B. No focused visual regard; the child appears disinterested in people because of apathy or perhaps very slow development.

   1. Refer to 4.01 (Regards colorful object momentarily) and to 4.03 (Regards colorful object for few seconds.)

   2. Refer the child for visual assessment.

5.05 MOLDS AND RELAXES BODY WHEN HELD; CUDDLES (0-3 mo.)

The child, when picked up and held, molds his body to the adult's and snuggles comfortably. It is very important that a child, who actively rejects being held, be helped to find a position he finds comfortable and acceptable.

1. Be sure the child feels secure when held. He may be held in cradled position, over an adult's shoulder, at the hip (facing toward or away from the adult), in sitting leaning against the adult's chest, or in prone lying face-to-face on an adult's stomach. (Different children prefer different positions at different times.) Do not be afraid to experiment.

2. Be sure the child feels comfortable and unrestricted when he is held. Very often, a young child struggles against being held in certain positions because he feels as if he cannot breathe, e.g., when breastfeeding, the child's nose may be blocked by the breast, or because he feels as if he cannot move, e.g., the active child, especially, may fight having his arms and legs trapped.

3. Hold the child so he can see your face or the faces of others as much as possible. Hold him over your head sometimes so he can look down at your face.

4. If the child has great difficulty accepting body contact, try lying down beside him and gently touch his arm or leg. See if he will allow you to place your arm around him, to touch his stomach, his head and his face. Make this an enjoyable activity by talking to and smiling at him. Stop the activity *before* the child begins to resist it. Work very gradually through the stages of making body contact.

5. A child who consistently avoids or rejects body contact is said to be tactile defensive. Do not allow this situation to continue. Obtain psychiatric, psychological, neurological or occupational therapy consultation.

5.06 DRAWS ATTENTION TO SELF WHEN IN DISTRESS (0-3 mo.)

The child may fuss, cry or scream when exposed to unpleasant environmental situations, e.g., loud noises or, when internally upset, e.g., hungry.

1. The child should not cry unattended. Crying is the child's attempt to communicate. Reinforce his attempts by fulfilling his needs if possible.

2. Do your best to respond appropriately to his crying and alleviate his distress. Often, your appropriate response is achieved by trial and error. The child may be hungry and the solution, of course, is to feed him. Then again, he may be having gas pains, the solution would be to bubble him or place pressure on his stomach. The child may be wet or soiled (a child may mind this very much). The child may be in pain; perhaps the diaper pin is not in place. The child may be lonely; cuddling would help. A frequent cause of crying is *tiredness* which is often overlooked. An overtired child may want to cry alone for a few minutes or may prefer being put to sleep by his parents.

3. The child who rarely cries or cries with little urgency is sometimes in danger of being ignored. Respond to any of his "sounds" or his vaguest cry with consistency. Let the child discover he can control your responses by his behavior.

4. Give plenty of attention, even if the child does not demand it. Play with, talk to, and cuddle the child.

5.07 RESPONDS WITH SMILE WHEN SOCIALLY APPROACHED (1½-4 mo.)

The child smiles fairly consistently now when an effort is made to "see her smile."

1. Spend some time each day in social play. Provide small, frequent doses of fun rather than a drawn-out, lengthy play period.
2. Place the child in supine. Lean over her with your face about eight to ten inches above her chest. Be sure your face is parallel with hers. Talk, smile, nod your head, and gently stroke her stomach. Stroke her cheek near her mouth, if necessary, to encourage her to smile. If the latter elicits a rooting reflex and frustrates the child, discontinue it.
3. Be sociable and enjoy the daily routines such as feeding, diaper-changing, dressing, bathing. Let the child know you enjoy her company.
4. A child who is overtired or too stimulated will attempt withdrawal by acting disinterested, looking away or even falling asleep. Respect her need for relaxation and do not demand social behavior until a later time.

5.08 STOPS UNEXPLAINED CRYING (3-6 mo.)

A child has usually outgrown his fretful, colicky crying that often characterizes the early months by age three months. This condition can last as long as five to six months, but this is rare. The following activities are for the child who is not yet over "periodic irritable crying."

1. A child may be comforted by the appearance of a face, soft talking, a hand gently placed on his abdomen, or by holding his two hands together over his abdomen and gently rocking him.
2. Quieting may often occur on a psychological, neurological level. You might consider:
   a. Swaddling the child firmly, but not tightly.
   b. Continuous motion, e.g., rocking, walking, bouncing.
   c. Continuous, monotonous sound, e.g., a clock ticking, low radio music, crooning.
   d. Turning on lights in the child's room, although this may not be suitable for an older child.
3. Do not become upset with yourself if you become too distraught or angry with your child and need to relax. This is very normal. Let the other parent hold the child for a while. Tension in a parent increases the child's tension and distress. If the parent is very upset and has no other choice, he can put the child down and walk away until he feels calmer.
4. Hold and comfort the child, as much as possible, when he has fussy periods or cries unconsolably. This may be colicky crying or just the result of stress and tiredness. If you find yourself tense, which makes the child's worse, leave the child alone, at least temporarily.
5. Meet the young child's need for company and attention when he cries just to be held. This is perfectly all right; meeting the child's need will not result in "spoiling" the child. The young child's major means of communication is crying. It is very important for the child's future development that his early attempts to communicate and to reach out are recognized.
6. Lack of tactile stimulation may cause the child's unexplained crying. A child who is carried much of the time, e.g., in a sling on the mother's back or chest, may cry much less.

5.09 VOCALIZES IN RESPONSE TO ADULT TALK AND SMILE (3-5 mo.)

The child vocalizes, coos or makes happy sounds in response to social interactions.

1. Imitate his noises; talk, smile and nod to him when the child spontaneously vocalizes.
2. Play vocal games with the child. Coo at him, make funny noises, sing little songs during feeding, diaper changing, bathing. Do not become too silent when with him. You can begin "talking" with sounds he already makes.
3. Pause at appropriate times when talking to the child. See if he makes any noises of his own. If he does, immediately respond by smiling and talking to him.

5.10 DISCRIMINATES STRANGERS (3-6 mo.)

The child freezes, stares, quiets or refuses to smile on sight of a stranger. He now discriminates among familiar and unfamiliar people.

1. Let the child closely acquaint himself with two or three people who visit the home regularly. This might lessen the stranger anxiety that is to come.
2. Make sure the father has frequent enjoyable contacts with the child. Allow the father to take over some caretaking.
3. Make sure the child sees new faces and environments by taking him shopping, to a park, for walks or to other homes.
4. A young child usually prefers high-pitched voices to low voices at some developmental ages. This may result in an acceptance of female figures and a fear of male figures. Do not worry over this; it is temporary. Fathers should not avoid contacts at this time, even if contacts must be brief or from a distance.
5. A child discriminates strangers by first learning the familiar. Visual recognition of the mother, family or primary caretakers comes first. A child must be cared for by a consistent figure to learn whom he knows and whom he does not.
6. Refer to 5.17 (Recognizes mother visually) for activities.

5.11 SOCIALIZES WITH STRANGERS/ANYONE (3-5 mo.)

The child can be exposed to any comfortable person and responds well.

5.0 SOCIAL-EMOTIONAL

1. Take the child on short outings occasionally such as to the store or park. It is important to let the child accustom himself to the sight and sound of other people in and out of the home. A little of this does go a long way; do not let a young child become overstimulated.
2. Introduce a regular sitter at this time. It may be frightening for the child to be left with a sitter later when in the period of stranger anxiety. Make sure the child sees the sitter often and enjoys her before the child becomes stranger anxious.
3. A child may resist strangers and may be upset over his mother's absence almost from the first month. This is not a cause for concern. It may be related to the amount of time the mother holds the child and the speed with which he becomes accustomed to her voice, smell, and manner of holding him. If the child is very distressed, he should be treated as if stranger anxious and not be forcefully separated, especially during vulnerable or tired periods. However, it is a good idea to accustom the child to at least one other person to free the mother once in a while.

5.12 DEMANDS SOCIAL ATTENTION (3-8 mo.)

The child becomes bored and fretful when left alone. She learns that crying brings attention. Crying for attention is a positive behavior and should be reinforced.

1. Attend to cries; do not leave a crying child alone. Help her.
2. Place the child in different positions and places such as the floor, chair or crib; move together about the house throughout the day.
3. Provide appropriate toys, especially ones small enough for manipulation.
4. Alternate social play and toy play with the child. Do not isolate the child to teach him independence. Isolation need never be provided. His development depends on social contact, not on learning to be alone. However, do not make the mistake of entertaining the child at all times. He should be able to enjoy your companionship without needing your direct interaction. Be in the same room with him if you both wish it, but busy yourself with other things for at least a couple of minutes.

5.13 VOCALIZES ATTITUDES—PLEASURE AND DISPLEASURE (3-6 mo.)

The child no longer cries for everything, although crying is still the usual response. Sometimes, the child whines, grunts or makes an unhappy noise instead of crying. Pleasure may be indicated by a coo, chuckle, laugh or any other sound. The child's vocalizations are not yet very consistent, especially those of displeasure.

1. Be sure to respond when the child vocalizes. The child may vocalize a little before actually wailing for attention when she first awakens to be fed. Do not wait until she is "serious" and crying hard. Go to her immediately if she makes any sounds and meet her needs. This teaches the child that crying need not be her only means of communication.
2. Give the child plenty of time to respond when you are socializing with her. Do not talk so constantly that she cannot participate. Let her respond, however minimally; then respond to her.
3. Listen for the child's voice. If at any time during the day she makes a sound, answer her. Call across the room to her or go over and talk with her briefly. Let your voice mirror hers. If she sounds happy, respond happily.
4. A child who is talked to constantly may not be able to "get a word in." "Talking" to each other is very important. Be sure there is sufficient silence for the child to "talk," and that he is finished "talking" before you respond.

5.14 BECOMES AWARE OF STRANGE SITUATIONS (3-6 mo.)

1. Take the child on outings away from home, such as to the store, park, neighborhood, shopping center, zoo, other homes.
2. Be sure other people are invited to the child's home fairly regularly.
3. Go on a bus ride if he is used to cars and vice versa.
4. Go on outdoor picnics where the child does a familiar activitiy, such as eating, in an unfamiliar surrounding.
5. Let the child lie on grass, feel sand, wade in water, lie on different textures, such as a rubber raft or beach mats made of straw. Experiment by supporting him in sitting or in standing in these situations.

5.15 ENJOYS SOCIAL PLAY (3-6 mo.)

1. Tickle, swing, and toss the child gently.
2. Sing little songs and play vocal games with him.
3. Play "This Little Piggy" and "Pat-a-cake" with the child's toes and hands.
4. Make silly, non-verbal sounds to him, e.g., cluck, whistle, etc. and see if he will smile.
5. Make a fun movement or activity contingent upon some activity of the child's, e.g., blow on his stomach whenever he kicks his legs, claps his hands or tickle him whenever he waves his arms. Align yourself so he looks straight at your face.
6. Let the child bounce on the parent's knees or stomach to the accompaniment of nursery rhymes, such as "This is the Way the Ladies Ride" or "Ride-a-Cock Horse."
7. Dance with the child.
8. Make silly faces if this does not frighten the child.
9. Do not overdo social play to the point of exhaustion for the child. Ten five-minute play periods spaced throughout the day are better than one or two hour-long sessions.

Let the child learn to amuse herself by giving her brief periods alone (at least two to five minutes).

10. Caution: Some of these activities are not appropriate for cerebral palsy children without special physical therapy consultation. All children need and enjoy frolic play, but certain positions and adaptations are very important in handling the CP child's rougher play. Special equipment, e.g., a net swing, can often be used for frolic play and can be adapted to prevent undesirable movement patterns.

5.16 MAKES APPROACH MOVEMENTS TO MIRROR (3-5½ mo.)

The child stares at and moves slightly toward the mirror. Her arms may activate. Her stare is usually very solemn.

1. Hang a mirror or a shiny aluminum cooky sheet to one side of the child's visual field in his crib or playpen.
2. Tap on the mirror to call the child's attention to it or hold the mirror directly in front of the child's eyes.
3. If the child still does not respond, refer to 5.02 (Regards face), 5.03 (Smiles reflexively), 5.07 (Responds with smile to social approach), 5.09 (Vocalizes to talk and smile), 5.04 (Establishes eye contact).

5.17 RECOGNIZES MOTHER VISUALLY (4-8 mo.)

The child may smile, activate, quiet, or cry at the sight of the mother. "Mother" is used to refer to whoever is the primary caretaker.

1. Attend to the child's cries and respond appropriately. At this age, the child should not be pushed to accept comforting from others. His most important need is to learn to adjust to his primary caretaker.
2. Attend to the child's cries; pick him up and place him over your shoulder to stimulate visual exploration, especially if the child is young and has trouble with visual regard.
3. Let the child see and explore your face with his hands, especially during feeding and dressing. Talk to him.
4. Stop and say "Hi," and pat the child whenever you pass him. Make sure he sees your face.
5. A child responds to a "gestalt" of recognition cues. Visual recognition may depend upon the "sameness" of the mother's appearance. A new hat, hair curlers, sunglasses, wet hair, or a facial bandage may completely destroy recognition and frighten the child under one year of age. Avoid these additions if possible. If the child becomes upset and the addition cannot be removed, the mother can hold the child in a position in which he cannot see her face and can talk to him. Her familiar voice, smell, and touch will reassure the child that she is really the "same old mother."

5.18 ENJOYS FROLIC PLAY (4-8 mo.)

1. Let the parent lift the child "way" above his head and shake her gently.
2. Begin slowly and gradually work up to rough play, e.g., swing the child very slowly at first, then faster and faster.
3. Watch the child's face. If she shows fear, stop immediately, bring her close to your body, and hold her securely. Drop back to much quieter play.
4. Use a blanket to swing the child. Two people are needed for this activity. Place the child in supine on the blanket. Each adult should stand at one end of the blanket, holding one corner in each hand. Lift the blanket (and the child) a few inches off the floor. Gently swing the blanket from side to side, forward and back, up and down. Increase your momentum as the child becomes comfortable and enjoys his "ride."
5. Play "Ride-a-Cock-Horse" with the child on your stomach or on your knees.
6. Get down on the floor and crawl around the child. A young child is often charmed by this.
7. Tickle the child gently. Laugh with her when she laughs.
8. Turn the child upside-down.
9. Bounce on the bed together.
10. Splash water in the tub. (Be sure there is no soap in it.)
11. Dance to music together.
12. Place the child on your shoulders and give her a ride. Hold the child tightly since she cannot hold on yet. Be sure to watch for low ceilings, doors and tree branches.
13. Refer to precautions for cerebral palsy children in 5.15 (Enjoys social play).

5.19 REPEATS ENJOYABLE ACTIVITIES (4-8 mo.)

The young child loves repetition and will repeat or attempt to repeat any "game" he enjoys.

1. Introduce games to the child and play them over and over:
   a. Sing "Row Row Row Your Boat," holding hands and rocking together.
   b. Bounce to music.
   c. Rock to music.
   d. Sing "Rock-a-bye Baby," rocking the child gently in your arms.
   e. Play "Pat-a-cake," clapping his hands for him if he does not imitate.
   f. Let the child give to you and you give back to him a toy he likes. Do this only with an older child who has learned release. Be sure to pass the toy back and forth.
2. Hold a conversation; first you talk, then he talks. Allow plenty of time for his response. Praise even a minimal response. Continue as long as the child responds.
3. Provide a mobile the child can activate by hitting or kicking. Let him play at this over and over again.
4. Provide pots and pans to bang on, drums to hit, bells to

131

ring. Anything that makes a good noise with minimal effort is acceptable. Encourage the child to "do it again."

5. Help the child learn that he can make fun things happen. A soft squeak toy he can hit to make a noise may interest him. Chime balls that move with the slightest touch are also good.

5.20 DISPLAYS STRANGER ANXIETY (5-8 mo.)

The child who is stranger anxious is evidencing real growth in discrimination and affection. Although difficult for parents and staff members, this is an important and positive stage.

1. The child is now actively frightened by strangers, cries in protest or rejects handling. Expose the child very slowly to different people and to being handled by them.
2. Do not leave a child alone with strangers at this stage unless he is evidently comfortable with them.
3. The mother or primary caretaker should hold the child when he is approached by strangers.
4. The mother must act relaxed and happy. Body tension or worry is communicated to the child and provides a good reason for the child to be afraid.
5. Let the child closely acquaint himself with two or three people who visit regularly in his own home. Ask them to ignore the child until he makes his first approach. They should not approach the child, but should talk to the mother, remain nearby, and make only brief eye contacts with the child.
6. Do not move suddenly or make loud noises near a child if you are a stranger.
7. If a child accepts a toy from you she has probably accepted you at least tentatively and will usually cooperate with your efforts in play, teaching or assessment.
8. Visual familiarity with a stranger comes before tactile familiarity.
9. If there is a fear of the father, it will eventually disappear. Father should be calm, quiet and cheerful, attempt no rough play and be around the child frequently so the child can observe him.
10. Stranger anxiety is built upon visual recognition of familiar people and discrimination of strangers. Refer to 5.17 (Recognizes mother visually) and 5.10 (Discriminates strangers).
11. A very outgoing child, who has experienced multiple caretakers, may never experience stranger anxiety. This is all right *only if* the child is positively attached to one or two primary caretakers and is discriminating in the amount of attention and affection he gives to those he does and does not know.

5.21 LIFTS ARMS TO MOTHER (5-6 mo.)

1. Cue the child before he is picked up. Lightly clap your hands, reach out to the child and say, "Up," invitingly. Wait for a response. If there is no response after five seconds, pick him up anyway. Do this whenever you pick up the child.

2. Language, whether gestural, vocal or verbal, is most likely to be used and expanded if it is its own reward, i.e., if it is effective for the child as a tool in achieving an aim such as being picked up.
3. Refer to 3.20 (Holds head in line with body when pulled to sitting) and to 3.37 (Lifts head and assists when pulled to sitting).

5.22 EXPLORES ADULT FEATURES (5-7 mo.)

1. Place the child's hands on your face and help him explore by touching your eyes, nose, mouth. If the child wants to taste your face, too, let him if you can stand it. Kiss him back.
2. Be sure not to discourage this exploratory behavior when it occurs spontaneously. Keep the child's fingernails short, so you will not be scratched!
3. Let the child explore and touch everything, such as different textures, toys, his body. If he does not explore, encourage him.
4. If the child pulls your hair and jerks, do not scold or yell. Bend his wrist down just enough so he will release his hold. Do not pull his fisted hand away.
5. Experiment by "decorating" your face with rouge, lipstick, stars, or sunglasses to attract the child to your face. Do not do this if the child is frightened by it.
6. Hold a cracker, celery stick, or some food items in your teeth and encourage the child to pull it out.
7. Let the child feel his father's beard.
8. Stick out your tongue and wiggle it. Let the child place his fingers in your mouth. Suck the child's fingers to let him feel the difference between your doing it and his own finger-sucking.
9. Place a feather, rolled up paper or unsharpened pencil between your upper lip and nose and keep it there by puckering your lips. Encourage the child to remove your "moustache."
10. Place a block on top of your head and let the child remove it.

5.23 SMILES AT MIRROR IMAGE (5½-8½ mo.)

1. Use activities from 5.16 (Makes approach movements to mirror). Allow ample time for a response from the child to build up.
2. Use a large mirror so both the adult and the child can be seen. Talk to and smile at the child's *image* in the mirror. Tap the glass to attract the child's attention.
3. Use a technique which usually elicits laughing and smiling, and do it in front of the mirror, e.g., tickle the child, blow on his stomach or make funny noises.
4. Dance with the child in front of a mirror.
5. Make a favorite toy, stuffed animal, object, doll, or pet "dance" near or "talk" to the mirror.
6. Position the child in front of the mirror in different ways. Experiment with placing him in puppy position, in sidelying, in supported sitting, on hands and knees, in supported standing or looking over your shoulder.

5.24 DISTINGUISHES SELF AS SEPARATE FROM MOTHER (6-9 mo.)

The child probably considers himself a part of his mother and his environment at first. By this age he has learned to distinguish himself from his environment. He knows he is a distinct individual as is his mother. This awareness fosters a real knowledge of his dependency on and love for his mother (or primary caretaker). It is through this attachment to one primary caretaker that the child develops his ability to love others and develops his own self-esteem.

1. Refer to 5.17 (Recognizes mother visually) for beginning activities.
2. Help the child contrast himself and his mother by stressing the child's individuality. This is best accomplished by consistently responding to and fulfilling his needs and by letting him discover that his actions bring results. If he cries or fusses, do not ignore him; respond to his distress and try to meet his needs. If he "talks," smiles, coos or laughs, respond to him in a happy way. Talk back and forth with him as much as possible.
3. Play games with the child's body parts. Find and lightly tickle his tummy; play "This Little Piggy" with his toes; let him "find" his mouth and your mouth; let him place your finger in his mouth and his finger in yours; let him "find" his hand and your hand and compare the fingers, size, and the difference in feel.
4. Help the child find himself and an adult in a mirror. Refer to 5.28 (Responds playfully to mirror).
5. Play a game of "Where's Mommy?" or "Where's Baby?" with an older child. Applaud when he is right.
6. Be prepared for the separation anxiety which accompanies this real love for the mother. Refer to 5.25 (Shows anxiety at separation from mother).

5.25 SHOWS ANXIETY OVER SEPARATION FROM MOTHER (6-9 mo.)

The child's fear of being separated from the mother at this time is evidence of his emotional normality as well as his cognitive awareness and his recognition of his great dependence upon her. Although the eventual goal for every child includes ability to separate and be independent, this is not the age at which to demand development of these skills. Separation takes a very long time, and the way in which we handle separation is quite dependent upon the child's developmental level. Working through separation fears is a gradual process which will probably being now, but continue until the child is age two-and-a-half or three or older.

A. If the child is *under* eighteen months of age, *do not forcefully separate:*
    1. The child who is *developmentally* under eighteen months, attached to her mother, and fearful when the mother is absent. The child at this age requires our respect of her fears. She needs to be dependent.

2. The child who has accepted separation in the past, but now has reached a temporary developmental stage of separation anxiety, e.g., eight or thirteen months.
3. The child under two-and-a-half or three who accepts center or school staff and activities when the mother is present. The child is happy to interact and participate as long as her mother does not leave, but is distressed at her absence. (Even though this child is over eighteen months, it is unnecessary for all concerned to forcefully separate her.)
4. The child who has recently undergone a traumatic separation of more than short-term duration. If the child is hospitalized between the ages of one and five years or if the mother leaves home for a visit, hospitalization or vacation for more than a day, the child will probably react dramatically once things have returned to normal. This situation requires special care. Some manifestations of the child's increased anxiety include: regression, such as soiling, wetting, thumb-sucking, demands for the bottle; sleep problems, such as crying when put into bed, inability to go to sleep, night awakenings, fear of the dark; clinging, excessive whining, initial hospitality toward the mother or others, aggression, and withdrawal.

    Parents must make a special effort to understand and console during the months the child is recovering from her disturbance. This can take months.
    a. A repeat separation is to be avoided if at all possible.
    b. Cheerfully allow, without shaming or scolding, any regressions; they are temporary.
    c. Sit with the fearful child in her room until she is soundly asleep.
    d. Let the child know you understand she is angry with her mother and upset about the separation. Mother must be reassuring about the anger, too. Mother should reassure the child she will not go again, if this is true.
    e. Let the child cling and provide the extra affection needed.
    f. Act cheerful and confident that there is nothing to fear.
    g. Play with a doll family and act out the fearful situation if the child is old enough to understand. Repeat the game as often as the child wishes.
    h. If the child understands, read some books about separation or make up stories about it. One good book on this subject is *The Runaway Bunny* by Margaret Wise Brown. Books about hospital experiences are available also.
B. If the child is *between* eighteen and thirty-six months of age, *work on gradual separation.* Separation takes place through sequential steps or in successive approximations. Begin where the child is and work through all of the following steps one at a time. The child often does not reach the last step until thirty to thirty-six months of age. Do not attempt to forcefully separate a child under eighteen months. *It may take a week or over a year to work through the stages of separation.* Follow the child's lead and your knowledge of her developmental level.

1. At home, the child should:
   a. Be left in a playpen or on the floor in a room where the mother is present but not attentive. See if the child can be left "alone" for about five minutes. Provide *fascinating* toys at first, e.g., lots of balloons or a coffee can full of novel and interesting kitchen items.
      Caution: If the child is likely to break and/or swallow balloon pieces, do not offer balloons without supervision.
   b. Be left alone in a room while the mother goes to another room. Provide fascinating and absorbing toys. If the child follows the mother, do not force the issue. Casually try again later. Start with very brief departures, ten seconds if necessary; work up to about five minutes. Mother should casually tell the child where and when she is going.
   c. Be left with another familiar person while the mother leaves the room for five minutes.
   d. Tolerate the visits of the mother's friends. Visits should occur two to three times a week so they become common place events to the child. The child will gradually approach these friends when he adjusts to them and feels "safe."
   e. Go for walks with the mother to the store, park or around the block.
   f. Stay with the father or a very familiar figure in his *own home* while the mother goes out.

2. Begin where the child is and work through the following steps one at a time. At the center or at school, the child should:
   a. Tolerate your presence without distress when her mother is with her. Start at a distance, if necessary. Sit still on the floor. Do not make eye contact too frequently. Gradually, even if it takes days, move closer until you can sit right beside the child. (With a normal child this process should only take a few minutes.) Talk to the mother, not to the child. The child's distress, or lack of it, determines your speed and distance.
   b. Accept a proffered toy from you. Give plenty of time for a slow, cautious response. If she takes a toy from your hand, she is ready for you to talk casually to her. If not, go back to 2.a.
   c. Let you touch her casually for brief moments while you are talking to her. Withdraw *before* she has a chance to be upset.
   d. Let you make the attempt to play with her. Use a toy that both of you can play with and that requires close contact. Talk, make suggestions, keep it light and easy.
   e. Let you hold her. Be ready to put her down as soon as she needs to return to her mother. Work on this step until the child lets you hold her comfortably. Do not get up and do not let the mother move away.
   f. Explore at a distance from her mother while the mother remains stationary. The child will make frequent returns to her mother for security. Attempt to join the child, moving slowly, when the child is playing a little distance away. Engage in social interaction and play. Do not hold the child, and accept any returns to "home base" (Mother). When the child is comfortably playing with you at a distance from her mother for five to ten minutes, go to the next step.
   f. Allow you to care for her while the mother remains stationary in the room, in the same spot all morning or follows along behind, whichever comes easiest for the child. The staff member should carry or walk the child to the toilet, sink, snack table. If you began with the mother following, change to the mother sitting stationary as soon as the child is comfortable. (At this stage, the mother might be advised to bring along a book or some needlepoint.) The child may still return to the mother temporarily, but the mother should make an effort to be very casual and boring when the child is with her. The mother should act as if there is nothing to do if the child remains with her, whereas the staff member has toys and activities to entice the child back to the group.
   h. Allow the mother to leave for very brief periods, no more than a minute, when engaged in some absorbing activity with you. The mother should leave her stationary spot, come to the child, and casually mention her need to get a diaper, go to the bathroom or get a drink of water. She must say she will be *right back*. Mother should then go, no matter how the child responds. If the child is screaming, she can stand outside the door, count to five, then immediately return. She should inform the child of her return and then resume her seat. If the mother can do this three or four times without causing distress in the child, go to the next step.
   i. Go outside for play periods, if this is part of the regular routine, and leave the mother behind in her usual spot. She should be there when you return.
   j. Let his mother leave now for periods of ten to fifteen minutes. She must always casually inform the child she is going (to do something) but will be right back. The leave-taking must be brief, cheerful, and confident. Return the child to the mother or have the mother return *before* the child begins to cry.
   k. Be able to tolerate these brief separations very well before continuing with the next step. Then, the mother can leave for about an hour. She *must* tell the child she is going but will be back soon. If the child becomes worried while the mother is absent, casually assure her that her mother will be back after the music session or before lunch or whatever is true. Distract her as quickly as possible with an interesting activity.

l. Be able to stay at school or the sitter's all morning without the mother and without distress. The mother can settle the child in and then cheerfully leave. Parting words should be brief, e.g., "So long! I'll see you at lunch time." The mother should leave quickly and without looking back. Sometimes the child may cry for a minute or two immediately after the mother departs. This is unimportant if separation has already been achieved.

C. If the child is *over* eighteen to twenty months of age, *use abrupt separation only as a last resort:*

1. If the mother cannot cooperate with gradual separation; if the child has been attending school for a number of months and all efforts to make friends and interact with him have failed; and if despite the mother's presence and interaction, the child refuses all school activities and staff approach.

2. The mother should enter the school room with the child, place him on the floor with an interesting toy, cheerfully and quickly say, "Good-bye. Mommy will come back to you after lunch [or whatever]," and leave immediately without looking back. A staff member should immediately approach the child and stay with him, comforting, reassuring, and distracting him throughout the day. It should be the same staff member each day.

5.26 COOPERATES IN GAMES (6-10 mo.)

The child enjoys the give-and-take of simple games, such as "Pat-a-cake" and cooperates with any efforts to initiate the games. The games should be fun.

1. Give the child plenty of time to respond to games and lavishly reinforce minimal responses.

2. Swing the child in a blanket. Stop periodically and wait for the child to make a movement or a sound to indicate he wants more. Refer to 5.18 (Enjoys frolic play).

3. Play a "Give me" game by handing some object back and forth.

4. Play ball. The child will not do very well at first. Chase the ball together by creeping after it before you roll it back and forth together.

5. Play "Peek-a-boo" with a cloth. See if the child will pull the cloth off his head in the spirit of the game.

6. Sing nursery rhymes and do gestures with your hands and with the child's hands. Let the child try the gestures by himself.

7. Play "Hid-and-seek" with a toy repetitively. Hide the toy while the child is watching and then encourage him to "find" it. Place the toy under a cloth so its shape obviously shows or hide it behind something leaving an edge of the toy in view. Exaggerate your "joy" when he "finds" the toy.

8. Put objects into and out of containers together.

5.27 STRUGGLES AGAINST SUPINE POSITION (6-12 mo.)

The child's activity level increases during the latter half of the first year. It is her increased need to explore motorically and her enjoyment of an upright posture which cause her to resist lying down.

1. Learn to change the child's diaper while she is in an upright position, e.g., while she is standing and holding onto crib rails. Diaper changing can become a real fight if the child becomes infuriated when placed in supine.

2. Offer the child a very interesting toy to play with just before you lay her down for changing or dressing. This may or may not work. If she still fusses, try to respect her need for an upright posture rather than engage in a battle.

3. Refer to 5.36 (Explores environment enthusiastically— safety precautions important).

4. Do not force the child into supine in the bathrub, e.g., to rinse her hair. Clean her head with a wet wash cloth and allow her to remain in sitting. A child may be terrified by the lack of security in the tub if she must lie on her back.

5.28 RESPONDS PLAYFULLY TO MIRROR (6-9 mo.)

The child pats, points to, laughs at, "talks" to or makes faces at his mirror image. Any positive response which is more than a smile is acceptable.

1. Let the child play "Pat-a-cake" or "Peek-a-boo" in front of a mirror.

2. Give the child a rattle or bell or some other toy she can shake in front of the mirror. Encourage the child to watch what is happening in the mirror. Tap the mirror to call her attention to it.

3. Make silly faces to the mirror together.

4. Kiss the child in the mirror.

5. Give ample opportunity for a response to build up; if there is no playful response, go back to 5.16 (Makes approach movements to mirror) and 5.23 (Smiles at mirror image).

5.29 MAY SHOW FEAR AND INSECURITY WITH PREVIOUSLY ACCEPTED SITUATIONS (6-18 mo.)

The child's growing awareness of her environment and her increased understanding of her helplessness seem to trigger new fears and insecurities. But, these are positive signs of her increased cognitive ability. Her most common fears include: the bath tub, hairwashing, vacuum cleaners, animals, things that move suddenly or things which make loud noises. The child may fear only one thing or many different things. At the same time, the child may be frightened of strangers and fearful of separation from the mother. So much fear may disturb parents who see it as a serious personality change in their once outgoing, fearless child. It is, however, a perfectly normal phase, one which the child gradually outgrows. This is not a stage which lasts from six to eighteen months. Rather, a sudden fear may crop up at any time within this age period and last for a few months. Long lasting, stubborn fears require special psychological help.

This is also a period when stranger anxiety and suspicion may crop up again, especially at age twelve or thirteen months. It is not a cause for concern and may be treated casually.

1. A sympathetic, but casual approach works best with the fearful child. Hold her closely and reassuringly in feared places or when faced with feared animals. Avoid using the vacuum, mixer, disposal when the child is around. She will not need to be taught to overcome her fears. In a few months she will forget her fears, even though she is not taught how to tolerate the feared objects now.
2. Give her a sponge bath or a sink bath for a few months. Rinse her hair with a washcloth or use a gentle spray. Avoid pouring water over her head if this terrifies her. It takes a little extra time, but it is worth it if the child's confidence is kept intact.
3. Joke about loud noises and frightening sounds that occur beyond your control. Use simple language to talk about the noise, e.g., "Oh, just an old truck!" Play a game of "Pop!" or "Bang!" imitating the noises, then laughing.
4. Fortunately, a fear of falling may arise now. This fear may reduce your need to worry about the child's climbing off things, but you still may have to put away the high chair.

5.30 SHOWS LIKE/DISLIKE FOR CERTAIN PEOPLE, OBJECTS, PLACES (7-12 mo.)

1. Respect the child's choices whenever possible. Do not push him towards people he dislikes. Commiserate with his dislike of the doctor's office, car, or whatever.
2. The child likes best those objects he has seen his parents "play" with and use with him. His favorite toys are usually those the parents have taught him are interesting. His drive to be grown-up like his parents determines very much his choice of toys or activities.
3. Point out familiar places: "Here's the park! Where are the swings we played on yesterday?" "There's the store. Remember when we saw a dog there?" The child may not understand all of this, but he may grasp the familiarity implied.
4. A child usually likes people who play with him. Relatives sometimes feel the child should "know him" and often expect immediate affection and interactive play. Relatives, especially those who visit infrequently, should be cautioned against an aggressive approach. A slow, but friendly and interested manner is most appealing. Presents and special playtimes help, too. Later, relatives and friends may help the child to like and enjoy them by playing directly with the child. Once trust is established, the child must not be ignored; he needs a playtime with adults, a playtime which is appropriate to his age

level and interests.

5.31 LETS ONLY MOTHER MEET HIS NEEDS (8-12 mo.)

The child refuses attention and caretaking from everyone except his mother. He cries, fusses, rejects, especially if the mother is in sight.

1. Respect the child's rejection of others and approach him slowly. Refer to 5.20 (Stranger anxiety appears) and 5.25 (Shows anxiety at spearation from mother).
2. The father may be rejected by the child at this time. This is a temporary condition. Let the father gradually take over responsibility for the child's favorite activities, such as bathing or feeding. The father should still take the time to play and have fun with the child. He will soon be accepted again.
3. The child may accept attention from other family members if the mother is not present. She should be out of sight and earshot.

5.32 EXTENDS TOY TO SHOW OTHERS, NOT FOR RELEASE (9-12 mo.)

The child is physically capable of release, but he is not developmentally or socially ready to do so. Toys are offered as a means of socializing; the child does not intend to give them up.

1. Look at and admire proffered objects. Touch them if the child allows it.
2. Help the child show a favored object or toy to a familiar person, e.g., his father. Help him hold the toy out to show to his father. The father should express his pleasure and interest in the toy the child shows him.
3. Ask the child to show you his toy and lavishly praise the toy.
4. Help the child show his toy to his dolls or to his stuffed animals.
5. Sometimes the child releases his toy accidentally. Return it immediately.

5.33 TESTS PARENTAL REACTIONS DURING FEEDING (9-12 mo.)

The child seems to act deliberately "naughty" or mischievous during this stage. He plays games with food just to see how his parents will react.

1. Do not urge the child to eat. If he begins to play or act restless, let him leave the table.
2. Allow finger feeding and tolerate much messiness. Refer to 6.25 (Finger feeds).
3. Allow the child to eat to please himself, not his parent.
4. Do not comment on his eating habits or the amount eaten. You might name foods, notice smells, comment on colors.

5. Introduce a variety of foods.
6. Offer a rejected food at a later time, perhaps in a few weeks.
7. The child eats very little at this age anyway. One good meal a day is adequate.
8. Do not say anything if the child throws food, spits foods, or engages in excessive play. Just calmly pull the food away and wait one to two minutes. You may give the child "one more chance" if he really seems to want his food back, but if the same behavior occurs, remove the food, and let the child leave the table. He is probably not hungry.
9. If the child attempts to grab your spoon from you, offer him another spoon to explore with and to practice his grasp. You may also allow him to take your spoon to experiment with while you get another spoon for yourself.

5.34 TESTS PARENTAL REACTIONS AT BED-TIME (9-12 mo.)

The child tries out new and mischievous behavior just to see how his parents will react. He is testing their confidence as well as his independence.

1. Remain cheerful and consistent. Now is the time to establish a little bedtime ritual, such as reading a story, tucking teddy in or singing songs. Stick to the routine. Do not hurry the child.
2. Do not engage in active, exciting play one hour before bedtime.
3. Resist checking on a fussing child and complying with more and more requests. These activities can extend bedtime rituals for an hour or more.
4. Use your voice and call to the child as a comfort instead of continually returning to him. Cheerfully call to him to let him know you are nearby.
5. The above items are appropriate only if you wish to teach the child to go to sleep alone. If you wish to put the child to sleep by rocking, walking, etc., by all means do so, but expect this habit to continue until three or four years of age.

5.35 ENGAGES IN SIMPLE IMITATIVE PLAY (9-12 mo.)

The child can do simple imitations at this age. She may clap her hands in imitation, grab at the spoon and try to feed herself, brush her hair if she can acquire the hairbrush. These activities do not last very long, and they are not usually complete behavior sequences.

1. Refer to 5.26 (Cooperates in games) for simple games which encourage early imitative behavior.
2. Acknowledge and admire imitative behavior even if the result is messy or non-productive. A child thrives on praise for his achievements.
3. Do not discourage spontaneous imitative behavior. Allow

the child to "use" the spoon, "comb" her hair, or "wipe" the table with a sponge if she attempts to grab these implements from you. Get another for yourself.
4. Give the child an extra washcloth in the bath and encourage her to wash her tummy, a favored spot because it is so visible. Praise any success.
5. Ring a bell, shake a rattle, squeeze a squeak toy. Give the object to the child and encourage her to repeat your behavior. Enjoy with her any noise she succeeds in producing.
6. Imitate the child, at first, if she has trouble imitating you. Sit beside her while she is playing with her toys and do what she does. Let her know you are really enjoying yourself. Call her attention to your imitative play. She may repeat herself just to get you to "do it again." You may also imitate her motor behavior by crawling and exploring with her, and imitate her verbal behavior by repeating the sounds she makes. You are demonstrating the concept of imitative play by your actions. If the child enjoys your mimicking she eventually learns to imitate you.

5.36 EXPLORES ENVIRONMENT ENTHUSIASTI-CALLY—SAFETY PRECAUTIONS IMPORTANT (9-12 mo.)

The child is more physically than socially oriented. His interest in people, language, and social games may decrease, although it definitely should not disappear. The child's interest focuses on his motor skills, his environment, and the objects he can explore and discover for himself. Do not dampen the child's excitement about his physical world and his increasing self-confidence by limiting or discouraging his active behavior.

1. Allow the child to explore in safety. Protect the child because he cannot be expected to obey prohibitions. The child should not be punished for his explorations and for getting into things.
2. Do not burden a child with many "No-no's" right now. He cannot understand or control himself yet. There should be no more than one or two prohibited objects within his reach. Everything else should be removed. He can be distracted from forbidden objects with novel toys or play. Never punish a child for exploring.
3. This is an important time to *childproof the home*.
   a. Keep in high places: roach and ant killers, cleaning materials, shampoos, medicines, vitamins, alcohol, aspirin, lighter fluid, cigarettes, matches, lighters, plastic bags. Cords attached to rice cookers, coffee pots, the television and appliances should be out of reach. Appliances can be placed flush against the wall.
   b. Remove breakable and valuable objects.
   c. Place good books on high shelves or jam them in tight. Let the child play with old magazines on lower shelves.
   d. Place protective gates at stairways and near the stove if the child can reach the knobs on the stove. Latch necessary doors.

5.0 SOCIAL-EMOTIONAL

e. Plug up or tape unused electrical outlets. Remove, hide or tape to the wall all electrical cords.

f. Tie cabinet doors shut with strings or rubber bands. Be sure the child does not go near the garbage disposal.

g. Place non-skid rugs or pillows at the foot of chairs, or whatever the child can climb on. Do not let the child walk on wet floors.

h. Remove sharp or dangerous objects the child might place in his mouth, e.g., pencils, scissors, chopsticks, popsicle sticks, forks, nuts, popcorn, small hard objects. Do not let him chew objects that may have lead-based paint on them.

i. Place objects in centers of tables, not on the edges. Do not use tablecloths that could be pulled off.

j. Fence in the yard and constantly supervise outdoor play.

k. Do not let the child have any toys with strings twelve inches or longer or mobiles and crib gyms he can reach and perhaps strangle on once he becomes very active.

l. Be sure the child cannot stick his head through cribs or playpen slats, balcony or porch railings.

m. Pad the corners of coffee tables slightly with "covers." These "covers" may be purchased in many retail, hardware, and drug stores.

5.37 LIKES TO BE IN CONSTANT SIGHT AND HEARING OF ADULT (12-13 mo.)

1. Allow the child this behavior during this period although it may drive his parents crazy. Do not isolate the child to "teach" him how to be alone. The child learns to enjoy being alone only if he is given the opportunity to be with people when he wants.

2. Leave the child alone with favored toys two or three minutes at a time. Gradually increase the time you are away from him.

3. Allow him to follow and "help" with tasks throughout the day. Let the child dust, sweep, or play with pots and pans while mother washes dishes.

5.38 GIVES TOY TO FAMILIAR ADULT SPONTANEOUSLY AND UPON REQUEST (12-15 mo.)

The child is already capable of voluntary and purposeful release. The child uses this interaction in a sociable way.

1. Hold out your hand invitingly and ask the child to give you the object. Praise success and return the toy to him.

2. Accept and thank the child for gifts of toys. A child often gives toys as a sign of friendship. Always return them immediately when the child asks for them. A child views his giving as very temporary. Admire his toys.

3. Play a game of trading objects with the child, but never tease a child into believing you intend to keep his toys.

4. A child who has physical involvement in the hands may take longer to release the object or may release it in an awkward manner. Refer to 4.50 (Releases object voluntarily).

5.39 DISPLAYS INDEPENDENT BEHAVIOR; IS DIFFICULT TO DISCIPLINE—THE "NO" STAGE (12-15 mo.)

The child seems to say, "No" to almost every suggestion. This extremely important stage is critical to the child's growth as an independent, self-confident person. This stage should be encouraged, not discouraged; it is the ability to say "No" that counts. This does not mean that parents should allow the child to "rule the roost." They must still use positive guidance to control the child and must not allow the child to control them.

1. Pay attention to the child's cooperative behavior. Ignore, as much as possible, the child's "No's" and negative responses.

2. Never ask a child at this stage if he wants to do anything unless he truly has a choice. Tell him or say "Let's" or just do it without comment. Move the child cheerfully, firmly, and matter-of-factly throughout the routines of the day.

3. Use distraction. It is a powerful tool. The child can be fascinated by many things; his attention span and memory are still short. Whisk him away from one thing and quickly interest him in another activity.

4. Cut down on the number of "No's" directed at the child. Be especially sure to childproof the home. The more "No's" the child hears, the more "No's" he will use.

5. Do not always take his "No" as final. He often does not really mean it. However, be sensitive: sometimes his decision needs to be respected.

6. The child who says "No" to a firm command will often be cooperative if quietly and gently asked to "Leave something alone" or inhibit some activity.

7. Whining may begin at this time, too. Do your best to ignore the whining, but not the child. Respond to the child's first request before she needs to whine.

8. A child should hear and be expected to attend to very few "No-no's" or restrictions in the home. It is possible to avoid the "No-no's" altogether if you arrange the home carefully and if you use gentle distraction instead of "No-no's" to control him.

9. Discipline is only guidance at this age. Punishment, because it so often angers the child, works poorly when compared with tactful suggestions, distractions, and an established, cheerful daily routine. The parent's modeling of appropriate behavior is also a powerful means of guidance. A child under two years of age should never be physically punished or spanked. He cannot control himself yet or even understand the cause-and-effect relationship between his behavior and negative consequences. The child can be very frightened by punishment or anger and therefore *temporarily* inhibit undesirable behavior. However the child cannot really *learn*

from punishment, i.e., produce a *lasting* behavior change, independent of adult control.

5.40 ACTS IMPULSIVELY, UNABLE TO RECOGNIZE RULES (12-15 mo.)

The child cannot really understand or attend to rules because he has such little control over his impulses. He does not ignore rules out of defiance, but because he cannot stop himself.

1. The child occasionally remembers restrictions, but he usually cannot control his actions without parental help. He is not being bad if he remembers but does not obey; he just does not have sufficient self-control to obey. He should not be ashamed or punished for this inability. Remove him from forbidden activities and interest him in something else.

2. Do not direct the child verbally; physically remove him when you want him to do something.

3. Allowing inappropriate throwing of objects is unnecessary. If the child throws toys, take them away and let him throw a ball. If he throws crayons or pencils, give the child a crayon and as soon as he draws a few times, ask him to give it to you. If possible, anticipate his throwing to prevent it. If he throws food, remove it cheerfully and let him leave the table.

4. Never leave a child unattended at home sleeping, outside, in a high chair, near streets, in a pool or bath, on the toilet. He is definitely not old enough to remember dangers or protect himself.

5. It may be important to inspect the home again and childproof it with a more active, curious, older child in mind.

6. Make rules for yourself, structure the environment, but do not expect the child to structure himself. Do not punish a child for "breaking the rules." He does not understand what rules are, and it is quite difficult for a one-year-old child to follow rules.

5.41 ATTEMPTS SELF—DIRECTION; RESISTS ADULT CONTROL (12-15 mo.)

The child learns to assert and control himself. This is just another facet of the "No" stage and the child's urge for independence.

1. Allow the child plenty of opportunity to exercise his newfound self-direction. Be sure he is not being controlled too much.

2. Childproof the home so he is not subjected to too much control in the way of touching forbidden or dangerous objects.

3. Teach the child to do things for himself if he is capable, such as fetching things; helping to dress and undress himself; washing himself; and after eighteen months of age, brushing his teeth and toileting himself. Give him pride in his accomplishments.

4. If you offer him a choice by asking if he wants to do something, accept his choice, which will usually be "No." Do not say, "Do you want to . . ." if you cannot stick by his decision.

5. Let him choose the book to read or the toy to play with. Do not always make suggestions or choose for him.

6. Let him decide when he is through eating and let him down right away.

7. If you have to exert control, as you often must, do it quickly, cheerfully, matter-of-factly and with a minimum of talk. Ignore his protests.

8. Be proud and pleased when the child reaches this stage of self-direction. It means growth and independence.

9. Do not punish the child for his newfound independence or negativity. There is no good reason to punish or spank a child under two years. You may frighten the child into temporary inhibition, but you will not stop the behavior permanently or teach the child anything valuable.

5.42 DISPLAYS FREQUENT TANTRUM BEHAVIORS (12-18 mo.)

The child exhibits tantrum behaviors which disturb adults. Almost everyone has a different idea of just what consitutes a tantrum. Perhaps the best way to define tantrums is according to the reaction of the adults who are subjected to them. If the adult feels distressed enough about a child's display of negative emotion to wish to "do something" about the behavior, then we will call it a tantrum. One adult may see any angry crying or frustrated yelling as a tantrum, even if the behavior lasts only a few seconds. Another may be referring to a kicking, screaming, hysterical scene of forty-five minutes duration which is repeated many times a day. Whatever the definition, the following suggestions are applicable if the child's behavior is disturbing.

A. Internally reinforced tantrum behavior: Most tantrums thrown by a child below three years of age are uncontrolled and the result of intolerable frustration for the child. A child this age can tolerate very little. The cause is internal. This does not mean the child is spoiled, badly trained or manipulative because his parents let him get away with "murder." The child is just releasing his unhappy feelings and expressing the very great difficulty of growing up and learning to cope with his environment. The child's frustration may arise not from some specific incident, but from his environment as a whole. The tantrum may be an indirect way of expressing frustrated needs. The environment as a whole will need consideration. Perhaps an indirect way to decrease the tantrums can be found.
   1. A child, when overtired, overstimulated or excited, may become cranky and tense. This is a prime cause of tantrum behaviors. The child may not be sleeping and resting enough. Check his hours of retiring and awakening, his night awakenings, his nap schedule.

5.0 SOCIAL-EMOTIONAL

139

See if his tantrums almost always occur after or during some special, exciting event. If so, the child may need some special help in relaxing, calming down, or engaging in some quiet activity. Periods of activity should be alternated with periods of relative inactivity. Regular periods of outside socializations should be alternated with times spent alone with an adult.

2. A child may also be irritable and tense because his nutrition is inadequate. Check on this with his parents.

3. Check the child's environment. An environment which demands too much conformity and self-control may also produce tension at any age at which self-control is minimal. The home or school should be child-proofed so the child can "get into things" without having to cope with a lot of restrictions. He should have plenty of opportunity to exercise his independence and decision-making ability.

4. A child needs consistency from the adults around him along with lots of love, affection, and positive attention. Inappropriate attention and expectations may also result in tantrums. Restrictions should be few, but firm, and understandable to the child. Toys should be developmentally appropriate to the child's age. Remove any which consistently upset the child. Behavioral demands should be age-appropriate, no one-or two-year-old can be a cooperative, self-controlled three-year-old.

5. The kind of attention a child receives in the midst of his temper tantrum is important, too. The child may need some sympathy, cuddling, and help in redirecting his attention. He may need distraction. He may need to be casually left alone until the worst of his feelings have passed. It is critical, however, that you *never* give into his tantrum, rescind a rule, or give the child what he threw the tantrum for. Otherwise, tantrums can quickly become manipulative and purposeful.

B. Externally reinforced tanrum behavior: These are tantrums thrown on purpose, either to obtain positive or negative attention or to control the environment. Usually these tantrums are very frequent, last a long time (over thirty minutes) and can be turned on or off at will. Often there are no tears.

1. If the child is throwing a manipulative tantrum, it is usually best handled by completely ignoring the child and his behavior. Do not talk to him, look at him, comfort him, or react to him in any way. Especially, do not look tense, upset or in any way affected by the performance. If it is impossible to look calm and relaxed, leave the room or even the house, if it is safe. Do not punish for tantrums. Go to the child as quickly as possible and reinforce him, by talking, smiling, picking him up and hugging him once he has stopped his tantrum (a child rarely lasts longer than forty-five minutes) or calmed down considerably. Perhaps give him some food or play with him. *Do not* discuss his previous behavior with him. Forget it. *Do not* give to him whatever he threw his tantrum for. This

approach will take two or three weeks to be really effective, depending upon the severity of the behavior. At first the behavior may get much worse, but this is very temporary, perhaps two to three days.

3. The self-destructive child or one who may really injure himself in any way during a tantrum cannot be left alone or ignored. Hold him in your arms like a baby, with one of your arms under his back and up and over his chest and arms; your other arm over his legs. If held firmly the child can hurt neither himself nor the adult. It is critical for the adult to look and feel calm, relaxed and unconcerned. Looking and/or feeling relaxed, while very important for the child, can be extremely difficult for a parent or staff member to accomplish. It is usually very helpful if a second adult is present to help you ease the strain. This person can sit with you to keep you company and talk and joke with you. Even a screaming child can be tolerated with some adult objectivity and companionship. You may also wish to talk quietly to the child whether or not he seems to hear you. Do not scold. Instead say things such as, "It's okay," "You'll be all right," "I'll just hold you like this until you calm down."

4. These kinds of handling of tantrums discussed in items #1, 2, and 3, are almost always necessary for a child under two years. Tantrums of frustration or unhappiness usually occur below this age and demand gentler and more helpful treatment. Use the treatment methods discussed in items #1, 2, and 3 for temper tantrums which are a) extreme, these are rare and occasional but often dangerous to the child or others and are usually terribly disruptive in the home or at school; or for those tantrums which are b) serious and frequent, these occur more than three or four times a day and at least fifteen minutes each time. Remember that manipulative tantrums can be prevented completely if early tantrum-like behavior never results in providing the child with a payoff. Comfort, sympathize, but do not give in.

5. Breathholding is a kind of tantrum or frustration response. Do not let the child see your fright. Try to ignore this behavior, too. The child really will not hurt himself. Attempt to help the child relax and settle down; distract him before he becomes so upset. However, do not give the child so much attention that he makes a habit of breathholding to receive attention.

6. Parental response to tantrums must be as consistent as possible, no matter how the behavior is being treated.

7. If it is difficult to determine why the tantrums are occurring, you may keep a little record of the number and times tantrums occur, what happens directly before and what happens after, e.g., parents' response. Look for a pattern.

5.43 NEEDS AND EXPECTS RITUALS AND ROUTINES (12-18 mo.)

The child becomes ritualistic about familiar routines and demands a repetitive pattern for some daily activities.

1. The child begins to demand that rituals be carried out exactly the same way every day because he is finally understanding and remembering the way things are done and in what order. This is particularly true for bedtime rituals. This is a harmless and natural phase. Rituals provide comfort and security for the child and can last quite some time.

2. Do not establish a ritual, especially at bedtime, that cannot be continued indefinitely. Keep a ritual short. Otherwise, if a parent reads six stories and gives four drinks one night, the parent will find himself doing it forever.

3. The child may object violently to a change if certain seating arrangements have been made in school or at home. Respect this.

4. A set time for certain routines, play, outings, baths or naps may become very important to the child. General routines are good for children who are trying to learn how their world is ordered.

5. Avoid a big change, such as moving, taking a vacation or going to the hospital if at all possible. It can be particularly difficult for the child at this time.

6. *CAUTION: Ritualistic concerns should occupy a minor part of the child's day. An excessive need for environmental sameness may be a serious abnormal sign.*

5.44 BEGINS TO SHOW A SENSE OF HUMOR— LAUGH AT INCONGRUITIES (12-18 mo.)

The child learns what things are normal and what are abnormal in his environment. If the unusual or strange events are not frightening, the child may see them as "silly" and laugh. This early sense of humor is usually evidenced in the familiar home environment.

1. Expose the child to a familiar but not rigid, routine at home as much as possible. Until he knows what is familiar and appropriate, a child cannot recognize and appreciate the humor of the unfamiliar. It is also important that the child feel comfortable with and non-threatened by the unfamiliar at least some of the time. The child who is startled by strange events all the time must be exposed to small unfamiliar happenings within the context of the very comfortable and familiar routine of his home.

2. Repeat funny situations with the child and laugh with him as long as he is enjoying them. A joke is funny over and over again at this age. Not only does the child enjoy repetition of humorous events, he also expects others to laugh again and again along with him. It is important that adults not discourage this budding sense of humor by ignoring a funny event just because the novelty is gone.

3. See if the child enjoys putting a piece of clothing on the "wrong" body part, either yours or his. Place a sock on your head, a hat on his foot, pants on his arm. Laugh at all the silliness.

4. Watch television commercials with him and laugh at the funny parts. At this age he may laugh because a cat is singing like a person or because someone is "wearing" bubbles on his head. Remember that a child's humor is different from an adult's. "Jokes" in an adult sense, verbal or non-verbal, go unappreciated. The child may laugh or cry when someone falls down or when he is startled. Do not push slapstick comedy, for instance, if it frightens the child.

5. Dance or walk around with the child's feet on yours.

6. Laugh with him if he laughs because you have dropped or spilled something. Play a game of dropping things with exaggerated reactions and "silly" distress.

7. Model appropriate amusement for the child. Very often, what is humorous to the child is discovered accidentally. He spontaneously laughs at something he perceives as funny which may go unnoticed by adults. When he laughs, it is important that adults acknowledge and react to the funny situation even if the situation does not strike the adult as particularly humorous.

5.45 ENJOYS IMITATING ADULT BEHAVIOR: RESPONDS WELL TO THE INTRODUCTION OF NEW TASKS (12-18 mo.)

1. Let the child "help" the mother around the house: dust, wash dishes, "cook" by sitrring and pouring things, "wash" the tub or the front porch, rake and pick up leaves, pull weeds, hand the parent tools to use (safe ones) or clothes to hang up, wash the car, water the garden with a hose. Do not ask for or expect task completion; these "jobs" should be fun and not forced.

2. Parent and child should companionably pick up toys at the end of the day. They should do it cheerfully and together. It is a wonderful way to establish a good habit, and later the child may do it alone.

3. Give the child a little job, such as bringing slippers to his father, bringing in the newspaper. Appreciate the child's willingness by telling him, "What a big help you are!"

4. This is an excellent time to introduce toilet training, brushing teeth, washing self. These are wonderful, fascinating activities to the child because he sees his parents doing them.

5. The child enjoys and benefits from doll play, in imitation of parental care for him or especially if there is a new baby. Both boys and girls should be allowed to have at least one baby doll. An anatomically correct "Baby Brother" doll is available through Mattel, Inc.

5.0 SOCIAL-EMOTIONAL

5.46 PLAYS BALL COOPERATIVELY (12-15 mo.)

The child cooperates happily in a give-and-take game. She can tolerate releasing the ball, knowing it will be rolled or tossed right back to her.

1. Play ball with the child in front of a mirror. Encourage her to use her hands to push or roll the ball.
2. Play ball while the child is on a wedge, on a prone board or in a standing table. She can also play in sitting, kneeling, or in standing, either with or without support. (Refer to the Gross Motor section for positioning where appropriate.)
3. Throw a soft cloth ball to each other.
4. Experiment with different kinds of balls, such as a small tennis ball, a clutch ball, a soft rubber ball, a large beach ball, to see which is easiest for the child to handle. Start with a large ball and decrease the size as the child's skill increases.
5. Introduce balloons; a child usually loves them. Laugh when they break, but remove the pieces quickly so the child does not put them in her mouth and choke on them.
6. If the child needs extra help in giving up the ball, play with two adults. Let one adult sit behind the child and help her throw. The second adult must always roll or throw the ball back immediately.
7. A child at this age can rarely catch a ball. "Ball" is a game of chase and throw or of rolling the ball to each other. Roll the ball between her legs for her to "catch" if she uses long leg sitting with legs abducted.
8. Throw a ball across the room and enjoy chasing it together. Be sure the child retrieves the ball and "wins the race."

5.47 SHOWS TOY PREFERENCES (12-18 mo.)

The child shows his developing individuality and his unique personality when compared to other children in his preferences for dolls versus books versus blocks versus trucks, active versus quiet play. Certain toys appeal to him; others are ignored.

1. Let the child play with brooms, safe tools, pots and pans, old magazines, cans, and unbreakable dishes. The child may prefer the "toys" he sees his parents using because he wants so much to be like them.
2. Make sure the child's toys are conveniently available to him. Toys placed in a toy box or on high shelves out of sight are gone forever. They do not exist as far as the child is concerned. Of course, too many toys in sight may be overwhelming, but a few visible and available toys allow the child to figure out what he would like to do and allow him to make his own decisions.
3. Comfort toys, cuddly objects, or "loveys" are very popular with about half of all children beginning at this age. Whether a child develops a strong attachment to a blanket or stuffed animal is not important. It is unnecessary

to help a child develop such an attachment, but neither is there a need to worry about a very strong attachment to such an object.

5.48 DISPLAYS DISTRACTIBLE BEHAVIOR (12-15 mo.)

A child at this age typically "flits" from one thing to another. He is quickly bored, easily distracted, and literally incapable of sitting still for extended periods of time. This is too normal to worry about as long as he plays or explores constructively at least some of the time.

1. Do not demand prolonged attention during quiet play. A quiet, fine motor or sedentary activity should not last longer than five minutes.
2. Alternate the child's quiet and active times throughout the day providing frequent chances for the child to work off his physical energy.
3. Do not expect the child to be "good" in "adult" places, such as restaurants or stores. The only true way to handle a fidgety, restless child in a restaurant is to avoid taking him there. If you do go, provide interesting things for him to do, bringing toys along and talking frequently to him. Do not expect to linger over coffee when the meal is over.
4. Play with the child's toys together with him. A child always attends longer when an adult participates.
5. Provide a quiet time each day, such as before bedtime. Play quiet games which require some attention. Talk about body parts making a game of it. Talk about pictures in books; read stories in the books if the child is interested; recite nursery rhymes. Tell stories about fun things the child did that day, e.g., what he did at the park.

5.49 TENDS TO BE QUITE MESSY (12-18 mo.)

The child does not have a sense of neatness or order. He usually revels in making messes with just about everything.

1. Let the child fingerpaint; let him use clay that is non-toxic. Occasionally, let him feel his food, his spilled milk, the juice in his cup.
2. Allow plenty of water and sand play.
3. Provide old clothes and let the child make mudpies, digging in the dirt. The child needs to get dirty.
4. Occasionally play with bowel movements is normal; do not scold or shame the child. After the child is eighteen months of age, it may be necessary or desirable to increase his aversion *a little*. Make casual statements to him about discomfort and being "nice and clean." Do not appear too concerned about discomfort or cleanliness for now.
5. Children who are excessively neat and finicky need gradual introduction to messy play. Play with mud, paint or flour and look cheerful and happy. Invite the child to join you. He may need to observe for awhile before joining in with you.

6. Do not leap to clean the child's hands, face or tray every time they get a little messy when the child is eating. Be calm and casual about dirt or mess on the child.
7. Let the child help you make cookies, play with dough or knead bread.
8. The child who is frightened of or dislikes any mess that clings to his hands, such as dough, paint or mud, may demand frequent cleaning. Keep a damp rag or sponge handy so his hands can be wiped immediately upon request. Verbally emphasize to him that the mess comes "right off!" This helps him learn to explore and enjoy messy things.
9. Refer to 1.68 (Enjoys Messy Activities such as finger painting).

5.50 ENJOYS BEING CENTER OF ATTENTION IN FAMILY GROUP (12-18 mo.)

The child loves to be admired and watched in the family group, even though he may be shy and self-conscious around others. He often repeats activities to attract attention, and, in general, is very demanding of this attention.

1. Recognize the child's behavioral repetition for attention for what it is. Certain behaviors increase directly as parents pay attention to them. It is especially important to remember that scolding, talking, spanking, and lecturing are forms of attention. These so-called punishments may very likely increase undesired behaviors. Attend only to those behaviors of which you approve.
   a. If punishment is necessary, do it with a minimum of attention and talking. Isolating the child for one to five minutes is often effective. Hopefully, punishment will be minimal at this age.
   b. Walk away or turn your back to the teasing, whining, and fussing the child is using to manipulate you.
   c. Talk a lot about and attend to the child's good behaviors. Teach him what *to* do, not just what *not* to do.
2. Much learning takes place because of parental attention. New words, new gestures, new skills, a big block tower, any accomplishment will be repeated if the parents notice and praise the child. Teach him to be proud of his abilities and successes.

5.51 HUGS AND KISSES PARENTS (14-15½ mo.)

1. Demonstrations of affection are learned directly through imitation. Hug and kiss the child often. Tell him what you are doing. Invite him to respond. Make a game of it.
2. A child often kisses with the mouth open. Do not withdraw from this.
3. Play with dolls or animals. Ask the child to hug or kiss them, as you do him.
4. Do not encourage the child to hug and kiss everyone he meets. These gestures of affection should be saved for

family members or others very close to the child. A habit of indiscriminate kissing upon greeting or saying good-bye may be very hard to break in later years, especially with the handicapped child.

5.52 IMITATES DOING HOUSEWORK (15-18 mo.)

The child's imitation is very simple, incomplete, and of short duration. He is copying his parents because he loves to do so. It is a good sign that he is developing normally in his identification with his parents.

1. Give the child simple tasks to do around the house, such as wiping one area of the table or putting away toys. These should not be chores; they should be games.
2. Let him pick any scraps of paper off the floor and place them in the rubbish can. Let him take things to the kitchen for you.
3. Let him fold newspapers and put them away.
4. Place pots and pans and other unbreakable objects on low shelves so the child can play with them in the kitchen.
5. Give the child a cloth of his own to "help" dust when the mother is dusting.
6. Give the child a sponge or cloth in the bathtub to "wash" the tub and walls.
7. Let the child help put things away, handing things to his parent or teacher.
8. The child cannot do tasks alone. He will enjoy his "work" if an adult keeps him company and works with him. It is a good age for putting toys away together; have a good time.
9. Both boys and girls love to imitate their mothers' work because it is most often visible to them. Either sex will enjoy brooms, dust pans, washing dishes, "cooking." The father should also involve the child in his work around the house whenever he can.

5.53 EXPRESSES AFFECTION (18-24 mo.)

1. Be affectionate with the child; he learns through imitation.
2. Do not reject affection; enjoy touching and hugging the child.
3. Boys are not "feminine" because they are affectionate. Touching is normal and healthy.
4. The child is still a baby; enjoy and talk to him.
5. Provide much body contact. Do not ignore handicapped parts, if the child is handicapped.
6. Play with and listen to the child. Respect his rights. Tell him he is "neat," good, "OK." Let him play with your toes. Tickle each other, bounce, swing, play "Hide-and-seek" together, tumble on the floor together, sing songs, enjoy each other!
7. Do not tease the child. He cannot handle it because he does not understand it. Even when it is done in a joking way, it confuses and upsets him. You may teach him to mistrust, reject adult play, and make him very negative,

5.0 SOCIAL-EMOTIONAL

143

e.g., do not hold toys or food out of reach as a game.

8. Affection is not overprotection. Allow as much independence and self-control as the child can handle.

9. Affection is not just hugs and kisses; it is a positive attitude. Do not interrupt a child to kiss and "love" him. You will only turn him off.

10. Sympathy and affection are learned mainly through imitation and experience. Parental sympathy and affection demonstrated to the child teach him to feel the same emotions for others. You do not make a child strong and brave by ignoring his need for love and sympathy.

5.54 SHOWS JEALOUSY AT ATTENTION GIVEN TO OTHERS, ESPECIALLY OTHER FAMILY MEMBERS (18-24 mo.)

The child evidences his jealousy not in words but in negative behavior. He may become aggressive, loud, noisy or destructive. He may become babyish, whiny, act overly dependent or demand parental help unnecessarily. His actions are proof of his need for extra attention, even though he does not know what is wrong with him.

1. This is natural, normal, and acceptable behavior. Never shame a child for his jealousy, especially of a new baby.

2. Give the child extra, loving attention. Assure him of your continued concern and care for him.

3. Humor the child's desires to be babied with diapers, a bottle, rocking. He will drop these activities on his own as he discovers they are not as wonderful as they look.

4. Be very interested in the child's age-appropriate activities. Occasionally comment admiringly on how big the child is and how much he can do.

5. Let the child "help" you in caring for the baby. Occasionally refer to the baby as helpless or not so capable.

6. Give the child a baby doll of his own to play with. Allow him to be abusive to it if he wishes. Encourage play with it when the mother is busy with the baby.

7. A child does become jealous of parents' affection for each other. The child must understand that he cannot interfere altogether, although the parents should sympathize with his feelings. Parents should not go through long displays of affection in front of their child, but they do not need to hide from him either.

8. One kind of jealousy is evidenced by the child's constant interruptions if his parent or teacher is talking to another adult, reading, or on the telephone. The child constantly tries to interfere, to attract the adult's attention or to be a part of whatever is going on. He may make attempts to join the conversation, mimicking adult words and trying to introduce new topics. Include the child whenever possible. If it is not possible, gently but firmly refuse the interaction. The mother may say, "I'm busy right now talking to Mrs. Smith [or reading]. You have to find something else to do." Help interest the child in something appropriate. Ignore any continued pesterings; remove him kindly from the room if absolutely necessary.

5.55 SHOWS A WIDE VARIETY OF EMOTIONS: FEAR, ANGER, SYMPATHY, MODESTY, GUILT, EMBARRASSMENT, ANXIETY, JOY (18-24 mo.)

The child pushes himself along toward being grown up and displays a wide range of emotions. This is a natural development. Negative emotions should be mild and occupy a minor portion of the child's day.

1. The child may demand that you leave him alone during toileting and urge you to go out and shut the door. Do not laugh at this desire, but solemnly respect his new-found individualism and modesty.

2. The child may suddenly resist being dressed and undressed in front of others, on the beach or in the living room. Respect this when it occurs.

3. Minimize, as much as possible, scolding or correcting the child in front of others, especially his peers. If correction is necessary, take him quietly aside or to another room.

4. The child may feel guilty about doing forbidden things some of the time. If the guilt is overwhelming, you may have to reassure and comfort him. However, a little guilt can be a good thing and a sign of a budding conscience. You might want to encourage this occasionally.

5. Never make a child feel guilty or embarrassed about toilet accidents, masturbation or his body in general. He will feel a little guilty on his own and further guilt should not be added. Do not turn him against his body.

6. Model excited, joyful behavior for the child. If something good happens, clap your hands; say, "Oh boy!" or some such phrase; show the child how to act excited.

7. Do not discourage natural excited behavior. Recognize and join in with the child's happy feelings.

8. Point out pictures of children with different facial expressions. Talk about how they feel.

9. Over-excitement for the child may lead to a full-blown tantrum if he cannot cope with these feelings. Even good feelings or experiences can be too much and become unpleasant, especially for the sensitive child. In such a case, the child may need help to calm down. Be relaxed and help him participate in a calm activity. Avoid doing too many exciting things in one day.

5.56 DESIRES CONTROL OF OTHERS—ORDERS, FIGHTS, RESISTS (18-24 mo.)

1. Follow the child's directions some of the time. He needs to be humored in his wish to be grown up.

2. Set few but firm limits.

3. He can direct and control dolls. Help him and encourage him in this kind of play.

4. Help him to joke and laugh about his scolding and fussing. Make a game out of it and pretend to be a "silly" child while he plays the "stern" adult.

5. Let him control the situation and even his parents and teachers sometimes.

6. Be calm about tantrums. Refer to 5.42 (Displays frequent

tantrum behaviors) for suggestions.

7. Ask what he wants at times and respect his choice.
8. Label and respect feelings, even if the child's actions must be held within limits, e.g., say, "You are angry. It's all right to be angry, but you cannot hit. People are not for hitting; punch clowns are for hitting."
9. Try kidding the child out of his angry moods sometimes; it often works.

5.57 FEELS EASILY FRUSTRATED (18-24 mo.)

The child can stand very little challenge or thwarting. He is as easily frustrated by his own inability as by his parents' limits or demands upon him.

1. Minimize demands and rules as much as possible. The child has enough difficulty living up to his own internal demands.
2. This is a prime age for temper tantrums. These are not manipulations, but real misery and frustration which cannot be held in or controlled. Distraction and a little comfort may be very helpful if the child will allow it. A child may need to be left alone at this time.
3. It may be necessary, either temporarily or permanently, to remove a toy which is frustrating the child because of its difficulty.
4. Make sure the child is getting enough rest and sleep. He needs a calm and relaxed environment which encourages short periods of quiet play.
5. If you have had to frustrate the child, e.g., by refusing a request or removing a toy, a little distraction and sympathy may be important. Do not respond to crying and screaming by giving in or changing your demands.
6. Never tease, even in play.
7. Refer to 5.42 (Displays frequent trantrum behaviors) for further suggestions.

5.58 INTERACTS WITH PEERS USING GESTURES (18-24 mo.)

The child may push, pull, or grab at toys. He may hit. Most of his interaction is still aggressive. Occasionally, he pats, offers toys, or waves "bye-bye" to another child.

1. Help the child interact with other children in "Row your boat" or "Choo-choo" games. Two children can sit facing each other holding hands and rocking together back and forth. The children can also hang on to one another at the waist and pretend to be a train, either sitting on stools or standing and moving on a "track" around the room.
2. Use a large box or carton filled with about two inches of various types of macaroni, rice or long noodles. Place two children in the box for "sand" play with various digging utensils. Allow the children to interact, which may include grabbing toys, without interfering very much.

3. Take the child to a park where other children play at least once or twice a week, more often, if possible. Allow the child to just watch without joining in as long as he wishes. It may be some weeks before the child can join in. A child may be too self-conscious to interact with others until he knows "all the rules" for sure. Whether or not he actively participates, a shy child can enjoy himself if he is not pressured by adults to do more than he is ready to do.
4. Parents should invite one other child to their home regularly. More than one child is usually too overwhelming at this age.
5. There will be much grabbing and snatching between children. This is okay; the children should be allowed to resolve their own battles unless a child is in real danger.

5.59 ENGAGES IN PARALLEL PLAY (18-24 mo.)

The child plays beside or around other children. He watches others intently. However, he does not really interact or play games with other children at this time.

1. A child of this age loves to play beside or around other children. This is preparation for future interactive play. However, the child should not be pushed to do things with the others yet. Let him play alone or just stand and watch.
2. Direct the child's interactive play if you want it to be positive. Usually unsupervised interaction involves pushing and grabbing. All children treat each other without empathy; they push, pull, and grab toys away whenever the spirit moves them. This is perfectly acceptable. It will not make the child "mean" or a "bully." Let the child fight his own battles, learn to stand up for himself, learn to get along without adult help.
3. Take the child to the park regularly where others his age play.
4. Place two or three children in a sandbox or a large carton with macaroni in it. Provide safe toys to use in this medium.
5. Interactively, a child can usually handle one child for each year of his age; for example, a one-year-old can enjoy only one other child; a three-year-old, three others. A larger group is tolerable only with a lot of adult help and direction.

5.60 ENJOYS SOLITARY PLAY COLORING, BUILDING, LOOKING AT PICTURE BOOKS FOR A FEW MINUTES (18-24 mo.)

The child cannot play alone, even for a few minutes, at all times. First, occasionally, and later, more and more frequently, he can attend to toys and amuse himself alone for longer and longer periods of time. Do not interrupt him!

1. If the child's attention span is always very short:
   a. Play with the child; this always makes the toys extra

5.0 SOCIAL-EMOTIONAL

145

fascinating for him. Withdraw your direct play gradually and start just watching the child; remain seated right beside him, praise and verbally interact with him when necessary. Start withdrawing altogether for very short periods, promising to be right back. For example, go to the kitchen for a few seconds, wash your hands, and come right back to join him. Gradually increase the length of time you are away.

b. A very short attention span may indicate overstimulation in the child. Let only two or three toys be visible to him at one time. Reduce noise and disorder in the household or classroom if necessary. Get the child off in a quiet corner. Speak quietly and simply. Relax and help him to do so.

c. Perhaps he is disinterested. Is the toy too easy, too hard, really dull? Provide very interesting toys; e.g., a bunch of balloons on the floor may be a powerful way to get interest.

2. Let the child watch television very occasionally and only good, child-oriented shows. Watch with him. He should be *doing* things, not *looking* at things most of the time.

5.61 ENJOYS ROUGH—AND—TUMBLE PLAY (18-24 mo.)

1. Teach the child to do somersaults; swing him around; give him piggy-back rides; let him touch the ceiling; help him stand on his head.

2. Avoid pretend games in which the father is a bear or chases the child; play at general acrobatics instead. The former is too real and scary for a young child.

3. Provide plenty of space and opportunity inside and out for active play. The child needs daily motor activity. Tyke-bikes, indoor-outdoor gyms, swings, monkey bars and sandboxes are all very popular and very beneficial.

4. A little rough play with parents goes a long way and can be too exciting for the child to handle. Do not overdo with "hysterical," giggly play, especially in the evening.

5. Handicapped children often miss out on rough-and-tumble play. Do not be afraid to encourage such play. Too many young handicapped children are overly passive because of lack of experience in this area.

5.62 EXPERIENCES A STRONG SENSE OF SELF—IMPORTANCE (18-24 mo.)

The child begins to feel he is the center of the universe and expects others to treat him as such. He is often described as "selfish," but he is actually learning to feel positive and good about himself, to develop self-respect and to become an individual. It is a very important stage of development if the child is to grow up to be an independent and happy adult.

1. A child may grab things, may demand things, cannot share, and may often hit other children. Do not shame the child for these activities. Sharing, in particular, does not come about until age three or later and, even then,

there are plenty of fights. Let the child snatch toys from other children and vice versa. Let him protect his own property. A child learns to share and take turns, not be being forced, but by feeling generous toward people he truly likes.

2. Suggest to the child that he give an unused toy or an old toy to another child. Praise positive responses, but do not act disappointed in him if he refuses.

3. The preceding is especially important for siblings if you are to avoid rivalry, jealousy, and constant battles.

4. Do not try to make the child feel guilty about hurting others. Firmly stop any such activity, but do not expect the child to understand pain in others as yet.

5. Allow the child to develop a strong sense of property and "mine." He needs your respect for his toys as his to do with as he wishes. Give him a special place he can call his own to keep his toys, his clothes, his shoes. Let the child learn that he owns things, but do not think he is ready to understand what is *yours*—he is not.

5.63 ATTEMPTS TO COMFORT OTHERS IN DISTRESS (22-24 mo.)

1. The child may cry when other children cry. Reassure him. Let him try to comfort the unhappy child occasionally.

2. Encourage the child to pat or console the other child, especially if he caused the other child's tears. This teaches appropriate sympathy for others and peer interaction.

3. A child cannot comfort others unless he has been comforted and treated with sympathy for his unhappiness or injuries. A child does not become a "sissy" because he is comforted when he cries or gets hurt. Neither does a child learn to be "brave" by having his distress ignored or ridiculed; he only learns that you do not care about his feelings. Even minor injuries may demand brief, but loving, attention. A child treated with sympathy does become brave and learn not to cry so much at a much later age, when all on his own, he wants to grow up and be "big." At this age, it is often hurt feelings, not real hurt, which cause most of the tears anyway.

4. Anger is also a form of distress. Especially, when parents argue, a young child is quite upset and may attempt to rectify matters. Parents should try not to rebuff the child's overtures at this time. They can help him cope with this fearful situation by giving extra contact, cuddling, and affection. They should speak of their anger, when they can, cheerfully and matter-of-factly. They can let the child know everyone gets "mad" sometimes, and it is all right because they still love each other.

5.64 DEFENDS POSSESSIONS (23-24 mo.)

The child has developed a sense of possession and ownership. He is also self confident enough to defend his things from others.

1. The child is still not sharing and may even try to defend his treasured things from his parents. Respect his property rights as you would want him to respect yours.
2. "Mine" becomes a very popular word. This helps the child see himself as an individual and helps develop a healthy ego. It even helps teach proper pronoun use. The child who never says "mine" should be taught to do so.
3. Each child in a family should have a few things, clothes or toys, and a place, bed, toy box or a corner of a room, which are really his and can be kept from everyone else. A child can share ownership of some things, but not everything. This is too confusing for him.
4. A child may hide things which belong to him so no one else can have them. This is all right; let him know he does not have to share unless he wants to.
5. A child of this age does not really steal, but may vigorously defend as his own an attractive possession of another. Sympathize with his feelings and desires, but let him know he cannot have the desired object. Calmly remove it from him even if you have to force it. Be matter-of-fact about the consequent tantrum.

5.65 DISTINGUISHES SELF AS A SEPARATE PERSON; CONTRASTS SELF WITH OTHERS (24-36 mo.)

The child begins to really understand now that he and his body are separate from his parents and the rest of the world. The dawning realization that he alone is responsible for himself and his body, this awareness of bodily integrity, is powerful and frightening. The child may become afraid of injury, fearful under some circumstances, worried about body differences, modest.

1. A little cut may produce screams, not of pain, but of simple upset. Always treat this with sympathetic concern, but be matter-of-fact and relaxed. A ritual Band-aid and kiss may work wonders, and then you can distract the child to something else. A child may fear Band-aids or tape because they are strange, alien things that stick to the body. Respect the child's fear and do not insist.
2. Temperature-taking may be experienced as a violation. Stop taking temperatures rectally; do it under the arm.
3. Do not provide dolls whose limbs and head are easily removed. The child may fear that the same can happen to him.
4. Be prepared to give simple and relaxed explanations about injuries or handicaps the child may see or ask about. His major concern is that the same thing could happen to him; he needs reassurance so that he will not become fearful of handicapped people.
5. Give simple answers to questions about differences between others and the child. Constantly reassure the child you like her just the way she is. Say, for example, "Mother has brown hair like Dr. Jones and Jamie. You have blond hair just like Daddy, George and Mrs. Smith.

I like your nice blond hair," or "Daddy has big hands because he is big. Your hands are little because you are little. When you get big, you will have big hands too." Or for the handicapped child, "When you were born something happened to your feet so they do not do all the things they should, just like I was born with crooked teeth. You were just born that way, but we have eyes just the same color." This kind of explanation, while appropriate now, will not do for the older or brighter child. As the comments get more complex, the responses must become more detailed. You can talk about how everyone has differences; you can sympathize with the child's frustrations, e.g., "I wish you could run, too, but you just can't. What else can you do together instead?" Do not intimate that things will change when the child grows up unless this is true. Do reassure the child that you like her just the way she is. Keep your remarks brief. A sentence or two is sufficient unless the child demands more. Do not make an issue of the handicap anymore than you would of more normal differences.

5.66 DISPLAYS SHYNESS WITH STRANGERS AND IN OUTSIDE SITUATIONS (24-30 mo.)

The child may place his fingers in his mouth, refuse eye contact, hide his face or hide behind and cling to his mother's skirts when approached by strangers or other children. He may seem especially shy at school.

1. Allow the child to hang back and take his time. Pushing the child to talk, relate or play only makes the child feel more shy and resistent. Be matter-of-fact about the inability to interact. Respect the child's need to choose when and with whom he will interact.
2. Mention occasionally that *some day* when he is big, the child will not be shy anymore or will be able to play.
3. The child may dawdle over or cling to the initial routines of the day at school. He wants to go very slowly in getting ready to start the day. This is not laziness, but a need to slowly take in and absorb the situation before joining in. Let the child take his time. Do not rush him.
4. The mother should stay at school until the child has "settled in" with a morning activity. Usually this takes no more than fifteen or twenty minutes.
5. Do not ask a child to "show off" or perform for others. This makes him very self-conscious. Should the child fail or refuse, the parents may feel embarrassed or unhappy with him and make him feel he is "bad" or a disappointment to them.

5.67 HOLDS PARENT'S HAND OUTDOORS (24-30 mo.)

1. Always offer your hand to the child when out walking, etc. Let go if it is safe and he wishes it.
2. Do not pull or drag a child by the hand. This can make a supposedly positive activity very unpleasant.

5.0 SOCIAL-EMOTIONAL

3. Do not insist the child "grow up" and let go of you. This will come later all by itself.

4. For the very shy child, holding his hand is a good substitute for carrying him or holding him when he feels fearful. Tell him you will hold his hand when he asks to be picked up so he will feel safe. Do not force this but try to encourage it.

5. The extroverted child may never want to hold his parent's hand and may always be running off. This is okay but watch him closely. Insist on holding his hand only when it is imperative, as in crossing the street.

5.68 FEELS STRONGLY POSSESSIVE OF LOVED ONES (24-36 mo.)

The child really knows now to whom he "belongs" and is strongly and permanently attached to the primary caretakers. He wants these loved ones to pay attention to only him and is often jealous of attention paid to others or of affection between parents. The birth of a sibling at this time can create strong feelings of jealousy.

1. Parents should try not to be overly affectionate toward one another in front of the child, but they should let him know firmly and positively that they have times when they want to be alone together or do things together.

2. Be sure the child receives enough positive attention. A quick hug or a few loving words can help a jealous child tremendously.

3. Make an effort to keep the older child in the center of attention, if there is a new baby at home. His parents should tell him they understand his jealous feelings but love him just as much as they always have. They should try to include him in activities with the baby and admire his "bigness" and skills. They can let him pretend to be a baby sometimes. The parents should spend some time alone with the child each day and let him know they truly love and need him as much as ever.

5.69 DISPLAYS DEPENDENT BEHAVIOR; CLINGS AND WHINES (24-30 mo.)

The child strongly feels his dependence upon and his need for his parents. The two-year-old child is at a peak age for whining, fussing, and clinging, especially at bedtime. At other times, he may feel independent and want to be left alone.

1. The child loves demonstrations of affection from his parents and loves giving them, too. This is a genuinely affectionate age.

2. Do not worry about a child's lack of independence or the "femininity" of a little boy's behavior. He is not yet ready to give up infantile behaviors, but this has *no* effect upon later "masculine" development. Parents should be as sympathetic and understanding as they can, and try to appreciate the child's need to know he can be dependent and cling.

3. Remember, a child will outgrow most of these behaviors when he reaches a developmental level of about three years. Try to tolerate his difficult behavior. If an issue is made of it, the child may continue these behaviors because they have been heavily reinforced by adult attention.

5.70 ENJOYS A WIDE RANGE OF RELATIONSHIPS; MEETS MORE PEOPLE (24-36 mo.)

1. Take the child to a play group regularly, if possible.

2. Leave him with a trusted adult, friend or relative, for the afternoon so he can have a good time away from you.

3. Make a special effort to make friends with children in the neighborhood. Invite them to your house.

4. One of the handicapped child's greatest lacks is in the area of peer relationships. A housebound child does not learn the skills he needs for school and later adulthood. Make a strong effort to have the child included in the neighborhood play group at his developmental level. Even if the parent has to drive for miles to get the child together with playmates, she should try to do it. The handicapped child is easily accepted by other children if playmates' questions are answered freely; a parent should take the time to sit down and explain the child's disability in simple terms; adults should not overprotect or provide special treatment for the child; the child can be taught to explain his disability in a free and unembarrassed way.

5.71 SAYS "NO," BUT SUBMITS ANYWAY (24-30 mo.)

1. The "no" stage continues, but it is no longer so definite. Ignore the words if the child's actions are compliant.

2. Do your best to be cheerful about the child's resistance. He is only trying to learn that he is a person in his own right with ideas of his own.

3. Try to see the humor of the situation and sometimes kid him out of his stubborn behavior.

4. Continue to make attempts to direct the child with actions instead of words. Do not lay down too many rules. This is a very stubborn age.

5. Compliance and cooperation finally begin to appear, but they are inconsistent and occasional at first. The "No," said in a mild tone helps the child assert his independence and comply at the same time. However, do not expect this mildness all the time; the child does not really outgrow his need to assert himself by being negative until about age three.

6. The child at this stage can sometimes be talked into cooperative behavior. If she wants to do something by herself, handling or physical forcing may make her very angry and defiant.

5.72 TENDS TO BE PHYSICALLY AGGRESSIVE (24-30 mo.)

The child can be very aggressive, hitting, biting, and pinching. She is not picking up bad habits from peers or from home. Most of this behavior is natural and disappears with adult encouragement.

1. Firmly prevent as many of these activities as you can *before* the child has a chance to carry them through. Do not scold or attempt to shame her. This only makes her worse. Tell her it is okay to be angry and to tell you about it; it is never okay to hit.
2. Do not bite, kick, or hit back. This only teaches the child that such behavior is acceptable.
3. Redirect the child by saying, "People arc not for hitting; punch toys [or any other appropriate objects] are for hitting." Give the child a few *weeks* to grasp this concept before you give it up as a failure.
4. If the aggression persists, calmly remove the child from the person he hits or remove yourself from him. Do not talk about the behavior; you may increase it through attention.
5. The child may attempt to act out his aggression and his anger with adults, but never allow him to physically attack you by hitting, pulling hair, pinching or biting in anger. Even at his angriest, the child senses underneath that such an attack on his powerful and needed support system (his parents or teachers) is wrong. He probably also fears the adult's anger. He imagines it to be as intense and retaliatory as his own. *For his own sake and for his feeling of security and safety, the child needs to be protected from his aggressive acts.* Very firmly prevent or stop any physical attack, especially against adults upon whom the child depends.

5.73 ENJOYS EXPERIMENTING WITH ADULT ACTIVITIES (24-30 mo.)

The child continues to love play that imitates adult activities. As the play is continued, it becomes more varied and complex. The mother and her activities around the house are usually the most visible and therefore the most imitated. The child thinks of his behavior as "real work" to be proud of, not as imitative play.

1. Let the child play dress-up with the parents' old clothes, hats, shoes, etc.
2. Let him help you with housework, wiping the table, putting away unbreakable dishes, sweeping the floor, polishing furniture, washing the car. He can not do a very good job, but praise his efforts anyway.
3. Let him help you cook by pouring ingredients, stirring, cleaning up *some* dishes.
4. Let him be creative in learning about adult activities. Give him a doll to imitate parent-child interactions.
5. Let him help put things away, especially your things; putting away his own things may seem too "boring."

6. Allow him to practice self-help skills. Let him brush his hair when the father does, pretend to shave, help care for the new baby by fetching things, experiment with dressing, even make-up.
7. If the parents appreciate his efforts, however clumsy, they set the stage for cooperative behavior.
8. Most of the child's interests may seem "feminine" at this time. Doll play and imitating the mother are very popular. This is perfectly all right. The little boy will begin identifying with and imitating his father at about three or four years of age.

5.74 FRUSTRATION TANTRUMS PEAK (24-30 mo.)

The child displays frustration tantrums which are internally caused. These tantrums are not a sign that negative behavior has been reinforced by adults.

1. The child who has never had tantrums before may begin now. Refer to 5.42 (Displays frequent tantrum behaviors).
2. As frustration tantrums peak in quantity, parental tolerance becomes harder to achieve. The mother, especially needs some time away from the child.

5.75 RELATES BEST TO ONE FAMILIAR ADULT AT A TIME (24-36 mo.)

1. A two-year-old is often overwhelmed, overstimulated, and unable to relate to two adults at a time even if both adults are his parents. Perhaps he is jealous. Perhaps he is torn by having to make a choice between them. Perhaps he feels too aware of their authority and is worried about being bossed around by two powerful adults.
2. Have each parent, if possible, play alone with the child for some period each day while the other quietly fades out of the picture.
3. Let one parent do the directing and managing when the family is together, not the same parent all the time.
4. Engage in quiet, understimulating activities when the family is together, especially at the end of the day when the child is fatigued.
5. Do your best to be understanding about the cranky, negative behavior that crops up at these times.
6. Be sure the child has experiences with "outside" adults fairly frequently.

5.76 ENGAGES BEST IN PEER INTERACTION WITH JUST ONE OLDER CHILD, NOT A SIBLING (24-36 mo.)

1. A five- or six-year-old may be the best playmate for the child at this age. The child plays best with only one playmate at a time, but usually not an older sibling. Look for a neighborhood child.

5.0 SOCIAL-EMOTIONAL

2. Give some opportunity for real peer play, but be constantly available for supervision and direction.

5.77 DRAMATIZES USING A DOLL (24-30 mo.)

The child's doll play is very helpful and important. The child learns to identify with adults by mimicking adult behavior with dolls.

1. Play with the child first and help him understand "pretend" games.
2. The best doll is very sturdy and simple. Dolls cannot be dressed yet. As a matter of fact, "naked" dolls are usually preferred. Get a doll with molded rather than rooted hair. A doll with rooted hair is quickly ruined. Provide a doll whose head and arms are not readily removable; parts that come off may frighten a young child into thinking he can come apart, too.
3. Provide the child with simple, sturdy equipment, e.g., a bed for the doll, a doll bottle, maybe a carriage or doll chair or a doll blanket.
4. Begin doll play very simply. For instance, use a toy bottle and feed the "baby." Then give the child the equipment and ask him to imitate you. "Graduate" to putting the doll into bed, taking it for a walk, feeding, toileting. Mirror the child's daily experiences when you assist him in doll play.
5. Do not be afraid to let little boys have dolls. It is a valuable experience for them.
6. Do not be upset by particularly violent treatment of the doll, especially if there is a baby at home. Jealousy can often be worked out with the use of a doll.

5.78 INITIATES OWN PLAY, BUT REQUIRES SUPERVISION TO CARRY OUT IDEAS (24-36 mo.)

The child thinks of things to do and then becomes frustrated because he cannot carry out his plans. He definitely needs tactful adult help.

1. Make sure the child is left to his own devices often enough that he has a chance to think up things to do.
2. Agree with and join the child when he asks you to play with him, but follow his lead. Usually just sitting, watching and making very occasional comments are enough.
3. Be "too busy" to play right away sometimes, but be sure to verbally indicate that you are busy doing some particular activity. This helps to gradually "wean" the child from dependence on your participation.
4. Provide enough creative toys, such as blocks, dolls, household equipment and trucks for beginning imaginative play. Play simple pretend games with the child.
5. If the child becomes frustrated in his play, help him gather his materials together, put things together, and get started. Fade out of the picture as soon as possible.
6. If the child is often frustrated, perhaps the toys are too

difficult and should be put away until they are age-appropriate. Perhaps he has too many toys around, and he cannot concentrate well on more than one or two. Remove some of his toys from sight, at least temporarily.

5.79 FATIGUES EASILY (24-30 mo.)

A child may be cranky, irritable, whiny, clingy, aggressive or throwing tantrums. Fatigue is the first thing to consider. A child can usually handle only thirty minutes or so of an exciting activity before falling apart. This is especially true of peer play, group activities or special events.

1. Do not punish a child for being tired. Arrange for some relaxing interactions with one adult immediately, such as reading, talking, singing or rocking.
2. Alternate quiet and relaxing times with more exciting play.
3. Provide adult supervision and guidance for group play.
4. Be sure the child obtains enough sleep both at nap-time and at night.
5. A child who has been "good" at school, visiting or at the sitter's may take it all out on his parents once he gets back to "safety" and home. Two-year-olds are usually very compliant outside and then express their feelings of anger, confusion, etc., at home. Parents will just have to be patient and take this tension release until the child can adjust and cope. Do not punish the child for his behavior.

5.80 DAWDLES AND PROCRASTINATES (24-30 mo.)

The child may continue this very difficult and frustrating habit of dawdling and procrastinating for years if it is not tackled now or prevented before it starts. There are many reasons for beginning this behavior, but they all originate with adults. A child is never naturally lazy or dawdling.

1. The child may be directed too much. His life may be interfered with constantly. Let him make decisions; let him play the way he wants; do not direct him constantly. Leave him alone and take it easy.
2. Too much may be expected of the child. Rules, chores, toys and expectations should be age-appropriate. Do not allow him to be constantly frustrated by an inability to do what is expected of him. He should often be successful.
3. *Completely ignore all eating behaviors.* Do not praise, urge, scold or withhold. Refer to 6.30 (May refuse foods—appetite decreases).
4. A child is naturally slow to do things, especially when he is just learning. Do not push or hurry the child. Allow plenty of time to get through tasks, such as dressing, bedtime, and eating in a relaxed way.
5. Let the child do for himself whenever he can.

150

5.81 VALUES OWN PROPERTY; USES WORD "MINE" (24-30 mo.)

1. Encourage the child to learn what is hers. Tell the child which clothes, toys, dishes, furniture are *hers*. Contrast these with her parents' things. You may need to point to her and say "Mine" or "My doll." See if she will imitate you.
2. Be sure each child in the family has a few things of her very own that she can do with as she wishes.
3. Do not force sharing. If an item is truly the child's, she can do whatever she wants with it.
4. If she orders you to leave her things alone, by all means do so.
5. Point out the things that are yours and explain in simple terms that you control these just as she controls hers. You may ask her to leave some things alone just as you will leave her things alone. Of course, she will not remember to do this, but is is a start.
6. Begin offering the use of some of your things and ask to use some of hers. This is the start of generosity.
7. Do not expect her to care for even treasured objects yet. The parents still have to bring toys in out of the rain.

5.82 TAKES PRIDE IN CLOTHING (24-30 mo.)

The child enjoys the compliments he receives about his appearance. This behavior is most common when encouraged as it often is in little girls' dressing up, but it is appropriate and important for both sexes.

1. Tell the child how pretty or nice he looks in his clothes or in a particular piece of clothing.
2. Ask friends and family to sometimes praise the child's clothing, especially when he is particularly proud of what he is wearing.
3. Remember that a child's taste differs from an adult's taste. The child may prefer a flashy shirt to one with tasteful little designs on it. If his clothing preferences seem gaudy to you, relax. "Good taste" comes with age and experience.
4. Teachers can help morning adjustments to school by noticing what the child is wearing and complimenting the child.
5. Remember to let the child choose his clothes for the day whenever possible. Let him choose between two alternatives which are equally acceptable to the parent.

5.83 BECOMING AWARE OF SEX DIFFERENCES (24-30 mo.)

The child knows his sex and that of others, although he may sometimes make mistakes. He also becomes aware of genital differences.

1. The child has had enough experience to be aware of and wonder about sex differences between boys and girls, adults and children, especially by two-and-a-half. It is a mistake to assume that the "innocent" child, who has not asked questions, does not want to know. Parents must be prepared to discuss freely at this time, both to avoid worry and to prepare an atmosphere for later, more difficult questions. Openness of communication between parent and child begins now.
2. The child typically wants to know, "Why am I different from [some child of the opposite sex]?" "Why do I look different from Mommy or Daddy?" "Is something wrong with me?" "Could that happen to me?" It is critical to provide answers to these questions.
3. The child often asks things in a roundabout way rather than directly. A little boy watching his mother bathe a new baby sister may simply express unusual interest in the procedure. The child may try to say the baby is hurt, try to pat or touch the baby's genitals, or handle his own genitals. All of these behaviors are really questions. Even the child who does not yet talk can benefit from a simple explanation at this time. If nothing else your reassuring tone of voice is helpful.
4. Keep your answers short. Take your cues from what the child says. Long complicated explanations are not necessary at this time. Say something like, "You are a boy and baby is a girl. You are like Daddy and baby is a girl. You are like Daddy and baby is like Mommy. We were all born this way and were meant to be the way we are. A little girl, like [baby's name] can be a mommy when she grows up and you can be a daddy when you grow up." Tell the child he or she is like the parent and like all the same-sex friends or relatives who are most familiar and well-liked. Tell the child he or she is made just right for a little boy or little girl.
5. The child who observes his parents, especially the little boy, sometimes worries about size differences. Go through the same explanations about the appropriateness of the child's genitals, if necessary. Emphasize that he is small all over, but will grow to be just like his father later.
6. A little girl may sometimes worry about how "plain" she is in relation to boys. Reassure the little girl how exactly right she is and how pleased you are with her just the way she is.
7. Remember that no child can incorporate a large amount of information at once. The child may repeat the same question, and you will have to repeat explanations many times before they "sink in."

5.84 MAY DEVELOP SUDDEN FEARS, ESPECIALLY OF LARGE ANIMALS (24-30 mo.)

The child may develop sudden fears which seem to arise out of the blue. Animals can be particularly frightening, but anything may be feared at this sensitive age.

1. Accept the child's feelings, and do not force him into a situation he fears, e.g., the water, bathtub, etc. You will only frighten him more and convince him you do not understand or care about his feelings.

5.0 SOCIAL-EMOTIONAL

2. Be calm, relaxed, and cheerful in fearful situations. If you are afraid that he will be afraid, he definitely will be.

3. If he fears an animal, offer the child a small stuffed animal which looks the same. Let him play with and abuse it if he wishes.

4. A child afraid of dogs may not fear a tiny puppy in a cage at the peg store. Experiment with, but do not force, this activity.

5. If he is afraid of water, dig a hole in the sand at the beach and play with the little bit of water that appears, or take a doll "swimming" in a plastic tub. Look for a comfortable and enjoyable play involving water.

6. See if he can admire feared objects from a considerable distance.

7. Read to him about the feared animal if he can enjoy this activity.

8. A sense of humor about the fear on the part of the parent can be very helpful. Sometimes a child can be "kidded" out of his fear. Be sure not to deride or make fun of the child because of his fears.

9. Most importantly, relax about the fear. If you do not make an issue of it, it will probably go away by itself eventually.

10. Apply the general suggestions about animal fears to any sudden fears that arise.

5.85 SEPARATES EASILY FROM MOTHER IN FAMILIAR SURROUNDINGS (30-36 mo.)

The child can cope with separation fairly well by now. The shy, dependent child may still have difficulty. This is a personality difference not necessarily due to "bad" handling.

1. Leave the child in his own home or in the home of an friendly person he knows very well if you expect him to separate happily. He should be very comfortable in school and feel very friendly toward his teachers before he is asked to let his mother go.

2. Remain in the background at school until the child is happily engaged in some play or interaction. This usually takes no more than fifteen minutes.

3. Act cheerful and relaxed when you leave the child. Keep your "good-bye's" very brief.

4. Leave the child for just an hour or so at first.

5. The child who is or has recently been ill, separated from a loved one, hospitalized, exposed to family upset or a big change, perhaps even after a trip will not be able to separate easily if at all. Respect the child's wishes because of the disturbance and give the child time to get over the traumatic event.

6. Refer to 5.25 (Shows anxiety over separation from mother) for methods of gradual separation.

5.86 SHOWS INDEPENDENCE; RUNS AHEAD OF MOTHER OUTDOORS; REFUSES TO HAVE HAND HELD (30-36 mo.)

The child feels proud and practices her independence by refusing "babyish" contact with her mother.

1. Insist upon holding her hand or carrying her in dangerous places, e.g., near streets.

2. Make a special effort to take her where she can run freely. A child will usually not run more than two hundred yards before returning to her mother.

3. Offer a simple explanation as to why you must hold her hand at certain times.

4. A child of this age often gets lost in stores. She must be watched carefully. Better yet, do not take the child shopping if you need to accomplish something which requires a lot of attention and time. *Never* "lose" a child on purpose to "teach her a lesson" or threaten to leave her in the store. Such behavior can only be damaging. At the very least, the child will soon learn that she cannot trust her mother or that her mother lies to her.

5. Make an effort to give up the stroller even if it is tempting to use it to restrict the child. Harnesses are not a very good idea either. The child needs the independence she is striving for and cannot achieve it if she is literally tied to her mother. A child can be embarrassed and shamed by such devices.

5.87 DEMONSTRATES EXTREME EMOTIONAL SHIFTS AND PARADOXICAL RESPONSES (30-36 mo.)

The child has emotional ups and downs which are indicative of how hard this third year is on the child as well as the parents. This is the age when the child really does not "know his own mind." He contradicts himself and is terribly frustrated by his indecision. His reactions are almost always intense.

1. The child should not be expected to make a decision and stick by it. At this age the child is not always able to decide whether or not to go somewhere even if it is someplace he usually enjoys, such as the park. He is torn between choices and is sometimes terribly distressed by the results of his choice. It is best to make the decision for the child in many instances. If, for example, you know the child will later be disappointed if he did not go somewhere, decide for him. If necessary, insist upon his going, knowing he will enjoy himself once he escapes the decision-making situation.

2. Resist becoming too involved in the extreme emotionality of this age. Make an effort to remain calm and relate to the child in a relaxed way when the child is . screaming or overly excited. Sympathizing with his feelings may help a little, but removal from the causal situation and ignoring protests may be better.

3. Avoid, if possible, choice-making situations over which the child must agonize.

4. Keep alternatives simple and few.

5. Avoid the phrase, "Do you want to . . .," since the probable answer will still be "No!" Sometimes, because of

his extreme indecisiveness and before you realize it, the child may erupt with a full blown tantrum.

6. Avoid using phrasing involving "or" since it is a difficult concept for the child and is especially frustrating when the child's desire may be for both choices.

7. Do not insist on sticking by the child's choice between two desirable objects. Very often he did not really mean it and cannot understand your insistence. Remove the other object from sight as soon as possible after the child makes a choice.

8. However, do stick by *your* decisions. Do not flip-flop between "Yes" and "No" just because the child flip-flops.

5.88 BEGINS TO OBEY AND RESPECT SIMPLE RULES (30 mo. and above)

1. The child is gradually and on occasion overcoming his negativity of the earlier age levels by age two-and-a-half or three. He now remembers, at times, to leave a forbidden object alone, come when called, and decide to cooperate. This period has its ups and downs so do not expect "good" behavior all the time.

2. The child may pick up and bring forbidden objects to his mother for removal. He is really trying to cooperate, although he cannot *not* touch them. The mother should let him know she appreciates his efforts.

3. A child will sometimes be amazingly cooperative if you remind him gently about a rule and ask him to "please" do something. Experiment with this rather than grabbing the forbidden object or demanding good behavior.

4. The child is still difficult to live with despite this occasional ability to follow rules. His emotional responses remain extreme. He is not an adult and should not be expected to behave like one.

5.89 TENDS TO BE DICTATORIAL AND DEMANDING (30-36 mo.)

The child constantly orders others around and exhibits generally irritating attitudes. He behaves like a "little king" and is furious if he is not obeyed. Despite its difficulty, this is an important time for the child. He is learning in this exaggerated way to be an assertive and competent individual who has confidence in himself and his ability. He is trying to learn how to care for and stand up for himself. It is hard on the child as well as the parents.

1. Try to develop a sense of humor about the child's behavior. The period from two-and-a-half to three is probably the most difficult for parents to live through. Spanking tends to reach a peak around this time although it is generally ineffective as far as the child is concerned. An easy going, good-humored approach still works best.

2. Do not make many demands on the child. This is not the time for it because the child is *not* ready to learn manners, follow orders, cooperate or be diplomatic.

3. Recognize that the child's dictatorial, demanding behav-

iors, like all other behaviors during this third year are normal and important for the child. Set a few, very firm limits, but also accept most of his behavior. A sense of humor and an understanding of this developmental stage are critical. The child *will* outgrow these behaviors.

5.90 TALKS WITH A LOUD, URGENT VOICE (30-36 mo.)

1. A child is usually not capable of speaking in low, well-modulated tones. Parents and teachers simply have to get used to this.

2. Unfortunately, the automatic reaction to a loud child is to raise one's voice. Avoid this, if possible. Lower the decibel level by responding especially quietly and in low tones to the loud child. The louder the child becomes, the softer you become. However, do not expect considerable success with this method.

3. Remind the child gently about lowering his voice. Although a real behavior change is unlikely, you may achieve some momentary success with a tactful reminder. You will have to repeat it many times, but may find it helpful for temporary control in restaurants, church or school.
   a. Distinguish between an "inside voice," a soft, quiet voice, and an "outside voice," yelling. Remind the child when necessary to use her "inside voice." This may not work with a child who cannot make such a fine distinction. Try whispering to the child when an "inside voice" is desired.
   b. Consider saying *very* quietly when the child is just too loud, "I can't hear you when you talk so loud. What did you say?" Even if the child thinks this is silly, you might focus his attention on speaking softly.

5.91 RESISTS CHANGE; IS EXTREMELY RITUALISTIC (30-36 mo.)

The child is very sure of the way things are supposed to be; any disruption appears to be quite threatening to the new-found understanding of order and routine.

1. The child's resistance to change is a period which must just be lived through and tolerated. It will not be permanent.

2. Ritualistic behavior may be so extreme that the child demands the same cup to drink out of at each meal, wants exactly the same story each night, demands the same person put him to bed each night, insists that each person sit in exactly the same chair every evening. The child may even be upset if he is dressed in the "wrong" order, e.g., his shirt first if he is used to diapers or pants being first. Any change may produce a violent reaction. Go along with his need for little rituals if they are not too prolonged or disrupting. His extremeness is not caused by poor parental handling.

3. Handle this stage by accepting it as a part of normal development and tolerate it as much as possible. The child

5.0 SOCIAL-EMOTIONAL

will outgrow it at about three years.

4. Refer to 5.43 (Needs and expects rituals and routines).
5. CAUTION: Ritualistic concerns should occupy only a minor portion of the child's day. A demand for environmental sameness which interferes with normal play or generalizes to too many situations is a sign of trouble. Seek professional help.

5.92 EXPERIENCES DIFFICULTY WITH TRANSITIONS (30-36 mo.)

The child experiences emotional distress of varying severity when faced with transitions. A transition involves any movement from one activity to another. The child usually experiences transitional problems between sleeping and awakening, playing and being asked to sleep, playing and being stopped for lunch, indoor and outdoor play, and upon first arrival at school or play group.

1. Give the child plenty of time to adjust mentally to new surroundings. Do not rush the child; give him time to gradually accustom himself to the idea of any new activity. Tantrums occur when the child is pushed too fast. Most importantly, take it easy and go slowly.
2. Transitions between sleeping and waking often produce very cranky behavior. Attempt the following to see if you can ease the transition for the child:
   a. Lie down beside the child when she first awakens. Be silent, then quietly start talking to her.
   b. Rock the child until she is completely awake.
   c. Offer the child food, quiet music, books, maybe a good television program.
3. Give the child arriving at school a few minutes to himself, if necessary, before greeting him and insisting he start activities or play. A consistent morning ritual helps. The mother should not leave until the child has "settled in." This process usually takes about fifteen minutes.
4. Be firm at bedtime if this is important to you. A little ritual and quiet time beforehand will help the child quiet, but it may not completely overcome the child's resistance to letting go of the day. Be calm and friendly, but insist upon sleep.
5. Be careful not to interrupt an absorbed child's activities too suddenly. When you first break into his play, just sit and make contact with him. Help him wind up his play; give a little warning of what is coming up next. Be sure to give him enough time to adjust to the idea. Then, tell him it is time for the next activity, lunch, outdoors, whatever, and take him. Do not ask his preference or if he wants to!
6. An insistence on instant obedience will usually fail and only serves to frustrate everyone. Give the child time. Children learn to obey later, when they have more self-control.
7. Do not fall into the habit of telling the child over and over and over again to do something. Once you have announced your intentions and given the child a gradual introduction, carry the child, bodily if necessary, into the planned situation. Do this in as friendly a way as possible.
8. Despite adult carefulness, there will probably be frequent upsets and tantrums. Do your best to ignore them. Do not allow them to sway you. Remain calm. Adult distress reinforces the child.

5.93 PARTICIPATES IN CIRCLE GAMES; PLAYS INTERACTIVE GAMES (30 mo. and above)

1. Help the child play very simple games with plenty of adult help and supervision. Give every child a chance to participate and be the "star" playing:
   a. "Ring Around the Rosie,"
   b. "The Farmer in the Dell,"
   c. "London Bridge,"
   d. "Hot Potato," pass a ball around,
   e. "Hide and Seek,"
   f. Tag-do not play competitively, but more as a fun chasing game.
2. Remove yourself gradually from the games, allowing a few days for complete withdrawal. Let the children play without interference, settle their own battles, etc.
3. Let the child run around, scream, shout, and yell during interactive play. Much of the child's play seems aimless and without purpose. The child, however, has a marvelous time. Do provide appropriate times and places for this activity. As the child grows older, his games will develop more order.
4. True interactive games with rules and cooperative efforts are not engaged in independently until the six to twelve year age period. Do not demand adherence to complex rules. Make even supervised, interactive games very flexible. Do not emphasize winning or losing. Preschoolers need to win *all* the time.

5.94 TAKES PRIDE IN OWN ACHIEVEMENTS; RESISTS HELP (30-36 mo.)

1. Encourage the child to do what he can do, such as partially dress, walk instead of being carried, wash himself, help around the house. Express satisfaction and pride in his accomplishments.
2. Tactfully arrange things and help with what he cannot do, such as buttoning. If his pants are on backwards, do not notice it or arrange his clothing in advance so he picks it up facing frontwards.
3. Help, if he asks. Ask if you can help.
4. Always be proud when the child feels proud of being a *big* boy or girl.
5. Emphasize to the child that she will grow up to be a woman just like Mommy; the boy, a man like Daddy.
6. Pick the child up bodily and remove her from any situation in which she is in a fury because she can not accomplish something to her satisfaction, will not give up, and is made more furious by your efforts to help.

7. If the child is always frustrated by her toys, perhaps they are too difficult for her. Make sure her playthings are age-appropriate. She should usually experience success in her play.

5.0 SOCIAL-EMOTIONAL

NOTE: Each child is unique and may master skills at a rate and age different from other children. The age references in this Guide are approximations. You should not be concerned if your child does not display skills exactly within the specified age ranges. See the Introduction for additional clarification.

6.01 OPENS AND CLOSES MOUTH IN RESPONSE TO FOOD STIMULUS (0-1 mo.)

The child opens and closes his mouth in response to the food stimulus when his cheek or the area around the mouth is touched with the nipple.

1. Sit in a comfortable chair with a back and armrest while feeding the child. A low footstool to support your feet may be helpful. Hold the child close to you during feeding and support him in a slightly reclined position.

2. Select a quiet environment and try to relax during the child's feeding period. Talk soothingly to the child while looking at him.
3. Breast feeding the child:
   a. Hold the child in a slightly reclined position. Let his head rest in the bend of your elbow. His face should be close to and turned slightly toward your breast.
   b. Guide the nipple to the child's mouth by taking the breast with your free hand and touching the nipple only to the side of his face nearest your breast. Encourage the baby to turn his head toward the breast to nuzzle for the nipple. Do not push his head toward the breast.
   c. Squeeze some milk out first and touch the child's lips to encourage.
4. Bottle feeding the child:
   a. Hold the child close to you in a slightly reclined position. Touch the child's cheek, on the side closest to you, and his lips with the nipple. Do not stimulate the baby's mouth on both sides at the same time. This may confuse and upset him. Stimulate only the side to which you present the food.
   b. Alternate holding the child to the right side and to the left side with different feedings. Do not always feed the child holding him only on one side, e.g., to your left side.
5. For the cerebral palsied child with feeding difficulties due to abnormal reflexes, posture and muscle tone:

   a. Consult a physical therapist, occupational therapist or speech therapist regarding positioning of the child to facilitate feeding.
   b. Sit at the table with the child on your lap facing you, using a wedge under the child. Place the wedge against the table edge and on your lap. Position him in a slightly reclined position with his head slightly flexed and his arms forward. Use a footstool to position or raise your knees to bring the child to a more upright position, if necessary. Bring the child's legs around your waist or flex his hips and knees to exhibit extensor pattern of the legs.

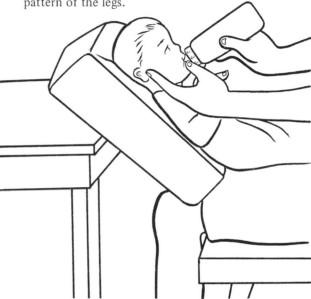

   c. Be sure to position the head slightly flexed at midline with arms and legs symmetrical.
   d. Open and close his mouth by applying slight pressure on the child's chin below his lower lip with your thumb.
   e. Sit at the same level as the child to avoid extensor pattern and to maintain eye contact with the child.
   f. Keep the food where the child can see it.

6.02 COORDINATES SUCKING, SWALLOWING, AND BREATHING (1-5 mo.)

The child sucks a number of times in succession, rests, sucks a number of times again and rests, developing a regular pattern of sucking, swallowing, and breathing while feeding at the breast or bottle.

1. Be sure the bottle nipple hole is not so large in size that the milk flows out too fast in a steady stream. Milk should drop freely through the nipple at approximately twenty drops per minute.
2. Hold the child close to you in a slightly reclined position. Do not hold the child in supine or let him lie flat on his back in the crib or on the floor. Do not prop the bottle, the child may choke or vomit.
3. Select a quiet environment and relax during the child's

157

feeding period. Talk soothingly to the child and make feeding as pleasant as possible.

4. Burp the child once or twice during each feeding, and once after the feeding. Hold him upright against your shoulder or lay him across your lap and pat or rub his back gently to help him burp up swallowed air.
5. Do not position the child so the breast presses against the child's nose. This may interfere with his breathing and make sucking difficult. Place a finger against the breast and press it away from the child's nose.
6. Break the suction from the child's mouth when he is finished feeding by pressing a finger at the base of the nipple or at the corner of the child's mouth. Do not pull the breast from the child's mouth.
7. For the child who has difficulty with sucking and swallowing:
   a. Close the child's lips manually around the nipple or press the lower lip upward with your thumb placed below his lower lip if the child has difficulty with lip closure.
   b. Stimulate the lips with a cold stimulus, such as a refrigerated nipple, cold cloth, or ice cube to encourage lip closure and sucking.
   c. Try the Nuk Orthodontic nipple, which is shaped like a breast nipple, if the child has poor lip closure, tongue thrust (pushing out of the tongue) or a bite reflex. Try a "preemie" nipple, which is softer than the regular nipple, if the child sucks very weakly. These nipples are available at retail and drug stores.
   d. Use a bottle straw device if the child has a strong extensor thrust pattern of the head and trunk. The child draws the liquid from the bottle as he sucks on the nipple. This device will allow the child to suck and swallow with his head at midline and with his head slightly flexed rather than in a hyperextended position.
   e. Let the child drink from a small cup if he has very poor sucking. Continue to provide close body contact, mouthing and oral stimulation experiences.
   f. Refer to 6.01 (Opens and closes mouth to food stimulus), Activity #5, for positioning of the older delayed child.

6.03 SLEEPS NIGHTS FOUR—TEN HOUR INTERVALS (1-3 mo.)

The child's sleep needs vary widely during the first year but each child will take as much sleep as he needs if his environment provides the opportunity. Sleep patterns may change from day to day. Nothing needs to be done about this.

1. Feed the child, formula or milk, when he awakens to be fed.
2. Do not awaken the child to feed him. He will awaken himself when he is hungry.

6.04 STAYS AWAKE FOR LONGER PERIODS WITHOUT CRYING—USUALLY IN P.M. (1-3 mo.)

1. Let the child be in the room with other people.
2. Offer small colorful toys for visual regard and grasp.
3. Put mobiles in rooms other than the child's room, such as the kitchen, living room, patio.
4. Offer social play. Smile, sing, talk to the child.
5. Refer to 4.08 (Stops unexplained crying) if the child's periods of evening wakefulness are accompanied by long crying episodes.

6.05 NAPS FREQUENTLY (1-3 mo.)

The child will take as much sleep as he needs. His sleep patterns can vary widely.

1. Do not expect the home to be absolutely quiet during the child's nap. The child will accustom himself to having normal household noises and voices during his nap.
2. Place the child on his stomach for his nap if he falls asleep while being fed and has not burped.

6.06 SUCK AND SWALLOW REFLEX INHIBITED (2-5 mo.)

The child automatically closes his lips around the nipple and sucks several times before swallowing. This is the suck and swallow reflex seen from birth to about two months. From about two months on, the child develops a more voluntary sucking and swallowing pattern.

Refer to 6.02 (Coordinates sucking, swallowing and breathing).

6.07 BRINGS HAND TO MOUTH (2-4 mo.)

The child brings his hand to his mouth for oral stimulation and explorations.

1. Allow the child to explore his hands and fingers by mouthing. Do not pull his finger or thumb out of his mouth if he begins to suck on them.
2. Place the child in supine or hold him so you can guide the child's hand to his mouth. Bring the child's shoulder forward by holding his elbow or forearm and bring his hand to his mouth.
3. Place the child in prone or in side-lying and bring the child's hand to his mouth.
4. Dip the child's fingers or hand in strained foods or baby cereal to encourage him to bring his hand to his mouth. Bring the child's hand to his mouth, if he does not do so himself. Repeatedly dip the child's fingers and let him enjoy the taste and mouthing of his hands and fingers.
5. Let the child produce different sounds by bringing his hand to his mouth, covering and uncovering his mouth for him when he is making sounds. Bring his hand to your mouth and produce "ahh-ahh-ahh" sounds for him.

Repeat at his mouth. Enjoy playing this with him.

6.08 SWALLOWS STRAINED OR PUREED FOODS (3-6 mo.)

The child swallows strained foods which are fed to him with a spoon.

1. Introduce the child to strained foods when it is recommended by the pediatrician. The child may try to suck and swallow the food as he did his formula.
2. Allow time for the child to become accustomed to the new food.
3. Offer milk before or after the strained food, whenever the child prefers it.
4. Introduce new foods one at a time in small amounts and increase the amount gradually. Continue the same food for three successive days before introducing another new strained food. If there is a question of food allergy it will usually manifest itself during this trial period.
5. Position the child for feeding by holding him as upright as possible in sitting or by placing child in an infant seat facing you.
6. Keep his food where he can see it.
7. Strained or pureed foods can be made at home by cooking the desired food well, mashing it, putting it through a sieve or in a blender. Do not add salt.
8. Encourage the child to open his mouth by:
   a. Giving verbal, visual, olfactory, tactile, and gustatory stimuli. Talk about his food. Make "ahh" or "mum-mum" sounds. Place the child's meal where he can see it. Show him the food on the spoon. Touch his lips lightly with the spoon so he can feel and smell the food before tasting it.
   b. Applying downward pressure with your thumb below the lower lip, if necessary, to open his mouth.
9. For the older delayed child:
   a. Use a baby spoon or a spoon with a small bowl, e.g., a demitasse spoon for feeding. Or, use a rubber coated spoon if the child has a strong bite reflex.
   b. Present the spoon to the center of the lips. Allow the child to take the food off the spoon with his lips.
   c. Place the spoon on the mid-portion of the tongue and gently press downward to encourage swallowing or if the child has a strong tongue thrust.
   d. Pull the spoon straight out and let the child use his upper lip to remove the food from the spoon. Swallowing is easier when the mouth is closed. Use jaw control, if necessary, to help the child open and close his mouth and swallow. Place your thumb under the lower lip on the chin, middle finger under his chin and index finger at the jaw bone. Refer to the illustration, next column.

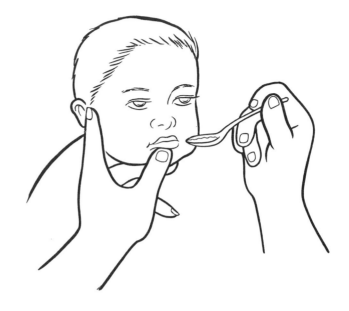

6.09 BRINGS HAND TO MOUTH WITH TOY OR OBJECT (3-5 mo.)

The child brings her hand to her mouth while grasping a toy.

1. Place a small toy or rattle in the child's hand. Be sure the toy or rattle is safe, non-toxic and that the child can hold it comfortably. Guide her hand with the toy to her mouth, if necessary, and encourage her to explore the toy with her mouth.
2. Give the child different textures to explore with her hands and mouth, such as plastic non-toxic toys, rubber toys, squeeze toys, soft, hard, smooth, fluffy, scratchy or rough textures.
3. Caution: Do not use tiny objects which she might swallow, such as beads, marbles, objects from which a portion may break off, or toys with sharp corners.

6.10 RECOGNIZES BOTTLE VISUALLY (3½-4½ mo.)

The child shows visual recognition of the bottle or breast by facial or body expression, by an open mouth, or by sucking motions.

1. Hold the bottle where the child can see it. Bring attention to the bottle visually and verbally before giving it to the child. Comment to the child, e.g., "Do you want your milk?" or "Here's your bottle." Bring the bottle gradually toward the child and insert it in her mouth. Do not simply stick the bottle into the child's mouth.
2. Keep the child nearby to watch and hear as you prepare the formula or milk in the bottles.
3. Hold the child when feeding her. Make it a pleasant, relaxed time.

4. For the visually handicapped child: Offer the bottle by letting her feel or touch the bottle, talk about the bottle or shake it so she can hear it.

6.11 USES TONGUE TO MOVE FOOD IN MOUTH (4-8½ mo.)

The child uses her tongue to move the food in her mouth before swallowing.

1. Offer the child strained foods by spoon. As you remove the spoon from her mouth, encourage her to remove the food from the spoon with her upper lip and not her teeth.
2. Use a spoon with a shallow bowl if the child has difficulty removing the food using her upper lip.
3. Use a teflon coated spoon if the child has a bite reflex so she will not hurt herself should she bite on the spoon.
4. Encourage the child to use her tongue to move the food in her mouth by:
   a. Placing the food to one side of her mouth or the inside of her cheek.
   b. Depressing the mid-portion of the tongue gently with the spoon. Do this before removing the spoon from the child's mouth if she pushes the food out with her tongue during feeding. Keep the lips closed if necessary.
   c. Pushing the child's tongue gently at each side with your finger, tongue blade or teflon coated spoon if the child has difficulty moving her tongue in her mouth. Be careful of your finger if the child has a bite reflex.
   d. Putting food on the corners of the child's mouth and upper lip. Let her use a mirror so she can see her tongue moving, or, let her imitate you moving your tongue.
   e. Introducing lumpy foods such as soft rice, mashed banana, tofu, cottage cheese. Encourage tongue movements and chewing motions by placing the foods to the side of the mouth.
5. Encourage mouthing of fingers and toys.

6.12 ROOTING REFLEX INHIBITED (4-6 mo.)

The child's cheek or the area around the mouth is touched and the rooting reflex is seen. The child turns his head toward

the stimulus with his mouth open as if in search of food. If this is the case it is not cause for concern. The rooting reflex may continue up to eight months of age.

1. For the older delayed child who continues to have the rooting reflex:
   a. Inhibit the rooting reflex by rubbing or touching the cheek close to the mouth. Do not give the child the bottle or spoon immediately after he responds with the rooting reflex; wait until the response diminishes.
   b. Avoid feeding positions in which the child's cheek might be stimulated. Feed the child in face to face position. Refer to 6.01 (Opens and closes mouth in response to food stimulus), Activity #5, b.
   c. Rub her cheek or touch around her lips after feeding when she is not hungry.

6.13 PATS BOTTLE (4-5 mo.)

The child periodically pats his bottle while it is held for him during feeding.

1. Help the child, if necessary, to touch or pat bottle by placing his hand or hands on the bottle while bottle feeding him.
2. Offer milk bottle warmed or at room temperature. A cold bottle may be too uncomfortable for the child to touch.
3. Use bottles with designs if he does not respond to the regular bottle.
4. Cover a plain bottle with different textures, e.g., insert it through a clean sock.
5. Hold the child and the bottle when feeding him. It is very important for the child to be held while being fed. Do not lay him down on his back and, especially, do not prop his bottle. This is an unsafe practice because the child may choke or vomit.

6.14 SLEEPS NIGHTS TEN—TWELVE HOURS WITH NIGHT AWAKENING (4-8 mo.)

The child sleeps ten to twelve hours at night and awakens at least once. The child who has been sleeping through the night may begin to awaken to play or perhaps to fuss a little. This, at times may be related to teething or it may be just a desire to have fun.

1. The child needs attention at this time if he is fussing. Be careful because too much attention may make for a long standing habit of awakenings. Be brief in comforting and do not get wrapped up in playing or having fun with the child if he awakens at night. Try to be "boring."
2. The child does not require any attention if he awakens to play alone in his crib.

6.15 NAPS TWO THREE TIMES EACH DAY ONE—FOUR HOURS (4-8 mo.)

The child takes two to three naps during the day of one to four hours duration, varying according to his needs.

6.16 PLACES BOTH HANDS ON BOTTLE (4½-5½ mo.)

The child places both hands on the bottle while the bottle is held for her during feeding.

1. Hold the child while feeding her from the bottle. It is very important for the child to be held. Refer to 5.01 (Enjoys and needs much holding, physical contact, tactile simulation).
2. Do not lay the child on her back while feeding her, and, especially, do not prop her bottle. This is an unsafe practice because the child may choke or vomit.
3. Refer to 6.13 (Pats bottle). Hold the bottle with your hands over the child's hands if necessary. Reduce assistance when the child begins to voluntarily place her hands on the bottle.
4. Hold the end of the bottle and let the child place her hands on the middle part of the bottle. The bottle should not be extremely cold and cause discomfort for the child.

6.17 MOUTHS AND GUMS SOLID FOODS (5-8 mo.)

The child mouths and gums solid foods, such as a teething biscuit or graham cracker.

1. Start introducing new food textures. It is not necessary to wait until the child's teeth come in to offer foods to gum, to bite or to encourage chewing motions. The younger child is more willing to accept different textures than an older child.
2. Introduce lumpy foods such as soft rice, cottage cheese, tofu, mashed bananas, Jello.
3. Offer her Zwieback, dry toast, teething biscuit, or a Graham Cracker. Encourage the child to grasp the food to mouth or gum.
4. Do not leave the child alone when solid food is offered. Choking may occur if too large a piece is bitten off.
5. For the older delayed child: Cheese spread or peanut butter may be spread on a slice of dry toast to give a variety of tastes and to encourage her to accept new textures.
6. Caution: If a small child chokes and is in great distress, use the Heimlich maneuver. Sit on a chair with your feet flat on the floor. Lay the child across your knee with your leg pressing against his abdomen below the rib cage with his head down. Use the heel of your palm and apply a downward and upward pressure thrust at the base of the child's neck. Repeat if necessary. For the older child or adult, stand behind the child and place your arms around him. Clasp your hands with your thumb side against his stomach below the rib cage. Apply pressure with an inward and upward thrusting motion. Repeat if necessary. Take the child to the physician after the incident if there are further complications.

6.18 HOLDS OWN BOTTLE (5½-9 mo.)

1. Give the child the opportunity to hold his own bottle. Help him as needed. Refer to 6.13 (Pats bottle) and 6.16 (Puts both hands on bottle.)
2. Let the child hold the bottle for part of the feeding.
3. Use plastic bottles which are lighter than glass bottles.
4. Use a smaller plastic bottle (four ounces) if the size and weight of the bottle are a problem.
5. Hold or position the child as upright as possible in sitting while he drinks from the bottle. Hold the child as often as possible when bottle feeding even after he can hold his own bottle. Do not let the child drink from the bottle lying down, he may choke or vomit.
6. Use a bottle straw for the older delayed child who has poor arm and hand control. He can hold and drink from the bottle without having to raise the bottle. Refer to 6.02 (Coordinates sucking, swallowing and breathing), Activity # 7, d.
7. Wean the breast fed child directly to a cup if he refuses to take a bottle. Refer to 6.20 (Drinks from cup held for him).

6.19 BITES FOOD VOLUNTARILY (6-8 mo.)

The child begins to develop voluntary biting, a controlled bite with vertical jaw movement. The bite reflex, the strong closure of the jaw when the gum or teeth is stimulated, is diminished.

1. Let the child bite rubber toys.
2. Let the child bite on a teething biscuit or bite off a graham cracker.
3. Let the child bite off food which will readily dissolve in his mouth.
4. For the older delayed child:
   a. Present the food to the side of the child's mouth.
   b. Use jaw control, if necessary, to assist the child in controlling or grading the opening and closing of the mouth. Refer to the illustrations in 6.24 (Chews food with munching pattern), Activity #9, b.
   c. If the child has a bite reflex, release the bite by:
      1) Loosening the jaw control.
      2) Applying firm pressure on his jaw bone.
      3) Rocking the child gently to decrease hypertonicity.
   d. If the child is hypersensitive around the face or mouth, consult a physical therapist, occupational therapist, or speech therapist.
5. Caution: Remain close by the child in case he chokes. Use the Heimlich maneuver should the child choke and is in great distress. Refer to 6.17 (Mouths and gums solid foods), Activity #6.

6.20 DRINKS FROM CUP HELD FOR HIM (6-12 mo.)

1. Acquaint the child with a cup by letting him look, touch, and handle it.

2. Offer some water or milk or some favorite liquid by cup gradually. Do not show concern if the child refuses the cup initially. Try again later. He may refuse milk from a cup but may take other liquids from a cup easily. This is all right, but continue to offer milk in a cup every few days.

3. Seat the child as upright as possible. This will help facilitate his drinking from a cup. Place him in a high chair or infant seat.

4. Use a small, short cup so the rim fits comfortably between the child's lips and requires only slight raising for the child to take the liquid. The *Tupperware* two ounce midget cup is easy to use as a starting cup.

5. Place the rim of the cup between the child's lips, not between his teeth, and raise the cup at short intervals as he drinks.

6. Let the child use the same cup he will later learn to hold himself.

7. For the older delayed child:
   a. If the child's lips are hypotonic, use firm pressure with your fingers around the child's lips to increase tone. If the child's lips are hypertonic, press and gently shake around the child's mouth with your finger to decrease tone.
   b. Use jaw control if necessary. Place your arm around the child. Put your index finger above his upper lip, the middle finger below his lower lip, your thumb on his jaw bone. Maintain his head in slight flexion. Place the rim of cup between his lips, not his teeth, and apply gentle pressure with your fingers to encourage lip closure. Remove the cup from the lips and maintain jaw control to encourage swallowing. Or use the face to face method. Refer to illustration in 6.08 (Swallows strained or pureed food), Activity #9, d.

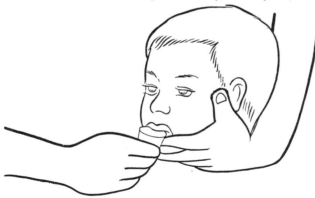

   c. Use thicker liquids, such as fruit nectars or milkshakes. Thicker liquids are easier to control in his mouth for swallowing.
   d. Consult a physical therapist, occupational therapist, or speech therapist for specific problems.

6.21 FEEDS SELF A CRACKER (6½-8½ mo.)

The child holds and feeds himself a cracker, hard toast, or cookie.

1. Let the child grasp a cracker and bring it to her mouth.

If she is unable to do this, place the cracker in her hand and guide her through the movements. Let the child use either hand or the hand of her preference.

2. Offer teething biscuit, hard dry toast, Graham Cracker or a baby's pretzel, which are shaped for easy grasp.

3. Do not leave the child alone when she is eating a cracker as she may take too large a bite and choke.

4. Refer to 6.17 (Mouths and gums solid food), Activity #6, if the child chokes and is in great distress.

6.22 BITES AND CHEWS TOYS (7-8 mo.)

The child mouths, bites and chews toys for sensory exploration.

1. Provide non-toxic flexible toys for the child to mouth, bite, and chew. Be careful that the toy or object is safe with no sharp corners, leakages, or pieces which can break off. Avoid tiny objects which are easily swallowed, such as marbles or beads.

2. Provide teething rings or squeeze toys made of rubber.

3. Offer toys or objects with various tactile, auditory, visual, or oral stimuli.

6.23 DROOLS LESS EXCEPT WHEN TEETHING (7-12 mo.)

The child drools less except when he is teething or when the child is concentrating on or attempting a particular gross or fine motor task.

1. For the child who drools excessively due to poor tongue, lips, and jaw control:
   a. Let the child imitate smacking lips and encourage swallowing with lips closed.
   b. Close the child's lips manually by using jaw control. Encourage swallowing. Refer to illustrations in 6.24 (Chews food with munching pattern), Activity #9, b.
   c. Encourage nasal breathing by using jaw control to help the child close his mouth and swallow. Check to see if the child is breathing through his nose by placing your finger by his nose or by placing a small mirror under his nose. See if the mirror fogs. Nasal breathing will be unsuccessful and he will breathe through his mouth if his nose is stuffed.
   d. Use various sensory stimuli in and around the mouth. Offer foods of different tastes, temperatures, textures, such as lemon slices or ice cubes, to make the child aware of his mouth and tongue.
   e. Wipe the child's mouth with a napkin, by applying pressure by pressing around the lips.

6.24 CHEWS FOOD WITH MUNCHING PATTERN
(8-13½ mo.)

The child begins to chew, the jaw movements are on the vertical place (up and down) with biting or munching movements.

1. Introduce junior foods, mashed foods, and chopped foods gradually. During the transition from strained foods to junior foods, offer the junior foods which are the child's favorite strained foods. This may avoid some fussing about accepting new textures.
2. Encourage the child to bite off a cracker, a banana, or a peeled apple slice.
3. Make chewing motions and let the child imitate you.
4. Let him imitate the repetitive opening and closing of the jaws as well as the clamping noise of your teeth.
5. Let the child feel your jaw movements by placing his hands on your jaws. Let him feel his own jaw movements with your hands on his hands.
6. Offer chewy strip of food such as a slice of good quality raw steak or a celery stick. Hold on to one end of the strip and place other end to the molar side of the mouth and encourage child to chew. Change over to the other side of the mouth with the other end of the food and let the child chew.
7. Use upward pressure below the lower lip to help the child keep his lips closed. Do this if the tongue pushes the food out of the mouth.
8. Offer foods which can be easily masticated and not foods which the child can easily choke on, such as raw carrots, nuts, or popcorn. Give these foods after the child can chew well. Remain close by to help the child in case he chokes.
9. For the older delayed child who has difficulty with chewing:
   a. Consult a physical therapist, occupational therapist, or speech therapist.
   b. Use jaw control, if necessary. Experiment with jaw control from the front or the side. Use whichever is appropriate or comfortable for the child. In using jaw control from the front, place your thumb on the child's chin, your middle finger under the chin, and your index finger on the jaw bone. Place the food on the side of the mouth or on the molars. Guide the jaw up and down with your hand.

Using jaw control from the side, place your thumb on the child's jaw bone, your index finger on the chin, and your middle finger under the chin.

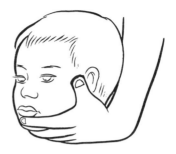

   c. Keep the child's head in slight flexion during feeding.
   d. Place the food to the side of the mouth or on the molars.
   e. Guide the child's jaw up and down with your hand.
   f. Maintain jaw control with the child's lips closed and wait until the child swallows.
   g. Reduce jaw control as the child improves in his chewing and swallowing skills.
10. Caution: If the child chokes and is in great distress use the Heimlich maneuver. Refer to 6.17 (Mouths and gums solid food), Activity #6.
11. Suggested foods to encourage chewing, finger feeding, self-feeding:
    a. Junior foods, table foods which are lumpy, mashed, thinly sliced, or choppoed.
    b. Meat, chicken, turkey, pork, ham, which are thinly sliced on a diagonal, chopped, or shredded.
    c. Ground meats, such as hamburger.
    d. Fish without any bones, tuna.
    e. Meat and chicken sticks.
    f. Eggs which are hard boiled, poached, scrambled.
    g. Cheese which is cubed or cut in strips for grasp; cottage cheese.
    h. Yogurt with fruit.
    i. Tofu, raw or cooked.
    j. Macaroni, spaghetti, rice.
    k. Cooked or canned vegetables, which are mashed, chopped, diced, or cut in strips for grasp, such as carrots, string beans, sweet potatoes, squash, spinach, beets, broccoli. Use raw celery sticks with caution. Pull out the celery stick as it starts to get chewed off. The strings of the celery can aid in pulling the celery stick from the child's mouth. This is to prevent the child from choking. Put peanut butter, creamed cheese or cheese spread on the celery. Do not give the child who is learning to chew a raw carrot, as it may crumble in the mouth and the child can easily choke.
    l. Fresh, canned or stewed fruits which are mashed, chopped, or sliced, with the skin peeled and the seeds removed, such as papaya, prunes, pear, banana, peach, orange, apple, star fruit, pineapple (the core can be sliced to use to grasp and chew), mango.

6.0 SELF HELP

m. Jello with cottage cheese or canned fruits, Jello with added gelatin to make it very firm or finger feeding and chewing, tapioca pudding.

n. Hard toast (oven toasted will dry out the toast nicely for coarse texture), Zwieback, teething biscuit, cracker (Graham, soda, cheese, wheat), dry cereal, bread sticks.

12. Caution: Hold off acidic fruits, spicy foods, egg whites until the child is older. Check with the mother or the pediatrician on known allergies.

6.25 FINGER FEEDS SELF (9-12 mo.)

The child feeds himself using his hands or fingers.

1. Assist the child with grasp and hand to mouth motions, if necessary.
2. Encourage the child and assist, if necessary, to suck, gum, bite off, chew and swallow food.
3. Offer the child finger foods which are easy for him to grasp. Slice, chop, cut, or dice foods appropriately for easy grasp.
4. Place the food on the tray, on the table in a bowl, or hand it to him to encourage reach, grasp, and the use of hand to mouth motions.
5. Let the child grasp the food with either hand.
6. Meats, cooked vegetables, fruits, baked goods may be appropriately sized for the child by slicing, dicing, or chopping to encourage finger feeding.
7. Let the child feed himself at least part of his meal with his hands.
8. Tolerate messiness as this is part of the child's learning experience.
9. Refer to 6.24 (Chews food with munching pattern), Activity #11, for a list of suggested finger foods.

6.26 HOLDS SPOON (9-12 mo.)

The child holds or grasps a spoon in his fisted hand.

1. Acquaint the child with a spoon. Let him look at it, touch it, grasp it and handle it. Let him do this as you feed him with another spoon, if this does not greatly interfere with his feeding.
2. Place the spoon on the table, let him reach and grasp for it, allowing him to use whichever hand he prefers. At first, he may not use the spoon instead, he may experiment with it by banging and waving it.
3. Place the spoon in the child's hand or guide his hand to the spoon and assist his grasp if he cannot hold onto the spoon. If he shows hand preference, place the spoon in that hand.
4. Offer a small wooden mixing spoon, a large serving spoon, or measuring spoons during play.
5. For the older delayed child:
   a. Offer a spoon with a built-up handle if the child's grasp is weak and he has difficulty grasping a regular spoon. Wrap a layer of sponge around the spoon handle with masking tape to build up the handle or use a commercially made built-up handle spoon.
   b. Place an elastic cuff around the palm of the hand. Insert a spoon handle into the cuff. This will assist the child who is physically incapable of maintaining grasp.

6.27 SLEEPS NIGHTS TWELVE—FOURTEEN HOURS (9-12 mo.)

The child's sleep pattern is usually fairly regular by now. The child sleeps through the night for about twelve to fourteen hours. Allow opportunity for the child to get as much sleep as he needs.

6.28 NAPS ONCE OR TWICE EACH DAY ONE— FOUR HOURS, MAY REFUSE MORNING NAP (9-12 mo.)

The child begins to give up his morning nap but gets desperately tired. It may help to move his lunch time to as early as 11 a.m., then put the child down for an early afternoon nap. The nap may be from one to four hours in duration.

6.29 COOPERATES WITH DRESSING BY EXTENDING ARM OR LEG (10½-12 mo.)

The child voluntarily moves his arms or legs while being dressed. This item does not refer to negative behavior which may cause the child to refuse to cooperate with dressing.

1. Dress the child by making it into a game. Distract him. Pulling the shirt over his head is usually disliked, so be very quick. Say "Boo!" when his head reappears.
2. Dress the child slowly enough so he has time to respond. Hold out the armhole or the leg of the clothing and ask him to put his arm or leg into the clothing. If there is no response, put it in for him. Hold a sock or a shoe out and encourage the child to extend his leg.
3. Talk to the child while dressing and undressing him. Talk about what you are doing and the parts of body involved such as, "Let's put your shirt on," "Arm through the sleeve."
4. Give tactile stimulation by lightly tapping the child's arm or leg to encourage cooperation.
5. For the older delayed child: Dress and undress the child in sitting whenever possible, in supported sitting if necessary, so the child can see the parts of his body and what is happening.
6. For the hemiplegic child, *undress* the unaffected arm before the affected arm. *Dress* the affected arm first, then the unaffected arm. It will be easier for the child to follow this procedure when he begins to dress himself.

6.30 MAY REFUSE FOODS—APPETITE DECREASES (12-18 mo.)

The child begins to refuse food. Refusing food is a behavior which may continue throughout the toddler stage. The behavior may be inconsistent. At some time the child may eat his meals then resume again the behavior of refusing foods. This is normal behavior for the toddler. This is a growth stage in which one good meal or the equivalent of one good meal from the three meals of the day is adequate. Food dislikes and inconsistency of appetite may continue throughout toddlerhood.

1. Try not to be overly concerned if the child does not eat much when he is otherwise well.
2. Some children may be fussy about foods related to taste, form, color, or consistency, such as:
   a. Casserole dishes. The child may prefer his foods separate.
   b. Sticky foods such as mashed potato.
   c. Highly seasoned foods. Avoid sour, strong or spicy foods. The child prefers bland foods.
   d. Raw vegetables or chewy meats. Prepare vegetables at least half cooked. Slice meats thin diagonally, into small pieces or shred it.
   e. Too large portions or pieces of foods. Serve small portions and keep foods at bite sizes.
3. Remember that mealtimes should be pleasant for all, so calmly accept the child's decision if he refuses food.
4. The following activities are for the mother to learn to tolerate her child's natural stage of being choosy about foods and to avoid future feeding problems:
   a. Do not force the child to eat if he shows strong dislikes of certain foods. Try again at a later date.
   b. Do not show your personal dislikes of certain foods overtly before the child. A child learns through imitation.
   c. Introduce a variety of foods of different tastes and textures.
   d. Do not insist that the child eat the foods he dislikes. Do not force feed him either. Otherwise, he will begin to distinguish between the foods he wants and the foods you insist he eat. Try to prepare a well balanced meal with the foods he likes or, let the child select certain foods from a well balanced meal you offer him.
   e. Do not comment on the amount or type of food the child eats or does not eat. Your attention to too little food or not enough variety may be reinforcing to the child. You want the child to eat because he is hungry, because his body needs it. Eating should be internally controlled. External control, e.g., praise or pushing, leads to obesity, feeding problems, food as a symbol for other things, excessive craving for certain types of food, etc.
   f. Talk about the taste, smell, color, and texture of a certain food the child is already eating. Do not discuss a food item to try to coax the child to eat it.
   g. Praising the child for eating may present the same problems as criticizing him for not eating. The child (or adult) should eat because he needs food, not to please or punish others. For the older child, do com-

ment on his style, if he is drinking well from the cup or using the spoon nicely.
   h. Do not withhold dessert as a punishment. A food withheld will increase its value to the child.

6.31 BRINGS SPOON TO MOUTH—TURNS SPOON OVER (12-15 mo.)

The child usually grasps the spoon with a fisted hand. He brings the spoon to his mouth, licks it, but has difficulty preventing the spoon from turning over.

1. Refer to 6.26 (Holds spoon).
2. Let the child grasp the spoon with either hand. Do not insist he use the right or left hand exclusively unless he shows a strong hand preference or he definitely has better use of one hand more than the other.
3. Sit next to the child in front or behind him when assisting him. Do not stand over him.
4. Scoop a favorite food or a food which will stick to the spoon. Encourage the child to bring the spoon to his mouth to lick it.
5. Assist or guide the child in bringing the spoon to his mouth, if necessary.
6. Continue to allow the child to finger feed while he is learning to hold and use the spoon.
7. Use a spoon which will meet the child's needs:
   a. Use a child's spoon. Be sure it is not too large for the child's mouth or hand.
   b. Use a spoon with a shallow bowl if the child has difficulty removing the food from the spoon with his upper lip.
   c. Use a teflon coated spoon for the child who has a strong bite reflex. Do not use a plastic spoon since it may break.
   d. Use a child's spoon in which the bowl of the spoon turns toward the child. With this type of spoon the child need not turn his hand to bring the spoon to his mouth. Commercially made spoon of this type are sold at drug stores.
   e. Use a spoon with a built-up handle if the child has a weak or poor grasp. Refer to 6.26 (Holds spoon), Activity #5, a. Check for proper thickness to allow for a comfortable grasp.

6.32 HOLDS AND DRINKS FROM CUP WITH SOME SPILLING (12-18 mo.)

The child holds and drinks from a child's cup with some spilling, especially when he drinks or when he puts it down on the table.

1. Seat the child as comfortably as possible in an upright position in a high chair with a tray or at the table in a chair the correct height for the child. Elbows should be resting on the table at ninety degrees, hips and knees at ninety degrees on the chair, feet flat on the floor or stool. A child with poor sitting balance may sit better supported

165

at a cut out table.
2. Guide and assist in the following steps as necessary, withdrawing your assistance as the child's ability increases in:
   a. Reaching and grasping the cup.
   b. Bringing the cup to the mouth and placing the lid of the cup between the lips on the lower lip, not between his teeth.
   c. Tilting the cup upward without the child leaning backward with his trunk or without hyperextension of head.
   d. Allowing for the coordination of swallowing and breathing while drinking by controlling the flow of the liquid. Control the flow or rest between sips as necessary. The child's lips should be closed so he can swallow.
   e. Giving the cup to mother or placing the cup on the table. The child may need some assistance in placing the cup back on table without spilling.
3. Use a child's cup depending on the individual child's needs and preference:
   a. *Tommee Tippee* cup with a plastic, weighted, non-tip,
   b. Plastic mug type cup with a flat bottom.
   c. Two handled cup for bilateral grasp.
   d. One handled cup for unilateral grasp.
   e. Cup with a lid which prevents spilling because the child has poor control in tilting the cup or placing it down on the table.
   f. Plastic cup without handles. The cup should be narrow enough to allow the child to comfortably grasp it using one or both hands. The cup should be short enough so the child need not tilt the cup too far back to drink from it.
   g. Tupperware or flexible plastic cup in which a "nose tunnel" or groove for the nose may be cut out of the rim of the cup. To clear the nose so the child's head does not go into hyperextension while drinking the liquid.
4. Fill the cup just a little at a time until the child can drink quite well from the cup.
5. Start training for cup drinking with a favorite liquid, either milk, juice or water. For the child with poor lip closure and swallowing patterns, use a thicker liquid, such as a fruit nectar or milkshake.
6. Be prepared with a large bib, a sponge, a mop, or place newspapers on the floor. Spilling accidents will occur often.
7. Make training pleasant. Praise successes, do not scold the child when accidents happen.

6.33 HOLDS CUP HANDLE (12-15½ mo.)

The child develops better control of his hands and can hold the handle or handles of a cup with his fingers.

1. Let the child grasp a one-handled cup with one hand and use his other hand around the cup for better support, if necessary.
2. Let the child use a lightweight unbreakable cup.

3. Use play tea cups with handles and have a tea party. Encourage the child to hold the cup handle.
4. Let the child grasp the strap or small handle of a toy radio, small pail, handbag or a purse.

6.34 SHOWS BLADDER AND BOWEL CONTROL PATTERN (12-18 mo.)

The child's frequency of urination will decrease and he will begin to show some regularity by being dry for about one to two hour intervals. Bowel movements may occur after a meal. A pattern of regularity and control is forming. At this point the child's pattern of elimination is still automatic, and not yet voluntary.

1. Determine if there is a pattern of regularity by noting the child's pattern of elimination. Record or chart on paper each time the child wets or soils his diapers during the day for about a week.
2. Keep the chart where you can easily record when the child is wet or soiled, e.g., where you always change his diapers.

6.35 INDICATES DISCOMFORT OVER SOILED PANTS VERBALLY OR BY GESTURE (12-18 mo.)

The child is psychologically aware of soiling and wetting when he indicates discomfort over soiled pants. Watch for signs such as the child hiding his face, showing you his wet pants, or trying to take them off. He may be indicating also if he stops during an activity, grimaces, strains, touches or holds his genitals, or squats. He may touch his wet diaper. He may hear the sound of his urination or look down as he makes a puddle. He may verbally say, "shi-shi," "wee-wee," or "do-do."

1. Watch for and respond to signals by acknowledging his indications by saying "shi-shi," "wee-wee," "do-do," or whatever the family word is used for urination or bowel movement. Use the same word consistently. Change him and mention his being wet or soiled. Do not scold. Be calm.
2. Praise the child if he tells you verbally or by gesture, that he soiled or wet his pants. Later, he will be able to tell you before he urinates.
3. Attend to the child and change him as soon as possible after his movement when he shows discomfort at soiled pants. This will prevent his becoming accustomed to staying in soiled pants.

6.36 SLEEPS NIGHTS TEN—TWELVE HOURS (13-18 mo.)

The child sleeps through the night for about ten to twelve hours.

1. Do not overstimulate the child before bedtime. Allow for

a quiet, calm time, such as reading bedtime stories or talking together.

2. The amount of sleep the child needs depends on the individual child. Be sure the child receives as much sleep as he needs.

6.37 NAPS ONCE IN AFTERNOON ONE–THREE HOURS (13-18 mo.)

The child takes one nap a day usually in the afternoon for about one to three hours.

1. Sleep patterns vary widely. Make sure opportunities are there for child to get the sleep he needs.
2. If the child awakens after one hour of nap and you feel he should sleep longer:
   a. Keep the noise level in the house down and keep out of sight. The child may look around, play briefly, then go back to sleep.
   b. If the child uses a "comforter" of some sort, have the child's "comforter" available to help him get back to sleep.
   c. Perhaps a little rocking and singing may help him get back to sleep as you assure him nothing is happening that he is missing.
3. If the child skips his regular afternoon nap, but falls asleep earlier in the evening than usual, provide a lot of active play the next morning to return him to his regular sleep schedule.
4. Let the child take his afternoon naps until he is ready to give them up especailly if he seems to need his naps. Afternoon naps may last beyond the age of eighteen months.
5. For the older child, if the nap interferes with his going to sleep at night or if he is very active until very late in the evening, shorten the nap by waking him. Do not eliminate the child's naps completely. He may need a nap until four or five years old.

6.38 SCOOPS FOOD, FEEDS SELF WITH SPOON WITH SOME SPILLING (15-24 mo.)

1. Refer to 6.26 (Holds spoon) and 6.31 (Brings spoon to mouth—spoon turns over.)
2. Let the child experiment and practice self feeding with a spoon. Do not scold or fuss about spills or messiness. Spread newspapers, an old sheet, or a plastic sheet on the floor to catch spills. Make mealtimes as pleasant as possible and do not pressure the child to feed himself completely.
3. Help the child take over before he becomes frustrated in his efforts to feed himself. Be sure to give the child the opportunity to do as much as possible by himself.
4. Allow the child to finger feed when he gives up the spoon during the meal.
5. Assist and guide the child as necessary in inserting the spoon into the dish, scooping and bringing it to his

mouth. He might remove the spoon from his mouth by tipping it upward. Mother should become less available, but still remain nearby as the child learns to be more independent.

6. Let the child practice at the beginning of the meal when he is hungriest.
7. Use a bowl with a high edge or a "scoop plate" with a high curved edge on one side. Position the scoop plate so the higher edge is on the side toward which he is scooping.

8. Let the child use a bowl with a non-slip bottom or suction cup which will prevent the bowl from skidding around while child is trying to scoop the food.
9. Serve foods which are easy to handle with a spoon. Thin soups and rolling peas are difficult for beginners. Foods which will stick to the spoon will make scooping and retaining food on the spoon easier. Some food suggestions: Stews with mashed or chopped meats, vegetables; stews with mashed or chopped meats, vegetables. Casserole or creamed dishes using hamburger, meats, poultry, pork, fish, vegetables which are chopped or thinly sliced. Rice may be added to make it stickier; vegetables which are mashed, chopped; macaroni and cheese; spaghetti (short noodles); cooked cereal; soft rice with chopped meats, vegetables; Spanish rice; junior or toddler foods; mashed pumpkin, squash, sweet potato; pudding; custard; poi; cream cheese; yogurt; cottage cheese; fruit sauces; ice cream.
10. Let the child practice scooping by:
    a. Scooping wet or dry sand with a large spoon, wooden spoon, or small spoon.
    b. Scooping soap suds, shaving cream from a pan or bowl with a large or small spoon.
    c. Scooping uncooked macaroni or rice in a large box with a large spoon.

6.39 REMOVES SOCKS (15-18 mo.)

The child pulls the socks off his feet.

1. Let the child begin with loose or slightly large sized socks. Cotton socks are easier to handle then nylon socks.
2. Sit behind the child on the floor. Position the child so one leg is extended and the other leg flexed at the knee with

her foot of the flexed leg over the extended leg. It may
be easier for the child to see what she is doing in this
position.

    a. Show the child how to remove her sock by pushing
the sock over the heel and pulling the sock off by pulling at the toe part of the sock.

    b. Let the child alternate leg and foot position and re-
peat. Encourage the child to pull off the second sock.

    c. Assist as needed; praise success.

    d. Assist or guide the child's hand as needed, letting him
use his thumb to remove the sock over the heel and
pulling it off at the toes. A loose fitting sock can be removed by just pulling at the toe part of the sock.

3. Let the child remove the sock with legs extended if he
can reach them comfortably. In supine, the sock can be
pulled off with the leg raised and the child reaching for
his foot.

4. Let the child lean against the wall if he cannot sit without support, then remove his sock.

5. Let the child try sitting on a low stool or a low chair.
Place one foot on the other knee and remove the sock.

6. Let the child remove other easy to remove items, such as
an untied bib or a hat.

6.40 REMOVES HAT (15-16½ mo.)

The child takes a hat off from his head.

1. Let the child bring his hands up to touch or tap his head.
2. Place some pieces of yarn on your head and let the child
take them off. Repeat with the yarn on the child's head.
3. Place a handkerchief, scarf, towel, small blanket or napkin on the child's head and let him take it off.
4. Place a hat on the child's head and let him take it off
while he watches himself in the mirror. Assist or guide as
necessary.
5. Use verbal cues, "Take hat off."
6. Show the child pictures, read stories about children with
hats.
7. Use novel hats for variety, such as Mickey Mouse ears,
cowboy hats, baseball hats, football helmets.
8. Let the child take a hat off from a doll or from your head.

6.41 PLACES HAT ON HEAD (16½-18½ mo.)

1. Let the child remove a hat you placed on his head. It is an
easier skill for the child to remove an object. Refer to
6.40 (Removes hat).
2. Place a hat on your head and let the child imitate you by
placing a hat on his head.
3. Let the child place a scarf, towel or small blanket on his
head.
4. Let the child look in the mirror and place a hat on his
head.
5. Use verbal cues such as "Put hat on" or "Put *your* hat on
your head."
6. Use a variety of novel hats.
7. Show him pictures of firemen, policemen, soldiers with
hats on their heads.

6.42 GIVES EMPTY DISH TO ADULT (18-19 mo.)

*The child hands the empty dish to the adult after she fin-
ishes eating or wants more food. The child will usually first
give the empty dish to a familiar person or whoever feeds her.
If the adult is not available, the child might drop the dish on
the floor.*

1. Remove the child's dish and say, "All done," or "More?"
when she finishes what she has in her dish. Do this at
snack or mealtimes to give her the idea that the dish is
going to be removed.
2. Give the child more food if she requests it by handing
you her dish.
3. Remove the dish and say, "All done," whether she indicates she is finished eating whether she is all done or not.
4. If there is another child who is able to give you his empty
dish on request, ask him for the dish, so the learning child
might imitate.
5. Ask the child for her empty dish and assist or guide as
necessary, saying "All done, give me your dish." Praise
him when he is successful or thank him.
6. Repeat the above to the point where the child will spontaneously hand the empty dish to Mom or another person
indicating he is finished or wants more food.

6.43 DISTINGUISHES BETWEEN EDIBLE AND
      INEDIBLE OBJECTS (18-23 mo.)

*The child knows what can be eaten. It is normal for a child
at this age to want to taste objects. It is important to keep
hazardous and poisonous objects away from him.*

1. Teach the child about inedible objects by letting him
imitate you. Stick out your tongue and say "Yuck" when
the child tastes an inedible object. Be expressive.
2. Play games. Show the child two objects, one edible and
one inedible, e.g., a toy and a cracker. Ask him to point
to or pick the one he can eat.
3. Let the child help in peeling bananas and oranges. Let him
taste the peels if he wants to experience them. Help him
put the peels aside or throw them away and eat the fruit.
4. Show him how to remove paper wrap from foods. Refer
to 6.59 (Unwraps food).
5. Caution: Even though the child may be able to distinguish
edible from inedible he is not safe unsupervised. Do not
leave him alone with soaps, paints, play dough. Always redirect the child's interest to something else when he tastes
something he should not so he will discontinue what he is
doing. He distinguishes only familiar things he has tasted
before. New, interesting fluids, e.g., bleach, paint, insecti-
cide *look* edible to him. For a child under five years of
age, poisoning is very common. Take extra precautions.
6. Do not scold the child for mouthing an inedible object.
Rather, tell her and show her what the appropriate use for
it is, such as "Hold the penny in your hand," or "Crayons
are for writing or coloring."

6.44 CHEWS COMPLETELY WITH ROTARY JAW MOVEMENTS (18-24 mo.)

The child chews food well with rotary jaw movements. The tongue moves the food in the mouth from side to side and front to back. She can chew meat and other tough foods.

1. Let the child eat a variety of foods to give her an opportunity for chewing. Refer to 6.24 (Chews food with munching pattern).
2. Place the food to the molar side of the mouth to encourage the child to chew with rotary jaw movements and to encourage her to move the food with her tongue from one side to the other. Repeat on the other side.
3. Use jaw control if necessary, using slight rotary motions. Refer to 6.24 (Chews food with munching pattern) Activities #9, b, c.

6.45 GIVES UP BOTTLE (18-24 mo.)

The child gives up drinking from the bottle. A child may want or ask for the bottle until age three or four. This is all right and he need not be deprived of it if parents do not wish to wean him. Very gradual weaning to perhaps one bottle a day may be necessary. Breast feeding should continue as long as mother and child are able to and/or want to continue.

1. Give the child the bottle less often as the child drinks liquids from the cup or as he learns to use the cup by himself. Let the child gradually and eventually eliminate the bottle.
2. Do not pour the child's milk from his bottle into a cup in his presence. He may refuse to drink it from the cup because he associates his milk with the bottle. Also, do not let him see you pouring it back into his bottle from the cup because he may now feel that that milk belongs to the cup.
3. Reduce the number of bottles the child has in a day very gradually. Slowly eliminate the bottle he will miss the least until he is down perhaps to one bottle.
4. Do not offer the child a bottle unless he asks for it.
5. Do not make it a habit to give the child a bottle with milk or juice in it when he is in his crib at bedtime in order to put him to sleep. The habit of taking the bottle into the crib with him will make it difficult for the child to give up this bottle. Also, milk or juice bathe the teeth while the child sucks during sleep and this promotes tooth decay. There is also the danger of the child choking or milk entering the lung if he drinks lying down. Hold him in an upright sitting position as he takes his bottle before putting him into his crib. Try to give the child water instead of milk or juice in this last evening bottle. Or, spend time with the child at bedtime, reading, rocking, or holding him without giving him the bottle, if possible.

6.46 REMOVES SHOES WHEN LACES UNDONE (18-24 mo.)

The child takes shoes off by himself. Shoes should be very easy to remove with laces loosened or removed, ready to slip off.

1. Refer to 6.39 (Removes socks) for positioning of the child.
2. Let the child enjoy removing slip-on shoes without backs. Put these shoes which are designed like house-slippers or sandals on the child's feet and let him remove them.
3. Let the child pull off a larger sized shoe from his foot after the laces are untied.
4. Remove the child's shoe until it is slightly over the heel, then let the child pull it off.
5. Let the child grasp the heel part of the shoe and pull it off. Help undo the laces or buckles; assist and guide the child as necessary.
6. Unlace and loosen high top shoes for the child.
7. Undo brace fastenings and laces for shoes with short leg braces. Assist or guide the child, if necessary, in removing the brace, by holding the cuff of the brace or by holding the back of the shoe.

6.47 UNZIPS, ZIPS LARGE ZIPPER (18-21 mo.)

1. Let the child pull down and pull up the zipper by holding the zipper tab. Assist as necessary.
2. Use skirt or neck opening zippers which are closed or attached at the bottom end.
3. Let the child begin unzipping with an easy moving heavy duty zipper.
4. Let the child unzip and zip a large handbag. Place a surprise in the bag for the child to discover.
5. Use a zipper board made with a zipper sewn on heavy fabric. Tack the fabric onto a board or within an eight inch by ten inch wooden frame. Place a picture underneath the fabric which will be revealed when the child unzips the zipper board.
6. Adapt the tab for easier grasp if the child has difficulty grasping or pulling the zipper tab. Place any of the following items through the hole of the tab: a zipper ring, a decorative zipper pull, a paper clip, a safety pin, a heavy string with a wooden bead, a ribbon, a key ring, or a chain.
7. For the child who has difficulty with zippers, *Velcro* can be placed on clothing at openings instead of a zipper.

6.48 SITS ON POTTY CHAIR OR ON ADAPTIVE SEAT ON TOILET WITH ASSISTANCE (18-24 mo.)

The child sits on the potty chair or adaptive seat on a regular toilet when placed or assisted by an adult. He may or may not be successful each time he sits on the potty.

1. Refer to 6.49 (May be toilet regulated by adult), Activity #1, for behaviors which indicate he is ready to begin toilet training.

2. Allow the child opportunities to play with his potty seat or become familiar with it by looking at it, touching it, and exploring it before actually using it for toilet training.

3. Select the type of toilet seat (potty chair or a child's adaptive seat placed on a regular toilet) according to physical needs or individual preference.

4. Make the child as relaxed and comfortable as possible on the seat. Use the safety belt, a foot rest or stool.

5. Help the child onto the seat and keep your hands on him until he becomes used to sitting on the toilet. Praise him for sitting on the potty.

6. Stay with the child throughout the time he sits on the toilet for safety and support.

7. Begin by putting the child on the toilet very briefly. If he resists strongly, discontinue. Try again a week or so later.

8. Do not leave the child on the seat longer than five minutes if he is unsuccessful.

9. Let the child see you or a sibling use the toilet.

10. Be as pleasant and calm as possible. Do not scold or shame him.

11. Praise attempts or successes.

12. Do not flush the toilet when the child is sitting on the seat. Flush after he is off the seat or let him flush the toilet. If the child seems frightened by the flushing, flush later, after he leaves the bathroom.

13. Talk naturally about his genitals, naming them "Vagina," or "Penis," as you would naturally name or label other parts of his body if the child makes reference to them. This is a natural time for the child to be curious about his genitals.

14. For the physically handicapped child, special adaptations for toileting may be necessary, such as.
    a. A footstool to bring his hips and knees at ninety degrees while in sitting. This is helpful for a child with tight leg adductors or with extensor pattern of the legs. It also gives the child more stability in sitting.
    b. A seat with good support if the child has very poor sitting balance.
    c. Hand bars for sitting balance.

6.49 MAY BE TOILET REGULATED BY ADULT (18-24 mo.)

The child can be considered toilet regulated even if he does not yet indicate his need to use the toilet, but can be "caught" in time by the adult.

1. The following behaviors are indications that the child is ready to begin toilet training:
   a. When he remains dry for about two hours at a time.
   b. When he understands simple directions.
   c. When he is aware of accomplishments.
   d. When he takes pride in new skills.
   e. When he likes to do things for himself.
   f. When he likes to please the adult.
   g. When he enjoys imitating an adult.
   h. When he has learned to indicate wet or dirty pants.

2. Keep a chart for about two weeks to establish the child's elimination pattern. Refer to 6.34 (Shows bladder and bowel control pattern). Record each time elimination occurs during the day. When you have established a time schedule, e.g., every two hours, watch the time carefully. Put the child on the potty when it is close to the time the child may be ready to eliminate. Stay with him and do not let him stay on the potty for longer than five minutes. Praise the child for sitting on the potty. Refer to 6.48 (Sits on the potty chair or on adaptive seat on toilet with assistance).

3. Be calm. Take him to the toilet without whisking him off or rushing him impatiently.

4. Be consistent with the words you use when you talk about toileting, e.g., "shi-shi," "do-do," or whatever family word is used. Be sure to praise the child's attempts and successes.

5. Let the child wear training pants which are easier and quicker to take off and put on than diapers after some successes over a period of time. The child may learn to associate diapers with wetting and underpants with removing to use the toilet.

6. Place the child on the potty if the child is dry when he wakes up from a nap or from a night's sleep. This may be a good time to achieve success.

7. It is not necessary to "catch" a child to toilet train him. Use this "catch" method only if you think it is important to train him *now*. Some children "self-train" themselves around age two and two and a half.

6.50 PLAYS WITH FOOD (19-23 mo.)

A child normally plays with his food. If food play becomes a problem, e.g., throwing or dumping, teach him that he cannot play with the food in such a way. If he continues, casually end the meal. Be consistent with your routine.

1. The following are tips to prevent excessive food play:
   a. Do not encourage play by putting too much food in the child's bowl.
   b. Place the child's food directly on the tray or table rather than in a bowl, especially if the child insists on dumping the food out of the bowl.
   c. Give the child his food one portion at a time during the meal.
   d. Let the child touch his foods to experience their texture and temperature. This is good but when play becomes excessive or becomes a problem, end the meal casually.
   e. Allow other times for appropriate messy play with finger paints, mud, sand, water. Refer to 1.68 (Enjoys messy activities such as fingerpainting).

6.51 WASHES AND DRIES HANDS PARTIALLY (19-24 mo.)

The child washes and dries his hands partially, requiring assistance to complete the job.

1. Fill a large plastic bowl with water and let the child practice washing his hands after a meal or messy play. Let him dry his hands with a towel.
2. Provide a stepstool so the child can reach the sink by himself.
3. Turn on the cold water or let the child turn the cold water on by himself. Warn him about the hot water faucet and remind him to be careful.
4. Wash your hands along with child and let him imitate. Give assistance and verbal instructions as necessary.
5. Let the child use a small bar of soap. Use hotel sized soap or cut a regular soap to the child's hand size. Use small novelty soaps of different shapes or figures.
6. Turn the water off or let the child turn the water off by himself after he rinses his hands.
7. Keep a towel within reach or hand it to her to dry her hands. Assist as necessary.
8. Let the child use a wet towel or a "wash and wipe" tissue when necessary during the day.
9. Use hand lotion or baby powder on the child's hands. Let him rub his hands together as if washing hands.
10. Let the child help bathe the parts of his body he can see, such as arms, hands, stomach, legs, feet.

6.52 ANTICIPATES NEED TO ELIMINATE— USES SAME WORD FOR BOTH FUNCTIONS (19-24 mo.)

The child shows awareness of wanting to urinate or have a bowel movement. He may use the same word for both urination or bowel movement.

1. Praise the child if he tells you he must urinate or have a bowel movement. Model the correct word when the child uses one word for both functions.
2. Be sure the child consistently hears the appropriate words, such as "Shi shi," "Do-do," or "Potty," whenever his diaper is being changed or whenever he uses the toilet. If the child is cared for by others, e.g., babysitter, request that the appropriate words for toileting be consistently used for the child.
3. Use the terms "Shi shi," "Wee wee," "Do-do" or "Potty" and let the child repeat it if he can, right at the time you see him anticipating the need to eliminate because of his facial expression or gesture. Be sure to attend to his anticipatory gesture and word. Refer to 6.35 (Indicates discomfort over soiled pants verbally or by gesture).
4. Give the child opportunities to become acquainted with his toilet seat before he actually uses it. Introduce the toilet seat to him casually, allowing him to look at it and explore it. Refer to 6.48 (Sits on potty chair or adaptive seat on toilet with assistance).
5. Toilet training can be started at this time by seating him on the potty and praising his willingness to sit. Refer to 6.49 (May be toilet regulated by adult).
6. Do not scold, shame, or punish the child when he wets or soils his diaper.

6.53 DELAYS SLEEPING BY DEMANDING THINGS (19-31 mo.)

The child refuses to sleep and fusses or demands things to delay bedtime.

1. If you wish to train the child to stay in his bed at this point:
   a. Be consistent in the way you put your child to bed. Keep the ritual short, e.g., one story, one song, be friendly, but avoid stimulating or exciting talk and activities. Do not rush through bedtime.
   b. Should he keep demanding one more drink, a kiss, or a trip to the potty, give him one only say firmly, "This is the last one," and stick to it.
   c. Tell the child it is all right to wet the bed if he resists sleep worrying about this.
   d. Leave the door open if he wishes and if it helps. A light, if needed, is harmless and often a big help to the fearful child.
   e. Do not go back to the child's room. If the child gets out of bed, cheerfully and promptly return him to his room every time he does so. Give no other attention.
2. If all of the above seems to be too much trouble and the parents are not worried about training the child now, this is perfectly okay and will not harm the child. He will learn to go to bed alone naturally by age three, four or five. Put the child to sleep by rocking or lying beside him or whatever works. It will not spoil him. He will naturally outgrow this later. A note of caution, unless it is not a problem to allow the child to make a consistent habit of it, do not let the child sleep in the parents' bed.

6.54 HOLDS SMALL CUP IN ONE HAND (20-30 mo.)

The child holds a small cup with or without a handle in one hand and drinks from it with minimal spilling.

1. Provide a one handled cup. Use a weighted bottom or non-tip cup, such as *Tommie Tippee*, if the child spills liquid when placing the cup on the table.
2. Provide a small, narrow cup that is easy to grasp, such as a *Tupperware* six ounce cup.
3. Give the child a cracker to hold in one hand, then offer a cup to the other hand.

6.55 OPENS DOORS BY TURNING KNOB (21-23 mo.)

1. Let the child turn the door knob with supervision and give him assistance as needed.
2. Provide toys with knobs to turn, such as a toy radio, a small jar, or film containers with a cover which the child can open and close. Put a surprise in the container or jar for the child.
3. Push a small plastic drinking cup without handles into sand with the bottom side up. Let the child grasp the

the end of the cup and turn it.

4. Let the child hold the bottom end of a cup and press the rim of cup into rolled out playdough. Let the child turn it to make cut-out "cookies."
5. Let the child dip the rim of a plastic cup into paint and make impressions on paper by giving the cup a turn before lifting it off the paper.
6. Prevent the child from opening doors you do not wish him to open by:
   a. Locking the door.
   b. Putting a sliding bolt-type or hook-type lock high on the door above the child's reach.
   c. Putting a plastic door knob cover over the door knob. This allows the child to turn only the cover, not the knob. Or put fabric or a knitted cover over the knob which will make the knob slippery and difficult for the child to turn.

6.56 HELPS WITH SIMPLE HOUSEHOLD TASKS (21-23 mo.)

The child has fun helping you and doing something "adult." Do not expect him to do a perfect job or insist that he do or complete the tasks. It may sometimes take you longer to finish your tasks or perhaps it will double your duties, but do not ignore or discourage his efforts. Much learning takes place for the child. Praise all his attempts.

1. Refer to 5.52 (Imitates doing housework).
2. Make the simple tasks enjoyable for the child Let the child imitate or "help" you as you do simple household tasks. Do them together or if he works by himself,
3. Let the child wipe the table with a wet sponge.
4. Let the child dust large furniture with a cloth or duster.
5. Let the child "help" or imitate you when folding clean clothes such as towels. He can help put away his clothes.
6. Provide a toy broom or sweeper and encourage the child to imitate you while you're sweeping.
7. Let the child put the napkins on the table when you set the table.
8. Let him help put his toys away.
9. Let him throw small rubbish items into the trash can.
10. Let the child pick up leaves, help rake leaves or sweep the walkway.
11. Let the child water plants using a small watering can or hose.

6.57 PUTS SHOES ON WITH ASSISTANCE (21-30 mo.)

The child needs assistance in putting his shoes on. The amount of assistance the child may need to put his shoes on will depend on the type of shoes he wears. Shoes with fastenings (buckles, laces) or special shoes with high tops or shoes with braces may require more assistance. The child will need help in putting his shoes on the correct foot.

1. Let the child sit on the floor, on a low stool or a low chair so his feet are on the floor.
2. Let the child bring his foot over his other knee and bring the shoe to his foot. Let him put his toes into the shoe and bring the shoe over the heel. Repeat with the other foot. Assist as needed.
3. Let the child practice with loose shoes.
4. Let the child begin with open back or slip-on type shoes.
5. Remove or loosen the shoe laces and bring the tongue of the shoe out so the child can put her foot easily into the shoe.
6. Place the shoes on the floor and let the child work his foot into the shoe while he is in sitting or in supported standing.
7. For the older delayed child:
   a. Let the child use a floor sitter (a seat with a back and sides which is placed on the floor) or let him lean against a wall or a corner wall if his sitting balance is poor.
   b. Let the child who is in a wheelchair bring one foot over the other knee to put his foot into the shoe. The shoe may also be placed on the footrest of the wheelchair so the child can try to place his foot into the shoe.
   c. Let the child see what you are doing and how you are putting his shoe on his foot if he is unable to do so by himself. Position him in supported sitting in front of you and put his shoe on for him as if he would be putting them on himself.

6.58 MAY HAVE DEFINITE FOOD PREFERENCES (23-25 mo.)

The child may have definite food preferences at this age. The child may crave one food, e.g., bananas, and eat it to the exclusion of everything else. This is normal although not all children do this. Some children under two and a half years have been found to have some fruit or vegetable as a preferred food. After two and a half years of age, meats gradually become favorites.

Refer to 6.30 (May refuse foods—appetite decreases).

6.59 UNWRAPS FOOD (23-25 mo.)

The child removes the wrapper from the food and puts the food into his mouth to eat.

1. Demonstrate with wrapped food. Unwrap and throw wrapper away while the child is watching. Place the food in your mouth.
2. Offer the child a wrapped food and let him imitate. Assist as necessary.
3. Avoid offering candies and too many sweets. Offer healthy, nutritious wrapped snack foods, such as a cracker, cheese, a fruit roll. You can also wrap your own foods, such as cereal or dried fruits in waxed paper, clear wrap or cellophane.
4. Show the child and talk to him about how certain foods are peeled. Let him discard the peelings and then eat the

food. Do this, rather than just giving the child the edible part. Let him taste the part to be discarded if he insists and tell him it does not taste good. Let the child help peel foods, such as:
a. A banana.
b. An orange. Cut the peel with a knife vertically by sections. Peel sections halfway down and let the child peel off as much as he can. Tangerines are easier to peel. Remove seeds before giving it to the child to eat.
c. A hard boiled egg.

6.60 UNDERSTANDS AND STAYS AWAY FROM COMMON DANGERS—STAIRS, GLASS, STRANGE ANIMALS (24-30 mo.)

1. Be careful about common dangers and remain within close range of the child.
2. Ask the child to be careful without frightening the child. Keep your voice firm when talking about dangers. Explain to the child why things are dangerous, e.g., hot, sharp.
3. Take the child away using simple explanations when the child is near danger.
4. Refer to 5.36 (Explores environment enthusiastically— safety precautions important) and 5.84 (May develop sudden fears, especially of large animals).

6.61 HANDLES FRAGILE ITEMS CAREFULLY (24-26 mo.)

The child can handle fragile items carefully and does not throw or break them.

1. Keep precious objects or dangerous objects out of reach or put them away. Let the child handle, manipulate, and explore safe objects.
2. Teach the child not to throw breakable objects. Demonstrate how to be gentle with babies, pets (kittens, puppies, etc.) and fragile items. Let the child "Touch with one finger" or let him touch or gently pat a baby's feet or hands.
3. Remain nearby to supervise or assist him if he does get hold of an object which should be handled carefully. Explore the object together. Do not snatch it away. Divert his attention to other things if it is necessary to take the object out of his grasp. Give him a replacement.
4. Expect accidents to happen.

6.62 HELPS PUT THINGS AWAY (24-29½ mo.)

1. Make a game of putting toys away after the child is through playing. Be enthusiastic, encouraging the child to join in. Do not expect the child to put everything away by himself.
2. Put things away as part of the routine so it might become part of his routine as he gets older.

3. Let the child help while you are putting away his clean folded clothes. Let him help put his soiled clothing into the hamper.
4. Refer to 6.56 (Helps with simple household tasks).

6.63 HOLDS SPOON IN FINGERS—PALM UP (24-30 mo.)

The child holds the spoon in his fingers or between thumb and index and middle fingers with forearm supination (palm up) in adult-like fashion. The child should have voluntary supination in order to hold spoon in this manner. He may still occasionally grasp the spoon in his fisted hand with forearm pronation (palm down).

1. Refer to 4.57 (Forearm supination).
2. Let the child scribble with the crayon held in his fingers. Refer to 4.78 (Holds crayons with thumb and fingers).
3. Let the child hold a child sized fork or a salad fork in his fingers with palm up and let him poke the food to eat.

6.64 PULLS PANTS DOWN WITH ASSISTANCE (24-26 mo.)

The child pulls his pants down with assistance over his hips.

1. Talk to him about what you are doing and let him co-cooperate as much as possible as you dress and undress the child. Gradually allow him to do as much as he can. Help him start and finish dressing as needed. Talk about body parts which are involved in the dressing procedure as well as positions and procedures, e.g., "Pushdown," "Leg up," or "Let's take your pants off."
2. Offer encouragement to the child; assist as needed, but allow the child time to do as much as he wants to by himself. Learning undressing and dressing skills requires repetition and practice.
3. Begin with the child assisting you; then as he does more, you assist him. Practice with the child wearing loose underpants or shorts for easy removal. Give the child enough time and assistance, as needed, before he becomes frustrated.
4. Let the child use both hands to grasp each side and to help pull his pants down. Let the child place his thumbs under the elastic waist on both sides and push down. You may need to help him pull his pants down over his hips at first, but decrease assistance as he becomes more capable. If he

6.0 SELF HELP

is unable to push down using both hands together, let him alternately push down on one side and then the other side and repeat.

5. Let the child wear pants with a loose elastic waist band without fastenings so he can remove it easily.

6. Let the child pull his pants down, then let him sit on a stool or the floor to remove his pants or let him lean against the wall and let him lift one leg, then the other leg.

7. For the older delayed child:
   a. Position the child in front of you in supported sitting with his legs extended if he is unable to sit unsupported to remove his pants. Shift his weight to one side and remove his pants from the non-weight bearing free hip; repeat on the other side. Let the child help you push his pants off his legs, if possible.
   b. Let the child hike his hips up while in supine and let him pull his pants down over his hips with both hands, if possible. Let him bring his knees up and pull off his pants. He may need to roll over to his right side, pull down the left side of his pants, roll over to the left side and pull down his right side. Repeat until his pants are down far enough over his hips. Let him flex his knees and pull off or kick off his pants.
   c. Let the child lean against the wall for support while sitting and let him remove his pants.
   d. Let the child lean against the wall while standing to pull his pants off. A handrail on the wall the child can grasp for standing balance may be helpful.
   e. Let the hemiplegic child use both hands, if possible, to pull his pants down.

6.65 UNBUTTONS LARGE BUTTONS (24-25 mo.)

The child unbuttons large flat round buttons least one inch in diameter.

1. Let the child put coins into bank or poker chips into slots cut into a covered box or through the lid of a coffee can.

2. Make a "button box." Use a cigar box, a shoe box or any other box and make the slots on the box-top. Let the child put flat buttons or poker chips through the slots. Make the slots vertical or horizontal. Place a few slots so the child can pass the button through one slot and pull it out through an adjacent slot with his other hand. Keep the buttons in the box.

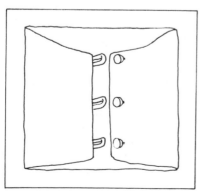

3. Make a "button board" with fabric and large buttons, one-inch to one-and-one-fourth inch in diameter. Make the button holes at least one-fourth inch larger than the button. Sew the button on loosely with strong thread. Place an attractive picture on the button board under the fabric so after the child unbuttons the buttons, the picture is revealed. Use loops instead of button holes, as an alternative (see diagram previous column).

4. Demonstrate and let the child unbutton the buttons. Assist as necessary. Do not hurry or rush the child.

5. Let the child unbutton large buttons on a doll's clothing.

6. Let the child wear clothing with large front buttons, such as a vest or smock and let him unbutton the buttons.

6.66 WASHES HANDS (24-30 mo.)

The child washes his hands by himself. He may need a little help to do a thorough job.

1. Refer to 6.51 (Washes and dries hands partially).

2. Place a step stool at the sink which the child can step upon to reach the sink and the faucet. If the child is independent, place the stool on the cold water side so the child will turn on the cold water rather than the hot water.

3. Stick red tape on the hot water faucet as a reminder for the child.

4. Place the soap within reach and let the child wash the front and back of his hands with rotary movements of the wrist, if possible. Let the child rinse and dry his hands thoroughly with a towel placed nearby within reach.

5. Put hand lotion or baby powder on the child's hands to practice hand and wrist movements involved in washing hands. Use a towel to wipe.

6. For the older delayed child:
   a. Remain in back of the child while he washes his hands, if he needs support to stand.
   b. Let him lean forward against the sink and give support or supervision as needed.
   c. Be sure the child who uses a wheelchair locks his wheelchair before he leans forward to wash his hands.

6.67 BRUSHES TEETH WITH ASSISTANCE (24 mo. and above)

The child begins to brush his teeth and requires assistance to brush thoroughly.

1. Use a clean wet gauze pad or clean wash cloth wrapped around your finger to wipe the child's teeth. This can be done from the time the child's first tooth appears until his teeth can be gently brushed with a soft toothbrush.

2. Introduce a child's soft toothbrush at about two to two and a half years of age. At first, let the child play with it and imitate while your brush your teeth. This is the stage when the child enjoys imitating adult behaviors. Continue to wipe his teeth with gauze.

3. Shave off part of the bristles at the base of the brush so that the brush easily and comfortably fits into the child's mouth.

4. Let the child gradually become accustomed to tooth brushing by making it a brief and casual experience at first.
5. Brush the child's teeth daily after each meal if possible from about two and a half years of age. Gradually add flouride toothpaste.
6. Position yourself behind the child. Let the child stand in front of you with his back to you. Place one hand around his chin to stabilize his head while brushing his teeth with your other hand. Or, you can brush his teeth in face to face position. Brush gently.
7. Let him brush his teeth first, if he wants to brush, then you can complete the brushing.
8. Let him learn to rinse his mouth with water by imitating you.
9. Floss the child's teeth to prevent accumulation of food particles between the teeth.
10. Let the child visit the dentist from about age two or two and a half.
11. Caution: Do not let the child sleep with a bottle of milk or juice, which can cause tooth decay. If the child needs a bottle, give it to him before he goes into the crib to sleep. If he insists on a bottle, give him water. Drinking from a bottle while lying down can cause choking.
12. For the older delayed child:
   a. Use a gauze wrapped around your finger, a tongue blade, or a cotton swab to wipe the child's gums and teeth. Do this for the child who is hypersensitive in the mouth.
   b. Use jaw control as used in feeding, if necessary, to open and close the child's mouth. For illustrations of jaw control, refer to 6.24 (Chews food with munching pattern), Activity #9, b.
   c. Brush the child's teeth with a soft toothbrush after every meal. Shave off part of the bristles at the base of the brush if necessary, to make it easier to brush the teeth.
   d. Keep the child's head in slight flexion to prevent gagging.
   e. Use an electric toothbrush, if possible.
   f. Rinse the child's mouth with water using jaw control, if necessary. Use a cup to rinse or use a squirt bottle with water. Flex the child's head gently over the sink to spit the water out. If the child is unable to spit, let him open his mouth to let the water out. He may swallow most of the water; this is not harmful.
   g. Floss the child's teeth, if possible.
   h. Avoid sugary or sticky foods which cause tooth decay if teeth cannot be brushed frequently.
   i. Regular visits should be made to the dentist.

6.68 ANTICIPATES NEED TO ELIMINATE ON TIME (24-36 mo.)

The child may indicate need to eliminate by gesture, signal, or verbally in time to use the toilet.

1. Encourage the child to say, "Potty" or whatever term, whenever he anticipates the need to use the toilet. Let him gesture or signal to you if he has no speech.
2. Take him to the bathroom. Carry him if he needs assistance with locomotion.
3. Remove his diapers or pants and put him on the toilet. Stay with him while he is on the toilet.
4. Flush the toilet after the child leaves the bathroom if the child is fearful of the flushing toilet. He may want to flush the toilet himself. Never flush the toilet while he is sitting on the seat.
5. Do not scold the child if he has accidents. Praise success!
6. Refer to 6.48 (Sits on potty chair or on adaptive seat on toilet with assistance), 6.49 (May be toilet regulated by adult), and 6.52 (Anticipates need to eliminate—uses same word for both functions).

6.69 USES TOILET WITH ASSISTANCE—HAS DAYTIME CONTROL (24-36 mo.)

The child uses the toilet during the day. She may still have occasional accidents. She may need reminding and assistance with her clothing and wiping herself.

1. Refer to 6.68 (Anticipates need to eliminate on time).
2. Go with the child to the bathroom and assist or supervise as needed.
3. Do not scold or shame the child for accidents. She may be too busy at an activity or may not ask to go to the bathroom if she is at a strange or unfamiliar place or with an unfamiliar person. She may refuse a strange toilet altogether out of fear.
4. Assist the child in getting her pants off, especially if she is in a hurry. Dress the child in easy to remove clothing. Let the child wear training pants.
5. Assist in wiping her with toilet tissue. After a bowel movement wipe toward the back, away from the genitals.
6. Go through the whole toileting routine together as pleasantly and casually as possible. Do not scold. Praise attempts and successes at being independent.
7. Refer to 5.83 (Becoming aware of sex differences).

6.70 UNDRESSES WITH ASSISTANCE (26-32 mo.)

The child undresses with physical and verbal help. He will also need help undoing fastenings.

1. Refer to 6.64 (Pulls pants down with assistance).
2. Let the child watch you or another child undress.
3. Let the child undress with assistance before bathtime or bedtime.
4. Let the child undress a doll.
5. Undress the child using a sequence of movements he would use in undressing himself.
6. Help him undo fastenings if necessary.
7. Let the child grasp both sides of clothing with front openings at the chest level and bring the clothing back over his shoulder area. Let him shrug it off or bring each arm out of the sleeve.

8. Let the child practice with sleeveless undershirts at first for overhead or pullover clothing. Let him next use T-shirts.
   a. Let him remove a pullover shirt by letting him grasp the shirt at the back of his neck, bring the shirt over his head and bring his arms out through the sleeves.
   b. Let him raise the clothing by grasping the lower part or hem of the clothing and raise his arms and bring the clothing over his head to remove.
   c. Let him remove one arm through one sleeve then the other within the clothing. Then raise the clothing above his head to remove.
9. For the older delayed child:
   a. Let the hemiplegic child remove the clothing from the unaffected side first. Then using the free unaffected hand, let him remove the clothing from the affected side.
   b. Position the child who is unable to undress himself at all, in front of you with his back facing you. Use movements and motions as *you* would undress. Remove the sleeves from the child's arm rather than trying to pull the child's arm from the sleeve.

6.71 PULLS PANTS UP WITH ASSISTANCE
(26-28 mo.)

The child pulls his pants up with assistance over his hips.

1. Let the child sit on the floor in front of you with his back to you. Bend over and place the child's pants in front of him with the appropriate leg openings in front of him. Assist him by holding his pants in position. Let the child put one foot then the other into the pant leg. Let him pull the pants to his knees. Ask him to stand and pull up his pants. Assist him as necessary.
2. Let the child put one foot through the pant leg, then the other, pulling his pants up to the knees while sitting on a low stool. Ask the child to stand and pull his pants up.
3. Let the child stand with his back to you and let him lean against you for support, if necessary. Hold one pant leg open and encourage the child to step into one leg, then the other. Encourage the child to pull his pants up, giving assistance as necessary. The child may also lean against the wall with you in front of him to assist him.
4. For the older delayed child:
   a. Let the child with poor sitting balance sit supported against you or against a wall. Put his legs through the pants. Let the child lie on his back and pull his pants up by hiking his hips or by moving from one side to the other, then pulling up his pants.
   b. Position the child in side-lying with hips and knees flexed. Put his legs into the pant legs, if necessary, and help him pull his pants up in side-lying or supine.
   c. Gather up the pant leg and bring the child's leg through the pant leg. Repeat on the other side.

6.72 DRESSES SELF WITH ASSISTANCE
(28-32 mo.)

1. Watch for readiness and interest. This is when the child can follow simple directions and can grasp and release objects. She should be able to do some undressing.
2. Give the child simple directions and break down the process into simple steps, doing it the same way each time. Let her start dressing doing one small step at first, such as putting one arm through a sleeve, then you should finish dressing her. Encourage her to do a little more as her skills will increase. Dressing skills require repetition and practice.
3. Remain with the child during dressing, giving assistance as needed.
4. Allow enough time for the child to dress herself. Make the effort to allow the child to do as much as she can, offering encouragement and praise. Do not insist that she always dress herself.
5. Talk about what you are doing, mentioning and touching the parts of the body involved.
6. Select loose clothing to make it easier for the child to dress herself without a struggle.
   a. Begin with easy clothing for the child to practice dressing, such as clothing with elastic waist bands, short pants, sleeveless undershirts sleeveless or short sleeve open front shirt, blouses or dresses.
   b. Put on easy fastenings, such as a pull tab or a plastic ring on zippers, *Velcro* tape at openings, large front buttons. *Velcro* can be used on the outside seams of pant legs for the child who has leg braces.
7. Assist with "front" and "back" of clothing by placing a label or X-mark on the back, telling and showing the child each time that the label goes on the back.
8. Let the child dress in front of the mirror. This may be helpful to some, but it can be distracting to others. Let her see herself in the mirror after she is dressed, if she does not use a mirror while dressing. Refer to 5.82 (Takes pride in clothing).
9. Keep this training light and fun. Make plans to go out after the child is all dressed. Let her practice with Daddy's, Mommy's, or older sibling's clothing.
10. Let the child dress and undress large dolls.
11. Provide a low stool or chair so child's feet rest securely on the floor while she sits to dress herself.
12. Remember to give the child physical affection and praise. There was much physical contact and handling when you dressed the child. The child may miss your attention when she starts to dress herself.
13. For pullover or overhead clothing:
    a. Practice first with a sleeveless undershirt. Use T-shirts next.
    b. Let the child place her arms through the sleeves. Then let her hold the bottom of the back of the shirt or let her gather up the back of the shirt, bringing the shirt over the head, and pulling it down into place.
    c. Or, let the child hold the bottom of the back side of the T-shirt, place the head opening on her head and pull down. Let the child place one arm then the other through the sleeves.

14. For an open front shirt, sweater or dress:
    a. Let the child put one arm through the sleeve or arm-hole and bring the clothing up to the shoulder. Then let the child reach in back to the other sleeve.
    b. Let the child use the overhead method. Place the open shirt facing up on the child's lap with the collar close to the body. Let her put her arms into the armholes, pulling the sleeves up. Let her raise her arms and bring the shirt over the head, bringing her arms down and arranging the collar and shirt.

15. Let the child start buttoning from the bottom upward to avoid mis-matching the buttons and the buttonholes.
16. For the hemiplegic child or for the child affected more on one side than the other:
    a. Dress the more affected arm or leg first, then the unaffected or less affected side.
    b. Undress the unaffected side first, by pulling off the clothing with the unaffected hand. Then remove the clothing from the affected side with the unaffected hand.

6.73 WIPES NOSE WITH ASSISTANCE (29-31 mo.)

The child wipes her nose with some help. She may not be able to blow her nose as yet.

1. Let the child look in the mirror when her nose is runny. Let her watch you wipe her nose with a tissue so she can see what is being done.
2. Let the child watch you wipe your nose.
3. Let the child take a facial tissue and wipe her own nose. You can complete the job for her.
4. Let the child look in the mirror and wipe her nose.
5. Let the child pretend to wipe the doll's or stuffed animal's nose.
6. Pat her nose if wiping annoys her.
7. Let the child observe you throw the facial tissue away in the trash can and let her throw her facial tissue away.
8. Let the child wipe her face with a wet towel during her bath or wipe her mouth with a napkin after a meal or snack.

6.74 MAY REJECT MANY FOODS (29½-31½ mo.)

The child may want only certain kinds of foods or will eat only one kind of food for several days in succession. The child's appetite may decrease according to his level of activity or motor development. He may eat only one good meal a day. This is all right as long as the child is not ill. Part of the reason for these demands is his increased cognitive awareness and memory. The child can remember a food he likes and asks for it. He requests foods he has had before but which are not directly visible. He is learning where things go and belong, so he may want to have dishes arranged the same or "correct" way. He may also notice any change in seating arrangement, or in his place at the table.

1. Refer to 6.30 (May refuse foods—appetite decreases) and 6.58 (May have definite food preferences).
2. Do not force the child to eat.
3. Ask him what he'd like for a meal sometimes.
4. Talk about foods or meals which he especially liked and suggest you will have them again sometime.

6.75 INSISTS ON DOING THINGS INDEPENDENTLY (30 mo. and above)

1. Let the child do as much as he can by himself. Try not to interfere or take over when he wants to do more for himself. If he is not allowed to or if everything is done for him, he may lose the desire to become more independent.
2. Allow the child time and be patient as he works on a task. Give him a start or help him along as he needs help, but let him complete the task as much as possible.
3. Encourage and praise his attempts at independence.

6.76 KNOWS PROPER PLACE FOR OWN THINGS (30-36 mo.)

The child knows where his possessions are kept and demonstrates this by fetching the object on request.

1. Use the classroom or home situations to learn whether the child knows where his things are kept. For example:
    a. Ask the child to get his sweater or bag before leaving the classroom for home.
    b. Ask the child to get a storybook so the parent can read to him.
2. Label with pictures where things are kept. For example, place a picture on the drawer for pants, skirt, and underwear, and on the wall hook where jacket or sweater is hung.
3. Put his things away with him, his toys, books, toothbrush, clothing.
4. Keep the child's things in the same place to help him learn the proper places for his things.
5. Provide one box or shelf with the child's name or picture on it. This shelf is for only his possessions.

6.77 POURS LIQUID FROM SMALL CONTAINER (30-36 mo.)

1. Let the child play in a wading pool or bath tub. Let him pour water from a small plastic pitcher or a cup into another cup or container.
2. Let the child pour uncooked rice, beans, macaroni or sand from a small pitcher or cup into a box, a cup or any other small container.
3. Let the child pour water over his feet while outdoors or while in the tub.
4. Let the child water plants pouring from a small container.
5. Let the child pour his own juice or other liquids at the table, using a small plastic lightweight pitcher under supervision.
6. Have a tea party and let the child pour "tea."
7. Keep water in a small plastic pitcher in the refrigerator at a low level where the child can easily reach it. Allow
• him to get it out and let him pour himself water when he is thirsty. Keep a cup in the refrigerator near the pitcher or elsewhere where it is easily accessible.

6.78 USES FORK (30-36 mo.)

The child uses a child sized fork or a salad fork to pierce or scoop his food.

1. Let the child use a fork when he can use a spoon well.
2. Provide a spoon and a fork at meal time. The child may need or prefer one utensil at the beginning of the meal and finish the meal with the other utensil. He may need assistance at times, but let him experiment on his own.
3. Let the child use the fork to pierce foods, such as an apple slice or a weiner and let him take bites from it.
4. Let the child use a fork to pierce pieces of food or scoop sticky foods.

6.79 USES NAPKIN (30-36 mo.)

The child uses a napkin to wipe his mouth and hands.

1. Place a napkin at the child's place setting at snack or mealtime.
2. Let the child learn by imitation watching everyone at the table use a napkin.
3. Remind the child once in awhile that he has food on his chin or face and ask him to wipe himself with his napkin. Let the child wipe his mouth and hands at the end of the meal or snack.
4. Use a mirror so the child can see himself wipe his mouth.

6.80 HANGS CLOTHING ON HOOK (30 mo. and above)

1. Make it part of the routine for the child to hang up her coat, sweater, jacket or clothing each time she removes it.
2. Model by hanging up your clothing.

3. Assist the child as needed.
4. Place the hook within easy reach for the child.
5. Sew on a short chain or heavy tape in the inside of the collar so the child's clothing can be hung on a hook.
6. Place a picture of her clothing on the wall where the hook is placed for her to hang her clothes.
7. Provide a clothes tree of the correct height, especially for her clothes.
8. Let the child get her clothing herself from the hook when she is to wear it.

6.81 BUTTONS LARGE BUTTONS (30-36 mo.)

The child buttons large round buttons, at least one inch in diameter.

1. Refer to 6.65 (Unbuttons large buttons).
2. Attach buttons with string, leaving about half-inch of string between the string and the fabric. This will give enough space between the button and the fabric so the child can pass the button through the buttonhole easily.
3. Pass the button halfway through the hole and let the child pull the button completely through the hole.
4. Let the child practice on dressing dolls with large buttons.
5. Let the child button front opening clothing with large buttons. Use a practice smock or a sleeveless vest with large buttons.
6. Use buttons with loops instead of buttonholes. Refer to 6.65 (Unbuttons large buttons), Activity #3 for illustration.

6.82 DRIES HANDS (30-36 mo.)

The child dries his own hands with a towel after washing them. He may need a little help to do a thorough job.

1. Hang a towel where the child can easily reach it to wipe his hands.
2. Keep paper towels within the child's reach. Place a wastebasket nearby for the child to dispose of the paper towel.
3. Let the child wipe his hands with a wet towel to "wash" his hands when water is not easily accessible.

6.83 HELPS WITH BATHING SELF (30 mos. and above)

1. Name or talk about parts of the body as you bathe the child. Talk naturally about his genitals, naming them, "Vagina" or "Penis" as you would naturally name or label other parts of his body. Refer to 5.83 (Becoming aware of sex differences).
2. Give simple directions, such as "Arm up," "Wash your stomach," "Turn around."
3. Soap the towel and let the child wash himself before or after you bathe him.
4. Let the child soap his hands to wash parts of his body he can see and reach.

5. Let the child use a mitten type wash cloth so the child can place his hand into the mitten washcloth and help wash himself.
6. Let the child watch you or his sibling bathe or bathe together.
7. Let the child bathe a bath toy in the bathtub.
8. For the older delayed child:
   a. Place the child in a bathchair, swim ring or inner tube inside the tub to bathe him if he has poor sitting balance.
   b. Lift the child from the bath wrapped in a towel. This will facilitate lifting and carrying the child with abnormal movement patterns when he is wet and slippery.
9. Caution: Do not leave the child alone no matter how little water is in the tub. Always test water temperature before putting the child into the bath water.

6.84 DISTINGUISHES BETWEEN URINATION AND BOWEL MOVEMENTS (30-36 mo.)

The child can verbally or by gesture distinguish between bladder and bowel movements. She may tell you before or after she has eliminated.

1. Use the same words consistently to distinguish between functions. Use the same words at home, at school or at the sitter's.
2. Ask her if she needs to go "Shi shi" or "Do-do" when she seems to want to use the toilet.
3. Show the child her bowel movement and name it. Do the same with her urine and name it. Let her repeat the word as she does it.
4. Encourage the child to tell you when she needs to eliminate by using words or sounds. Do not pressure the child for verbal performance. Praise success.

6.85 SERVES SELF AT TABLE WITH LITTLE SPILLING (31 mo. and above)

The child serves himself finger foods or small portions of some foods under supervision.

1. Let the child serve himself rolls, or sandwiches, or finger foods.
2. Let the child serve himself cold or warm foods which are easily scooped with a serving spoon or pierced with a fork. Supervise or assist as necessary.
3. Try not to make an issue if the child serves herself too much at first. Do not insist that what is taken must be eaten; do not act as if the child is greedy. She can only learn about proper amounts by trial-and-error. If it's a big problem, you might make a rule about "one spoonful" for everyone at a time.
4. Have a tea party or luncheon. Let the child serve play foods.
5. Let the child use a spoon to scoop sand, dirt, uncooked rice, uncooked beans or macaroni into containers, such as small boxes, buckets, or bowls.

6.86 SHOWS INTEREST IN SETTING TABLE (31 mo. and above)

The child enjoys feeling "grown up" helping with grown-up activities, such as setting the table.

1. Give the child simple tasks to do which can give the child a sense of accomplishment. Refer to 6.56 (Helps with simple household tasks)
2. Encourage his interest by letting him help you, although it may take more time for you. He can "help" you.
   a. Wipe the table.
   b. Place the napkins at each place setting.
   c. Place the utensils at each place setting.
   d. Set his own place, using plastic or unbreakable dishes.
3. Talk about the seating arrangements at the table, e.g., Daddy's place, Mommy's place, Brian's place, Sara's place.
4. Have a tea party with play dishes and let the child set the table.

6.87 VERBALIZES NEED TO USE TOILET— HAS OCCASIONAL ACCIDENTS (31 mo. and above)

The child tells you when he needs to use the toilet but still has occasional accidents.

1. Refer to 6.68 (Anticipates need to eliminate on time).
2. Remind the child or direct him to the bathroom if you see any signs of his needing to use the toilet. He may be too involved in an activity and may wait until the very last moment and result in an accident.
3. Do not scold or shame him if he has an accident.
4. Show the child where the bathroom is or tell him to let you know when he needs to use the toilet when he is in a new environment or situation.
5. Let the child use the toilet before going somewhere where toilets are not easily accessible, e.g., a car ride, shopping, church, or theatre. If he refuses, do not force him.

6.88 TAKES RESPONSIBILITY FOR TOILETING; REQUIRES ASSISTANCE IN WIPING (31 mo. and above)

The child goes to the bathroom and removes his underpants to use the toilet. He may need assistance getting on and off the toilet. He may also need help wiping himself. Teach the child to flush the toilet, if flushing is not a frightening experience, and to wash and dry his hands.

1. Let the child wear underpants which are not too tight, but comfortably loose for easy and quick removal. Refer to 6.69 (Uses toilet with assistance—has daytime control).
2. Encourage the child to start toward the bathroom and follow him at first.
3. Let the child wear simple and easy to remove clothing:

179

6.0 SELF HELP

a. A girl may wear a dress or a shirt so underpants are easily accessible for removal.

b. A boy may wear loose elastic waisted pants or shorts without fastenings so he can manage by himself.

c. Let the child wear only underpants and a shirt when he does not need to "dress up." This will make it easier for the child during the toilet training period.

4. Use a low footstool which the child can use to get on and off the toilet, if this is helpful.

5. Help the child wipe himself with tissue paper. Wipe away from the genitals. This is important for girls to avoid possible vaginal infection.

6. Let the child wipe himself. Be casual and quick if he needs help. Pay attention to his sitting balance.

7. Teach the child to flush the toilet, if flushing is not a frightening experience for the child.

8. Let the child wash and dry his hands. Refer to 6.67 (Washes hands) and 6.82 (Dries hands).

6.89 SLEEPS TEN—FIFTEEN HOURS DAILY (31 mo. and above)

The child is sleeping enough if he is not terribly fussy or cranky. The amount of sleep the child needs will vary according to the child. Schedule changes made upon the child, such as school, new situations or demands, should be taken into consideration. There are times when the child may need more rest.

6.90 MAY AWAKEN, CRYING FROM DREAMS (31 mo. and above)

The child's crying from dreaming is usually distinguishable from other crying. It sounds very distressed and fearful.

1. Go to the child and comfort him. Label his experience for him as a "dream," and tell him it is not real. It's important to tell him it is "All right," "All gone," "No more." Use a phrase that is familiar and comforting to him.

2. Talk soothingly to the child so he will go back to sleep. Usually the child is not completely awake so "talking" him back to sleep may be easily done. However, if the child is hysterical, try to gently wake him so he does not go back to his dream. Comfort him and put him back down to sleep.

3. Nightmares are very common and normal at this age and do not indicate an emotional disturbance. Very happy, well-adjusted children can have nightmares. However, if the child always has bad dreams after seeing a certain television show or a movie, this exposure is too much. Restrict his visual experiences in seeing movies or television shows.

6.91 MAY ELIMINATE NAPS (31 mo. and above)

The child may take only occasional naps and then gradually take no naps at all. He may need only to lie down and rest or engage in a quiet activity like listening to a story or a record. The child may nap only when he is especially tired.

This might be the time when a short nap may be too much nap and the child will keep awake and active until very late in the evening. Or, if he does not take a nap during the day, he may go to sleep very early in the evening and awaken after a couple of hours. This becomes the child's nap and he is awake and alert until much later in the evening. This period will pass shortly. Try to tolerate and handle this period by continuously adjusting the child's schedule.

6.92 DRESSES WITH SUPERVISION, REQUIRES ASSISTANCE WITH FASTENINGS (32 mo. and above)

The child undresses and dresses himself with minimal assistance, but still needs supervision and some verbal assistance. He will need help with fastenings.

1. Refer to 6.64 (Pulls pants down with assistance), 6.70 (Undresses with assistance) 6.71 (Pulls pants up with assistance) and 6.72 (Dresses self with assistance).

2. Let the child dress and undress himself as much as he can. Allow enough time within to dress.

3. Do not always insist he dress himself completely.

4. Provide simple, loose clothing.

5. Allow the child's choice of clothing, perhaps between two sets of appropriate clothes. If choice does not matter, such as for play, let him choose or ask him to select his own clothing.

6. Help the child distinguish the back and the front as well as the right side out. He may get distracted. Give simple verbal directions and physical help as needed. Do not rush or take over completely.

7. Lay clothing out ahead of time and place them in the order in which he will put them on.

8. Supply shelves or hooks at the child's height so he can reach for or hang up his own clothing.

6.93 BLOWS NOSE WITH ASSISTANCE (32-34 mo.)

The child blows his nose with help. He may need a demonstration or reminder to blow his nose. He may need help with wiping after he blows his nose.

1. Remind the child when he needs to blow his nose.
2. Keep the tissue box easily accessible for him.
3. Let the child hold the tissue to his nose and ask him to blow his nose by exhaling through his nose with his mouth closed. Demonstrate, if necessary.
4. Let the child wipe his nose. Refer to 6.73 (Wipes nose with help).

GLOSSARY

Abduction — Movement of a limb away from the midline of the body. Finger abduction is done with lateral movements of the fingers.

Adduction — Movement of a limb toward the midline of the body. The opposite motion is abduction.

Articulation — The production of individual sounds in connected speech; the movement and placement of the speech organs which serve to modify the air stream into meaningful speech sounds.

Asymmetrical tonic neck reflex (ATNR) — A primitive response to head movement, where turning the head to one side causes the arm and leg of the face side to extend and the opposite arm and leg to flex.

Babble — Repetition of consonant-vowel combinations in play.

Bilateral — Pertaining to, affecting, or relating to two sides of the body.

Bite reflex — Strong closure of the jaw when the gums or teeth are stimulated.

Concentric — Having a common center, as circles or spheres.

Coo — Vowel sounds produced by the child in pleasure.

Copy — The child is shown a model (e.g., a cross, a circle) and asked to draw one like it, without a demonstration. See Imitate.

Crawl — To move by using the extremities with the abdomen resting on the floor.

Creep — To move on hands and knees with the abdomen off the floor.

Dipthongs — A speech sound gliding continuously from one vowel to another in the same syllable, "oy" in boy.

Do-Do — Colloquial expression referring to bowel movement.

Dysfluency — A pause, hesitation, repetition or other behavior which interrupts the normal flow of speech.

Expansion — In language, an adult utterance that uses what the child has said to form a more adult-like utterance. "Ball" could be expanded to "Linda wants the ball," or "I see the ball."

Expressive language — The ability to express one's thoughts, ideas and feelings through any means, including gestures, talking and writing.

Extension — The straightening of trunk and limbs. Total extension is the straightening out of all joints of the body. The opposite of flexion.

Extensor thrust — The strong extension of one or more limbs in response to a stimulus.

Flexion — Decreasing the angle or bending of a joint. The opposite of extension.

Hemiplegia — A condition affecting one side of the body due to brain damage.

181

Hitching — Movement in a sitting position where the child pushes or pulls with his legs.

Hypertonia — Increased tension of muscles making movements difficult.

Hypotonia — Decreased tension of muscles making upright postures difficult to hold.

Imitate — The child is asked to repeat an activity after observing a demonstration. See *Copy*.

Inflection — Pitch changes used in connected speech to add meaning to speech. For example, there is a rise in pitch at the end of questions, "Are you tired?"

Inhibition — The prevention or diminution of a reflex muscle contraction. Stopping patterns of movement which interfere with normal activity.

Intelligibility — Capability of being understood or comprehended. A child can have many articulation errors but his speech may still be understood.

Intonation — Changes in volume or quality used in connected speech to add meaning to speech.

Jargon — The use of assorted meaningless syllables with speech inflection patterns; production of sentence-like utterances without using words.

Linguistics — The study of the origin, structure and modifications of language, including grammar and use of functional language.

Long leg sitting — Sitting with the legs straight out in front and somewhat apart.

Midline — An imaginary line down the center of the body. This is the basic reference point for all body parts.

Midsupination — Forearm turned midway of full supination with little finger down and thumb up.

Misarticulation — Incorrect production of an individual speech sound, i.e., an error of articulation which may be described as an omission, distortion or substitution of the sound. This is different from a mispronunciation, where the sounds may be produced correctly but not in the correct order, such as "pasgetti" for "spaghetti."

Model — To give an example to be imitated. Adults model words and sentences when they label objects or use sentences for the child to imitate.

Mother — See *Primary caretaker*.

Passive — Movements done to a child without his help.

Phonation — The production of voiced sound by means of vocal cord vibration.

Poi — A Hawaiian food; pounded taro. Taro is a staple vegetable food; when the taro root is steamed or boiled then pounded, it is called poi.

Primary caretaker — The adult who cares for and is best known by the young child during his early years. To this adult the child gives his most intense love and dependence. In our culture, the primary caretaker is usually the mother, but it may be the father, a grandparent, foster parent, or elder sibling. A babysitter, even one who cares for the child most of the day, does not usually qualify as the primary caretaker for the child; the quality of the love and the attention from a parent is more important than the amount of time a child spends with a sitter. In this Guide, the word "mother" is used synonymously with "primary caretaker," primarily for the sake of convenience.

Prolonged regard — Looks for four to five seconds.

Pronation — The hand, wrist, or forearm is rotated so the palm faces downward. The opposite of supination.

Prone – Lying on the stomach.

Protective extension – A reaction to the sudden movement of the body; arm(s) and/or leg(s) extend to try and protect self from a fall.

Puppy position – Prone position with weight on forearms, head extended.

Radial – Pertaining to the thumb side of the forearm and the hand.

Receptive language – The ability to understand what is being communicated, usually through verbal communication.

Reciprocal – Moving one extremity at a time in alternation.

Regard – To look or gaze.

Rooting reflex – Stroke the upper and lower lip and the corners of the mouth. The head, lips and jaw turn in the direction of the side that is stroked in a food seeking movement. The tongue, lips and jaw also move in the direction of the stimulus.

Shi-Shi – Colloquial expression referring to urination.

Sibling – A brother or sister.

Side sitting – Sitting with both legs flexed to one side.

Spasticity – Hypertonicity or tightness of muscles causing stiff and awkward movements.

Supination – Turning of the forearm with palm upward. The opposite of pronation.

Supine – Lying on the back.

Symmetrical movements – Moving corresponding parts of the body simultaneously and in the same direction.

Tactile defensive – Resistant to, avoidance of, fearful of or actively rejecting touching and handling. This is seriously abnormal behavior.

Tofu – Soybean curd or cake.

Tongue thrust – The strong protrusion of the tongue.

Transfer – To move an object from one hand to the other hand.

Unilateral – Affecting or occurring on only one side of the body.

Ventral suspension – The body is held horizontally in the air face down.

Verbalize – To express something in words.

Vestibular board – A large platform on rockers which may be tilted to change child's body position in space and require balancing reactions.

Visual regard – See *Regard*.

Vocalize – To produce consonant or vowel speech sounds, or to use words.

Withdrawal position – Simultaneous flexion of all extremities, in supine.

REFERENCE LIST (PARTIAL) TO
COMMERCIALLY AVAILABLE MATERIALS

Baby Bouncer

    Creative Playthings
    Princeton, NJ 08504

Baby Brother doll

    Mattel, Inc.

Ball — Large, inflatable treatment ball

    J. A. Preston Corporation
    71 Fifth Avenue
    New York, NY 10003

Bathchair

    J. A. Preston Corporation
    71 Fifth Avenue
    New York, NY 10003

Bolsters & Wedges

    Skill Development Equipment Company
    Box 6300, 1340 North Jefferson
    Anaheim, CA 92807

    United Canvas & Sling, Inc.
    155 State Street
    Hackensack, NJ 07601

Crawler/Creeper

    J. A. Preston Corporation
    71 Fifth Avenue
    New York, NY 10003

Crawligator

    Creative Playthings
    Princeton, NJ 08540

First Rider

    Childcraft Education Corporation
    20 Kilmer Road
    Edison, NJ 08817

    Creative Playthings
    Princeton, NJ 08540

Floor sitter

>   J. A. Preston Corporation
>   71 Fifth Avenue
>   New York, NY 10003

Nerf Balls

>   Developmental Learning Materials
>   7440 Natchez Avenue
>   Niles, IL 60648

Nuk Orthodontic nipple

>   Drugstores

>   Reliance Products Corporation
>   108 Mason Street
>   Woonsocket, RI 02895

Premie nipple

>   Drugstores

Prone Stander

>   J. A. Preston Corporation
>   71 Fifth Avenue
>   New York, NY 10003

>   Kaye Products, Inc.
>   2819 Hillsborough Road
>   Durham, NC 27705

>   Adaptive Therapeutic Systems, Inc.
>   36 Howe Street
>   New Haven, CT 06511

>   For do-it-yourself instructions, see
>   *Physical Therapy*, 52, 10, October 1972, page 1058.

Rollator Walker

>   Educational Teaching Aids
>   159 West Kinzie Street
>   Chicago, IL 60610

Scoop Plate — Plastic scoop dish with a high curved edge on one side which aids in filling the utensil and low edge on the other side for easy access to food. It has a no-slip bottom.

>   B and L Engineering
>   8332 Iowa Street
>   Downey, CA 90241

Spoons with built-up handles

> J. A. Preston Corporation
> 71 Fifth Avenue
> New York, NY 10003

> Fred Sammons, Inc.
> Box 32
> Brookfield, IL 60513

The Runaway Bunny — children's book by Margaret Wise Brown (new edition), 1972

> Harper & Row
> New York, N.Y.

Theraplast — Moldable exercise material for strengthening fingers, hands, and wrist muscles.

> J. A. Preston Corporation
> 71 Fifth Avenue
> New York, NY 10003

Thumper

> Playtentials

Tommee Tippee Cup

> Drugstores

> Department stores

Training walkers

> Invacare Corporation
> 1200 Taylor Street
> Elyria, OH 44035

Tunnels

> Educational Teaching Aids
> 159 West Kinzie Street
> Chicago, IL 60610

Tupperware cup

> Tupperware local dealers

> Tupperware World Headquarters
> Orlando, FL 32802

Tyke Bike

> Playskool

Vestibular Board

J. A. Preston Corporation
71 Fifth Avenue
New York, NY 10003

Educational Teaching Aids
159 West Kinzie Street
Chicago, IL 60610

Consult VORT's Guides to Instructional Materials
for other possible references.

BIBLIOGRAPHY

Alpern, G. D., & Boll, T. J. *Developmental profile*. Indianapolis, Indiana: Psychological Development Publications, 1972.

Banus, B. S., et al. *The developmental therapist*. Thorofare, New Jersey: Charles B. Slack, Inc., 1971.

Bayley, N. *Bayley Scales of Infant Development*. New York: Psychological Corporation, 1969.

Bettelheim, B. *Love is not enough*. New York: Free Press, 1950.

Bobath, K. *The motor deficits in patients with cerebral palsy*. London: The Spastic Society Medical Education and Information Unit in association with William Heinemann Medical Books Ltd., 1966.

Bobath, B. *Table of child development*. Unpublished manuscript, The Western Cerebral Palsy Centre, London, undated.

Bowlby, J. *Attachment and loss* (2 vols.). New York: Basic Books, Inc., 1969-1973.

Brackbill, Y. (Ed.). *Infancy and early childhood*. New York: The Free Press, 1967.

Brackbill, Y. & Thompson, G. G. *Behavior in infancy and early childhood*. New York: The Free Press, 1967.

Brazelton, T. B. *Infants and mothers*. New York: Dell Publishing Co., 1969.

Brazelton, T. B. *Neonatal Behavioral Assessment Scale*. Philadelphia: J. B. Lippincott Co., 1973.

Caldwell, B. M. *Home inventory for infants*. Unpublished manuscript, University of Arkansas, 1970.

Caplan, F. & T. *The Power of Play,* Anchor Books, 1973, pp. 1-26.

Carey, W. B. A simplified method for measuring infant temperament. *Journal of Pediatrics*, 1970, 7, 188-194.

Conner, F. P., & Williamson, G. G., & Siepp, J. M., (Eds.). *Program Guide for Infants and Toddlers with Neuromotor and Other Developmental Disabilities*, New York: Teachers College Press, Columbia University, 1978.

Crickmay, M. C. *Speech therapy and the Bobath approach to cerebral palsy*. Springfield, Illinois: Charles C. Thomas, 1966.

Culver, B., Rollefson, V., Gortiz, J., Stevens, E., & Tickton, A. *The Special Children's Center, Inc. developmental chart*. Unpublished manuscript, Ithaca, New York, undated.

Dodson, F. *How to father*. Los Angeles: Nash Publishing Corp., 1974.

Dodson, F. *How to parent*. Los Angeles: Nash Publishing Co., 1970.

Donahue, M., et al. *Parent/child home stimulation: Manual I, behavioral developmental profile.* Unpublished manuscript, Department of Special Education, Marshall-Powesiek Joint County School System, Marshalltown, Iowa, undated.

E'Eugenio, D. B., & Rogers, S. J., *Developmental Screening of Handicapped Infants: A Manual.* Early Intervention Project for Handicapped Infants and Young Children. Ann Arbor, Michigan, University of Michigan, 1976.

Engel, R. C. *Language motivating experiences for young children.* Van Nuys, California: DFA Publishers, 1968.

Erhardt, R. P. "Sequential Levels in Development of Prehension." *American Journal of Occupational Therapy.* November-December, 1974, *28*, No. 10, 592-596.

Fantz, R. L. "Visual Perception from Birth as Shown by Pattern Selectivity." Annals of the New York Academy of Sciences, 118 (1965) 793-814.

Feeding suggestions for the training of the cerebral palsied. *American Journal of Occupational Therapy*, 1953, *7, 5,* 199-204.

Finnie, N. R. *Handling the young cerebral palsied child at home.* New York: E. P. Dutton & Co., Inc., 1968.

Fiorentino, M. R. *Reflex testing methods for evaluating C.N.S. development.* Springfield, Illinois: Charles C. Thomas, 1963.

Fraiberg, S. H. *The magic years.* New York: Charles Scribner's Sons. 1959.

Frankenburg, W. K., & Dodds, J. B. *Denver Developmental Screening Test.* Denver: University of Colorado Medical Center, 1969.

Fredericks, H. D., Baldwin, V. L., Doughty, P., & Walter, L. J. *The teaching research motor-development scale for moderately to severely retarded children.* Springfield, Illinois: Charles C. Thomas, 1972.

Freud, S. "The Sexual Enlightenment of Children," *Collected Papers*, Vol. 2, New York: Basic Books, Inc. (third printing), 1960.

Gawiser, P., et al. *Piagetian based infant stimulation curriculum.* Unpublished manuscript, Developmentally Delayed Infant Education Project, Nisonger Center, Ohio State University, 1972.

George Peabody College. *A manual for the development of self help skills in multiple handicapped children* (Experimental edition). Unpublished manuscript, Nashville, Tennessee, 1971.

Gesell, A., & Ilg, F. L. *Infant and child in the culture of today.* New York: Harper & Brothers Publishers, 1943.

Gesell, A. L., et al. *The first five years of life.* New York: Harper and Row, 1940.

Ginott, H. G. *Between parent and child.* New York: Macmillan, 1965.

Gordon, T. *Parent effectiveness training.* New York: Peter Wyden, Inc., 1970.

Hershenson, M., Munsinger, H., Kessen, W. "Preference for Shapes of Intermediate Variability in the Newborn Human." *Science*, 147, 5 Feb. 1965, pp 630-631.

Hoskins, T. A., & Squires, J. E. Developmental Assessment: A Test for Gross Motor and Reflex Development. *Physical Therapy*, 1973, 53, 117-126.

Illingworth, R. S. *The development of the infant and young child: Normal and abnormal* (2nd ed.). Baltimore, Md.: Williams and Wilkins Company, 1963.

Knobloch, H. & Pasamanick, B. (Eds.). *Gesell & Amatruda's Developmental Diagnosis.* San Francisco: Harper & Row, 1974.

LaCross, E., et al. *Meyer Children's Rehabilitation Institute teaching program for young children: Skills sequence checklist.* Omaha, Nebraska: University of Nebraska Medical Center, 1972.

Levy, J. [*The baby exercise book: for the first fifteen months*] (Eira Gleasure, trans.). New York: Pantheon Books, 1973. (Originally published, 1972.)

McGraw, M. B. *The neuro-muscular maturation of the human infant.* New York: Hafner Publishing Company, 1945.

Milani-Comparetti, A., & Gidoni, E. A. Routine Developmental Examination in Normal and Retarded Children. *Developmental Medicine and Child Neurology,* 1967, *9,* 631-638.

Morris, S. E. *Program Guidelines for Children with Feeding Problems.* Edison, New Jersey: Childcraft Education Corporation, 1977.

Paine, R. S., & Oppe, T. E. *Neurological examination of children.* London: The Spastics Society Medical Education and Information Unit in association with William Heinemann Medical Books Ltd., 1966.

Pearson, P. H., & Williams, C. E. (Eds.). *Physical therapy services in the developmental disabilities.* Springfield, Illinois: Charles C. Thomas, 1972.

Piaget, J. *Play and development.* New York: W. W. Norton & Co., Inc. 1972.

Piaget, J. & Inhelder, B. [*The psychology of the child*] (Helen Weaver, trans.). New York: Basic Books, Inc. 1969.

Redl, F. & Wineman, D. *Children who hate.* New York: Free Press, 1951.

Rogers, S. J., et al. *Early Intervention Developmental Profile.* Early Intervention Project for Handicapped Infants and Young Children. Ann Arbor, Michigan: University of Michigan, 1975.

Seal Bluff Center. *Feeding.* (Instructional paper.) Concord, California, undated.

Shearer, D. *Portage guide to early education.* Portage, Wisconsin: Cooperative Educational Service Agency (No. 12), 1972.

Sheridan, M. D. *The developmental progress of infants and young children.* London: Her Majesty's Stationary Office, 1968.

Spock, B. *Baby and child care.* New York: Pocket Books, 1972.

Staff of Developmental Language and Speech Center. *Teach your child to talk.* Grand Rapids, Michigan, undated.

Stone, L. J., Smith, H., & Murphy, L. B. (Eds.). *The competent infant.* New York: Basic Books, Inc., 1973.

Tesauro, P. A., & Takeshita, C. K. *Criterion reference checklist: Birth to five.* Unpublished manuscript, Project Parent-Child, Department of Speech Pathology and Audiology, Speech and Hearing Center, University of Denver, undated.

Tharp, R. & Wetzel, R. *Behavior modification in the natural environment.* New York: Academic Press, 1969.

Tilton, J. R., Liska, D. C., & Bourland, J. D. (Eds.). *Guide to early development training.* Unpublished manuscript, Wabash Center Sheltered Workshop, Lafayette, Indiana, 1972.

Uzgiris, I. C., & Hunt, J. McV. *Assessment in infancy: Ordinal scales of psychological development.* Urbana, Illinois: University of Illinois Press, 1975.

Wilson, J. M. (Ed.). *Oral-Motor Function and Dysfunction in Children.* University of North Carolina at Chapel Hill, North Carolina, 1978.

Zimmerman, I. L., Steiner, V. G., & Evatt, R. L. *Preschool language manual.* Columbus, Ohio: Charles E. Merrill Publishing Co., 1969.

SKILLS REFERENCE LISTING

COGNITIVE

1.01   Quiets when picked up (0-1 mo.)
1.02   Shows pleasure when touched and handled (0-6 mo.)
1.03   Responds to sounds (0-1 mo.)
1.04   Responds to voice (0-2½ mo.)
1.05   Inspects surroundings (1-2 mo.)
1.06   Shows active interest in person or object for at least 1 minute (1-6 mo.)
1.07   Listens to voice for 30 seconds (1-3 mo.)
1.08   Shows anticipatory excitement (1½-4 mo.)
1.09   Reacts to disappearance of slowly moving object (2-3 mo.)
1.10   Searches with eyes for sound (2-3½ mo.)
1.11   Inspects own hands (2-3 mo.)
1.12   Watches speaker's eyes and mouth (2-3 mo.)
1.13   Begins play with rattle (2½-4 mo.)
1.14   Enjoys repeating newly learned activity (3-4 mo.)
1.15   Uses hands and mouth for sensory exploration of objects (3-6 mo.)
1.16   Turns eyes and head to sound of hidden voice (3-7 mo.)
1.17   Plays with own hands, feet, fingers, toes (3-5 mo.)
1.18   Awakens or quiets to mother's voice (3-6 mo.)
1.19   Localizes sound with eyes (3½-5 mo.)
1.20   Finds a partially hidden object (4-6 mo.)
1.21   Continues a familiar activity by initiating movements involved (4-5 mo.)
1.22   Localizes tactile stimulation by touching the same spot or searching for object that touched body (4-6 mo.)
1.23   Plays with paper (4½-7 mo.)
1.24   Touches toy or adult's hand to restart an activity (5-9 mo.)
1.25   Reaches for second object purposefully (5-6½ mo.)
1.26   Works for desired, out of reach object (5-9 mo.)
1.27   Distinguishes between friendly and angry voices (5-6½ mo.)
1.28   Hand regard no longer present (5-6 mo.)
1.29   Brings feet to mouth (5-6 mo.)
1.30   Shows interest in sounds of objects (5½-8 mo.)
1.31   Anticipates visually the trajectory of a slowly moving object (5½-7½ mo.)
1.32   Finds hidden object using 1 screen, 2 screens, then 3 screens (6-9 mo.)
1.33   Plays peek-a-boo (6-10 mo.)
1.34   Smells different things (6-12 mo.)
1.35   Plays 2-3 minutes with single toy (6-9 mo.)
1.36   Slides toy or object on surface (6-11 mo.)
1.37   Follows trajectory of fast moving object (6-8 mo.)
1.38   Looks for family members or pets when named (6-8 mo.)
1.39   Responds to facial expressions (6-7 mo.)
1.40   Retains two of three objects offered (6½-7½ mo.)

1.41   Turns head and shoulders to find hidden sound (7–10 mo.)
1.42   Imitates familiar, then new gesture (7–11 mo.)
1.43   Responds to simple requests with gestures (7–9 mo.)
1.44   Looks at pictures one minute when named (8–9 mo.)
1.45   Retains two and reaches for third object (8–10 mo.)
1.46   Overcomes obstacle to obtain object (8–11 mo.)
1.47   Retrieves object using other material (8–10 mo.)
1.48   Listens selectively to familiar words (8–12 mo.)
1.49   Finds hidden object under three superimposed screens (9–10 mo.)
1.50   Guides action on toy manually (9–12 mo.)
1.51   Throws objects (9–12 mo.)
1.52   Drops objects systematically (9–12 mo.)
1.53   Uses locomotion to regain object and resumes play (9–12 mo.)
1.54   Listens to speech without being distracted by other sources (9–11 mo.)
1.55   Knows what "no-no" means and reacts (9–12 mo.)
1.56   Responds to simple verbal requests (9–14 mo.)
1.57   Removes round piece from formboard (10–11 mo.)
1.58   Takes ring stack apart (10–11 mo.)
1.59   Demonstrates drinking from a cup (10–15 mo.)
1.60   Enjoys looking at pictures in books (10–14 mo.)
1.61   Unwraps a toy (10½–12 mo.)
1.62   Hidden displacement one screen (11–13 mo.)
1.63   Places cylinders in matching hole in container (11–12 mo.)
1.64   Stacks rings (11–12 mo.)
1.65   Moves to rhythms (11–12 mo.)
1.66   Imitates several new gestures (11–14 mo.)
1.67   Hands toy back to adult (12–15 mo.)
1.68   Enjoys messy activities such as fingerpainting (12–18 mo.)
1.69   Reacts to various sensations such as extremes in temperature and taste (12–18 mo.)
1.70   Shows understanding of color and size (12–18 mo.)
1.71   Places round piece in formboard (12–15 mo.)
1.72   Nests two then three cans (12–19 mo.)
1.73   Understands pointing (12–14 mo.)
1.74   Pulls string horizontally to obtain toy (12–13 mo.)
1.75   Makes detours to retrieve objects (12–18 mo.)
1.76   Looks at place where ball rolls out of sight (12–13 mo.)
1.77   Recognizes several people in addition to immediate family (12–18 mo.)
1.78   Hidden displacement two screens (13–14 mo.)
1.79   Pulls string vertically to obtain toy (13–15 mo.)
1.80   Hidden displacement three screens (14–15 mo.)
1.81   Hidden displacement two screens alternately (14–15 mo.)
1.82   Pats picture (14–15 mo.)
1.83   Helps turn pages (14–15 mo.)
1.84   Imitates "invisible" gesture (14–17 mo.)
1.85   Matches objects (15–19 mo.)
1.86   Places square piece in formboard (15–21 mo.)
1.87   Indicates two objects from group of familiar objects (15–18 mo.)
1.88   Brings objects from another room on request (15–18 mo.)
1.89   Turns two or three pages at a time (15–18 mo.)
1.90   Identifies self in mirror (15–16 mo.)

1.91   Identifies one body part (15-19 mo.)
1.92   Recognizes and points to four animal pictures (16-21 mo.)
1.93   Understands most noun objects (16-19 mo.)
1.94   Series of hidden displacements: object under last screen (17-18 mo.)
1.95   Solves simple problems using tools (17-24 mo.)
1.96   Imitates several "invisible" gestures (17-20 mo.)
1.97   Points to distant objects outdoors (17½-18½ mo.)
1.98   Attempts and then succeeds in activating mechanical toy (18-22 mo.)
1.99   Uses playdough and paints (18-24 mo.)
1.100   Pastes on one side (18-24 mo.)
1.101   Paints within limits of paper (18-24 mo.)
1.102   Points to several clothing items on request (18-20 mo.)
1.103   Explores cabinets and drawers (18-24 mo.)
1.104   Matches sounds to animals (18-22 mo.)
1.105   Rights familiar picture (18-24 mo.)
1.106   Enjoys nursery rhymes, nonsense rhymes, fingerplays, poetry (18-30 mo.)
1.107   Matches objects to picture (19-27 mo.)
1.108   Sorts objects (19-24 mo.)
1.109   Assembles four nesting blocks (19-24 mo.)
1.110   Recognizes self in photograph (19-24 mo.)
1.111   Identifies three body parts (19-22 mo.)
1.112   Understands personal pronouns, some action verbs and adjectives (20-24 mo.)
1.113   Series of hidden displacements: object under first screen (21-22 mo.)
1.114   Places triangular piece in formboard (21-24 mo.)
1.115   Remembers where objects belong (21-24 mo.)
1.116   Turns pages one at a time (21-24 mo.)
1.117   Points to five-seven pictures of familiar objects and people (21-30 mo.)
1.118   Matches sounds to pictures of animals (22-24 mo.)
1.119   Identifies six body parts (22-24 mo.)
1.120   Plays with water and sand (24-36 mo.)
1.121   Pastes on appropriate side (24-30 mo.)
1.122   Demonstrates awareness of class routines (24-27 mo.)
1.123   Understands concept of one (24-30 mo.)
1.124   Identifies rooms in own house (24-28 mo.)
1.125   Demonstrates use of objects (24-28 mo.)
1.126   Identifies clothing items for different occasions (24-28 mo.)
1.127   Enjoys tactile books (24-29 mo.)
1.128   Finds details in favorite picture book (24-27 mo.)
1.129   Recognizes familiar adult in photograph (24-28 mo.)
1.130   Engages in simple make-believe activities (24-30 mo.)
1.131   Knows more body parts (24-28 mo.)
1.132   Selects pictures involving action words (24-30 mo.)
1.133   Obeys two part commands (24-29 mo.)
1.134   Understands complex and compound sentences (24-27 mo.)
1.135   Gives one out of many (25-30 mo.)
1.136   Matches shapes — circle, triangle, square (toys) (26-30 mo.)
1.137   Matches colors — black, white (26-29 mo.)
1.138   Knows own sex or sex of others (26-33 mo.)
1.139   Matches identical simple pictures of objects (27-30 mo.)
1.140   Listens to stories (27-30 mo.)

1.141   Understands many action verbs (27-30 mo.)
1.142   Identifies objects with their use (28-34 mo.)
1.143   Identifies body parts with their function (28-34 mo.)
1.144   Matches primary colors (29-33 mo.)
1.145   Matches similar pictures of objects (30-36 mo.)
1.146   Sorts shapes — circle, triangle, square (toys) (30-36 mo.)
1.147   Completes three-four piece puzzle (30-36 mo.)
1.148   Stacks rings in correct order (30-36 mo.)
1.149   Points to larger or smaller of two spoons (30-36 mo.)
1.150   Understands concept of two (30-36 mo.)
1.151   Identifies familiar objects by touch (30-36 mo.)
1.152   Enjoys being read to and looks at books independently (30-36 mo.)
1.153   Plays house (30-36 mo.)
1.154   Points to six body parts on picture of a doll (30-36 mo.)
1.155   Understands more adjectives (30-33 mo.)
1.156   Sorts colors and points to several colors when named (33 mo. and above)
1.157   Identifies longer stick (33 mo. and above)
1.158   Begins to pick longer of two lines (33-36 mo.)
1.159   Understands all common verbs, most common adjectives (33-36 mo.)

2.0   EXPRESSIVE LANGUAGE

2.01   Cry is monotonous, nasal, one breath long (0-1½ mo.)
2.02   Cries when hungry or uncomfortable (0-1 mo.)
2.03   Makes comfort sounds — reflexive vocal (0-2½ mo.)
2.04   Makes sucking sounds (½-3 mo.)
2.05   Cry varies in pitch, length and volume to indicate needs such as hunger, pain (1-5 mo.)
2.06   Laughs (1½-4 mo.)
2.07   Coos open vowels (aah), closed vowels (ee), diphthongs (oy as in boy) (2-7 mo.)
2.08   Disassociates vocalizations from bodily movement (2-3 mo.)
2.09   Cries more rhythmically with mouth opening and closing (2½-4½ mo.)
2.10   Squeals (2½-5½ mo.)
2.11   Responds to sound stimulation or speech by vocalizing (3-6 mo.)
2.12   Laughs when head is covered with a cloth (3½-4½ mo.)
2.13   Babbles consonant chains "baba-baba" (4-6½ mo.)
2.14   Vocalizes attitudes other than crying — joy, displeasure (5-6 mo.)
2.15   Reacts to music by cooing (5-6 mo.)
2.16   Looks and vocalizes to own name (5-7 mo.)
2.17   Babbles double consonants "baba" (5-8 mo.)
2.18   Babbles to people (5½-6½ mo.)
2.19   Waves or responds to bye-bye (6-9 mo.)
2.20   Says "dada" or "mama," nonspecifically (6½-11½ mo.)
2.21   Shouts for attention (6½-8 mo.)
2.22   Produces these sounds frequently in babbling: b, m, p, d, t, n, g, k, w, h, f, v, th, s, z, l, r (7-15 mo.)
2.23   Vocalizes in interjectional manner (7½-9 mo.)
2.24   Babbles with inflection similar to adult speech (7½-12 mo.)
2.25   Babbles single consonant "ba" (8-12 mo.)
2.26   Shows understanding of words by appropriate behavior or gesture (9-14 mo.)
2.27   Babbles in response to human voice (11-15 mo.)
2.28   Babbles monologue when left alone (11-12 mo.)

2.29   Says "dada" or "mama," specifically (11-14 mo.)
2.30   Repeats sounds or gestures if laughed at (11-12½ mo.)
2.31   Speech may plateau as child learns to walk (11½-15 mo.)
2.32   Unable to talk while walking (11½-15 mo.)
2.33   Omits final and some initial consonants (12-17 mo.)
2.34   Babbles intricate inflection (12-18 mo.)
2.35   Experiments with communication — not frustrated when not understood (12-17½ mo.)
2.36   Uses single word sentences (12-14 mo.)
2.37   Uses expressive vocabulary one-three words (12-15 mo.)
2.38   Vocalizes or gestures spontaneously to indicate needs (12-19 mo.)
2.39   Greets with verbal cues (12-15 mo.)
2.40   Uses exclamatory expressions — "oh-oh," "no-no" (12½-14½ mo.)
2.41   Says "no" meaningfully (13-15 mo.)
2.42   Names one or two familiar objects (13-18 mo.)
2.43   Attempts to sing sounds to music (13-16 mo.)
2.44   Uses voice in conjunction with pointing or gesturing (14-20 mo.)
2.45   Uses ten-fifteen words spontaneously (15-17½ mo.)
2.46   Vocalizes wishes and needs at the table: names desired items (15-17½ mo.)
2.47   Makes sounds in babbling, but often substitutes those sounds in words (15½-21 mo.)
2.48   Jabbers tunefully at play (17-19 mo.)
2.49   Echoes prominent or last word spoken (17-19 mo.)
2.50   Uses expressive vocabulary of fifteen-twenty words (17½-20½ mo.)
2.51   Uses jargon with good inflection and rate (18-22 mo.)
2.52   Uses own name to refer to self (18-24 mo.)
2.53   Imitates environmental sounds (18-21 mo.)
2.54   Imitates two word phrases (18-21 mo.)
2.55   Attempts to sing songs with words (18-23 mo.)
2.56   Names two pictures (19-21½ mo.)
2.57   Uses two-word sentences (20½-24 mo.)
2.58   Uses nouns, verbs, modifiers (20½-24 mo.)
2.59   Tells experience using jargon and words (21-24 mo.)
2.60   Uses intelligible words about 65 percent of the time (21½-24 mo.)
2.61   Names three pictures (21½-24 mo.)
2.62   Uses elaborate jargon (22-24 mo.)
2.63   Imitates four word phrases (22-24 mo.)
2.64   Sings phrases of songs (23-27 mo.)
2.65   Produces the following sounds clearly: p, b, m, k, g, w, h, n, t, d (24-27½ mo.)
2.66   Uses pronouns (24-30 mo.)
2.67   Uses three word sentences (24-30 mo.)
2.68   Uses past tense (24-30 mo.)
2.69   Uses expressive vocabulary of fifty or more words (24-30½ mo.)
2.70   Names five pictures (24-29 mo.)
2.71   Imitates spontaneously or requests new words (24-27 mo.)
2.72   Experiments with communication — frustrated when not understood (24-28½ mo.)
2.73   Relates experiences using short sentences (24-34 mo.)
2.74   Answers questions (24-36 mo.)
2.75   Formulates negative reasoning (24-36 mo.)
2.76   Uses size words (25-30 mo.)
2.77   Uses plurals (27-36 mo.)
2.78   Refers to self using pronoun (27-40 mo.)
2.79   Produces sounds correctly at beginning of words (27½-32 mo.)
2.80   Verbalizes one preposition (28-33 mo.)

2.81   Frustrated if not understood — utterances have communicative intent (28½–36 mo.)
2.82   Replaces jargon with sentences (29–31 mo.)
2.83   Names eight or more pictures (29–36 mo.)
2.84   Repeats words and sounds (29–36 mo.)
2.85   Talks intelligently to self (29½–36 mo.)
2.86   Uses most basic grammatical structures (30–36 mo.)
2.87   Over regulates and systemizes plurals and verbs (foots, doed) (30–36 mo.)
2.88   Vocalizes for all needs (30–31½ mo.)
2.89   Gives full name on request (30–33 mo.)
2.90   Participates in storytelling (30–36 mo.)
2.91   Recites a few nursery rhymes (30–36 mo.)
2.92   Uses expressive vocabulary of 200 or more words (30½–35 mo.)
2.93   Verbalizes two prepositions (33–35½ mo.)
2.94   Begins to respond to opposite analogies (33–36 mo.)
2.95   Repeats five word sentences (33½–36 mo.)
2.96   Relates experiences more frequently using short sentences (34 mo. and above)
2.97   Asks questions beginning with "what," "where," "when" (34½ mo. and above)
2.98   Uses intelligible words about eighty percent of the time (35 mo. and above)
2.99   Uses expressive vocabulary of 300–1,000 words (35 mo. and above)
2.100   Verbalizes three prepositions (35½ mo. and above)

3.0   GROSS MOTOR

3.01   Neck righting reactions (0–2 mo.)
3.02   Turns head to both sides in supine (0–2 mo.)
3.03   Lifts head in prone (0–2 mo.)
3.04   Holds head up 45 degrees in prone (0–2½ mo.)
3.05   Holds head to one side in prone (0–2 mo.)
3.06   Lifts head when held at shoulder (0–1 mo.)
3.07   Holds head up 90 degrees in prone (1–3 mo.)
3.08   Holds head in same plane as body when held in ventral suspension (1½–2½ mo.)
3.09   Extends both legs (1½–2½ mo.)
3.10   Rolls side to supine (1½–2 mo.)
3.11   Kicks reciprocally (1½–2½ mo.)
3.12   Extensor thrust inhibited (2–4 mo.)
3.13   Flexor withdrawal inhibited (2–4 mo.)
3.14   Assumes withdrawal position (2–3½ mo.)
3.15   Holds chest up in prone — weight on forearms (2–4 mo.)
3.16   Rotates and extends head (2–3 mo.)
3.17   Rolls prone to supine (2–5 mo.)
3.18   Holds head beyond plane of body when held in ventral suspension (2½–3½ mo.)
3.19   Asymmetrical tonic neck reflex inhibited (3–5 mo.)
3.20   Holds head in line with body when pulled to sitting (3–6½ mo.)
3.21   Holds head steady in supported sitting (3–5 mo.)
3.22   Sits with slight support (3–5 mo.)
3.23   Bears some weight on legs (3–5 mo.)
3.24   Moro reflex inhibited (4–5 mo.)
3.25   Protective extension of arms and legs downward (4–6 mo.)
3.26   Bears weight on hands in prone (4–6 mo.)
3.27   Extends head, back and hips when held in ventral suspension (4–6 mo.)
3.28   Rolls supine to side (4–5½ mo.)
3.29   Sits momentarily leaning on hands (4½–5½ mo.)

3.30   Demonstrates balance reactions in prone (5-6 mo.)
3.31   Circular pivoting in prone (5-6 mo.)
3.32   Moves head actively in supported sitting (5-6 mo.)
3.33   Holds head erect when leaning forward (5-6 mo.)
3.34   Sits independently indefinitely but may use hands (5-8 mo.)
3.35   Raises hips pushing with feet in supine (5-6½ mo.)
3.36   Bears almost all weight on legs (5-6 mo.)
3.37   Lifts head and assists when pulled to sitting (5½-7½ mo.)
3.38   Rolls supine to prone (5½-7½ mo.)
3.39   Body righting on body reaction (6-8 mo.)
3.40   Demonstrates balance reactions in supine (6-7 mo.)
3.41   Protective extension of arms to side and front (6-8 mo.)
3.42   Lifts head in supine (6-8 mo.)
3.43   Holds weight on one hand in prone (6-7½ mo.)
3.44   Gets to sitting without assistance (6-10 mo.)
3.45   Bears large fraction of weight on legs and bounces (6-7 mo.)
3.46   Stands, holding on (6-10½ mo.)
3.47   Pulls to standing at furniture (6-10 mo.)
3.48   Brings one knee forward beside trunk in prone (6-8 mo.)
3.49   Crawls backward (7-8 mo.)
3.50   Demonstrates balance reactions on hands and knees (8-9 mo.)
3.51   Sits without hand support for ten minutes (8-9 mo.)
3.52   Crawls forward (8-9½ mo.)
3.53   Makes stepping movements (8-10 mo.)
3.54   Assumes hand-knee position (8-9 mo.)
3.55   Demonstrates balance reactions in sitting (9-10 mo.)
3.56   Protective extension of arms to back (9-11 mo.)
3.57   Goes from sitting to prone (9-10 mo.)
3.58   Lowers to sitting from furniture (9-10 mo.)
3.59   Creeps on hands and knees (9-11 mo.)
3.60   Stands momentarily (9½-11 mo.)
3.61   Walks holding on to furniture (9½-13 mo.)
3.62   Extends head, back, hips and legs in ventral suspension (10-11 mo.)
3.63   Pivots in sitting — twists to pick up objects (10-11 mo.)
3.64   Creeps on hands and feet (10-12 mo.)
3.65   Walks with both hands held (10-12 mo.)
3.66   Stoops and recovers (10½-14 mo.)
3.67   Stands by lifting one foot (11-12 mo.)
3.68   Stands a few seconds (11-13 mo.)
3.69   Assumes and maintains kneeling (11-13 mo.)
3.70   Walks with one hand held (11-13 mo.)
3.71   Stands alone well (11½-14 mo.)
3.72   Walks alone two to three steps (11½-13½ mo.)
3.73   Demonstrates balance reactions in kneeling (12-15 mo.)
3.74   Falls by sitting (12-14 mo.)
3.75   Stands from supine by turning on all fours (12½-15 mo.)
3.76   Walks backwards (12½-21 mo.)
3.77   Throws ball underhand in sitting (13-16 mo.)
3.78   Creeps or hitches upstairs (13½-15 mo.)
3.79   Walks without support (13-15 mo.)
3.80   Walks sideways (14-15 mo.)

3.81   Runs — hurried walk (14–18 mo.)

3.82   Bends over and looks through legs (14½–15½ mo.)

3.83   Demonstrates balance reactions in standing (15–18 mo.)

3.84   Walks into large ball while trying to kick it (15–18 mo.)

3.85   Throws ball forward (15–18 mo.)

3.86   Walks with assistance on eight inch board (15–17 mo.)

3.87   Pulls toy behind while walking (15–18 mo.)

3.88   Throws ball overhand landing within three feet of target (16–22 mo.)

3.89   Stands on one foot with help (16–17 mo.)

3.90   Walks upstairs with one hand held (17–19 mo.)

3.91   Carries large toy while walking (17–18½ mo.)

3.92   Pushes and pulls large toys or boxes around the floor (17–18½ mo.)

3.93   Walks independently on eight inch board (17½–19½ mo.)

3.94   Tries to stand on two inch balance beam (17½–18½ mo.)

3.95   Backs into small chair or slides sideways (17½–19 mo.)

3.96   Kicks ball forward (18–24½ mo.)

3.97   Throws ball into a box (18–20 mo.)

3.98   Moves on "ride on" toys without pedals (18–24 mo.)

3.99   Runs fairly well (18–24 mo.)

3.100   Climbs forward on adult chair, turns around and sits (18–21 mo.)

3.101   Walks downstairs with one hand held (19–21 mo.)

3.102   Picks up toy from floor without falling (19–24 mo.)

3.103   Squats in play (20–21 mo.)

3.104   Stands from supine by rolling to side (20–22 mo.)

3.105   Walks a few steps with one foot on two inch balance beam (20½–21½ mo.)

3.106   Walks upstairs holding rail — both feet on step (22–24 mo.)

3.107   Jumps in place both feet (22–30 mo.)

3.108   Goes up and down slide (23–26 mo.)

3.109   Stands on tiptoes (23–25½ mo.)

3.110   Walks with legs closer together (23–25 mo.)

3.111   Catches large ball (24–26 mo.)

3.112   Rides tricycle (24–30 mo.)

3.113   Imitates simple bilateral movements of limbs, head and trunk (24–36 mo.)

3.114   Walks upstairs alone — both feet on step (24–25½ mo.)

3.115   Walks downstairs holding rail — both feet on step (24–26 mo.)

3.116   Jumps a distance of eight inches to fourteen inches (24–30 mo.)

3.117   Jumps from bottom step (24–26½ mo.)

3.118   Runs — stops without holding and avoids obstacles (24–30 mo.)

3.119   Walks on line in general direction (24–26 mo.)

3.120   Walks between parallel lines eight inches apart (24–30 mo.)

3.121   Stands on two inch balance beam with both feet (24½–26 mo.)

3.122   Imitates one foot standing (24–30 mo.)

3.123   Walks downstairs alone — both feet on step (25½–27 mo.)

3.124   Walks on tip-toes a few steps (25½–30 mo.)

3.125   Jumps backwards (27–29 mo.)

3.126   Attempts step on two inch balance beam (27½–28½ mo.)

3.127   Walks backward ten feet (28–29½ mo.)

3.128   Jumps sidewards (29–32 mo.)

3.129   Jumps on trampoline with adult holding hands (29–31 mo.)

3.130   Alternates steps part way on two inch balance beam (30–32 mo.)

3.131   Walks upstairs alternating feet (30-34 mo.)

3.132   Jumps over string two to eight inches high (30-36 mo.)

3.133   Hops on one foot (30-36 mo.)

3.134   Jumps a distance of fourteen inches to twenty-four inches (30-34½ mo.)

3.135   Stands from supine using a sit-up (30-33 mo.)

3.136   Stands on one foot one second to five seconds (30-36 mo.)

3.137   Walks on tiptoes ten feet (30-36 mo.)

3.138   Keeps feet on line for ten feet (30-32 mo.)

3.139   Uses pedals on tricycle alternately (32-36 mo.)

3.140   Walks downstairs alternating feet (34 mo. and above)

3.141   Climbs jungle gyms and ladders (34½-36 mo.)

3.142   Catches eight inch ball (35+ mo.)

3.143   Jumps a distance of 24 inches to 34 inches (34½-36 mo.)

3.144   Avoids obstacles in path (34½-36 mo.)

3.145   Runs on toes (34½-36 mo.)

3.146   Makes sharp turns around corners when running (34½-36 mo.)

4.0   FINE MOTOR

4.01   Regards colorful object momentarily (0-1 mo.)

4.02   Moves arms symmetrically (0-2 mo.)

4.03   Regards colorful object for few seconds (½-2½ mo.)

4.04   Follows with eyes moving person while in supine (½-1½ mo.)

4.05   Stares and gazes (1-2 mo.)

4.06   Follows with eyes to midline (1-3 mo.)

4.07   Brings hands to midline in supine (1-3½ mo.)

4.08   Activates arms on sight of toy (1-3 mo.)

4.09   Blinks at sudden visual stimulus (2-3 mo.)

4.10   Follows with eyes past midline (2-3 mo.)

4.11   Follows with eyes downward (2-3 mo.)

4.12   Indwelling thumb no longer present (2-3 mo.)

4.13   Grasps toy actively (2-4 mo.)

4.14   Looks from one object to another (2½-3½ mo.)

4.15   Keeps hands open fifty percent of the time (2½-3½ mo.)

4.16   Reaches toward toy without grasping (2½-4½ mo.)

4.17   Follows with eyes 180 degrees (3-5 mo.)

4.18   Follows with eyes, moving object in supported sitting (3-4½ mo.)

4.19   Follows with eyes upward (3-4 mo.)

4.20   Grasp reflex inhibited (3-4 mo.)

4.21   Clasps hands (3½-5 mo.)

4.22   Uses ulnar palmar grasp (3½-4½ mo.)

4.23   Looks with head in midline (4-5 mo.)

4.24   Follows with eyes without head movement (4-6 mo.)

4.25   Keeps hands open most of the time (4-8 mo.)

4.26   Reaches for object bilaterally (4-5 mo.)

4.27   Reaches for toy followed by momentary grasp (4-5 mo.)

4.28   Uses palmar grasp (4-5 mo.)

4.29   Reaches and grasps object (4½-5½ mo.)

4.30   Uses radial palmar grasp (4½-6 mo.)

4.31   Regards tiny object (4½-5½ mo.)

4.32   Looks at distant objects (5-6 mo.)

4.33   Drops object (5-6 mo.)
4.34   Recovers object (5-6 mo.)
4.35   Retains small object in each hand (5-6 mo.)
4.36   Watches adult scribble (5½-7 mo.)
4.37   Reaches for object unilaterally (5½-7 mo.)
4.38   Transfers object (5½-7 mo.)
4.39   Bangs object on table (5½-7 mo.)
4.40   Attempts to secure tiny object (5½-7 mo.)
4.41   Manipulates toy actively with wrist movements (6-8 mo.)
4.42   Reaches and grasps object with extended elbow (7-8½ mo.)
4.43   Uses radial digital grasp (7-9 mo.)
4.44   Rakes tiny object (7-8 mo.)
4.45   Uses inferior pincher grasp (7½-10 mo.)
4.46   Bangs two cubes held in hands (8½-12 mo.)
4.47   Removes pegs from pegboard (8½-10 mo.)
4.48   Takes objects out of container (9-11 mo.)
4.49   Extends wrist (9-10 mo.)
4.50   Releases object voluntarily (9-11 mo.)
4.51   Pokes with index finger (9-12 mo.)
4.52   Uses neat pincer grasp (10-12 mo.)
4.53   Tries to imitate scribble (10½-12 mo.)
4.54   Uses both hands freely; may show preference for one (11-13 mo.)
4.55   Grasps crayon adaptively (11-12 mo.)
4.56   Puts objects into container (11-12 mo.)
4.57   Supinates forearm (11-12 mo.)
4.58   Places one block on top of another without balancing (11-12 mo.)
4.59   Marks paper with crayon (12-13 mo.)
4.60   Puts three or more objects into container (12-13 mo.)
4.61   Builds tower using two cubes (12-16 mo.)
4.62   Places one round peg in pegboard (12-15 mo.)
4.63   Points with index finger (12-16 mo.)
4.64   Inverts small container to obtain tiny object after demonstration (12½-18 mo.)
4.65   Scribbles spontaneously (13-18 mo.)
4.66   Inverts small container spontaneously to obtain tiny object (13½-19 mo.)
4.67   Puts many objects into container without removing any (14-15 mo.)
4.68   Uses both hands in midline — one holds, other manipulates (16-18 mo.)
4.69   Builds tower using three cubes (16-18 mo.)
4.70   Places six round pegs in pegboard (16-19 mo.)
4.71   Imitates vertical stroke (18-24 mo.)
4.72   Builds tower using four cubes (18-22 mo.)
4.73   Imitates circular scribble (20-24 mo.)
4.74   Strings one one-inch bead (20-23 mo.)
4.75   Imitates horizontal stroke (21-24 mo.)
4.76   Folds paper imitatively, not precisely (21-24 mo.)
4.77   Builds tower using six cubes (22-24 mo.)
4.78   Holds crayon with thumb and fingers (23-25 mo.)
4.79   Imitates three block train using cubes (23-26 mo.)
4.80   Strings three one-inch beads (23-25 mo.)
4.81   Snips with scissors (23-25 mo.)
4.82   Imitates a cross (24-36 mo.)
4.83   Makes first designs or spontaneous forms (24-35 mo.)

4.84   Puts tiny object into small container (24-30 mo.)
4.85   Folds paper in half (24-30 mo.)
4.86   Copies a circle (25-36 mo.)
4.87   Builds tower using eight cubes (28-31 mo.)
4.88   Snips on line using scissors (28-35 mo.)
4.89   Holds pencil with thumb and fingers – adult-like grasp (29-31 mo.)
4.90   Places six square pegs in pegboard (29-31 mo.)
4.91   Imitates three block bridge using cubes (31 mo. and above)
4.92   Builds tower using nine cubes (32-36 mo.)
4.93   Strings one-half-inch beads (33½ mo. and above)

5.0   SOCIAL-EMOTIONAL

5.01   Enjoys and needs a great deal of physical contact and tactile stimulation (0-3 mo.)
5.02   Regards face (0-1 mo.)
5.03   Smiles reflexively (0-1½ mo.)
5.04   Establishes eye contact (0-2 mo.)
5.05   Molds and relaxes body when held; cuddles (0-3 mo.)
5.06   Draws attention to self when in distress (0-3 mo.)
5.07   Responds with smile when socially approached (1½-4 mo.)
5.08   Stops unexplained crying (3-6 mo.)
5.09   Vocalizes in response to adult talk and smile (3-5 mo.)
5.10   Discriminates strangers (3-6 mo.)
5.11   Socializes with strangers/anyone (3-5 mo.)
5.12   Demands social attention (3-8 mo.)
5.13   Vocalizes attitudes – pleasure and displeasure (3-6 mo.)
5.14   Becomes aware of strange situations (3-6 mo.)
5.15   Enjoys social play (3-6 mo.)
5.16   Makes approach movements to mirror (3-5½ mo.)
5.17   Recognizes mother visually (4-8 mo.)
5.18   Enjoys frolic play (4-8 mo.)
5.19   Repeats enjoyable activities (4-8 mo.)
5.20   Displays stranger anxiety (5-8 mo.)
5.21   Lifts arms to mother (5-6 mo.)
5.22   Explores adult features (5-7 mo.)
5.23   Smiles at mirror image (5½-8½ mo.)
5.24   Distinguishes self as separate from mother (6-9 mo.)
5.25   Shows anxiety over separation from mother (6-9 mo.)
5.26   Cooperates in games (6-10 mo.)
5.27   Struggles against supine position (6-12 mo.)
5.28   Responds playfully to mirror (6-9 mo.)
5.29   May show fear and insecurity with previously accepted situations (6-18 mo.)
5.30   Shows like/dislike for certain people, objects, places (7-12 mo.)
5.31   Lets only mother meet his needs (8-12 mo.)
5.32   Extends toy to show others, not for release (9-12 mo.)
5.33   Tests parental reactions during feeding (9-12 mo.)
5.34   Tests parental reactions at bedtime (9-12 mo.)
5.35   Engages in simple imitative play (9-12 mo.)
5.36   Explores environment enthusiastically – safety precautions important (9-12 mo.)
5.37   Likes to be in constant sight and hearing of adult (12-13 mo.)
5.38   Gives toy to familiar adult spontaneously and upon request (12-15 mo.)

5.39   Displays independent behavior; is difficult to discipline — the "no" stage (12-15 mo.)

5.40   Acts impulsively, unable to recognize rules (12-15 mo.)

5.41   Attempts self-direction; resists adult control (12-15 mo.)

5.42   Displays frequent tantrum behaviors (12-18 mo.)

5.43   Needs and expects rituals and routines (12-18 mo.)

5.44   Begins to show a sense of humor — laugh at incongruities (12-18 mo.)

5.45   Enjoys imitating adult behavior: responds well to the introduction of new tasks (12-18 mo.)

5.46   Plays ball cooperatively (12-15 mo.)

5.47   Shows toy preferences (12-18 mo.)

5.48   Displays distractible behavior (12-15 mo.)

5.49   Tends to be quite messy (12-18 mo.)

5.50   Enjoys being center of attention in family group (12-18 mo.)

5.51   Hugs and kisses parents (14-15½ mo.)

5.52   Imitates doing housework (15-18 mo.)

5.53   Expresses affection (18-24 mo.)

5.54   Shows jealousy at attention given to others, especially other family members (18-24 mo.)

5.55   Shows a wide variety of emotions: fear, anger, sympathy, modesty, guilt, embarrassment, anxiety, joy (18-24 mo.)

5.56   Desires control of others — orders, fights, resists (18-24 mo.)

5.57   Feels easily frustrated (18-24 mo.)

5.58   Interacts with peers using gestures (18-24 mo.)

5.59   Engages in parallel play (18-24 mo.)

5.60   Enjoys solitary play coloring, building, looking at picture books for a few minutes (18-24 mo.)

5.61   Enjoys rough-and-tumble play (18-24 mo.)

5.62   Experiences a strong sense of self-importance (18-24 mo.)

5.63   Attempts to comfort others in distress (22-24 mo.)

5.64   Defends possessions (23-24 mo.)

5.65   Distinguishes self as a separate person; contrasts self with others (24-36 mo.)

5.66   Displays shyness with strangers and in outside situations (24-30 mo.)

5.67   Holds parent's hand outdoors (24-30 mo.)

5.68   Feels strongly possessive of loved ones (24-36 mo.)

5.69   Displays dependent behavior; clings and whines (24-30 mo.)

5.70   Enjoys a wide range of relationships; meets more people (24-36 mo.)

5.71   Says "no," but submits anyway (24-30 mo.)

5.72   Tends to be physically aggressive (24-30 mo.)

5.73   Enjoys experimenting with adult activities (24-30 mo.)

5.74   Frustration tantrums peak (24-30 mo.)

5.75   Relatives best to one familiar adult at a time (24-36 mo.)

5.76   Engages best in peer interaction with just one older child, not a sibling (24-36 mo.)

5.77   Dramatizes using a doll (24-30 mo.)

5.78   Initiates own play, but requires supervision to carry out ideas (24-36 mo.)

5.79   Fatigues easily (24-30 mo.)

5.80   Dawdles and procrastinates (24-30 mo.)

5.81   Values own property; uses word "mine" (24-30 mo.)

5.82   Takes pride in clothing (24-30 mo.)

5.83   Becoming aware of sex differences (24-30 mo.)

5.84   May develop sudden fears, especially of large animals (24-30 mo.)

5.85   Separates easily from mother in familiar surroundings (30-36 mo.)

5.86   Shows independence; runs ahead of mother outdoors, refuses to have hand held (30-36 mo.)

5.87   Demonstrates extreme emotional shifts and paradoxical responses (30-36 mo.)
5.88   Begins to obey and respect simple rules (30 mo. and above)
5.89   Tends to be dictatorial and demanding (30-36 mo.)
5.90   Talks with a loud, urgent voice (30-36 mo.)
5.91   Resists change; is extremely ritualistic (30-36 mo.)
5.92   Experiences difficulty with transitions (30-36 mo.)
5.93   Participates in circle games; plays interactive games (30 mo. and above)
5.94   Takes pride in own achievements; resists help (30-36 mo.)

6.0   SELF HELP

6.01   Opens and closes mouth in responds to food stimulus (0-1 mo.)
6.02   Coordinates sucking, swallowing, and breathing (1-5 mo.)
6.03   Sleeps nights four-ten hour intervals (1-3 mo.)
6.04   Stays awake for longer periods without crying — usually in p.m. (1-3 mo.)
6.05   Naps frequently (1-3 mo.)
6.06   Suck and swallow reflex inhibited (2-5 mo.)
6.07   Brings hand to mouth (2-4 mo.)
6.08   Swallows strained or pureed foods (3-6 mo.)
6.09   Brings hand to mouth with toy or object (3-5 mo.)
6.10   Recognizes bottle visually (3½-4½ mo.)
6.11   Uses tongue to move food in mouth (4-8½ mo.)
6.12   Rooting reflex inhibited (4-6 mo.)
6.13   Pats bottle (4-5 mo.)
6.14   Sleeps nights ten-twelve hours with night awakening (4-8 mo.)
6.15   Naps two-three times each day one-four hours (4-8 mo.)
6.16   Places both hands on bottle (4½-5½ mo.)
6.17   Mouths and gums solid foods (5-8 mo.)
6.18   Holds own bottle (5½-9 mo.)
6.19   Bites food voluntarily (6-8 mo.)
6.20   Drinks from cup held for him (6-12 mo.)
6.21   Feeds self a cracker (6½-8½ mo.)
6.22   Bites and chews toys (7-8 mo.)
6.23   Drools less except when teething (7-12 mo.)
6.24   Chews food with munching pattern (8-13½ mo.)
6.25   Finger feeds self (9-12 mo.)
6.26   Holds spoon (9-12 mo.)
6.27   Sleeps nights twelve-fourteen hours (9-12 mo.)
6.28   Naps once or twice each day one-four hours, may refuse morning nap (9-12 mo.)
6.29   Cooperates with dressing by extending arm or leg (10½-12 mo.)
6.30   May refuse foods — appetite decreases (12-18 mo.)
6.31   Brings spoon to mouth — turns spoon over (12-15 mo.)
6.32   Holds and drinks from cup with some spilling (12-18 mo.)
6.33   Holds cup handle (12-15½ mo.)
6.34   Shows bladder and bowel control pattern (12-18 mo.)
6.35   Indicates discomfort over soiled pants verbally or by gesture (12-18 mo.)
6.36   Sleeps nights ten-twelve hours (13-18 mo.)
6.37   Naps once in afternoon one-three hours (13-18 mo.)
6.38   Scoops food, feeds self with spoon with some spilling (15-24 mo.)
6.39   Removes socks (15-18 mo.)
6.40   Removes hat (15-16½ mo.)

6.41   Places hat on head (16½–18½ mo.)
6.42   Gives empty dish to adult (18–19 mo.)
6.43   Distinguishes between edible and inedible objects (18–23 mo.)
6.44   Chews completely with rotary jaw movements (18–24 mo.)
6.45   Gives up bottle (18–24 mo.)
6.46   Removes shoes when laces undone (18–24 mo.)
6.47   Unzips, zips large zipper (18–21 mo.)
6.48   Sits on potty chair or on adaptive seat on toilet with assistance (18–24 mo.)
6.49   May be toilet regulated by adult (18–24 mo.)
6.50   Plays with food (19–23 mo.)
6.51   Washes and dries hands partially (19–24 mo.)
6.52   Anticipates need to eliminate — uses same word for both functions (19–24 mo.)
6.53   Delays sleeping by demanding things (19–31 mo.)
6.54   Holds small cup in one hand (20–30 mo.)
6.55   Opens doors by turning knob (21–23 mo.)
6.56   Helps with simple household tasks (21–23 mo.)
6.57   Puts shoes on with assistance (21–30 mo.)
6.58   May have definite food preferences (23–25 mo.)
6.59   Unwraps food (23–25 mo.)
6.60   Understands and stays away from common dangers — stairs, glass, strange animals (24–30 mo.)
6.61   Handles fragile items carefully (24–26 mo.)
6.62   Helps put things away (24–29½ mo.)
6.63   Holds spoon in fingers — palm up (24–30 mo.)
6.64   Pulls pants down with assistance (24–26 mo.)
6.65   Unbuttons large buttons (24–25 mo.)
6.66   Washes hands (24–30 mo.)
6.67   Brushes teeth with assistance (24 mo. and above)
6.68   Anticipates need to eliminate on time (24–36 mo.)
6.69   Uses toilet with assistance — has daytime control (24–36 mo.)
6.70   Undresses with assistance (26–32 mo.)
6.71   Pulls pants up with assistance (26–28 mo.)
6.72   Dresses self with assistance (28–32 mo.)
6.73   Wipes nose with assistance (29–31 mo.)
6.74   May reject many foods (29½–31½ mo.)
6.75   Insists on doing things independently (30 mo. and above)
6.76   Knows proper place for own things (30–36 mo.)
6.77   Pours liquid from small container (30–36 mo.)
6.78   Uses fork (30–36 mo.)
6.79   Uses napkin (30–36 mo.)
6.80   Hangs clothing on hook (30 mo. and above)
6.81   Buttons large buttons (30–36 mo.)
6.82   Dries hands (30–36 mo.)
6.83   Helps with bathing self (30 mos. and above)
6.84   Distinguishes between urination and bowel movements (30–36 mo.)
6.85   Serves self at table with little spilling (31 mo. and above)
6.86   Shows interest in setting table (31 mo. and above)
6.87   Verbalizes need to use toilet — has occasional accidents (31 mo. and above)
6.88   Takes responsibility for toileting; requires assistance in wiping (31 mo. and above)
6.89   Sleeps ten–fifteen hours daily (31 mo. and above)